MARTYRDOM AND MEMORY

GENDER, THEORY, AND RELIGION

GENDER, THEORY, AND RELIGION

Amy Hollywood, Editor

THE GENDER, THEORY, AND RELIGION series provides a forum for interdisciplinary scholarship at the intersection of the study of gender, sexuality, and religion.

WHEN HEROES LOVE: THE AMBIGUITY OF EROS IN THE STORIES OF GILGAMESH AND DAVID

Susan Ackerman

ABANDONED TO LUST: SEXUAL SLANDER AND ANCIENT CHRISTIANITY

Jennifer Wright Knust

MARTYRDOM AND MEMORY

Early Christian Culture Making

Elizabeth A. Castelli

COLUMBIA UNIVERSITY PRESS   NEW YORK

COLUMBIA UNIVERSITY PRESS

Publishers Since 1893

NEW YORK,   CHICHESTER, WEST SUSSEX

Library of Congress Cataloging-in-Publication Data

Castelli, Elizabeth A. (Elizabeth Anne), 1958–

Martyrdom and memory : early Christian culture making / Elizabeth A. Castelli.

p. cm. — (Gender, Theory, and Religion)

Includes bibliographical references (p. 283) and index.

ISBN 0-231-12986-6 (cloth : alk. paper)

1 Martyrdom—Christianity. 2. Memory—Social aspects. 3. Church history.   I. Title.

II. Religion and gender (Columbia University Press)

BR1601.3.C37 2004

272′.1—dc22

2004056033

Columbia University Press books are printed on permanent and durable
acid-free paper.

Printed in the United States of America

c 10 9 8 7 6 5 4 3 2

For my sister, Teresa.

CONTENTS

ILLUSTRATIONS

ACKNOWLEDGMENTS

MANY FRIENDS AND COLLEAGUES have been intellectually present in the conceptualizing, writing, and completion of this project. The Barnard College Center for Research on Women provided several different occasions for presenting aspects of this project, both in its Lunchtime Lecture Series and in a session of the Faculty Gender Seminar sponsored by the center. In this latter context, Janet Jakobsen, Wendi Adamek, Elisa Biagini, Natalie Boymel Kampen, Dorothy Ko, Michael Levine, Lesley Sharp, Paula Loscocco, and Timea Szell were generous critical readers of one chapter of the book, voices of encouragement in finishing the project, and models of collegiality and intellectual camaraderie. Other members of this seminar—Elizabeth Bernstein, Helene Foley, Elisabeth Friedman, Jason James, Kathryn Jay, Anu Rao, Paige West, Nancy Worman—have helped to create a rich and valuable intellectual community within the walls of Barnard.

Several other seminars and collaborative working groups provided important challenges and encouragement for the project. Professor Phyllis Mack of Rutgers University chaired a wonderfully rigorous and engaging seminar at the Center for Historical Analysis from 1995 through 1997, and I was honored to pursue work on this project in that setting during a postdoctoral fellowship in 1996 and 1997. In addition to Phyllis, I would like to thank the other members of that seminar, especially Michal Govrin, Alicia Ostriker, Cleo Kearns, Anthony Lioi, Carole Slade, and Gerdien Jonker. "The Scholars' Colloquium on Michel Foucault and the Study of Religion," led by James Bernauer and Jeremy Carrette at Loyola University in April 2000 was a welcoming forum for the portions of this project devoted to a rereading of Foucault's arguments concerning the technologies and writing of the self.

Portions of this project have been presented in other public fora: I thank Professor Denise Buell of Williams College for hosting my visits there in May 1998 and March 2003; Dr. Regina Mooney and Professor Michael Foat of Reed College for inviting me to deliver the Eliot Lecture in Religion in February 2000; Professor Dale Martin for welcoming me to Yale University in October 2000; Professors Christia Mercer, Alice Kessler-Harris, and Rosalind Morris of the Institute for Research on Women and Gender at Columbia University for the opportunity to present portions of this project in a colloquium there in November 2000; Professor Patricia Cox Miller and the Religious Studies Department at Syracuse University for the challenge and honor of speaking there on the first anniversary of September 11; Professor Laura Nasrallah of the Religious Studies Department and Professor Marla Stone of the History Department at Occidental College for the kind invitation to give a lecture there in November 2002.

The members of the 1996 NEH Summer Seminar on "The Art of Ancient Spectacle" at the American Academy in Rome helped me to ground this project in Roman cultural history and the history of ancient art and representation. I especially want to thank Dr. Christine Kondoleon and Professor Bettina Bergmann for their inspiring leadership of this seminar and their encouragement of this project. The academy library's staff was extremely helpful, both during that summer and in the summer of 1998.

Numerous other colleagues have been especially generous conversation partners and readers of different parts of this manuscript, and I am very grateful to them for their time and attention to my work: Beth Berkowitz, Daniel Boyarin, Virginia Burrus, Elizabeth A. Clark, Celia Deutsch, David Frankfurter, Jennifer Glancy, Amy Hollywood, Beth Katz, Lynette Jackson, Jennifer Wright Knust, Lois Lorentzen, Minoo Moallem, Kelly Moore, Afsaneh Najmabadi, Ann Pellegrini, James Rives, Rosamond C. Rodman, Erin Runions, Michael Schuessler, Susan E. Shapiro, Marla Stone, Randall Styers, Judith Weisenfeld, Vincent L. Wimbush, and Angela Zito.

I am particularly grateful to several people at Columbia University Press for their professionalism, enthusiasm, and hard work on behalf of this project: Wendy Lochner, senior executive editor; Michael Haskell, manuscript and production editor; and Suzanne Ryan, assistant editor.

My family of origin and extended family of friends have been among the most patient and supporting as this project came to completion. Thanks especially to my sister Teresa Castelli (to whom this book is dedicated) and my mother Rosemarie Castelli, both of whose sharp wits and countless generosities have made many things possible. Special thanks are also due to Sharon Krengel and Chuck Liebling, along with Simon and Elliott, for their weekly hospitality in Highland Park during my year at Rutgers; Neil Ludman and Terry King, for making Bernal Heights and Ravenna such models of hospitality; Eve Borenstein, Candace Falk, and Allie and Jacob Wilde, for restorative stolen days down the shore over the course of several summers; David Cohen and Lee Klosinski, for southern California hospitality over many a winter break; Jenifer Ward, for her world-class camaraderie from practically the beginning; Jerry Phillips, whose discipline as an artist and unparalleled friendship are inspiring; Randall Styers, for his intellect, empathy, and contagious love for all things New York; and Vincent Wimbush, whose steady presence over two decades as teacher, colleague, and friend have made all the difference.

ABBREVIATIONS

Note that all quotations from the New Testament are my translations of the standard Greek edition, the 27th edition of the Nestle-Aland *Novum Testamentum Graecae*. All references to the Old Testament are to the New Revised Standard Version.

ACW	Ancient Christian Writers
AHR	*American Historical Review*
AJA	*American Journal of Archaeology*
AnBoll	*Analecta Bollandiana*
ANF	*Ante-Nicene Fathers*
ANRW	*Aufstieg und Niedergang der römischen Welt*
BAGD	Walter Bauer et al., eds., *Greek-English Lexicon of the New Testament and Other Early Christian Literature*
BDAG	Frederick William Danker, ed. *A Greek-English Lexicon of the New Testament and Other Early Christian Literature*
BJS	Brown Judaic Studies
CCSL	Corpus Christianorum, Series Latina (Turnhout: Brepols, 1953–)
CH	*Church History*
ClAnt	*Classical Antiquity*
CPh	*Classical Philology*
CQ	*Classical Quarterly*
CRAI	*Comptes rendus de l'Académie des inscriptions et belles-lettres*
CSEL	Corpus scriptorum ecclesiasticorum latinorum (Vienna: Geroldi, 1866–)
DACL	Fernand Cabrol and Henri Leclercq, eds., *Dictionnaire d'archéologie chrétienne et de liturgie*

DOP	Dumbarton Oaks Papers
FZPhTh	Freiburger Zeitschrift für Philosophie und Theologie
GCS	Die griechischen christlichen Schriftsteller der ersten drei Jahrhunderte
HDR	Harvard Dissertations in Religion
HTR	Harvard Theological Review
ISPh	International Studies in Philosophy
JAAR	Journal of the American Academy of Religion
JAC	Jahrbuch für Antike und Christentum
JBL	Journal of Biblical Literature
JECS	Journal of Early Christian Studies
JFSR	Journal of Feminist Studies in Religion
JHS	Journal of the History of Sexuality
JJS	Journal of Jewish Studies
JR	Journal of Religion
JRA	Journal of Roman Archaeology
JRS	Journal of Roman Studies
JSNTSup	Journal for the Study of the New Testament: Supplement Series
JSOT	Journal for the Study of the Old Testament
JTS	Journal of Theological Studies
Lampe	G. W. H. Lampe, ed., A Patristic Greek Lexicon with Addenda et Corrigenda
LCL	Loeb Classical Library
LSJ	H. G. Liddell, R. Scott, and H. S. Jones, A Greek-English Dictionary, 9th ed., with rev. supp.
MEFRA	Mélanges d'archéologie et d'histoire de l'École Française de Rome. Antiquité
NPNF	Nicene and Post-Nicene Fathers
PG	Migne, J.-P., ed. Patrologiae cursus completus [Series Graeca]
PL	Migne, J.-P., ed. Patrologiae cursus completus [Series Latina]
PTS	Patristische Texte und Studien
RAC	T. Kluser et al., eds., Reallexicon für Antike und Christentum
RB	Revue biblique
RHE	Revue d'histoire ecclésiastique
RevScRel	Revue des sciences religieuses
RivAC	Rivista di archeologia cristiana
RQ	Römische Quartalschrift für christliche Alterthumskunde und für Kirchengeschichte
RTP	Revue de théologie et de philosophie
SANT	Studien zum Alten und Neuen Testaments

SC   Sources chrétiennes
SHR   Studies in the History of Religions
StPatr   *Studia Patristica*
TAPA   *Transactions of the American Philological Association*
TDNT   G. Kittel and G. Friedrich, eds., *Theological Dictionary of the New Testament*
ThH   Théologie historique
TSAJ   Texte und Studien zum antiken Judentum
TUGAL   Texte und Untersuchungen zur Geschichte der altchristlichen Literatur
USQR   *Union Seminary Quarterly Review*
VC   *Vigiliae Christianae*
WUNT   Wissenschaftliche Untersuchungen zum Neuen Testament
ZRGG   *Zeitschrift für Religions- und Geistesgeschichte*

MARTYRDOM AND MEMORY

"WHO'S YOUR SAINT?" we asked each other as we settled into our desks—more expectantly and conspiratorially, "What *happened* to her?"

The scene was a catechism class in Corpus Christi, Texas, in the early 1970s. I was twelve years old. The exchange took place within a circle of anxious girls preparing to be initiated into spiritual adulthood in the Roman Catholic Church through the sacrament of confirmation. As a part of this process, we had collectively studied a compendium of the church's teachings, and we had each passed an examination to demonstrate our mastery of this catechetical material. In the culminating moment of the initiation, when the sacrament would be dispensed, each of us, kneeling on the altar at the feet of the bishop, would express our free and willing acceptance of these teachings and their implications for our adult lives.

This was heady and serious business. Yet, for most, if not all of the girls in my class, the most compelling part of the preparation process involved choosing our confirmation names, the names we would utter when the bishop posed the ritual question: "What is your name?" The name each of us would offer in response to this question would be the name of a saint whose life we had researched in the church school's library. Writing out our reports in our still-emerging adolescent longhand and laying claim to the story of a life that we reinscribed on blue-lined notebook paper, we expected through the ritual of confirmation to enter into a special relationship with the saints whose names we would bear.

As with all ritual processes, there were complex dynamics involved in our preparatory efforts and their sacramental culmination. Insofar as we were each choosing our own names, we became imbued with some form of spiritual agency. The names we chose were secret names, not names to be used when fill-ing out bureaucratic forms or presenting ourselves to the world in ordinary ways. Our confirmation names would be those by which God would know us and through which God would communicate with us. In taking up these names, we were entering into a realm that struck many of us as tantalizingly mysterious. At the same time, we were engaged in a remarkable process of self-positioning in relation to the Catholic tradition as a whole because the names we chose would establish connections between ourselves and various saintly lineages. The choosing of our confirmation names wrote us into a communal history, organizing our spiritual identities in continuity with a geographically and temporally distant past. We were taking part in a ritualized practice of collective memory.

We were, of course, more than likely largely unaware of these dynamics. But we were thoroughly conscious of the potential adventure involved in choosing a name, and many of us undertook the task very seriously. The questions we asked each other suggested our interests and investments: "Who is your saint? What *happened* to her?" These questions pointed to the broad frameworks within which we assigned value: the realms of aesthetics, piety, and narrative. We wanted names that "went with" our other, given names. But we also wanted names that reflected our heightened adolescent certainty (or ambivalence) concerning our religious identities. (As I have already mentioned, the girls took this task rather seriously. The boys, generally speaking, seemed confoundingly unmoved by the drama of the moment. They took predictable and easily researched names—Anthony, Thomas, Peter, or Paul—and wrote their perfunctory reports on their saints, angling to be excused at the earliest justifiable moment to go to the gym to play basketball.) For many of the girls, the search for "my saint" became a search for a secret connection, a hidden narrative, an obscure but therefore especially true story.

The gendered differences that characterized the responses of the boys and girls in our class were, at the time, both strikingly obvious and predictably clichéd. The only comment they inspired involved the girls' complaining and/or worried incomprehension at the boys' apparent lack of investment and the teacher's knowing indulgence of it. From my current vantage point, well on the far and long-crested side of feminism's second wave, these differences are more interesting, evocative, and suggestive. Quite apart from the psychosocial dimensions of our creation as gendered subjects by means of our family systems, our schooling, and our daily lives in mid-twentieth-century U.S. society, the process of religious and spiritual formation in which we were engaged was also leaving the indelible imprint of gender.

What was most striking about the saint-selecting process, in retrospect, was the sort of narrative that most attracted us. For, as it happened, the stories most of the girls sought to make their own were stories of torture bravely endured and death heroically met. If there were gory illustrations accompanying these violent hagiographies, so much the better. As I have considered this attraction from a safe and distant vantage point (surrounded by scholarly books in my study, writing a generation after the fact), I do not think that our relationship to these stories was primarily or solely one of identification. I think that something more complex concerning historical difference and traditional continuity was being worked out in this process. After all, the selection of one's saint was not a matter of locating someone whose story was decidedly similar to one's own. The saints' lives were not *our* lives; indeed, their *differences* were precisely the point. The chance to choose one's own name was rather an opportunity to embrace a new story, one that appeared in higher contrast and brighter intensity in the illustrations of the books where hagiographies were found. *Their* lives were *not* ours, but we could bask in their reflected glory by taking their names and copying out their stories into our notebooks. Our fledgling "research" was an attempt to reach across time, to acknowledge the yawning abyss between their "then" and our "now" and to find a way, however provisionally, to bridge the gap.[1] Of course, there is no question that our labors in the church library were naïve and risibly partial approximations of "research." Moreover, if any of us actually had a fledgling critical historiographical method, it certainly never got in the way of our telling our compelling stories. And even if we had had such a method, the idiosyncratic collection of sources at our disposal would certainly have remained stubbornly resistant to its magic. Our research obviously was not historiography in any recognizable sense of the professional practice of writing the past. But it was, I would argue, an important form of collective memory work. And it was a form of memory work that linked in our imaginations undeserved suffering, heroism, violence, religious conviction, gender, and identity.

This entire liturgical process of laying claim to the past of another through self-naming was, I now argue, a contemporary example of earlier processes in Christian practice whereby spectacular lives and the extremes of torture and death became emblems of Christian identity. Moreover, the retellings that were required of us were just a contemporary manifestation of earlier practices of liturgical renarration.[2] Our report writing involved virtually no critical engagement beyond the exercise of our own intuitions and tastes (which we could, nevertheless, articulate with considerable fervor when struggling with each other over who was going to "have" St. Lucy or St. Agatha as "her" saint). In this emphasis on aesthetics and piety and narrative, our writing replicated the processes of reinscription that had been taking place in the preservation of martyrs' stories from the start. That the stories often bore remarkable structural similarities to one another, the varied details of a particular torture or death notwithstanding, raised no historiographical suspicions. The fact that these repetitions bordered on the formulaic was indeed telling, but only in the sense that it confirmed what we were already sure we knew: that the story bore within itself a deep-seated truth. What made the story compelling was its mythic scope and impact: although the powerful and evil seem everywhere and always to triumph through their exercise of brute strength, in a broader interpretive framework one could see that the suffering their brutality inaugurated was in fact a necessary sacrifice that promised the ultimate vindication of the weak and innocent. Understanding the true dynamics of the martyr's tale situated us in a long, nearly unbroken line of interpretation. Reinscribing those dynamics within the context of the sacramental cycle in the religious narratives of our lives, we reconstituted our individual identities and our stories about the present in relation to this socially constituted memory of the distant past.

The aim of this current project is to look in a more systematic way at the workings of such practices of collective memory in relation to early Christian martyrdom. My thesis is that the memory work done by early Christians on the historical experience of persecution and martyrdom was a form of culture making, whereby Christian identity was indelibly marked by the collective memory of the religious suffering of others. This book is not a history of early Christian martyrdom but an exploration of the culture-making aspects of its representations. The category of collective memory helps to illuminate why martyrdom was—and continues to be—such a critical building block of Christian culture.

Collective memory provides the central interpretive framework for this project, but it is not the only theoretically relevant category for understanding the rhetorical and ideological power of the martyrological. As the personal reflection recounted above suggests, gender plays a central role both in the generation of the idea of martyrdom and in its ongoing reception and commemoration. The centrality of gender in configuring martyrdom and its memory is, I argue, neither incidental nor capricious.[3] Rather, gender plays a significant role precisely because martyrdom has to do foundationally with competing ideas about the character and legitimacy of different systems of power. As Joan Scott has argued persuasively, gender is not only a mode of expressing the cultural meanings attributed to perceived sexual difference but also a "primary way of signifying relationships of power."[4] As a critical aperture onto questions of identity and power, the category "gender" reminds us to ask: Who remembers? Who is remembered? How? How are identities constituted and reconstituted in suffering and its remembrance? How are the contours of memory—both its content and its cultural forms—shaped by notions of difference and practices of power? Moreover, the conflict between the dominant imperial culture and the Christian counterculture that one finds reflected in the ancient sources concerning martyrdom is frequently staged as a conflict over the character of the proper and reasonable civil subject. These debates over subjectivity were almost always coded by gender, just as the polemics on both sides of the conflict used gender deviance as one of the standard forms of vituperation against their opponents. Gender pulses through the remnants of these debates and provides an analytical lens for reading them.

Martyrdom and Memory explores the generative quality of a social memory of suffering in the early Christian context. In the first chapter of the book, I explore the theoretical framework of "collective memory," a category that has been increasingly influential in cultural history in recent years. I begin with a discussion of the foundational work of Maurice Halbwachs, one of Durkheim's many students and a theorist whose work on religious collective memory is especially illuminating for a study such as mine. (Indeed, Halbwachs used early Christianity as a case study in one of his most important works, *La topographie légendaire des évangiles en terre sainte: Étude de mémoire collective* [1941].) Although Halbwachs's model has been critiqued and refined by subsequent scholars and although it poses but does not resolve some still-difficult theoretical problems, I argue that the idea of collective (or social) memory remains especially compatible with early Christian (and other ancient) forms of history writing and conceptualization of the past. Most important for making sense of the ancient sources that tell the story of early Christian martyrdom, the notion of collective memory allows one to move past often unresolveable questions of "what really happened" to questions of how particular ways of construing the past enable later communities to constitute and sustain themselves.

Chapter 2 seeks to provide a historical framework for understanding the conflict between the Roman imperial powers and the subject Christian population from the second through the fourth centuries. In addition to providing a historical summary of the conflicts, I focus in particular on the competing Roman and Christian interpretations of power, submission, resistance, and victory. I argue that several critical elements of the historical conflict were appropriated and ideologically transformed by Christians. The historical conflict had primarily to do with contestations over notions of law and piety. The political, legal, and religious systems of Roman imperial society were understood to be organized in a precise analogical relationship, and these systems were highly articulated and relentlessly hierarchical. The social order required that these different systems be in close and rational alignment. When they were not, when challenges to the coherence of these systems were brought into play, the hegemony of imperial power seemed to be called into question. The resulting threat of chaos was repeatedly figured as analogous to and essentially interchangeable with forms of deviance: gender deviance, deviance from systems of rationality (that is, accusations of madness), and religious deviance (that is, accusations of superstition and magic). Christians, meanwhile, made use of precisely the same forms of vituperation and critique, claiming for themselves the superior manifestations of gender identity, rationality, and religious piety. Moreover, this chapter emphasizes the discursive character of martyrdom from its earliest manifestations within Christian collective memory: martyrdom is the product of commemorative interpretation, and it provides a comprehensive frame for interpreting a wide array of historical encounters between Christians and the dominant imperial culture.

Chapter 3 focuses in on the production of the figure of the martyr through the practice of autobiographical writing and the inscription of memory. The chapter is framed by a critical engagement with Foucault's later work on technologies of the self, especially his essays on self-writing. In this work, Foucault focused on a literary history of personal ethical writing in late antiquity. This tradition, he argued, began with the personal reading notebooks (*hypomnēmata*) and correspondence of philosophers during the Roman period and ended with the emergence of self-conscious (and increasingly interiorized) self-writing of fourth-century Christian ascetics and monastics. According to Foucault, the trajectory of this tradition moves increasingly and inexorably from the public realm toward the private. In this chapter, I offer readings of three early Christian texts in which literary first-person accounts of the preparation for martyrdom complicate Foucault's historical narrative. The three Christian writers are Ignatius of Antioch, a bishop who wrote letters to various Christian churches while on his way to martyrdom in Rome; Perpetua of Carthage, a young wife and mother who records her increasingly complex visionary life in a prison diary; and Pionius of Smyrna, a presbyter whose rhetoric of resistance is preserved in lengthy speeches recorded as he prepared for execution. Central to the self-portraiture of the martyr-in-the-making is the privilege accorded masculinity and public performance. This chapter supplements, problematizes, and ultimately challenges Foucault's suggestion that the self-writing of this period moves straightforwardly from public (exteriorized) to private (interiorized) forms of writing. My reading suggests instead that the self-writing in which these Christian martyrs engaged was undertaken explicitly in the service of leaving a written remainder, an inscribed trace that would serve as a public memory text for those left behind.

Chapter 4 attends to the question of the public in a different way. It is devoted to questions of performance and spectacle as they serve as flash points in the debate over the politics of culture between Christians and non-Christians. Spectacle is a crucial dimension of martyrology—martyrs, after all, need an audience—and the Christian critique of spectacle is here read with and against the Christian tendency to appropriate and deploy the discourse and practice of spectacle when remembering the martyrs. Here, several different concepts and problematics overlap: in critiquing spectacle, Christian apologists and polemicists drew attention to the religious or idolatrous origins and associations of theater and the games; they asserted sexual and gender deviance on the parts of performers and spectators and, by implication and contrast, reaffirmed Christian normalcy; and they theorized the dangers of the gaze and worried over the blurred boundaries between fiction and reality. At the same time, the broader problematic of representation emerged in the memory works concerning martyrs. An apologist-historian like Eusebius would distinguish his commemorative work as distinctively Christian by characterizing it as word rather than as image. Meanwhile, Augustine the preacher would exhort Christians to divert their friends from attending the spectacles on the basis of the competition with pagan culture that Christian martyr stories could provide as a source of pleasure and entertainment. Christian culture found itself in direct competition with a wide range of forms of entertainment—the games, the circus, the theatre, the races. The arena became an especially charged venue where this competition came to be staged, since it was also the place where the executions of Christians could take place. As a consequence, the contest over the meanings of spectacle in this context was especially amplified. In a different venue, Christian debates over visual representations and the moral impact of graphic portraits of martyrs' sufferings emerged in this framework but continued well into the period of iconoclasm. These debates provide a complex historical record of the anxiety and paradox embedded in the practices of memorializing and the ethically charged—and often ethically ambivalent—power of the visual.

Chapter 5 draws upon visual representations as it explores the shifting and malleable character of collective memory in relation to one particular and important early Christian example: the female protomartyr, Thecla. Thecla is an especially appropriate figure for exploring the dynamics of collective memory because the evidence for her commemoration and her cult is sufficient in scope and range for analysis and comparison. There are strong literary traditions, both in the earlier *Acts of Paul and Thecla* and in the later *Life and Miracles of Saint Thecla*, alongside diffused artistic traditions involving cult objects from sites around the Mediterranean where Thecla was venerated. Because these texts and artifacts can be dated with some degree of certainty, it is possible to make a historical argument about the emergence of trajectories of collective memory. That Thecla is called a "martyr" at all opens the discussion as a problem, since the earliest source concerning her, the apocryphal *Acts of Thecla*, represents a more ambivalent tradition. It is a tradition in which Thecla suffers for her religious commitments but in which she also miraculously escapes persecution and takes up a life of ascetic renunciation (including the dramatic renunciation of the conventional markers of gender) and a life of public teaching. By the time she is venerated as a martyr-healer in Asia Minor, Egypt, and elsewhere, some centuries later, her representation emphasizes both her martyr status and her unambiguously feminine status. Paired with Paul in the literary tradition, she emerges in the artistic tradition paired most often with Saint Menas and with the biblical Daniel. The malleability and associative character of the commemorative traditions associated with Thecla open up a broader discussion of the workings of collective memory as a process of generating a useable past.

Chapter 6 makes what will likely seem to some readers to be an unexpected move, connecting early Christian culture making in relation to martyrdom with contemporary Christian commemorative practices organized around the figure of "the martyr." In Colorado in 1999, the early Christian martyrological tradition emerged dramatically in contemporary American culture as an as yet untapped resource for some evangelical Protestants to imagine their own experience in continuity with the Christian past. Almost immediately in the wake of the shootings at Columbine High School in Littleton that spring, martyr cults emerged around two of the young women who were killed in the incident. But with the rise of the martyr cults also came controversy over the veracity of the backstory. Focusing on the figure of Cassie Bernall, one of the two girls whose deaths at Columbine came to be interpreted as a Christian martyrdom, I explore the processes by which narrative and interpretation proliferate in the generation of a martyr cult. I also seek to place this phenomenon in historical and political context, arguing that the emergence of the Columbine martyrs *as* martyrs was a logical outgrowth of the historical situation of evangelical Protestantism in the United States in the 1990s. During that decade, the political activism of some evangelicals who organized themselves around the globalized idea of "the persecuted church" prepared the ideological ground in which the narrative seed of the martyrs of Columbine could germinate and flourish.

In reading the contemporary U.S. example in tandem with the early Christian situation, I do not argue that there is a simple, continuous historical line connecting the fourth century with the twentieth. Rather, I argue that the Columbine story demonstrates in a contemporary situation many of the dynamics of collective memory as they emerged in a distant cultural and historical setting. Moreover, the early Christian tradition itself was used in the Columbine aftermath as an ambivalent resource for interpreting contemporary circumstances—no longer evidence for the emergence of collective memory historically but rather a source for a new instance of the generation of collective memory. I read the emergent hagiographic literature and analyze some of the diverse material and cultural remnants that were produced in the wake of the tragedy alongside the public media debate over the authenticity of the stories that emerged from Columbine. This reading opens up an exploration of the ongoing power of collective memory constructed around a process of rendering tragic and meaningless suffering redemptive and meaningful. It also raises the question of the ethical ambivalence that resides at the heart of martyrdom, where privileged meanings emerge only out of death.

The epilogue of this book reflects further on the contemporary legacies of martyrdom's ethical ambivalence, raising questions about the meanings of this theological and ideological inheritance whose global impact in the early twenty-first century is incontestable. For, as the twentieth century's secularism hypothesis sits irrelevantly in the wings, "religion" returns to center stage. The martyr, meanwhile, is one of this drama's most contentious yet riveting stars, the one who packs the house for every performance. The epilogue raises a series of questions that will have to be answered in another context, questions about the deep and contradictory intersections between religion, suffering, and violence.

This book seeks to contribute to a range of different discussions: the burgeoning scholarly discussion about martyrdom in late antiquity,[5] the growing body of theoretically inflected work on early Christian culture, and, more broadly, the emergent field of religion and cultural studies.[6] This book is not exhaustive in its treatment of all possible sources for evidence concerning martyrdom in the early Christian setting nor does it seek to generate a comprehensive narrative of early Christian martyrdom. There already exist ample scholarly attempts at such reconstructions from the last two centuries. Instead, this book focuses on exemplary figures, moments, and debates in order to chart a broader theoretical course through the rich body of evidence that survives into our own time. Moreover, it seeks to illustrate the fruitfulness of the interpretive category of "collective memory" for understanding the work that the past does in the present, work that is necessarily ambivalent, contingent, and contested. This study of collective memory and early Christian martyrdom ends in a setting—twentieth-century America—geographically and temporally remote from the Roman Empire. This move intends to draw attention to the remarkable capacity of collective memory to collapse time and simultaneously to amplify and critique (whether implicitly or explicitly) the great divides of historical difference. The contemporary American example also helps to render visible the ongoing and powerful influence of shared memories of past suffering even in our own social world.

1

COLLECTIVE MEMORY AND
THE MEANINGS OF THE PAST

The solution to the question . . . —how is the memory of groups conveyed
and sustained?—involves bringing these two things (recollection and bodies) together.

—PAUL CONNERTON, *How Societies Remember*

Was der Raum für die Gedächtniskunst, ist die Zeit für die Erin-
nerungskultur.

—JAN ASSMANN, *Das kulturelle Gedächtnis*

WHAT DOES IT MEAN for a group to constitute its identity through the memory of past suffering? How is that memory constructed, refined, and maintained
over time? What are the dynamics of authority and authenticity that govern this
memory work? What is the relationship between the knowledge built upon collective memory and historical knowledge? What modes of interpretation and
meaning construction are at work in these different ways of thinking about and
reconstructing the past? Is it incidental that collective memory seems often to be
particularly focused on the experience of violence, a meaning-shattering occur-
rence?[1] These are some of the questions that frame this book's exploration of
early Christian martyrdom and collective memory.

In the last twenty years, the theoretical language of collective memory has
become increasingly important to interdisciplinary historical and sociological
discussions of how groups and societies construct and understand the past.[2]
This orientation to the study of how collectivities make sense of their own pres-

ent through recourse to constructed narratives of their pasts offers important insights to students of early Christianity. In what follows, I will seek to provide a brief history of the idea of collective memory or social memory, paying special attention to the historiographical challenges that this way of thinking about the past raises.

MAURICE HALBWACHS'S THEORY OF SOCIAL MEMORY

A theory of collective memory was first articulated in the modern period by the French sociologist Maurice Halbwachs (1877–1945).[3] A disciple, first, of philosopher Henri Bergson and later of sociologist Emile Durkheim, Halbwachs sought to create a systematic model for social memory. Positioning himself explicitly against Freudian psychoanalysis and its emphasis on the individual unconscious and on the psychic processes of repression and forgetfulness, Halbwachs was interested in how the past comes to be apprehended and rendered meaningful by individuals.[4] Halbwachs argued that memory is a social construction, the product of the individual's interaction with his or her group—be this family, social class, religious community, or some other collectivity with which the individual is affiliated. Halbwachs published his views on these matters in three major works over the course of a twenty-five-year period: *Les cadres sociaux de la mémoire*, published in 1925,[5] *La topographie légendaire des évangiles en terre sainte*, which appeared in 1941,[6] and *La mémoire collective*, published posthumously in 1950.[7]

As its title suggests, *The Social Frameworks of Memory* argues that individual memory is necessarily produced within a social frame. Here, Halbwachs asserts that individuals remember things only in relation to the memories of others. Individuals obviously possess personal memories peculiar to their own psychologies and experiences, yet even these memories are filtered through the social field. Their meanings derive their intelligibility from context and collectively generated frameworks of significance. Given that individuals are embedded in different and multiple social groupings, even the most personal memory cannot help but derive its sense from the collective context. Moreover, in a precursor to later poststructuralist theorizing, Halbwachs observes that even the most private memories are preserved in language, which renders them social entities rather than the products of autonomous individual consciousness. Memories are processed through language, which provides the conventional and customary meanings that then refract back onto the memory. Through retelling—whether narrative, performative, representational, even liturgical—memory accrues meaning through discursive and embodied repetition.[8]

In situating personal consciousness of the past within a collective context, Halbwachs argues that "memory" in essence performs a socially conservative function—that is, memory (a particular, socially constructed version of the past) operates as an ideological ground for the present. This tendency toward conservation—or, perhaps better, preservation—emphasizes continuity between the past and the present, establishing an attachment or bond across time. In this way, collective memory does the work of "tradition," providing the conceptual and cognitive constraints that render past experience meaningful in and for present contexts.[9]

Social memory offers one important way for groups to situate themselves temporally and topographically.[10] Individuals, as members of groups (families, social classes, religious communities, political parties), generate their own sense of the past out of the different groups' accountings of the past. Halbwachs is particularly interested in the structuring work that memory does socially, politically, and culturally. Therefore, individuals figure in his analysis only insofar as they are participants in groups, never as distinct and detached memory holders. He steers away from the physiological and philosophical questions that captivated his early teacher, Henri Bergson, about the dualistic relationship between matter and memory.[11] Instead, Halbwachs is very much a disciple of Durkheim, seeing the individual only in terms of the collectivities of which he or she is a part.

In this same early work, Halbwachs pays special attention to the conservative aspect of memory within religious communities in particular. In a chapter entitled "Religious Collective Memory," he observes the dual character of ancient Greek and Roman religions, organized around the household, on the one hand, and around public, political institutions, on the other. Both forms of religion—domestic and civic—involve positioning the collective (the family or the city) in relationship to its own past. But Halbwachs expends the bulk of his energy devoted to analyzing religion on a lengthy discussion of the origins of Christianity. This discussion, although constrained by the limits of the scholarship on early Christianity of his day, nevertheless offers some intriguing points of departure for this discussion.

Religion as a generic category and as a dimension of human life is, not surprisingly given his allegiance to Durkheim, for Halbwachs a foundationally social enterprise. Moreover, in the spirit of his time, he is not afraid to make sweeping statements about *all* religions and their collective relationship(s) to the(ir) past(s). "Every religion ... reproduces in more or less symbolic forms the history of migrations and fusions of races and tribes, of great events, wars, establishments, discoveries, and reforms that we can find at the origin of the societies that practice them," he writes.[12] Religion, in Halbwachs's account of it, is in essence a form of cultural memory work. What makes it different from the cultural memory work of other collectivities or modes of social life is the heightened importance attached to religion's complex and potentially paradoxical relationship with the past. This is particularly amplified at moments of ideological and institutional stress or change. On the one hand, religious transformations involve a sort of displacement of a society's or group's historical center of gravity and a reconfiguration of its core assessments of the past. That is, when religious change occurs, narratives of origins may be problematized, historical legitimations for contemporary practices may be questioned, and lineages and genealogies may be challenged. On the other hand, religious innovation must always be couched in the past's terms, Halbwachs argues, and so religious reforms will most often be described not as departures from but as reclamations of the past. "Even at the moment that it is evolving, society returns to its past," he writes. "It enframes the new elements that it pushes to the forefront in a totality of remembrances, traditions, and familiar ideas."[13]

For the religions of Mediterranean antiquity and late antiquity, this view seems to hold true—the Augustan restoration, for example, was an innovative movement whose author consciously cloaked it in the authorizing garments of the distant past.[14] The emergence of rabbinic Judaism—a radical reimagining of the law in the light of the destruction of the temple—used the language of conservation rather than innovation, building up in the process a new collective memory of a remote past.[15] Early Christianity, for all its talk of a "new covenant" and a "new creation," nevertheless rooted itself in existing national narratives and epic pasts.[16] Moreover, one of the important rhetorical strategies of early Christian apologists was to argue for their movement's superior embodiment of the highest virtues from the classical world.[17] Ultimately, Christianity generated its own myth of origin, which itself became the touchstone for all subsequent narratives of Christian collective memory. Claims to collective memory, here and elsewhere, operate in part to rationalize innovations in societies where ruptures with the past create cultural anxiety.

In exploring Christianity as an example of collective memory, Halbwachs observes this tradition's peculiar relationship to time. Although all religions, in Halbwachs's view, are wholly oriented toward the past, Christianity's relationship to time is different because it claims to be simultaneously *both* historical at its root *and* outside of time, eternal. The liturgy of Christianity embodies this paradox. The Eucharist is a ritual restaging of a purported historical event; both event and ritual reenactment take place in history, in time. The cultic, commemorative repetition, however paradoxically, seeks to remember something that recedes ever more persistently into the past the more it is reenacted.[18] Moreover, part of

Christianity's moral force resides precisely in its claim to exist outside history, beyond the confines of historical contingency. Halbwachs emphasizes the Christian negotiation with time by focusing on the power of repetition, not only in the ritual of the eucharist ("the successive sacrifices—celebrated at distinct moments and in distinct places—are one and the same sacrifice"[19]), but also in the idea of revelation's simultaneous eternity and constant renewal. "Dogma, just as the cult, is ageless; within the duration of passage of time of the changing world, it imitates the eternity and the immutability of God."[20]

But perhaps most important for this study is how Christianity negotiates its relationship to time and history through its engagement with the idea of Christian origins. Halbwachs notices the critical role played by the collective memory of the early years of the church in subsequent social formations and theological commitments. Just as the religious innovation embodied in the founding of Christianity situates itself in relation to its precursors, so any subsequent innovation comes to be measured in terms of an imagined past. "Every time that the Church was called upon to judge new theses, new cults or new details of the cult, new modes of life and religious thought, it asked itself first of all whether these conformed with the body of usages and beliefs of this first period. . . . *The Church repeats itself indefinitely, or at least it claims to repeat itself.*"[21] In the early centuries of Christianity, apologists and heresiologists alike would generate a portrait of the movement as one with an unbroken, monolithic tie to the past. Collective memory—at once deeply conservative and terrifically malleable— would serve this ideological project with great facility.

Some years after the publication of *The Social Frameworks of Memory*, Halbwachs continued his explorations of Christian collective memory in a work entitled *La topographie légendaire des évangiles en terre sainte: Étude de mémoire collective* (The legendary topography of the gospels in the Holy Land: A study of collective memory), published in 1941. In *The Social Frameworks*, Halbwachs had devoted a chapter to "The Localization of Memories."[22] In *The Legendary Topography of the Gospels*, he developed this idea of "localization" by analyzing the production of Christian origins through the memory work of Christian pilgrims, travelers, and crusaders. Mapping their notions of the Christian past onto the topography of the Holy Land, these travelers constructed a useable Christian past for their own Christian present. For the fourth-century pilgrims who initially mapped the Christian world of the Holy Land, this Christian past often was built directly on top of important Jewish sites. Like the allegorical and typological interpreters of scripture who found the Christian message embedded in the Hebrew Bible, these pilgrims produced a continuous Christian meaning out of Jewish precursors.

Halbwachs depends in his analysis of the gospels primarily on the work of Ernest Renan (1823–1892) whose influential *Vie de Jesus* (Life of Jesus) participated in the broader nineteenth-century destabilization of dogmatic accounts of the historical Jesus.[23] Despite the fact that this whole body of work from the original "quest of the historical Jesus" has been relegated largely to the realm of the artifactual,[24] Halbwachs's use of it offers some insights that remain critical to the contemporary project. Halbwachs reads the history of gospel writing as an occasion of collective memory, noting that there is a broad "framework of resemblances" shared by the gospels with respect to locations and narrated events as well as to the meanings attributed to these places and happenings. The multiplicity of memories present in the gospel accounts need not be seen as a problem requiring a solution, Halbwachs argues. There is, instead, a brand of paradox embedded in the very claims to historicity in the texts. As Halbwachs understands it, "It is precisely the presence of direct witnesses which increases the chances that some of [an event's] features will be changed so that it becomes quite difficult to determine its characteristics. This is especially the case when the event is of a nature that arouses deep emotions in groups of people, giving rise to passionate discussions."[25]

The multiplicity of collective memories is not the only feature of the gospel accounts and their later rendering in space by travelers, pilgrims, and crusaders. The gospels as examples of collective memory are also partial, in both senses of this term: they preserve only a selection of what the first followers of Jesus might have remembered about him, and they are filtered through religious and ideological interests. They are partial rather than complete or comprehensive, and they are partial rather than disinterested or objective. This rather straightforward observation can be seen as the interpretive and historiographic motor driving much of twentieth-century gospels research.

When localized through the activities of later visitors to the Holy Land, these memories link stories about the past with emergent theological and dogmatic claims. Because he understands collective memory as a social construction, Halbwachs has no problem questioning or indeed fully dismissing the historicity of important elements of the gospel narratives. The setting of the infancy narratives at Bethlehem, he notes, is completely dependent upon the prior importance accorded this town in Jewish tradition: "There is nothing indicating that Jesus was born at Bethlehem, that Joseph and Mary ever passed through or stayed there, or that they were ever in Egypt. The authors of the Gospels seem entirely to have invented this poetic history."[26] Moreover, the only places that are noteworthy in the Jerusalem of the gospels are those affiliated specifically with supernatural occurrences in the narrative. Hence, the collective memory tied to these places is the memory of "Christ" rather than "Jesus."[27] When later Christians travel to these locations, they are caught up in the time warp that Christian collective memory activates. Halbwachs reports on the many visitors to the Holy Land who record their impressions in a time-collapsing fashion as though, by travelling great distances, they have also engaged in a journey through time into the distant past.[28] Moreover, Halbwachs points out that the Jerusalem of these pilgrims is not the Jerusalem of Jesus' first century but a much more archaic Jerusalem tied to more ancient biblical narratives and distanced from the Judaism of the first century itself. "Let me add that the Jerusalem detested by the Christians was the Jerusalem of the Sadducees and the Phari-sees. . . . Christianity had to try to evoke—in the places it now occupied and to which it now wished to give a new sacred aura—the great figures of the early days, the symbols and rites that had been neglected by contemporary Jews."[29]

Many of the observations made by Halbwachs about the gospels as texts of religious conviction rather than historical narration may seem self-evident from our vantage point on the other side of historical criticism's century-and-a-half-long engagement with the gospel traditions. Yet his remarkable contribution as a sociologist who takes Christian origins seriously as an object of study should not be minimized. In this gesture, he moves far beyond his teacher and mentor, Durkheim, who limited himself to a study of "elementary forms" of religious life, albeit as a template for theorizing and understanding the social function of religion as a whole. Halbwachs rendered Christianity an object of critical social analysis, a move that remains provocative and controversial even into our own time. The emergence of Christianity, despite its own claims, could be histori-cized and mapped according to discernible social patterns. There is no question that Halbwachs's argument implies a potentially troubling logical slippage between Christianity as a particular, historical, culturally specific manifestation of "a religion" and the category of "religion" in general, a slippage that might well (indeed should) inspire a wave of suspicion or at least caution. Neverthe-less, I would suggest that Halbwachs's insights into the collective memory of Christianity are sufficiently compelling to justify bracketing these broader theo-retical problems, at least temporarily.

In his treatment of the gospel traditions and their ongoing reception and recapitulation through bodily practices (e.g., ritual, pilgrimage, and so on), Halbwachs does not ignore the challenges raised by the passage of time and by changing circumstances. Indeed, as he understands it, religious collective mem-ory is paradoxically and simultaneously open to change and vulnerable to stasis, and both potentialities can pose a threat to the ongoing viability of a shared memory. This danger can be seen clearly in Halbwachs's rendering of collective memory as a component of Christianity. Here, Halbwachs operates with a doubled vision of collective memory. On the one hand, he sees that collective memory always operates under the threat of change, disintegration, and loss. On the other hand, he argues that collective memory also tends toward atrophy, fixity, and stasis. This tendency toward solidity—although the apparent opposite of the tendency toward deterioration that Halbwachs also diagnoses—can present a problem for memory in shifting circumstances. That is, a memory can lose its tone and texture; as a consequence, it can potentially become insufficiently malleable to survive changing social and historical circumstances. To describe what happens in the historical development of early Christianity, Halbwachs invokes his technical notion of "permeability of memory," arguing that the story of Christian origins is a narrative of movement from the permeability of memory borders to ever increasing levels of impermeability.[30] Hence, the fluidity of collective memory gels over time, and the past's story becomes increasingly fixed.

This tendency toward a solidifying of collective memory is not simply an unconscious and inevitable result of the passage of time. According to Halbwachs, collective memory—which one might describe as a form of Foucault's history of the present *avant la lettre*—is articulated through attempts to secure it by means of localization and commemoration. That is, social practices of reinscription render collective memory available; collective memory is sustained through the agency of a group and its members. Nevertheless, collective memory is also always potentially vulnerable to transformation through changes in everything from topography and architecture to ritual and narrative. Moreover, since time does not stand still, collective memory is susceptible to the inevitable processes by which the object of memory recedes ever-backwards in time, placing the memory itself at risk. In his developing vision of collective memory as manifest most poignantly in "the places of memory," to use Pierre Nora's later formulation,[31] Halbwachs recognizes the paradox that both stability and decay are present simultaneously in memory and its material embodiments. Jerusalem

> was a city built with stones and made of houses and streets that were familiar to them [Jerusalem's Christian inhabitants]. It is on account of the stability of these things that their memories endured. But that stability is at the mercy of all the material accidents that slowly transform or even destroy cities—just as the memories we constantly compose regarding a person with whom we live are at the mercy of the physiological accidents that slowly transform or even destroy an organism.[32]

For those who do not live with this daily transformation of material memory, the memory itself becomes more easily fixed within symbolic representations. Here, ideology—or what Halbwachs calls dogma or doctrine (terms he uses interchangeably)—takes on the central and determinative role. This symbolic value is repeatedly projected back upon the locales in question. As Halbwachs puts it in relation to Jerusalem, "The Christians outside Palestine could invoke Jerusalem without fear of being contradicted by a clashing reality. The image had to adjust itself to beliefs, not to real places."[33] Whether this fixing of memory ought to be read as a consolidating, stabilizing effect or as an ossification depends upon how the memory is preserved. "It is of the nature of remembrances," Halbwachs writes, "when they cannot be renewed by resuming contact with the realities from which they arose, to become impoverished and congealed."[34] It is not fully clear from Halbwachs's explication whether the freezing of an impoverished collective memory is a natural or inevitable part of memory's life cycle. But one is left with the impression of collective memory as a constantly changing element in social life, changing either to adapt to new circumstances or to wither away when not needed or nurtured.[35]

Of course, Halbwachs's ideas about collective memory emerge out of their own social and intellectual milieu, and it is worth noting that he is constrained by tensions inherent in his own radically social understanding of religion. Throughout his discussions of religion, it becomes clear that he works with a broadly evolutionary view of social formation. Collective memory survives to the extent that it is adaptive to the present social situation. It changes or dies when the present needs of a group or a society change. But this evolutionary view tends toward making a causal, indeed deterministic claim about social formation. Christianity becomes, in some measure, a historical inevitability grounded in a process of cultural adaptation analogous to a biological one: "In a sense," he writes, "Christianity was the coronation and the result of an entire civilization."[36]

If "the social" was always Halbwach's starting point, "the historical" remained a troubled ground for him. Halbwachs struggled throughout his career with the vexing relationship between collective memory and historical memory. In the essay "Historical Memory and Collective Memory," which appeared in *La mémoire collective* (published posthumously in 1950),[37] Halbwachs renders the differences separating these two concepts in his most explicit terms:

> History can be represented as the universal memory of the human species. But there is no universal memory. Every collective memory requires the support of a group delimited in space and time. The totality of past events can be put together in a single record only by separating them from the memory of the groups who preserved them and by severing the bonds that held them close to the psychological life of the social milieus where they occurred, while retaining only the group's chronological and spatial out-

line of them. . . . History is interested primarily in differences and disregards the resemblances without which there would have been no memory, since the only facts remembered are those having the common trait of belonging to the same consciousness.[38]

The contrasts continue throughout the discussion: collective memory is dependent upon living testimonial; it is continuous, present, and multiple. Historical memory, by contrast, tends toward the unitary and seeks to represent a lost, broken, even irretrievable connection with the past. It is worth considering whether Halbwachs's theoretical framework had to end up in this binary opposition with memory/continuity/sameness/life on one side of the opposition and history/rupture/difference/death on the other. As will be seen below, the relationship between memory and history has many complex facets that fail to come fully into view when it is charted in such stark, binary terms.

HALBWACHS'S THEORY CRITIQUED AND REFINED

His peers, colleagues, and subsequent readers did not wholeheartedly embrace Halbwachs's theses about collective memory, and many have subsequently sought to refine and elaborate aspects of his theory. For example, very soon after the appearance of *The Social Frameworks of Memory*, the historian Marc Bloch (one of Halbwachs's colleagues at Strasbourg and a founder of the influential *Annales* school of cultural historiography) published a cautionary critique of the terms of Halbwachs's argument. Most centrally, he remarked upon the potential perils of attaching the adjective "collective" to terms drawn from individual psychology (collective mentalities, collective consciousness, and collective memory).[39] Years later, the French sociologist of religion Roger Bastide joined his voice to this critique of Halbwachs's unrecuperated and unapologetic Durkheimianism. At the end of his reading of Halbwachs's posthumously published *La mémoire collective*, Bastide observes: "We find again the old Durkheimian problem of the existence of a collective consciousness, exterior and superior to individuals, and in which individuals come to dissolve/coalesce, being nothing but an emanation when they take consciousness of themselves."[40] In a related but more recent critique, social theorists James Fentress and Chris Wickham call attention to the "concept of collective consciousness curiously disconnected from the actual thought processes of any particular person" whereby the individual is reduced to "a sort of automaton, passively obeying the interiorized collective will."[41]

Whereas some critics have challenged the very category of collective memory, others have sought either to elaborate its contours by magnifying its varying manifestations or to reframe collective memory as a process rather than as a reified object. In his work *Das kulturelle Gedächtnis*, for example, Jan Assmann differentiates between different forms of memory, those involving imitation and repetition, objects, modes of communication or language, and finally culture. Moreover, having at his disposal the nuances and subtleties of the German language in which he writes, he can make an ongoing distinction between *Gedächtnis* and *Erinnerung*—between a generalizable memory and multiple, multiform memories. Assmann seeks to solve the problem that some diagnose with the category of "collective memory" via a semantic and conceptual shift, embracing the notion of "cultural memory" over "collective memory."[42]

The epistemological problems that some have raised concerning Halbwachs's work on collective memory, in particular the concerns raised over the implicit claims about consciousness, have been engaged by scholars and theorists at a range of different levels and through a number of different suggestions for their resolution. Many would embrace as a salutary corrective Olick and Robbins's characterization of the field of inquiry when they write that it focuses on "the varieties of forms through which we are shaped by the past, conscious and unconscious, public and private, material and communicative, consensual and challenged," referring "to distinct sets of mnemonic practices in various social sites, rather than to collective memory as a thing."[43] Such a framing of the field allows Halbwachs's important and lasting contribution to remain in view: his insistence that individuals within social groups routinely and inevitably lay claim to a much wider and deeper past than the one constituted by their own personal or historical experience *and* that they discern the meanings of that past through the group's accounting of it. The fruits of this insight have been abundant in the many studies that have appeared in the last twenty years or so, studies that chart the proliferation of cultural practices and artifacts that produce and support collective memory. These studies move beyond Halbwachs in different ways, often emphasizing the ideological work that collective memory and commemorative practices have done to undergird political claims. Collective memory as an analytic category has offered a particularly useful explanatory framework when the object of study has been a highly contested event or period of history. Many of the major political and military events of the twentieth century, from World War I to the Spanish Civil War to the Shoah and the bombing of Hiroshima and Nagasaki to the Vietnam War and beyond, have been read through the lenses of collective memory.[44] The emergence of nationalist movements and new state formations in the modern and postmodern periods has also been charted with reference to the idea of collective memory.[45] Collective memory's emergence as a major interpretive framework in recent years has been explained in various ways, linked to seismic shifts in the theoretical orientations in historiography.[46] Multiculturalist, postmodernist, and ideological critiques have all in different ways called unified grand narratives of the past into question. Collective memory offers a way for thinking about the shifting perspectives that make up what is knowable about the past, and it also offers insight into the power dynamics involved in producing reigning accounts of the past.[47] Moreover, collective memory has been a dominant modality for situating emergent artistic and cultural forms around contemporary experience.[48]

The main arena in which Halbwachs's thought continues to stir controversy has to do with his framing of the relationship between "memory" and "history," as has already been seen. Some readers of Halbwachs have drawn especially critical attention to the tendency in his writing to create a stark division between collective memory (as social construction) and objective history (as a positivist narrative). Indeed, the temptation is strong to fall back into a conceptual opposition whereby "history" becomes coterminous with "what really happened" and "memory" signifies an imperfect simulacrum, a mere distortion.[49] Such a distinction, however, remains deeply fraught and increasingly difficult to sustain in the era of postmodern historiography.[50]

Yet those who would make use of the interpretive category of collective memory (or social/cultural memory) face an ongoing challenge to articulate their understanding of the character of the relationship between "memory" and "history." As has already become apparent, Halbwachs held onto a stark separation between the two, operating as he was within the confines of and in response to an intellectual inheritance that placed a high value on scientific positivism and objectivity in historical writing. Different scholars have, not surprisingly, sought to grapple with this question in a range of different ways. For example, in French historian Jacques LeGoff's framing of the problematic, memory functions as history's precursor or ancestor. In his study *History and Memory*, he maps a temporally shifting terrain on which memory is eventually displaced by forms of increasingly professionalized historiography and technological advances in the preservation of memory. Writing becomes one critically necessary technology required for memory to become or, sometimes, to give way to history.[51] Alternatively, some have articulated an opposition between the two terms such that history is understood as a form of science (understood as objectively constituted and retrievable), whereas memory is a matter of ideology (understood as politically interested and therefore perennially suspect).[52] Memory's version of truth in both of these ways of viewing its relationship to historical truth is either contingent or suspicious, giving way to a view of history as a more sophisticated, professionalized, and purportedly objectivist practice.

In recent years, however, the relationship between these two categories has lost a significant portion of its oppositional character. No one argues that memory and history are completely overlapping and coterminous, yet it is increasingly difficult to impose upon them the easy and impermeable divisions of the past. Some historians have used the category of "memory" as a way of expressing the impossibility of ever producing an utterly objective, exhaustive, and complete account of the past and, as a consequence, as a mode of critiquing historicist claims. In a recent forum among historians, for example, Susan A. Crane characterized the relationship between history and collective memory as one of simultaneity and competition.[53] Others have emphasized the ethical dimensions of memory, especially when engaging particularly charged historical events such as massive warfare, genocide, and culture-destroying imperialism.[54] In this context, "memory" attempts to put history telling into the hands of those who were the victims of disastrous and tragic historical forces. "Memory" here also implies "commemoration," demanding that the past not be forgotten and also calling for history telling as a kind of ritual mourning and remembrance.[55] Meanwhile, oral historians and anthropologists, among others, have emphasized the importance of memory as a source for an otherwise unrecorded past—the histories of individuals and communities whose stories have not been preserved because they lie outside of the dominant, public narrative of political or institutional history.[56] Indeed, memory can take on the force of "counter-memory" (in Foucault's terminology),[57] offering a powerful alternative to official narratives that may mask social suffering.[58] "Memory" can also interact with "mythmaking" in some historical projects, when events in the past are, with greater or lesser intentionality, reclaimed in the process of the building-up of a collective identity.[59] Indeed, it is precisely this relationship—between memory and mythmaking—that is so crucial to understanding how early Christian culture came to be built out of martyrdom, as this book seeks to demonstrate.

Postmodern challenges to the stark binarism of memory versus history have, in these various ways, produced a more subtle and nuanced vision of the relationship of these two critical categories. But it would be misleading to suggest, as a consequence, that memory is therefore easily reducible to a benign alternative gloss on the past, especially when charged political realities provide the framework within which memory is articulated and authorized. Recent debates over the slipperiness of individual memory, especially those involving trauma, can serve as a cautionary tale here, having generated an ample body of literature in which memory serves primarily as a cipher for unreliability.[60] Meanwhile, in a different political frame altogether, memory emerges as a critical player in the negotiations over national futures. In collective attempts to come to terms with national histories of violence and atrocity—the South African experiment stands out most dramatically—memory has come to bear a tremendous moral burden, serving both as a discourse of justice for the victimized and as an

authorizing framework for victims and perpetrators to move forward in recon-
stituting a social and political order. Publicly articulated memory in this context,
with its recognition of different registers of truth, stands as a bulwark against an
endless spiral of retributive violence.[61] It is striking to notice that violence itself
is the privileged object of memory when the political stakes are most intense.

Memory's authority is what is at stake in these different examples, and when
it is simplistically reified and left unqualified or uninflected, memory as a category can do potentially dangerous political work. Some, for example, under-
standably fear that memory as a heuristic category can run the risk of under-
writing revisionist impulses and in this sense become like the category
"experience" in other contexts—unchallengeable and sui generis.[62] Others have
suggested that the question is one of proportion, as does the writer and critic
Gabriel Josipovici in a brief but very suggestive essay, "Rethinking Memory: Too
Much/Too Little."[63] Contrasting dialogic/communal memory with mono-
logic/mythic memory, Josipovici argues that "when communal memory—dialogic memory—breaks down or disappears, myth rushes in to fill the gap."[64]
Here, "myth" bears the connotation of "invented past," as convenient as it is
unreliable. Meanwhile, communal/dialogic memory in this argument is the stuff
of history, preserved and transmitted through a process of exchange and debate.
It occupies the middle ground (in Josipovici's schema) between two other perilous entities: "too much memory" (paralyzed or compulsive memory, which is
to say, myth) and "too little memory" (forgetfulness, amnesia).[65]

While some have worried about the political implications of the notion of
collective memory, others have focused more centrally on the methodological
challenges presented by the term. Observing that memory has become "perhaps
the leading term in cultural history," Alon Confino draws attention to the
undertheorized character of this term, the lack of cohesion in the field, and the
consequent challenges to cultural historiography.[66] Linking the study of memory to earlier attempts to trace the history of mentalities, Confino worries about
the potential reductionism of memory studies. The history of mentalities was
criticized for its psychologizing tendencies and its reduction of beliefs and values to "a social structure established *a priori*."[67] The history of memory, he
argues, flirts with similar reductionism and memory risks becoming simply con-
flated with ideology. Confino argues that three methodological steps are
required as a bulwark against such reductionism. First, historians of memory
must pay attention to both the political and the social in considering how memory is produced and then how it works in specific social locations. Second, they
must consider the question of the reception of memory—how memory work is
received in the broader culture. Third, they must examine the relationship
among different representations and memories in a given society, paying atten-

tion to the places of memory as sites of contestation.[68] These questions of context and contest are crucial, and not only as refinements of the theory of collective memory in the direction of more nuance and subtlety. They are also a salutary reminder of Halbwachs's anxiety over the reification of memory *and* a corrective to the tendency Josipovici diagnosed in memory giving way to myth.

All of these thinkers, from Halbwachs on, are struggling in different ways with the epistemological and evidentiary challenges embedded in the term "memory." By adopting the language of collective (or social) memory for my own work, I do not frame my analysis as an *example* of collective/social/cultural memory but rather as a *study* of it. That is, I read the ancient Christian sources as themselves the creators and purveyors of collective memory. In reading them this way, I will suggest that collective memory, as a theoretical category for characterizing the story of the past, is in many respects indigenous to early Christian culture. Although the relevant modern terms—"collective," "social," "cultural" memory—are not found in the ancient sources, the concern for the preservation of Christian memory is at the heart of early Christian culture. Indeed, in some important respect, the contemporary emphasis on historical criticism of ancient religious texts can be read as a resistance to the predominance of memory as a governing value in these texts. Yet the critical exploration of the production and reception of memory is not unhistorical or antihistorical. Instead, it draws attention to the ways in which the story of the past has been generated, sustained, and interpreted.

COLLECTIVE MEMORY AND THE STUDY
OF EARLY CHRISTIANITY

This line of argument does not mean that memory should remain, as a category, immune from critique or interrogation. As Josipovici and Confino make clear, there are both practical and theoretical challenges embedded in the term that require careful attention by anyone who attempts to use the concept analytically. For a study of early Christian sources, attention must certainly be paid to how memory implies an almost naturalized continuity with the past and with tradition. Since Christianity in its formative stages (and beyond) engaged in a series of contests over how the past should be understood and who should possess the legitimate claim to tradition (and the authority that accompanied it), it should not be surprising to discover that Christian memory work also participated in this process of contestation. Moreover, texts that concern Christians who are understood to be models of piety—martyrs, ascetics, and so on—might reasonably be expected to do an extra share of the labor in these memory-steeped conflicts over authority.

These critical caveats notwithstanding, I argue that memory remains an especially fruitful category for thinking about the interpretation of martyrdom in the early Christian world. From the earliest of sources onward, it becomes clear that early Christians positioned the historical experience of persecution almost immediately within a framework of meaning that drew upon broader metanarratives about temporality, suffering and sacrifice, and identity.[69] Many scholars who have worked on these sources have expended a good deal of energy on separating out the "historical" from the "legendary" in the salutary service of producing a historically verifiable narrative of what we can know about what happened to Christians in the early centuries of the church. As we have already seen, however, the category of memory complicates this distinction. When early Christians generated texts, artistic representations, liturgies, and architectural installations devoted to the martyred, "memory" in its fullest sense was at the heart of the project. Of course, there are some texts that claim greater authority for having been written by eyewitnesses and others that display their encomiastic investments boldly and unapologetically. But the "historical" and the "legendary" are categories foreign to the world that generated the sources themselves. Early Christian writers seeking to preserve the story of Christian martyrdom (and, one might add, the story of the church's past as a whole) wrote with a broad metanarrative in mind, which framed every detail and interpretation.[70] Even the use of purportedly documentary evidence by early Christian writers, both in relation to persecution and martyrdom and in relation to other elements of the Christian past, served the rhetorical interests of creating a persuasive and continuous narrative about this history.[71] The task of early Christian historians was the production of Christian collective memory, a memory characterized by striking degrees of continuity over temporal and geographical distances.

One might even go so far as to argue that they did not simply *preserve* the story of persecution and martyrdom but, in fact, *created* it. It is not a story that becomes visible through the application of the tools of contemporary professional historians. Indeed, as the next chapter suggests, those tools have produced a significantly different story, one profoundly diminished in both scope and drama. Moreover, the lived experience of persecution could produce a wide range of alternative responses, from silence to ignoring the persecutors to portraying those at risk for persecution as actually far more powerful than they in fact are.[72] Yet the Christian story maintains a remarkable ascendancy and resiliency in spite of both historicist challenges and the range of available alternative responses to the problem of persecution. Indeed, as a Roman historian friend argued recently, the collective memory of Christians actually won the contest of legitimacy and remains the compelling account against which professional historians find themselves positioned rather defensively.[73] The project of this book is to ask how that collective memory became so pervasive and so persuasive.

COLLECTIVE MEMORY AND THE PRACTICES
OF ANCIENT HISTORIOGRAPHY

In focusing on collective memory, I continue to take seriously the accounts that modern historians offer about the Roman opposition to Christians as it is manifest in sources from across the empire, sources that can be critically engaged and used to generate a plausible reconstruction of events—if only in the broadest of terms. This critical engagement implies acceptance of particular contemporary historiographical standards, such as the supremacy of the rules of evidence and the importance of veiling or minimizing perspective. It is helpful to remember, however, that these standards are conventional and themselves historically specific. This is not to diminish their value for the professional work of historians, but it does suggest that it is unhistorical to hold ancient sources to these same standards. One does not need to venture far into the ancient historiographical project to recognize different governing values at work, values that also governed ancient Christian writing about the past.

Although this is not the setting in which to engage in a thoroughgoing discussion of ancient and contemporary historiographical theory and practice, I will make two brief observations.[74] The first is this: for Graeco-Roman writers, the practice of preserving the past in "history," "annals," and other genres served broad commemorative, ethical, and ideological purposes. The second is related to the first: the texts that remain for us to interpret from the early Christian world are overwhelmingly rhetorical in their character, and they require approaches that treat them in their textuality rather than approaches that presume their documentary status.[75]

To gloss the first observation, one can turn to the opening pages of some of the ancient historians. Herodotus, for example, begins his sweeping *Histories* with his declared commitment that the things that have come into being from human beings (τὰ γενόμενα ἐξ ἀνθρώπων) not become extinct (μήτε . . . ἐξίτηλα) and that great and marvelous works (ἔργα μεγάλα τε καὶ θωμαστά) of the Greeks and barbarians not be without fame (μήτε . . . ἀκλέα).[76] Herodotus does not explicitly use the language of memory, but his positive valuation of lineage and continuity (as opposites of extinction) and fame (as the opposite of obscurity) suggests that history for him is a form of writing that functions as a bulwark against collective forgetfulness. The work itself has been characterized variously as a source of ethnography, natural history, medicine, and rhetoric, while Herodotus, from antiquity onward, has also been accused of being a liar.[77] This latter charge can, of course, be read as a deauthorizing indictment of Herodotus's project, but it might also rather be understood as a commentary on the problem of the fictive "likely story" in ancient genres of history writing.

Centuries later, in the Roman period, Diodorus Siculus prefaces his *Library of History* with a reflection on the importance of writing a universal history, one that brings all human beings—who are of one race (συγγενεία) despite their separation by place and time—into one and the same organized arrangement (σύνταξις). Those historians who do this are "ministers of divine providence (ὑπουργοὶ τῆς θείας προνοίας)."[78] History for Diodorus is a resource for ethics, providing positive models to imitate and negative ones to eschew. It is by means of the memory of the good that history provides inspiration to human beings to found cities, write laws, and make scientific discoveries and artistic innovations.[79] History provides the tools for transforming mortal toil or suffering (θνητῶν πόνων) into immortal fame (τὴν ἀθάνατον εὐφημίαν).[80] Contrasting historical speech with poetry and law codes, Diodorus asserts that only in history are words and works in complete harmony (μόνην δὲ τὴν ἱστορίαν, συμφωνούντων ἐν αὐτῇ τῶν λόγων τοῖς ἔργοις); history thereby exhorts people toward justice, denounces the evil, and praises the good.[81]

The preface of Livy's *From the Founding of the City* (*Ab urbe condita*) also displays a commitment to commemoration while using the glories of the historical past to critique the present situation.[82] "Here are the questions to which I would have every reader give his close attention—what life and morals were like; through what men and by what policies, in peace and in war, empire was established and enlarged; then let him note how, with the gradual relaxation of disciplines, morals first gave way, as it were, then sank lower and lower, and finally began the downward plunge which has brought us to the present time, when we can endure neither our vices nor their cure."[83] Livy's history is hardly a neutral or objectivist document. Instead, it uses the memory of the past to explain and critique the present.

None of these examples needs to be read as evidence for bad or deficient history writing in antiquity. They can, instead, be understood as contributing to a broader methodological framework that governed writing about the past. As Greek historian Paul Veyne puts it, "In its own genre, ancient history was . . . a means of creating belief."[84] Christian history writing (whatever its precise genre) shared the commemorative, ethical, and ideological interests of its broader cultural context. Christian writing about the past was interested in plotting events along a recognizable teleological trajectory, remembering events in light of a belief of the role of God in history, generating pious models for imitation, and providing a traditional ground for contemporary debates over doctrine and institutional life.[85]

As a consequence, when reading these texts, it is necessary to keep their rhetoricity in full view.[86] In the context of this exploration of early Christian sources on martyrdom, the distinction between "texts" and "documents" advocated by Elizabeth Clark becomes critically important, for virtually all the Christian sources bear a deep imprint of their impulse to persuade. Even those martyr acts thought to be closest to the events that inspired them—acts that present themselves as documentary evidence in the form of court transcripts—are framed by the rhetorical interests of their production and transmission and by the rhetorical impact of their reception. The testifying words of the accused in such documents, even if they could be proven to be a straightforward transcription of words actually spoken (which they cannot), themselves bear the weight of rhetoric.[87] Moreover, their placement within collections of acts and passions of the martyrs embeds them within literary and hagiographic frameworks that significantly complicate any straightforward claims concerning their documentary status. The argument of this book does not concern the verifiable historicity of particular texts about persecution and martyrdom. It concerns the rhetorical and ideological work that these texts did in the early Christian world and continue to do in other contexts by establishing a foundational narrative framework for interpreting social violence and unjust suffering.

Memory, History, Myth

In the debates over the relationship between memory and history, a third term emerged that requires some discussion: "myth."[88] The strong pejorative connotations that emanate from this term in everyday language make it a difficult category for critical analysis, to say nothing of the rich and complex theoretical baggage the term carries with it. This is not the place to review all of the scholarly engagements with this category, but since I argue mythmaking is a by-product of Christian martyrological discourse and collective memory, the terminology requires some explication and glossing.

The use of the language of mythmaking may seem provocative in relation to Christianity. After all, Christianity is a historical religion that explains its origins by reference to a set of events believed to have taken place in the concrete and real historical past and that organizes itself in a clear linear, teleological progression. Beginning with the life and death of Jesus, Christianity moves relentlessly and single-mindedly to culmination and fulfillment in his promised return. This projected return will bring history itself to an end, inaugurating a new age characterized by the reign of God. Moreover, the ongoing theological significance for many Christians, whether Catholic, Orthodox, or Protestant, of "tradition"—events and teachings deemed authoritative even though they emerge in between the founding events and the present—reminds us that "history" continues to be a category of real consequence within the framework of Christian self-understanding. Yet, as has already been seen, this way of telling the story of the Christian past is no simple example of objective, exhaustive historiography. From the beginning, the traditional, mainstream Christian vision of history imprints explicit theological claims upon the past, producing a metanarrative of a meaningful, useable past. This metanarrative is the Christian story, itself a product of a long process of mythmaking. For some people, the invocation of this sort of language necessarily implies some indictment of the Christian story—and depending upon their theological and ideological positions, this indictment is either salutary or deeply threatening. But for the kind of history I am proposing in this book, a history of Christian memory and memorializing, the "what really happened?" questions that motivate many scholars across the spectrum are displaced by questions of "what meanings are produced?" and "what ideological impulses are satisfied?" However compelling the question "what really happened?" might be in a different context, whether a particular martyr actually died in a particular spot on a particular date matters much less to this study than the work that the *memory* of that event does at later points. What I argue is that the work of that memory is tied to the broader Christian project of producing a useable story—the project of mythmaking.

I am not unaware that the language of myth continues to be fraught, even among its technical users. In everyday language, "myth" is often linked to its weightier and more substantial competitor, "reality." Most frequently the two are bound together ominously by the oppositional preposition "versus." Such a usage assures us that we know the difference between fact and fancy, the real and the illusory. In other contexts, the invocation of "myth" is often a way to render certain cultural artifacts innocuous and benign. It comes to stand in the position of the "primitive" in an evolutionary narrative that tells us about how far "we" have come over the course of centuries of cultural development and sophistication. So collections of stories about, say, gods turning into humans or humans into beasts that travel under the generic title of "myth" can be safely allegorized out of reach and significance. These stories are equally charming and distant. They may entertain, but they are sufficiently removed from the reigning episteme that they fail to inspire credulity or serious reception. Even in contexts where some measure of intellectual self-consciousness about such matters obtains, the term often continues to echo some vestigial cultural chauvinism. "We" have our (good/true) religion and theology, while "they" have their (bad/false) myths.[89]

In spite of the difficulties presented by the terms, "myth" and "mythmaking" are nevertheless important for thinking about the emergence of early Christianity precisely because of the impasses categories like "the historical" create for understanding the genesis of new religious movements. I use the term "mythmaking" here not to trivialize Christian origins but to place them in a framework more amenable to explanation. "Myth," in this context, refers to narratives that promote a coherent portrait of the past and that forge links within a community among its members and between the community and its claimed past. Myth is the product of collective imagination, a compelling answer to urgent questions about foundations and identities. Myth produces a *unified* account of the past and a *unifying* account for the present and an imagined future. Myth is the text of a utopian dream, a dream about a complete and seamless story that has the capacity to suture the present (and the future) to the past.

The twin offspring of mythmaking—a unified past and a unifying present/future—are the products of subtle and not-so-subtle processes of framing and sifting, emphasis and supression. Myth necessarily involves a heightened narrativizing of the past and a careful linking of particular stories to larger, cultural master narratives. Myth has a timeless quality to it, a quality that is complicated when it is possible to trace the generation of myth to a particular historical period—as is the case with the generation of the Christian myth. Yet myths can interact with other ways of viewing the past by imposing historical frameworks that generate meaning. For example, the framework of historical periodization might lend itself well to mythmaking—a golden age in the mythic past might be invoked, or time passing could be seen as either the relentless march of progress or the inevitable disintegration of decline.

Importantly, the generation of myth may well also involve the veiling or muting of dimensions of a story that may not accommodate the reigning impulses of a particular social formation or the needs of a community constructing its own identity.[90] In the context of early Christian mythmaking, these processes are often linked to practices of reading and scriptural interpretation and to a wide range of practices of cultural inscription—writing, the creation of ritual, the construction and appropriation of sacred spaces, the generation of art, and the formation of institutional life.

Of course, mythmaking does not take place in a social or historical vacuum. It occurs in relationship to concrete processes of social and cultural formation, even when the traces of those processes may no longer be immediately apparent or accessible to us. Christianity is somewhat remarkable in this regard. It is possible to trace historically the emergence of Christian communities and rituals in the first and second centuries of the common era alongside the emergence of the foundational Christian myth that explained what these communities were and why they performed the ritual acts they did. Unlike many cycles of myth in different cultures, where the origins of the stories are elusive and, indeed, untraceable, the Christian myth is fixable to a geographical region and a series of historical moments. This important difference notwithstanding, the Christian story of origins remains mythic in its ideological orientation and its social function.

Burton Mack has been the most systematic among students of Christian origins in documenting the historical circumstances, political pressures, and ideological resources that gave shape to the founding myth of Christianity. Indeed, he argues definitively and persuasively that what one finds in the New Testament narratives and other writings is quintessentially mythological discourse.[91] Christianity did not burst full-blown onto the historical scene as an absolutely radical alternative to everything that had ever happened before—despite the fact that all-too-many accounts of Christian origins, both popular and scholarly, so intimate or argue outright. Ancient Christians, including those who wrote the texts that would become part of the Christian Bible, were participants in a culturally complex world. This world's rich diversity of ideas, politics, literary genres, rhetorical strategies, modes of relating socially and behaving ritually, and views of history often contested and sometimes blended with each other with a particular vigor during the first centuries of the common era. The stories early Christians told themselves about themselves and about their shared past borrowed widely from this rich cultural repertoire. Although early Christians expressed varying degrees of suspicion and critique of the surrounding cultures, ultimately these very expressions of suspicion were articulated through rhetorical, iconographic, and social strategies with close cultural cognates to be found in the immediate context. The early Christian process of mythmaking is no exception.

The writer and critic Gabriel Josipovici warned that "myth" was the result of "too much memory" and the absence of dialogical processes that can keep collective memory from ossifying into a potentially dangerous, monologic "invented past." Meanwhile, in a recent critical history of theories of myth, the historian of religion Bruce Lincoln has called myth "ideology in narrative form."[92] Such characterizations urge upon us a cautionary stance in relation to the language and content of "myth." In pursuing the history of Christian collective memory in this book, I remain open to the prospective conclusion that the martyrological tradition suffers from "too much memory" and therefore tends toward myth or, in Lincoln's words, "ideology in narrative form." By using the language of mythmaking in relation to the early Christian martyr traditions, I seek to draw attention to the ways that the memory of suffering became a resource for culture making and identity formation in other settings and contexts. I most certainly acknowledge that the resulting formations may not be salutary or benign and that they must remain open to critical assessment. But it is precisely because of the power of the figure of the (mythologized, memorialized) martyr that a careful consideration of how that figure comes to be produced and sustained in the collective imaginary is necessary. Regardless of the historicity of the martyr's story, it is a story that can both make an ethical demand and lend legitimacy to other forms of power claims. Hence, an analysis of how that story becomes part of a tradition's collective memory—as usable past, as living tradition, as myth—remains both urgent and significant.

2

PERFORMING PERSECUTION,
THEORIZING MARTYRDOM

WILLING AND SELF-SACRIFICING DEATH on behalf of one's religion, one's political ideals, or one's community—martyrdom—is hardwired into the collective consciousness of Western culture and is one of the central legacies of the Christian tradition.[1] The ideological content of martyrdom and its political, moral, and emotional force are familiar dynamics in contests where domination and submission are pitted against each other. It is perhaps hard for contemporary westerners to recognize that the ideological inheritance embedded in the idea of "martyrdom" has not always been self-evident. If Western (and notably American) culture is steeped in ideas of martyrdom, it has become so only after centuries of repetition and reinscription. Of course, like every other element of ideology—a term I use here nonpejoratively to signify assumptions that both go without saying and buttress the organization and power relations of a society— martyrdom, too, has a history.

The broader project of this book is to examine some key elements in this genealogy of Christian martyrdom. This book does not purport to offer a story about martyrdom's origins, since it is neither possible nor particularly illuminating to identify a single historical moment in which "martyrdom" came into existence. Instead, it seeks to consider some of the textual and artifactual traces of martyrdom's ongoing cultural production. Various ideas coalesce around the facts of violence and the feelings of marginalization and oppression. These ideas, in turn, produce narratives, social formations, practices, and representations. In the process of making sense of fact and feeling, of generating a collectively livable story, culture is produced. This book is about how these processes came to organize Christian culture around the memory of past suffering, the memory of martyrdom.

Martyrdom is not simply an action. Martyrdom requires audience (whether real or fictive), retelling, interpretation, and world- and meaning-making activity. Suffering violence in and of itself is not enough. In order for martyrdom to emerge, both the violence and its suffering must be infused with particular meanings. Indeed, martyrdom can be understood as one form of refusing the *meaninglessness* of death itself, of insisting that suffering and death do not signify emptiness and nothingness, which they might otherwise seem to imply. Martyrdom always implies a broader narrative that invokes notions of justice and the right ordering of the cosmos. By turning the chaos and meaninglessness of violence into martyrdom, one reasserts the priority and superiority of an imagined or longed-for order and a privileged and idealized system of meaning. Part of what I will argue is that at the heart of the conflict between early Christians and Roman imperial authorities is precisely this conflict over order and narrative, over whose sense of right relationship and justice would prevail, over whose story would dominate the cultural scene.

This chapter explores the competing theories of religion, power, and violence that were at work in the first centuries of the common era when Christians came into conflict with their neighbors, their society, and the representatives of imperial power. The two main features of this conflict focus on the contests over "law" and "sacrifice"—two foundational aspects of civic and religious existence that are both sources for metanarratives concerning justice. The intricacies of the numerous individual conflicts between Christians and Romans as they are preserved in ancient sources are important in this discussion primarily as they reflect the broader strategies that characterize the conflict as a whole. I will argue that both Christians and their opponents were drawing upon different (but sometimes strikingly overlapping) reservoirs of tradition and interpretation, competing understandings of power, and radically different notions of collectivity and its obligations. I will also argue that crucial dimensions of these conflicts relied upon contrasting stories about the past—different modes of collective memory. As each side in the conflict sought to make its perspective the true and righteous one, different versions of the past (and its relationship to the present and future) became critical resources for rendering present circumstances meaningful. It is precisely because of this tendency to refract the present through recourse to the past that it becomes impossible to generate a stable originary narrative concerning Christian martyrdom. Meaningful suffering is always already present in the Christian worldview as a fundamental interpretive category, and Christian theorists repeatedly connect it to earlier textual remnants of such suffering. So, although the cultural production that will take place in the early centuries of Christian culture making elaborates and complicates this central dimension of Christian storytelling, it is all glossing an idea without a precise origin, an idea whose preexistence is the sine qua non of the Christian project.

One final note by way of introduction: The categories of identity traditionally invoked in histories of Roman persecution and early Christian martyrdom tend to reinforce an oversimplifying and potentially misleading binarism: Roman vs. Christian. Obviously, these two categories are not structurally parallel, nor are they in lived experience necessarily mutually exclusive. At the same time, "Romanness" and "Christianness," as fantasies, stereotypes, and ideals, cast a long shadow over the ancient sources. Both are ideals that required constant reinscription, categories whose borders demanded heavy guarding and strategic shoring up through repeated and sustained rhetorical and ritual performances.[2] Indeed, from the Christian point of view, the commemorative practices associated with the production of "martyrdom" were a major defense of the borders of "Christianness," and that defense necessarily involved the production of a Roman imperial other whose political and cultural dominance bore the caricaturing stamp of oppositionality. As ideals, (utopian or paranoid) fantasies, and stereotypes, "Chrsitianness" and "Romanness" shaped the contours of social experience and collective memory, even as the historical experience of these categories most certainly was more complex and potentially contradictory than the idealizations would have willed.

HISTORICAL SUMMARY

The history and memory of Roman persecutions and early Christian martyrdom have been written, rewritten, and preserved many times over by Roman historians, early Christian writers, generations of church historians and artists, and popular culture and popular piety. Although there is no need to rehearse this narrative in great detail here, a general overview will help to situate the more detailed discussion of martyrdom's ideological and cultural resonances.[3]

Christians from the earliest generations onward found a compelling articulation of their circumstances in a narrative of persecution and redemptive suffering. New Testament authors shaped a mythic framework for meaningful suffering and also developed the raw material of self-fulfilling prophecy in repeating predictions of persecutions to come.[4] Paul's interpretation of the death of Jesus as an expiatory sacrifice for others both drew upon available models of suffering for others and also provided a template for later theorizing about

Christian martyrdom.[5] Moreover, Paul himself made use of the authority that came from imprisonment by the Romans, laying the groundwork for a complex martyrological tradition that would accrue to him in the decades and centuries after his death.[6] The Gospel of Mark offered up a narrative of martyrdom *avant la lettre* to which later Christians would attach their identifications and emulations.[7] The first narrative of the church, Luke-Acts, made the predictions of persecution an organizing feature of the triumphant story it told.[8] The gruesome portraits of righteous suffering and vindication in the book of Revelation wrote the story of Christian suffering within the broadest framework imaginable with a driving apocalyptic beat establishing the rhythms for understanding historical experience in cosmic terms.[9] As it did in so many other ways as well, the New Testament provided an interpretive framework for Christians who came afterward both to constitute the meaningfulness of suffering and to trace the contours of their own self-understanding and self-identity.

Christian sources routinely portray the Christian communities that emerged around the Mediterranean basin as embattled enclaves of right teaching and innocent practice positioned amidst profound and hostile error. Although the rhetoric may be the fruit of a propagandistic impulse, it is also likely that these texts reflect the fierce and alienated sentiments of members of these small, sectarian communities—even as the same texts generate and sustain such sentiments. It is also probable that a range of influences and internal impulses intensified such a perspective. Most centrally, the Christian tendency to generate identity through rhetorical strategies of differentiation and assertions of radical superiority intersected with the social and political realities implied by quite small numbers and significant social marginality. As Roman historian Keith Hopkins has argued, the demographics involved (however speculative they must necessarily be) seem to point to a small and extremely marginal group.[10] Moreover, as Hopkins has observed, even if one concedes a larger percentage of literate people to Christian communities than in the general Roman population (a concession complicated by the fact that Christians in the first two centuries did not come from highly educated classes), it is impossible to reconstruct a portrait of early Christianity with more than a handful of literate Christians in any given community at any given time.[11] Hence, the sources that preserve this heightened sense of embattlement are most likely simultaneously deeply sincere and necessarily perspectival. Read through Christian lenses, the story of Christian encounters with their Roman others is a cosmic battle narrative in which the opposition embodied by the Roman authorities takes on demonic auras and resonances. Read through Roman lenses, this same story is often an incidental account of a minor set of skirmishes with unruly subjects—or, indeed, a story that does not even merit being recorded.[12]

Historians of the conflict between Christians and imperial authorities generally agree that, prior to the mid-third century, violence against Christians was sporadic, decentralized, and the product primarily of local conditions and hostilities.[13] Local authorities possessed considerable latitude in applying very general principles to the circumstances that obtained in their jurisdictions. The year 250, meanwhile, is generally considered a pivotal point in the periodization of Roman persecution and Christian martyrdom, marking the occasion of the decree of Decius. This decree required that everyone in the empire offer sacrifice to the gods and secure a receipt affirming that one had done so. For obvious reasons, Decius's decree presented a peculiar challenge to Christians and resulted in the first centralized persecution of Christians. Significantly, an important percentage of the Christian evidence for this persecution produces a portrait not of Christian constancy but of accomodation, evasion, and failure.[14] Moreover, as Roman historian James Rives has shown, the decree of Decius was aimed more centrally toward religious reform within the Roman world, grounded more in Decius's desire to unify diverse and local religious observances around a common practice (e.g., sacrifice) than in the persecution of Christians per se.[15] The Valerian persecution (257–60) and the so-called Great Persecution of Diocletian and others in the early years of the fourth century (303–14) followed Decius's decree.[16]

The persecution under Diocletian had roots in broader conflicts over competing notions of religious obligation, political responsibility, and the nature of Roman society's relationship to the divine. Diocletian had inherited a broad set of political instabilities from his predecessors, and these inspired sweeping military, economic, and administrative reforms alongside an intensification of conservative religious and moral programs.[17] Christians were growing in numbers and influence, and the anti-Christian edicts that were issued in 303 and 304 were aimed at containing the threat this growth represented, a threat to political order, social stability, and religious conformity. Although much of what can be known of Diocletian's reign has been filtered through Christian lenses, contemporary historians have nevertheless proposed plausible reconstructions of the stakes involved in Diocletian's religious, military, and political restoration.

Central to any reconstruction must be the recognition of how thoroughly Roman law, civic identity, and religious obligation overlapped in the ideology of empire. This can be seen in Diocletian's political reforms (e.g., the formation of the imperial tetrarchy); his religious innovations (e.g., intensification of the imperial cult); and his attempts to rein in Christians through both civil penalties (e.g., loss of status and citizenship rights) and ritual demands (e.g., sacrifice). In forming the tetrarchy, itself a pragmatic gesture aimed at restoring some stability to the succession of emperors, Diocletian named himself not only Augustus but also son of Jupiter, aligning his political role and his imperial persona with the deity responsible for order and law.[18] In a world in which religious observance was inextricably interwoven with political security and civic loyalty, Christian affiliation served as a serious challenge to the religious traditions that assured order, stability, and peace. Diocletian sought to restore Christians to the traditional religious observances of Rome or, failing that, to place Christians outside of the boundaries of citizenship.

In the traditional periodization of persecution, the year 250 operates as a watershed. But even after 250, the shift to more top-down and systematic attempts at suppression did not result in wholesale violence against all Christians everywhere. This observation does not mean to diminish the sufferings of those who did endure torture and execution, but it suggests that these experiences were likely those of a very small minority within the minority communities of Christians. The precise number of people involved will always be elusive, of course. Like the demographics of early Christians *tout court*, it is not possible to reconstruct with great certainty the numbers of Christians who suffered persecution during the first four centuries of the Christian era. As G. E. M. de Ste. Croix pointed out a half-century ago, "No estimate of the total number of martyrs can profitably be attempted, but the considerations brought forward here [in an article on the "Great Persecution" of the early fourth century] certainly reinforce the arguments of those who have maintained that in the Great persecution, at any rate, the number was not large."[19] Even if one accepts the earlier argument, put forward by Henri Leclercq, whose reconstructive calculations resulted in the conclusion that some persecution of Christians was happening somewhere in the Roman empire during some 129 years out of a total of 249 years between 64 and 313, one need not conclude on the basis of such statistics that persecutions were generally speaking either large-scale or carried out against all Christians in general.[20] Again, this is not to diminish the lived experience of those who suffered violence at the hands of the civil authorities but rather to provide a context for interpreting it (as a historical experience) and understanding how that experience figured into Christian attempts to render it meaningful. Indeed, one might argue that the capriciousness of state violence— the mere presence of the imperial judicial apparatus with its omnipresent threat of violence, whether or not it was actually carried out—performed a critical kind of psychological work for all manner of subjected peoples, Christians included. As Ramsay MacMullen puts it, "Common or not, depending on time and place, pictures of brutal routines of law in action were no doubt stored away in the memory of every citizen."[21] It may be precisely because of the unpredictability of persecution as a practice that it came to loom even more largely in the Christian imagination.

It remains the case that the memory of persecution and martyrdom played a pivotal role in the generation of Christian culture in the early centuries of the church. The argument of this chapter is that Christian ideology interacted with the structures and practices of Roman imperial society in such a way as to wrest control of the power to name and redescribe the experience of state suppression away from the dominant culture. This took place in a variety of arenas from the legal to the religious. The discussion that follows explores some of the ways in which this process of rearticulation through cultural memory work took place.

PERSECUTION AND MARTYRDOM AS A CONTEST OVER POWER AND REASON, LAW AND ORDER

The imperial judicial apparatus, law and punishment under the Roman empire, provide the broad backdrop for considering the situation of those Christians who were arrested, tried, and punished by imperial authorities. This apparatus and its workings were simultaneously a simple social and material fact in the experience of subject peoples *and* an element in the Christian imagination of martyrdom. The imperial criminal-justice system reinscribed the social hierarchies that were central to other aspects of Roman social order.[22] Punishments varied both in substance and in significance, and they were based not only on the nature and severity of the crime but also on the status of the offender. Those of higher status could escape the more humiliating and cruel punishments—beatings and floggings, exposure to the beasts, crucifixion—while those of lowly free status and slave status could anticipate exceptionally painful punishments, condemnation to hard labor, and most likely an ignominious death.

Humiliores, people of lower ranks, could suffer a range of painful and humiliating punishments. Capital punishment in particular could take a wide diversity of particularly cruel forms. One could be thrown to the beasts, set afire, forced to drink molten lead, crucified, beaten to death, sewn into a sack with a number of animals and drowned, hurled from the Tarpeian Rock, condemned to become a gladiator, and so on. For *honestiores*, people of high rank, the options could include decapitation, the opportunity to commit suicide (or, in the language of the laws, "free choice of the form of death [*liberum mortis arbitrium*]"), or exile. Punishment had a largely propagandistic value, and its spectacular nature seems to have had both didactic and entertainment value attached to it.

A diverse range of social distinctions came into play in deciding what sorts of rights and penalties were available. Citizens, for example, had certain rights that noncitizens did not enjoy. For example, if in good standing, they could remain free during the investigatory phase of a trial.[23] In the realm of criminal penalties, status and position determined the appropriate punishments. Decurions avoided certain especially humilitating and excruciating punishments—relegation to the mines or to hard labor, crucifixion, and being burnt alive.[24] Soldiers were not to be sentenced to the mines or tortured, though they could suffer loss of money and status.[25] Veterans were exempt from the penalty of *ad bestias* and from being beaten with rods.[26] Vestal virgins who were convicted of breaking their vows of virginity were buried alive in what, according to the ancient sources, was a highly ritualized procedure.[27] The men who were convicted of sharing in their crime were beaten to death; on one occasion, at least, they had the option of choosing exile.[28] The broader point here is that the legal and social structures mutually implicated each other, and the punishments recorded in the Christian martyrological sources remind readers that competing narratives of identity and status were being negotiated in the penal system, using the body of the condemned as the field of contest.

A particularly striking dimension of Roman punishment is that imprisonment was not itself a form of punishment; it constituted a temporary detention while the accused awaited trial or the execution of a sentence. This said, some Christian sources nevertheless provide evidence for the fact that Christians themselves sometimes died in prison—but were nevertheless accorded the title "martyr," dying ignominiously if not spectacularly for their faith.[29] For example, in a famous letter written from his place of hiding, Cyprian encourages the commemoration and ritual celebration of "martyrs" who have died in prison:

> You should pay special care and solicitude also to the bodies of all those who, without being tortured, nevertheless die in prison, departing this life in glory. They are inferior neither in valor nor in honor, so that they, too, should be added to the company of the blessed martyrs. They have endured, in so far as they are able, whatever they were prepared and ready to endure. A man who, under the eyes of God, has offered himself to torture and to death, has in fact suffered whatever he was willing to suffer. He did not fail the tortures; they failed him. . . . Accordingly, you should keep note of the days on which they depart this life; we will then be able to include the celebration of their memories in our commemoration of the martyrs.[30]

Punishments, meanwhile, were simultaneously bodily, material, and social. Corporal punishments, loss of property, and loss of status emphasized the social and public character of both crime and punishment. The human body was the explicit site of punishment as the full weight of the state's authority came to be inscribed on the flesh of the criminal. Meanwhile, a second important aspect of

Roman penalties is that they not only reflected social status but also transformed status both practically and symbolically. Any person who was convicted of a criminal offense lost reputation (*existimatio*), an effect that was felt at both practical and symbolic levels. Those who were condemned to the mines, for example, lost their free status, their property, and their ability to make a will or to inherit property from another.[31] A person condemned to death for his or her crimes became at the time of condemnation an outsider to the social order. For those who would argue that an aura of sacrifice surrounded Roman capital punishment, the social and symbolic distancing of the condemned serves as a compelling piece of evidence.

The centrality of status to the Roman legal system is ironically central to the Christian framing of the ideology of martyrdom. If Roman law controlled its citizenry and subject populations (in part, at least) through the threat of loss of status, the Christian rejection of conventionally recognized social status as a meaningful measure of human value implicitly undermined the effectiveness of the system of law. Even if the Christian relationship to categories of social status was complex, sometimes contradictory, and often not completely coherent (especially around gender and around slave status), the view that vindication and salvation were achieved in and through the public humiliation involved in ignominious execution certainly played a significant role in the ideology of martyrdom. At the same time, this valorization of submission would certainly have been a shocking and unintelligible one to the average Roman. Even if the ancient philosophical schools from Plato forward promoted an understanding of philosophy as a rehearsal for death, it would be surprising if this ascetic impulse had translated into the idiom of ordinary interpretations of the systems of criminal law.

If Roman law provided the ideological and practical framework for the persecution of Christians, then what precisely were the legal foundations for the arrests, trials, and punishments of Christians by imperial authorities? In the last century, the debate on this question came to be organized around two quite different sets of assumptions concerning and readings of the (admittedly fragmentary) evidence. French and Italian scholars tended to argue that the persecutions before 250 were formal, centralized, and grounded in precise legal prescriptions; British, German, and American scholars have generated a consensus that there was no formal basis in law for the persecutions that did take place in this early period. Within this latter group, some scholars have argued further that even the more systematic suppression of Christian activity in the decades before the Christianization of the Roman Empire did not result from legal proscriptions against Christianity itself but from imperial rescripts promoting traditional religious observances.[32]

Before the issuance of imperial rescripts by Decius and Valerian, the prosecution of Christians was undertaken by governors who possessed no concrete code of law in which to ground their actions.[33] They were instead dependent upon practical precedents and general guidelines for proper government that then required interpretation in particular situations. As a practical matter, they were also dependent upon specific accusations or charges being brought against individuals or groups of purported Christians. Individual governors could reasonably respond to particular situations with considerable latitude, a situation that could produce diverse understandings depending on the value placed on such flexibility and the effects of relative degrees of inflexibility and latitude in practice.[34] Meanwhile, much of the evidence that we have concerning the activity of governors in this regard comes from early Christian sources, which obviously had an interest in portraying Roman authorities in ideologically charged ways. Rather than argue, however, that the matter should be framed as a question of separating the kernel of historical truth from the chaff of Christian rhetorical excess, I will suggest here that Christian writers appropriated the fact of legal latitude and recast it in theological and cosmic terms.

The historical precedent that established "being a Christian" as an actionable offense punishable by death was likely the execution of Christians by Nero in the wake of the fire that devastated Rome in 64 C.E.[35] Henceforth, courts that possessed *imperium* held both jurisdiction over any charges that might be brought and the power to carry out resulting sentences.[36] The precise nature of the charges that might be brought has been the subject of some debate. Some have suggested that the offense was primarily religious and that Christians were seen as responsible for the introduction of an alien cult that caused people to turn away from the traditional Roman religions.[37] Others have argued that the widespread rhetoric of vituperation that Christian apologists sought to counter, a rhetoric replete with dramatic accusations of cannibalism, infanticide, incest and other sexual excesses, magic, and treasonous conspiracy, was mirrored in the application of laws against such practices in actions against the Christians.[38] Still others emphasize the public claiming of Christian identity and the concomitant refusal of other identities and allegiances, including religiopolitical ones, as a source of social discord demanding discipline and punishment.[39] As the Christian sources themselves suggest, there was a strong degree of malleability in individual cases of prosecution, which mirrored the discretion accorded governors in dealing with such matters and provided for a range of potentially legitimate charges.

The pre-Decian martyr acts offer a compelling set of portraits for the malleability of the legal circumstances in which some Christians found themselves caught.[40] In addition to providing evidence for the historical facticity of the legal situation in the second and early third centuries, these texts engage in a narratively and rhetorically subtle appropriation of the historical reality in the service of a broader Christian interpretive activity. Here, as elsewhere, the historically verifiable elements of the Roman prosecution of Christians are complexly interwoven with the emergent Christian theory of martyrdom. The absence of precise legal foundations for charging Christians with a crime becomes, in the hands of Christian writers, fruitful evidence for the lawlessness of the hostile world in which they are but temporary sojourners.

In the *Martyrdom of Polycarp*, which narrates events in Smyrna in the mid-second century, there is no mention of any particular charge against Polycarp and the others who have died before him.[41] The accusation of "atheism" appears in the mouths of both the angry mob and the governor.[42] The attempts to persuade and, later, to coerce the Christians to recant include the command to sacrifice and to swear by the genius of the emperor; these suggest that such religious gestures could signal a change of heart. Neither the accusation of "atheism" nor the command to sacrifice and to swear by the emperor's genius suggests a codified prohibition or requirement that Polycarp or the others have violated. The religious dimension of the conflict seems to draw upon a broad and inchoate sensibility on the part of the blood-thirsty crowd, and the governor meanwhile consistently seeks to resolve the conflict, first through persuasion and only secondarily through threats. Meanwhile, prior to Polycarp's arrest, the governor has failed to persuade "the most noble Germanicus" to recant; instead the young man enthusiastically embraces martyrdom, dragging a wild beast on top of him, "wishing to be released sooner from unjust and lawless life [τοῦ ἀδίκου καὶ ἀνόμου βίου]."[43] Lawfulness and lawlessness, in this text, appear to be in the eye of the beholder.

Another second-century *acta* suggests something of the role that private accusations and judicial flexibility played in the processes in which Christians were prosecuted. The *Acts of Ptolemaeus and Lucius* contains the story of Ptolemaeus, who is accused by an irate husband whose wife has been his student. The woman has left her husband as a consequence of her repentance, and she too is the object of a complaint. (An intriguing narrative detail appears in the text: the woman had sought legal relief from her husband's complaint directly from the emperor, who granted her petition. It was as a result of the woman's foiling of her husband's legal maneuver against her that he sought vengeance against Ptolemaeus.) Once Ptolemaeus has been arrested by a centurion, and later when he is brought before the prefect, the emphasis in this account focuses on the posing of the question, "Are you a Christian?" and Ptolemaeus's forthright confession of his identity.[44] The text emphasizes that "a true Christian" neither denies his identity nor avoids answering the question.[45] When Urbicus, the prefect, condemns Ptolemaeus to death, the Christian Lucius brazenly raises an objection against what he sees to be "an unreasonable judgment."[46] The brief speech he delivers is illuminating, for he explicitly asserts that Ptolemaeus has not been found guilty of any crime—and he goes on to provide a list of crimes of which his fellow Christian is innocent: adultery, sexual immorality, murder, clothes stealing, robbery, and "any crime whatsoever." He then challenges the honor of the prefect, the emperor, his son, and the senate, arguing that the sentence imposed is unworthy of all of them. The contrast Lucius sets up is explicit: Ptolemaeus has not violated any recognizable social or legal norms—neither those governing proper sexual practice nor those constraining violence nor those that protect private property. Being innocent of all crimes, he has nevertheless been condemned "because he confesses the name of Christian."[47] The logic of the story depends upon the complete and *recognizable* innocence of Ptolemaeus, including the absence of a precise law that Ptolemaeus might be seen to have violated. Lucius's impertinent speech—which results, perhaps predictably, in his own accusation and condemnation—suggests that Urbicus potentially could have been open to persuasion and, more importantly, would have actually possessed the reasonable latitude to change Ptolemaeus's sentence. Moreover, the swiftness of Lucius's own condemnation, followed immediately in the short narrative with what amounts to a postscript ("Next, a third man also deserted and was sentenced to be punished"[48]), demonstrates that the prefect's power here was grounded less in precise legal prescriptions than in his broad capacity to pass judgment swiftly and ruthlessly.[49]

The short recension of the *Acts of Justin and his Companions* provides an even more intensified narrative concerning the centrality of Christian confession and identity at the heart of the prosecution of the seven Christians named in this text.[50] This text is generally included among the more historically reliable of the pre-Decian *acta*, and it emphasizes the confessional character of Christian guilt.[51] Rusticus, the prefect, asks each of the Christians in turn whether he is a Christian; each one confesses forthrightly. Rusticus follows this exchange with a short question about what Justin believes his fate will be after having been flogged and beheaded (to which Justin responds with certainty that he will ascend to heaven).[52] Rusticus concludes the exchange with a final threat—"If you do not obey, you will be punished"[53]—and then pronounces the sentence: "Those who have refused to sacrifice to the gods are to be scourged and executed in accordance with the laws."[54]

Although this text focuses on the exchange between the Christians and the prefect, it also sets the scene by describing the context in which the events take place: "In the days of the lawless ordinances of idolatry, the remembered saints being arrested were brought before Rusticus, the prefect of Rome."[55] Several commentators have suggested that this narrative framing is a later addition, rationalizing the second-century events to a later period of Christian history.[56] It certainly has nothing to do with the ensuing interrogation and testimony. It is true that the sentence includes Rusticus's condemnation of "those who have refused to sacrifice to the gods" as an action "in accordance with the laws." The sacrifice would, however, most certainly function as an ex post facto sign of recantation. The punishment "in accordance with the laws" signals not a particular law that the Christians have violated but the broader discretion possessed by Rusticus (and others who shared his legal authority) to impose a penalty on those who confess Christian identity.

The narrative remains of what happened to the Christian community in Vienne and Lugdunum/Lyon (Gaul) in 177 are recorded in a letter written soon after the events themselves and preserved in Eusebius's *Historia Ecclesiastica*.[57] This text offers yet another example of how pliable and adaptable civic and state authority could be in any particular situation of prosecution. Indeed, the absence of any sort of legal precision in rationalizing the violence that took place is especially striking in this text. Meanwhile, the writers of this letter emphasize the extragovernmental—indeed, extrahuman—causes of the persecutions of Christians in this pogromlike incident. The anger, mania, and cruelty of the mob are the main impulses behind the tortures, imprisonments, and executions narrated here. The writers of the letter understand these strong and irrational emotions to be the products of the devil's intervention in human events and to serve, ultimately, to fulfill scripture's assurances concerning the motives and the fates of the lawless and the righteous. Where more precise discussion of the charges brought against the Christians appears, it is quite clear that these charges are incidental to a process that serves primarily to respond to the bloodthirstiness of the crowd.

An initial public interrogation of arrested Christians under the oversight of the tribune (χιλίαρχος) and in the presence of the crowd in the agora results in public confession by the Christians. The confessions provide sufficient rationale for the Christians to be imprisoned until the governor (ἡγεμών) arrives. When the governor displays cruelty against the Christians, a young Christian man who believes the sentence to be unreasonable steps forward to request a hearing so that he might offer an apologia for the Christians, claiming their innocence of both atheism (ἄθεος) and impiety (ἀσέβης).[58] This is the first occasion in the text where any sort of concrete charge is suggested, and it is the crowd that shouts the young man down, resulting in his own interrogation, confession, and condemnation. Later references to anti-Christian charges emphasize their capriciousness or outright falsehood. Non-Christian slaves of Christian households are arrested; their fears of torture (and the influence of Satan) result in their making false accusations of incest, cannibalism, and other unspeakable/unthinkable/unimaginable crimes against their masters.[59] Later, a Christian woman who had initially denied her religious identity is the target of demonic attempts to use torture to coerce her to say "ungodly things about us."[60] The absence of concrete charges, beyond the general charge of "being a Christian," serves as evidence for the letter's writers of a divinely ordered dispensation: those who had confessed at the beginning had no further charges brought against them whereas those who had initially denied were accused of being murderers and defiled persons who would be punished twice as much as the faithful Christians.[61]

There are just a few places in the text where a glimpse of a more orderly legal process appears. Upon learning that Attalus, one of the Christians, may also be a Roman citizen, the governor sends him back to prison and waits for a reply from the emperor to an inquiry about what to do with such people.[62] It soon becomes clear, however, that such legal niceties are secondary to the governor's desire to satisfy (or appease) the mob. Within a few paragraphs, Attalus finds himself accompanying another Christian in the arena, where the governor has sent him in order "to please the mob."[63] The only other mention of any sort of legal grounding for the events taking place appears in the middle of the letter: "For Caesar had written that they should be tortured to death, but if any should recant they should be let go." As a consequence, the governor makes a public show of bringing the Christians before the judgment seat, reinterrogating them, and dispatching them with striking efficiency. "He accordingly examined them again, beheaded all who appeared to possess Roman citizenship and sent the rest to the beasts."[64]

The absence of any clear legal foundation for what is happening is, on the one hand, most likely simply a reflection of the facts of the matter at this time and place. On the other hand, it also serves an important narrative function within the letter itself, since it appears alongside the irrationality and diabolical character attributed to the persecutors by the Christian writers. Moreover, the fluidity of the legal situation needs to be read against the scripturally based argument in the text according to which the actions of both the governor and the people are understood as necessarily "lawless" acts whose essential nature renders the "righteous" character of the Christians equally essential.[65] If the madness and cruelty of the crowd and the authorities in this text suggest a disorderly and capricious escalation of violence, the authors' attribution of the ultimate responsibility for what transpires to the devil promotes a sense of inevitability of the proceedings. The absence of a precise legal foundation for the prosecution of Christians here is simultaneously, then, a likely historical reality *and* an ideologically useful narrative element that actually serves Christian rhetorical interests. It allows for an indictment of the ruling authorities as themselves not governed by "law" and for the vindication of Christians as embodiments of innocence— hence the repeated assurances by figures in the narrative that, no matter what the accusation, Christians are always innocent of it.[66]

The other two texts recounting pre-Decian martyrdoms—*The Acts of the Scillitan Martyrs*[67] and *The Passion of Perpetua and Felicitas*[68]—are familiarly lacking in any precision concerning the reasons for the arrest and prosecution of these groups of North African Christians. In both of these Latin texts, Christian confession—the forthright and public claiming of a Christian identity—lies at the heart of the proceeding. In both texts, the persecutors press the Christians to engage in religious activity in accordance with traditional Roman piety and observance; in both cases, the Christians are condemned for their refusal to do so. *The Acts of the Scillitan Martyrs*, in its brevity and lack of narrative development, suggests the genre of a court report. As such, it includes a quotation of the sentence meted out by the proconsul: "Since Speratus, Nartzalus, Cittinus, Donata, Vestia, Secunda, and the others confess that they live according to the Christian rite, and although the opportunity to return to the custom of the Romans was offered to them, they persevere in obstinance, they are sentenced to die by the sword."[69] *The Passion of Perpetua and Felicitas* simply reports that in response to the confessions of the Christians, Hilarianus sentenced them to death by the beasts.[70] Like the other early evidence concerning the prosecution of Christians, these texts also intimate a lack of legal precision and a concomitant degree of discretion residing in the persons of the local representatives of state authority.

It is worth reflecting on the ideological and practical impact of the flexibility inherent in this construction of the governors' powers. On the one hand, absent a particular law that articulated the state's position on the matter of the Christians, a governor's latitude could as easily result in a live-and-let-live sort of policy of benign tolerance as it might produce a virulent (if still local) persecution. On the other hand, the dependence of the process on the vagaries of precedent, interpretation, accusation, and personal sensibilities likely inflected the entire situation with a tone of capriciousness. The state's power here came to be enacted not through the equal imposition of precise and predictable legal constraints but in response to particular circumstances. The impulsive flare of anger or prejudice on the part of an accuser, the varying degrees of hostility or anxiety residing in a governor's assessment of the Christian threat, or the presumed practical impact of a well-timed public execution could well have fed the decision making that grounded particular occasions of prosecution and punishment.

From the perspective of social control, such an organization of authority could have a policing impact quite in excess of any discernible physical force.[71] That the governor possessed considerable discretion meant that his actions were potentially less predictable than if he were acting within the framework of an articulated law code. As a consequence, his discretion could produce a particular kind of docility within a subject population insofar as that subject population sought to escape both notice and prosecution/punishment. Where this power dynamic broke down in the conflicts between governing authorities and Christian communities was at a critical point of interpretation. Judicial authorities might reasonably have thought the mere threat of torture and execution a sufficient deterrent. What they could not have foreseen, however, was the degree to which the resulting suffering and death (for the authorities, the by-product rather than the goal of the whole legal proceeding) would become for Christians the desired outcome and indeed the principal aim of the whole performance. By reinterpreting suffering as salvation, Christian theorists interrupted the circuit of power created by Roman judicial structures and articulated a competing theory of power.[72] Whether one interprets this move through the lenses of Foucault's theory of power (which always implies resistance),[73] through James C. Scott's "arts of resistance,"[74] or through some other interpretive framework, it is clear that the inversions of value that are at the heart of Christian thinking here are central to transforming "persecution" into "martyrdom" and powerlessness into power.

A different situation might be expected to obtain from the mid-third century on, once emperors began issuing edicts that, when carried out, could cause Christians to face threats, coercion, accusation, trial, and sometimes punishment.[75] The Christian sources concerning the persecutions resulting from imperial edicts emphasize the legal character of the prescriptions toward sacrifice but portray the Christians who refuse to acquiesce as answering to a higher law. In *The Passion of Julius the Veteran*, for example, the portrait of Julius sets the identity of "Christian" in opposition to the legal requirements handed down by the emperor (in this case, Diocletian).[76] When the prefect asks who has been brought before him, one of the officials responds, "This is a Christian, and he will not obey legal decrees."[77] In the ongoing debate between Maximus the prefect and Julius the Christian, Maximus threatens ("If you do not respect the imperial decrees and sacrifice, I will cut off your head") and Julius welcomes the punishment as an answer to his prayers.[78] Meanwhile, as the political conflict intensifies, the ideological conflict takes on starker contours. When Maximus informs Julius that he will enjoy perpetual praise if he endures for the sake of civic laws (*nam si pro patriae legibus patereris, haberes perpetuam laudem*), Julius responds that he most certainly does suffer for the laws, but for divine laws (*pro legibus certe haec patior, sed pro diuinis*).[79] As the conflict comes to a resolution in the condemnation of Julius, the narrator emphasizes the diabolical nature of the execution, calling the executioner "the devil's servant [*minister diaboli*]."[80]

Other narratives that represent Christian martyrdom in this later period also emphasize these two arenas of the conflict—law and piety. For example, in the *Martyrdom of Felix the Bishop* (of Tibiuca in North Africa), Diocletian's first edict generates heated conflict between Christian clerics and imperial authorities over the Christians' refusal to hand over their books; a contest over whose law (the emperor's or God's) is preeminent; and finally Felix's execution, which he figures in a final prayer as a sacrifice.[81] Meanwhile, the *Martyrdom of Crispina* (also North African) reports that Crispina is charged with showing contempt for the imperial laws (*quae legem dominorum nostrorum principum contempsit*) in her insistent loyalty to superstition, figured as both madness and folly. In a direct debate between Anullinus the proconsul and Crispina, the Roman official demands her observance of "the sacred edict" (*sacrum praeceptum*), to which Crispina responds her willingness to observe the *praeceptum* of Jesus Christ, "my lord [*meus dominus*]."[82]

In what appears to have become almost a cliché for Christian writers, Roman authorities are repeatedly deemed "lawless and impious" in these texts and moreover are understood to be doing the devil's work.[83] Here, as in the texts concerning earlier occasions of persecution, the historical bases for the events that are narrated are immediately filtered through and interwoven with Christian expectations and interpretations. As a consequence, the authorities' attempts to achieve Christian compliance through various expedient means appear in Christian writings as sure signs of the authorities' sheer lack of both moral constancy and theological coherence. The persecutors are routinely portrayed as the servants of the devil, as madmen inspired by the folly of their error, as savage beasts whose thirst for blood is nearly insatiable.[84] Meanwhile, what most certainly must have appeared to their opponents as pure stubbornness, obstinacy, and even suicidal madness on the part of Christians is translated into a dramatic portrait of endurance, tenacity, and faith-filled intensity in which the conventional values of life and death are radically inverted. In this way, the debate over the obligations of piety and the moral force of the law was staged between two opponents who appear, at first glance, to be speaking the same language but whose ideological frames are altogether different. As we will see with the Christian use of the language of sacrifice in this context, the worldviews that clashed in this conflict were simultaneously overlapping and profoundly incommensurate with each other.

READING THE HISTORY THROUGH COMPETITION OVER NOTIONS OF SACRIFICE

Just as Christian theorists remade the facts of Roman legal constraint through reinterpretations of the character of law and the nature of power itself, they also performed complex reinterpretations of the character and nature of religious observance and practice. Nowhere is this clearer than in the ways that sacrifice was variously deployed in Christian sources concerning martyrdom. Drawing upon the profound resources of the biblical tradition about sacrifice and responding to the concrete demand on the part of civic authorities to prove their recantation through sacrifice to the Roman gods, Christians sought to disrupt the dominant culture's assessment of sacrifice. They did so through rhetoric, interpretation, and theorizing, all of which were aimed at reconfiguring the idea of meaningful sacrifice as being solely the domain of the Christian.

In the framework of the Roman Empire, sacrifice was the centerpiece of a public piety that was both "civic" and "religious," in the conventional senses of these terms. Sacrifice to the traditional gods signaled one's commitment to the shared enterprise of collective life and one's participation in and submission to the complex bonds of allegiance and protection that linked the social and political world to the realm of the divine. Sacrifice was a force that kept power in circulation in Roman society, and it sustained in good working order complex networks of relationship and patronage. In the imperial period, sacrifice also served as a means of unifying a disparate and far-flung empire, linking the imperial center (Rome) and the colonized periphery (the provinces).[85] From the vantage point of a post-Enlightenment society that understands the separation of the political and the religious as an ideal to be protected, the Roman imperial situation requires careful attention to the myriad ways in which "Roman religion" might, it could be defensibly argued, not quite exist. That is, insofar as practices that could conventionally be called "religious" intersected so thoroughly with political institutions, social structures, familial commitments, and recognition of the self-in-society, there is very little in ancient Roman society that would not as a consequence qualify as "religious."

Sacrifice was the consummate gesture of piety and, at the level of ritual, it helped to maintain networks of relationship and patterns of order that were simultaneously social, political, and religious. At the level of the symbolic, it signaled a commitment to traditional values, public institutions, and hierarchically organized social and political relationships—the status quo, underwritten by divine favor and sustained through regular ritual reinscription. Sacrifice in the Roman religious system was simultaneously absolutely central and completely self-evident and naturalized. Therefore, a refusal to participate in this sacrificial order—for whatever reason—would have been viewed by the vast majority of the empire's population as a rejection of all manner of socially ordering elements—kinship, gender identities, and so on—and therefore as utterly nonsensical, irrational, foolhardy, impudent, sacrilegious, and antisocial.[86]

Meanwhile, the notion of sacrifice that was emerging from Christian practice and theorizing was, from the start, at odds with the dominant culture's assumptions and values. On the one hand, Christians possessed a rich heritage concerning sacrifice deriving from the Hebrew scriptures. On the other, Christians from a very early point in their history interpreted the death of Jesus in dual terms: as a profound and decisive interruption in the sacrificial logic and economy and as itself an expiatory sacrifice.[87] Moreover, sacrifice also came to play a complex historical and ideological role in the ancient Christian literature on martyrdom. From the earliest evidence documenting the conflict between Roman officials and Christian stalwarts, sacrifice frequently functioned as a convenient way for a person to authenticate his or her recantation of Christian identity through a public ritual performance.[88] In sources from the period of the Decian persecution in the mid-third century, sacrifice also operated as a central provocation of persecution and martyrdom. As has already been noted, under the edict of the emperor Decius, all imperial subjects were required to perform sacrifice; those who refused would suffer the penalty of their obstinacy. It was in this persecution that the conflict of religious worldviews between sacrificing Romans and nonsacrificing Christians first came into particularly high relief.

The Christian understanding of sacrifice was clearly distinct from and incommensurate with the broader cultural view. Simultaneously more metaphorical and more literal, Christian assessments of the content and meaning of sacrifice were radically different from the symbolic content and the sociopolitical significance and functions of Roman sacrifice. In the Roman context, sacrifice sustained the social, political, and religious equilibrium of a steeply hierarchical social order. In the Christian view, sacrifice had been definitively brought to an end by the death of Jesus; continued sacrifice after this history-shattering event could only signal idolatry and demon worship. Ironically, despite their emerging theory of the end of sacrifice, Christians simultaneously appropriated the language of sacrifice to describe their experience of persecution at the hands of the Romans, seeing their own deaths as parallel imitations of the death of Jesus. In refusing to perform sacrifice, Christians removed themselves from the position of agent (sacrificer) to the position of victim (sacrificed). Yet at the same time, by aligning themselves with Jesus's own victimhood, they claimed as well the immediate divine vindication that Jesus himself, according to Christian teaching, enjoyed. They deprived the Roman gods of sacrifices and became, themselves, willing sacrifices to the one true God.

Performing Sacrifice, Becoming Sacrifice: The Metaphorical Range of Martyrdom

In his famous early third-century *Exhortation to Martyrdom*, the Alexandrian church father Origen articulates a theology of martyrdom in which, among other things, martyrdom functions as an expiatory, atoning sacrifice. In particular, at one point in the treatise, he makes a series of connections between ancient Israelite sacrifice, the death of Jesus interpreted through the figure of Jesus as the high priest offering himself as sacrifice, and the deaths of martyrs expressed as priestly imitations of this same sacrifice. The passage reads:

> For just as those who served the altar according to the Law of Moses thought they were ministering forgiveness of sins to the people by the blood of goats and bulls [Heb. 9:13, 10:4; Ps. 50:13], so also the souls of those who have been beheaded for their witness to Jesus [Rev. 20:4, 6:9] do not serve the heavenly altar in vain and minister forgiveness of sins to those who pray. At the same time we also know that just as the High Priest Jesus the Christ offered Himself as a sacrifice [cf. Heb. 5:1, 7:27, 8:3, 10:12], so also the priests of whom He is High Priest offer themselves as a sacrifice. This is why they are seen near the altar as near their own place. Moreover, blameless priests served the Godhead by offering blameless sacrifices, while those who were blemished and offered blemished sacrifices and whom Moses described in Leviticus were separated from the altar [Lev. 21:17–21]. And who else is the blameless priest offering a blameless sacrifice than the person who holds fast his confession and fulfills every requirement the account of martyrdom demands?[89]

The argument of this passage of Origen's treatise is predicated on a series of analogies drawing upon several different biblical sources and arguing for a precise parallelism between the meanings accruing to ancient Israelite practice and those deriving from early Christian experience. The first analogy claims that animal blood spilled on an altar is like the souls of martyred Christians insofar as both generate the forgiveness of sins. The second analogy is twofold: on the one hand, Jesus is the "High Priest," implicitly linked with the ancient Israelite high priest; on the other, the Christian martyrs are themselves priests alongside the archetypal figure of Jesus, the high priest. But, in addition, Jesus and the faithful Christians are not only those who sacrifice but those who are sacrificed—they are not only like the high priest of the Israelite sacrificial cult but also like the animals whose shed blood assures the forgiveness of sins. The purity of the priests and the wholeness and holiness of their offerings translate into the pure and undefiled character of the Christian martyr's sacrifice. Placed within the framework of sacrifice, martyrdom in this discussion requires an ethical version of cultic purity—the confession of the Christian must be unadulterated and undefiled, just as the Israelite priest must be ritually pure and his victim unblemished. The naturalized character of Christian ideas about sacrifice may unduly mute the peculiarity and strangeness of this move from cultic to ethical purity, a move predicated simultaneously on analogy (sameness) and contrast (difference). As the material practice of sacrifice becomes the raw material of Christian metaphor, the term itself becomes increasingly elastic and capacious.

In one sense, the sacrificial associations of Origen's argument seem straightforward; in another, they defy a commonsense logic. The sacrificer and the sacrificed fuse into a single figure whose pure offering of self constitutes a complete and acceptable sacrifice. Meanwhile, the actual historical executioners of Christians recede completely from view, those whom they execute rendered the grammatical subjects of a passive construction ("the souls of those who have been beheaded for their witness"), the action itself decisively detached from its agent.[90] Of course, the sacrificial logic in large measure demands this detachment, for there is no way that the cultic purity ascribed to the priest could be transferred onto the state's executioner. It is as though, in this sacrificial economy, the realities of the world recede altogether while the crucial exchange between faithful humans and the sacrifice-accepting divine takes center stage.

More than a century before Origen's exhortation, Ignatius of Antioch wrote on his way to martyrdom in Rome to the Christians of that city, exhorting them not to intervene to save his life. In pleading with them, Ignatius deployed the heady language of sacrifice to describe his desired fate. In this letter, he says that he wants to be "poured out as an offering to God while an altar is still ready" and to be found to be a "sacrifice to God through these instruments [of torture and execution]."[91] In other letters he wrote during the same journey, Ignatius characterizes his death as a ransom for others, paralleling the salvific function of Jesus' own sacrificial death.[92] Meanwhile, numerous other early Christian martyrological sources deriving from the second half of the second century and into the early third century mobilize the language of sacrifice in the service of the martyrological narrative. The public spectacle of Polycarp's death, for example, is explicitly characterized as a sacrifice by its narrator:

> Then he, having placed his hands behind him and having been bound, like
> a splendid ram chosen from a great flock for a sacrifice, a burnt offering

prepared and acceptable to God, looked up to heaven and said: "O Lord God Almighty, Father of your beloved and blessed Son Jesus Christ, . . . I bless you because you have considered me worthy of this day and hour, that I might receive a place among the number of the martyrs in the cup of your Christ, to the resurrection to eternal life, both of soul and of body, in the incorruptibility of the Holy Spirit. May I be received among them in your presence today, as a rich and acceptable sacrifice, as you have prepared and revealed beforehand, and have now accomplished, you who are the undeceiving and true God. . . . I praise you, I bless you, I glorify you, through the eternal and heavenly High Priest, Jesus Christ."[93]

Of several of the martyrs of Lyon who died in 177, the narrator of the eyewitness account makes numerous sacrificial references. Of the deaths of Alexander and Attalus, he writes: "On the following day he [Alexander] went in [to the arena] with Attalus. . . . Finally, they were sacrificed [τοῦσχατον ἐτύθησαν]." The burning flesh of Attalus meanwhile is described as having the odor of a burnt sacrifice (κνῖσα).[94] When the slave girl Blandina is executed, the narrator states simply, "She too was sacrificed (ἐτύθη καὶ αὐτή)."[95]

The examples could be multiplied, but the point is clear—martyrdom and sacrifice are integrally linked in the early Christian sources. Indeed, numerous scholars have documented the relationship between martyrdom and sacrifice in early Christian thought.[96] This scholarly discussion has tended to focus on the different terminology for sacrifice used in ancient texts concerning martyrdom, on the specific types of sacrifice analogized by Christian martyrdom, and on the theology of sacrifice that underlies the reigning analogies. Some authors emphasize the *imitatio Christi* dimension of martyrological sacrifice; others suggest that each martyr's death functions as a sacrifice of atonement; still others distinguish the martyr's sacrifice from other forms of sacrifice by calling it "spiritual."[97]

The mobilization of sacrifice as metaphor by early Christian theorists of martyrdom is enabled by the historical construction of sacrifice as a recognized practice and as a part of the Roman religious system. As it did with legal discourses and notions of lawfulness and orderliness, the conflict between the dominant Roman social order and Christians used the field of "sacrifice" as a staging ground. Moreover, just as Christians were able to neutralize the judicial threat of loss of social status ideologically (albeit not practically) by declaring status loss as a central marker of faithful Christian identity, so they troubled the sacrificial system of Roman piety by reconfiguring the sacrificial relationship in other terms. In this way, they called upon the collective memory of Hebrew sacrifice, which Christians claimed as their heritage, now interrupted by the ultimate sacrifice in the form of the death of Jesus. But they also inverted the expected social framework by embracing the characteristics of the sacrificial victim—willing-ness, passivity, and submission—and, indeed, using gender to inflect their appropriation of the sacrificial economy. This ideological move was available because certain dynamics were already in play—notably, the arena's operating as a sacrificial staging ground and the dominant discourses of gender providing a broader language for signifying power.[98]

In recent years, more scholarly attention has been paid to situating Christian martyrdom in the cultural and political context of the Roman arena. A few scholars have sought to explore the potential sacrificial resonances of the arena, though the Christian appropriation of those sacrificial echoes has received less treatment. And although gender as a category of analysis has certainly played a significant role in recent years in scholarly treatments of Christian martyrdom,[99] gender and sacrifice have generally not been brought together in these discus-sions.[100] The argument that follows seeks to bring these dimensions—sacrifice, arena, and gender—together within the framework of theorizing martyrdom. Sacrifice is a mobile metaphor in this context, rooted in the sociopolitical and religious foundations of Roman society but also having the capacity to travel into other realms of meaning production.

This discussion cannot settle all the complex theoretical, historical, and interpretive questions that arise out of the complicated intersections of these categories, a task that far exceeds the limits of its particular context. What I hope to do, instead, is to discuss the broader ideological stakes involved. To what question does the elevation to a high status and value of political/religious per-secution and physical suffering provide the answer? How does or can "gender" contribute to this answer or complicate it?

Roman-Style Sacrifice and Christian Resistance

To consider the character of the conflict between Christians and the imperial authorities, it is crucial to take note of the differences in their theories of sacri-fice. The Christian theory of sacrifice was built simultaneously on a critique of the Jewish temple cult, on explicit contrast with surrounding Graeco-Roman culture, on an emergent belief in the culminating effects of Jesus' ultimate sacri-fice, and on an increasingly metaphorical notion of sacrifice (sometimes ren-dered literal in the deaths of the Christians as martyrs). To be a Christian meant to believe that the sacrificial order inaugurated and codified in biblical texts had been undermined by the death of Jesus and rearticulated as ritual substitution and reenactment in the practice of the Eucharist. And although "sacrifice" con-tinued to function as a crucial interpretive framework for making sense of the experience (or fear) of persecution, it—along with martyrdom—operated in a framework "not of this world." Hence, the Christian theory of martyrdom qua sacrifice detached the experience of persecution from the historical context and resituated it in a cosmic realm, rendering it meaningful only in a divine register.

Meanwhile, the Roman conception of sacrifice was not about the ephemerality of this world and one's longing to claim one's true identity and community in some other realm. Rather, it was about ritualizing political relationships and sanctifying them through the act of sacrifice. Blood sacrifice was only one version of this form of exchange, though it was also the quintessential, idealized version of sacrifice. (Christians, in their critique of Roman practices, would collapse distinctions among the various forms of sacrifice, arguing that a pinch of incense thrown into a fire was much the same as animal sacrifice, each offering being equally worthy of condemnation for its collusion with idolatry.) Whatever the sacrifice, its performance served to build and sustain the relationships between the civic and divine orders. Indeed, sacrifice's proper performance reinscribed the essential quality of the society, its Romanness. As Mary Beard, John North, and Simon Price have pointed out in their history of Roman religion,

> distinctions between proper and improper religious activity were one means by which different social groups in the Roman empire constructed their identities. . . . The Roman empire raised in a particularly acute form the question of "Roman-ness": What did it mean in this vast multicultural territory to *be* Roman, or to *feel* Roman?
>
> The answer varied according to the standing, ethnic origin and gender of the individual; but for men, at least, an important part of the answer was religious.[101]

And since the answer was religious—particularly in the context of civic cults that linked religious observance to the well-being of the social order—it was also necessarily and foundationally sacrificial. At the top of the sacrificial hierarchy, the shedding of the blood of sacrificial victims and the consumption of their roasted flesh brought participants into the protection and community of the deity and reinforced their political and social bonds. Other, less bloody offerings also served to honor the gods, to invite their protections upon the imperial leaders, to demonstrate allegiance to a shared civic order. The complex ritual life undertaken by Roman citizens (perhaps particularly elites, since we know much less about the lives of nonelites) undergirded networks of patronage and power in the political, civic, and imperial institutions. As has already been noticed in the earlier discussion of Decius's and Diocletian's edicts, sacrifice was seen by these emperors as a particularly effective way to unify the widely divergent religious practices of a far-flung empire. Sacrifices undertaken in these contexts were not about detaching from or interrupting the ordinary rhythms of worldly existence; they were, rather, the ritual acts that maintained social and political relationships and, indeed, sought to underwrite and strengthen imperial hegemony.[102]

Christian theorists would attempt to develop the contrast between Christian and Roman sacrifice as one between a positively valenced spiritual and altruistic Christian sacrifice, on the one hand, and a negatively valenced idolatrous and calculating Roman sacrifice, on the other. Such a contrastive framing was, of course, profoundly polemical. Despite this, similarities between the two theories of sacrifice are also visible: both forms of sacrifice involve the mapping of the world, its internal relationships, and its relationship to the divine. Nevertheless, the contrasts rather than the points of similarity and continuity apparently dominated the debate. From a Christian perspective, Roman sacrifice was nothing but idolatry or demon worship, worse yet when performed in the service of deified political leaders. From a Roman perspective, Christian resistance to Roman modes of sacrifice was itself a sign of religious deviance or, indeed, failure. Christian privileging of interiority in developing a theory of sacrifice willfully misapprehended the materialism of Roman religiosity, uncannily echoing those earlier biblical writers who purposefully mischaracterized Canaanite worship. This same valorization of interiority rendered the Christian understanding of sacrifice illegible and confounding for Roman observers.

The Sacrificial Character of Violence in State-Sponsored Executions and the Arena

A number of recent studies of public violence in Rome, including capital punishment, have emphasized its sacrificial character. In order to understand the nature of public violence in imperial Rome, including gladiatorial games and other such spectacles alongside capital punishment, one must engage issues of theatricality, spectacle, and the religious frameworks within which such events were staged.[103] For example, Paul Plass's *The Game of Death in Ancient Rome* appeals to the theoretical framework articulated by René Girard in his *Violence and the Sacred* in presenting his own analysis of the ideological and psychological work public violence performed in the Roman context.[104] Although predominantly concerned with the socially marginal figure of the gladiator, Plass also extends his analysis to at least one significant example of capital punishment: crucifixion, which he describes as "another tool for managing violence through homeopathic counterterror."[105] In his appropriation of Girardian categories, Plass asserts that the "sacrificial-gladiatorial orgy of violence" is merely one example of the "need to process violence . . . [that] is a cultural universal."[106] The metaphor of violence as a homeopathic booster administered to the Roman social system (as immune system) appears throughout Plass's discussion.[107] According to Plass, arena violence, political suicide, and state-sponsored executions (a category that actually cuts across the first two) perform the ritual work of simultaneously spilling blood and containing the spilling of blood, both in the service of undergirding the structures of social and political life.

Alison Futrell's *Blood in the Arena* also makes connections between the Roman public spectacles of violence, including executions, and a sacrificial logic.[108] Sidestepping the question of whether such violence is a transcultural, transhistorical given (as Plass argues it is), Futrell grounds her thesis primarily in two different bodies of evidence. Ancient architectural evidence and the related topographical arrangements provide one crucial set of evidence. Here, Futrell reexamines the material evidence of arenas throughout the empire and offers an intriguing reinterpretation of the physical remains of the culture of violence. According to her argument, the amphitheater itself was a material articulation of the process of "Romanization" and participated in the establishment and maintenance of Roman political hegemony.[109] Going further than this, Futrell seeks to explain how public spectacles of violence, and the gladiatorial games in particular, functioned as "an innovative means of expiation."[110] Here, she calls her method "ethnographic analogy," where examples from different historical periods and geographical locations (Aztec, Incan, Carthaginian, Sumerian, Chinese, and Dahomean human sacrifice) provide a wide field for comparison and, indeed, function as her secondary set of evidence. Working with a (perhaps not wholly satisfying) functionalist definition of religion, Futrell argues against some historians of the arena and gladiatorial spectacle who argue for an increasingly secular character of the games; her counterthesis is that the spectacle of public violence was central to Roman ritual articulations of imperial power.[111] Futrell's focus is on the gladiator's death as an especially apt human sacrifice in the service of Roman statehood.[112] Yet she also discusses capital punishment in a brief passage where she notes that Roman law itself implied a relationship between the state's execution of a criminal and the expiatory effects of sacrifice: the condemned prisoner is " 'a *homo sacer* whom the People have condemned because of criminal activity.' "[113] She points out some occasions when capital punishment was "openly ritualistic" and notes that criminals were routinely condemned to participate in the games—and probably die there.[114]

That what happened in the arena or on the executioner's block could be read as sacrifice does not answer the question of whether the Romans themselves understood their actions in sacrificial terms. Indeed, the notion of human sacrifice was a contentious one, and accusing someone else of performing it was a fairly effective use of vituperative rhetoric and disciplining opprobrium.[115] As Beard, North, and Price note, human sacrifice was categorized by the Romans as a form of "magic," which is to say, a form of illegitimate religion.[116] If "Roman-ness" was linked to the proper performance of certain ritual and religious acts, then "human sacrifice" and "magic" were rhetorically charged signifiers for out-sider status. Pliny, for example, observes that Rome is owed a great debt for its civilizing gesture of wiping out magical ritual killing.[117] The Roman historian Livy, moreover, goes to great lengths to emphasize the singularly "un-Roman" character of human sacrifices that had been offered in Rome in the third century BCE.[118] As Beard, North and Price observe, whatever actually happened in the events that are narrated by Livy (and in a similar but different set of circum-stances a century later, narrated later still by Plutarch[119]), the killings do not fol-low the pattern of a "normal" Roman sacrificial rite.[120] The logic of the ancient sources seems to be that either the killings were not sacrifices (if they were Roman) or (if they were sacrifices) they were not Roman.[121]

The difficulty here is twofold: first of all, it is virtually impossible to detach Roman "religion" from other aspects of Roman life, so the language of ritual expands to fill an ample range of discursive space. Second, there is the question of whether "sacrifice" is (or should be) understood in a narrowly construed way or more broadly, embracing more occasions of ritualized killing than simply those that might immediately come to mind with a minimalist working defini-tion of Roman religion.[122] In some sense, this difference involves a more literal-ist or realist notion of sacrifice over against a more metaphorical or analogical notion of sacrifice. In interpreting particular cases or examples, it may be useful not to choose the narrower or broader definition abstractly but rather to give consideration to what sort of light one sort of definition or another might cast on the particular case. It seems possible that one might well call an event or a performance sacrificial even when its participants might not call their actions by this name. The question seems to be what work that naming does and how it either sheds light or obscures the view.

The Gender of Sacrifice

Sacrifice was a critical and central feature of Roman religion, and gender was fre-quently a crucial dividing line in the ritual life, especially the sacrificial life, of Roman society. In the realm of blood sacrifice in particular, Roman practice mirrored that of virtually every other sacrificial society in its exclusion of women from blood-shedding rituals.[123] For the historians Beard, North, and Price, this exclusion involved a high cost for Roman women at the level of civic participa-tion. According to them, "much more fundamentally (though the evidence is not entirely clear), they [women] may have been banned—in theory, at any rate—from carrying out animal sacrifice; and so prohibited from any officiating role in *the* central defining ritual of civic religious activity."[124] Meanwhile, in her suggestive discussion of the ritual roles of the vestal virgins, Ariadne Staples observes that exclusion itself was a component of sacrificial practice in Roman religion, one component in a system she describes as "an ever-shifting pattern of different permutations and combinations of categories."[125] Such exclusions did sometimes take place along gendered lines: women were excluded from making sacrifice to Hercules at the *Ara Maxima*, for example, and men were excluded from making sacrifice to the Bona Dea. Staples argues, however, that scholars have too quickly extrapolated a sweeping generalization from one particular ritual formula that excludes women from "certain" sacrifices to assume that women were excluded from them all.[126]

Two points might be made here: first, for the purposes of the comparison between sacrifice and martyrdom, blood sacrifice is the particular ritual form that is implied. Second, not all sacrifices were blood sacrifices—hence, the rituals devoted by women to the Bona Dea involved sacrificial elements (milk and honey, for example) but not the slaughtering of animals. Therefore, it may be possible to talk about the gender of sacrifice in different ways: at the more abstracted and ideological level whereby blood sacrifice stands as a synecdoche for sacrifice as a whole, on the one hand, and at the more variegated and practical level where a wide range of sacrificial elements (from slaughtered animals to pinches of incense) were used in a wide range of sacrificial settings, on the other. The gender of sacrifice at the ideological level involves coding the ritual violence performed in oppositional and symbolic terms. At the practical level, gender is only one of a range of possible distinctions that governs the dynamics of ritual.

When Christian sources invoke the language of sacrifice in relation to martyrdom, they most often disengage the sacrifice from its immediate and literal context—the arena or the executioner's bier—and resituate it within a different, cultic context: the rules governing the Jerusalem temple, for example, or the idea of Jesus' death as an expiatory sacrifice that martyrs imitate. As part of the systems of blood sacrifice, these sacrificial contexts are coded with gender. The blood sacrificial cults of pre–70 CE Jerusalem and of archaic and imperial Rome were the domains of male practitioners; the act of sacrificial killing belonged in the realm of men. Moreover, in the Roman context, the intersections between ritualized killing (whether as sacrifice or as sport) and state-sponsored execution crisscrossed public life and involved male actors and masculine virtues. Women are sometimes present as victims, and it is indeed an ambivalent and much-noticed aspect of the Christian sources that women are remarkably well represented among the condemned. Meanwhile, the "feminine" is present in the sources only as a shame-steeped other—the embodiment of a failure of masculine nerve.[127]

In the Christian theorizing of martyrdom as sacrifice, gender works in a number of different (and not always ideologically coherent) ways. Within the interpretive framework of sacrifice, martyrdom draws upon and generates ideals of "masculinity." Martyrdom figured as sacrifice, however, also generates a value-inverting understanding of victimhood as virtue. Hence, passivity and submission—quintessentially feminine values in the dominant culture—are elevated from their lowly status and given a privileged status by Christian theorists. Yet, if the sacrifice of martyrdom requires myriad practical renunciations (of family bonds, ties to the world, and so on), it also promises a vindication where the rewards are sometimes figured as amplified versions of gender privilege. Finally, gender figures prominently as either an intractable problem or a remarkably malleable dimension of contingent earthly identity as the sacrificial character of martyrdom is elaborated in the sources. These complex dynamics where martyrdom, sacrifice, and gender intersect and mutually implicate one another invite further exploration.

Martyrdom and the Gender of Self-Sacrifice

When Christian theorists of martyrdom use the available languages of sacrifice and gender to frame the Christian experience of persecution, they are working in a citational mode rather than developing a general theory that is always coherent and noncontradictory. As a consequence, there is a provisional quality to many of the claims made by Christian writers about the character of martyrdom—not because they are ambivalent about its significance but because they are generating that significance out of available rhetorical idioms and cultural systems of meaning. This citational, provisional mode emerges most visibly in the borrowing and invocation of gender categories from the dominant culture—particularly the category of masculinity.

It has already been suggested that gender categories and, in particular, masculinity are crucial for understanding the sacrificial component of martyrological discourses. But masculinity is not a fixed essence; it must be produced and sustained through various practical and conceptual means. In the martyrological sources, masculinity is repeatedly figured as a heightened state of being, potentially attainable by both men and women, but one that requires repeated shoring up. It cannot be taken for granted but must be pursued and protected.

The dramatic invocation of the masculine as a pivotal dimension of the martyr's state of preparedness appears in numerous sources, quite notably intersecting with the sacrificial in a text like *The Martyrdom of Polycarp*. The sacrificial components of *The Martyrdom of Polycarp* have already come into view earlier in this chapter. The whole text mimetically reflects upon the biblical passion narratives so that Polycarp and Jesus stand in analogous positions in the two stories of the sacrificial death of an innocent. Meanwhile, toward the end of the narrative, Polycarp is bound like a ram prepared for sacrifice, and he prays that he will become an acceptable sacrifice to God. By this point in the text, the reader can be assured that Polycarp is an unflinching and willing victim in the sacrifice that will be staged in the arena, his whole body becoming a burnt offering to God. But earlier in the text, one encounters a hint of potential ambivalence, a reminder that the masculine endurance required of those who populate the arena is not to be taken for granted. Here, a voice from heaven interrupts the action to urge Polycarp on. Quoting scripture, the voice exhorts: " Ἴσχυε, Πολύκαρπε, καὶ ἀνδρίζου [Be strong, Polycarp, and play the man]."[128] Thus begins a tradition whereby the martyr's endurance comes to be linked explicitly with masculinity and tied also to images of masculinized athleticism and militarism.

But it is not the case that this sentence merely generates a new tradition and set of associations. It also recalls a series of earlier traditions and links Polycarp's struggle to a long lineage of other struggles. The phrase, "be strong and be manly," is, after all, a scriptural quotation and connects Polycarp to a set of biblical traditions reaching beyond and behind the passion of Jesus. "Be strong and be manly" appears repeatedly in a variety of Septuagint texts, from the militarist conquest narratives in Deuteronomy and Joshua, to hymns seeking relief from persecution by one's enemies in the Psalms, to an apocalyptic vision of the end times in Daniel.[129] Echoing these different contexts, the Polycarp text links the martyr's masculine endurance with texts calling for military strength and imbued with the stark dualism of discourses of persecution and end times.

The willing death of the philosopher, the warrior, and the martyr is coded with and for gender.[130] The martyr's death is a masculine death, even when (or perhaps especially when) it is suffered by a woman.[131] But the character of this version of masculinity is complicated by the ambivalent and radically unstable character of gender itself—simultaneously malleable and contingent in its attachment to particular human bodies *and* durable and immutable in its capacity to signify difference.

Clement of Alexandria, in the fourth book of his *Stromateis*, discusses the ideology and genealogy of martyrdom, strikingly framing his discussion with assertions of the availability of the gnostic's life to all, regardless of their status (slave or free) and their sex (male or female).[132] Martyrdom, indeed, comes to stand for the possibility of undermining these social, cultural, and anatomical contingencies precisely because a worthy death definitively uncouples the soul from the body. Hence, gender in this context is simply a dimension of worldliness that can be left behind with enthusiasm and without regret. Such ideas about gender possess a considerable history in Christian thought: Paul, in Galatians 3:28, repeats the early Christian baptismal formula, in which Christian oneness overrides ethnic, status, and gender differences. The Coptic *Gospel of Thomas* closes notoriously with a saying attributed to Jesus in which, against a protesting Peter, he promises to "make Mary [Magdalene] male" so that she can be a "living spirit like you males" and thereby "enter the kingdom of heaven."[133] Gender's contingency and capacity to be overridden by spiritual prowess appear in numerous early martyr stories and in narratives about the ascetic specialists whose singular achievements are marked by the successful abandonment of femininity. These ideas represent a double-edged ideological and theological realization on the part of Christianity: the gender binary need not always be binding though its intrinsic value system (the masculine is always necessarily more positively charged than the feminine) remains relentlessly intact.[134]

When Clement links martyrdom and the true gnostic existence to the dissolution of meaningful gender distinctions, he also struggles with the tensions embedded in the gender constructions he invokes. On the one hand, Clement emphasizes men's and women's shared capacity to philosophize and to die nobly, and indeed the two abilities are integrally linked in Clement's understanding:

> Therefore the whole church is full of both chaste men and women rehearsing all their lives life-making death in Christ. For it is possible to the one who lives as a free citizen according to our ways to philosophize without learning, whether barbarian, Greek, slave, old man, boy, or woman. For moderation is common to all human beings who have chosen it. We confess that the same nature exists for each race, and the same virtue. As far as human nature is concerned, the woman does not have one and the man does not exhibit another, but the same one, as with virtue.[135]

Clement's framing of gender (and, indeed, numerous other forms of social distinction) and martyrdom here emphasizes the overarching sameness to be found in the embrace of virtue and wisdom. One can hear echoes of figures like the Stoic philosopher Musonius Rufus in Clement's insistence on the contingency of gender (or other worldly, material distinctions) in the realms that really matter.

A bit later in his argument, one reads: "But just as it is noble for a man to die for virtue, for freedom, and for himself, just so is it for woman. For it is not peculiar to the nature of males, but to the nature of the good. Therefore, the elder and the young person and the house-slave submitting to the commandments will live faithfully and, if it is necessary die, which is to say through death be made alive. We know that children and slaves and women often against the wills of

fathers and masters and husbands become the most excellent."[136] Precisely those
who occupy the traditionally subordinate positions in the household are those
who, when resisting the domination of their "superiors" in pursuit of faith and
life-generating death, may achieve excellence.

Yet, for all his insistence on the shared moral nature and virtue of men and
women (and old and young, slave and free, Greek and barbarian), Clement is
also certain that there are important and determinative gender differences,
marked by women's physical capacity for pregnancy, parturition, and lactation.
These are contingent but nevertheless quite compelling elements of difference—
that is, elements of femaleness, not humanness.[137] "If there were no difference
between man and woman, they would do and suffer the same things. As there is
sameness with respect to the soul, she will attain to the same virtue. But as there
is difference with respect to the peculiar nature of the body, she will pursue
childbearing and housekeeping (ἡ οἰκουρία)."[138] That "housekeeping" is the
proper purview of woman because of "the peculiar nature of her body" suggests
that Clement's separation of the contingent and the essential may be straining
against its own limits here. One sees this strain elsewhere, where Clement argues
simultaneously that men and women possess the same potential and capacity for
morality (virtue, moderation, and righteousness), and hence women should
philosophize equally with men whereas males continue to remain in possession
of the better things in everything, unless they are effeminate.[139]

Clement's position on the sameness/difference divide causes him to offer
women a place next to men in the field of virtue and to inscribe that place in
masculine terms. Because Clement believes that women have access to philosophy and virtue in like measure to men *and* that martyrdom is a privileged way to
enact the separation between soul and body for which the true gnostic longs,
women's participation in the martyrs' sufferings is predictably masculinized.
But the masculinity involved is, it appears, one constituted by a different difference—a Christian difference. The Stoic virtue of manliness (ἀνδρεία) is,
according to Clement, a prerequisite for both good courage (εὐθαρσής) and
patient endurance (ὑπομονή).[140] That ἀνδρεία and εὐθαρσής are connected in
Clement's discourse is unremarkable, but there is something still a bit startling
about ἀνδρεία keeping easy company with ὑπομονή, active courage finding a
peer in passive perseverance. In his discussion of the virtue of patient endurance
in 4 Maccabees and other Jewish and early Christian texts, Brent Shaw has
demonstrated how the linkage of ἀνδρεία and ὑπομονή or ὑπομονή and
γενναιότης (nobility) would most certainly have troubled the gender assumptions of "the classic male ideologue of the city state" who would have read this
juxtaposition "as contradictory, a moral oxymoron."[141] And just so, Clement
must immediately emphasize that the ἀνδρεία of Christian women is not like

that of women warriors from other cultures precisely because Christian masculinity itself is of a different order. But the pressure of ideologies of masculine
mastery and violence creates tension in Clement's argument here as well.

Good courage and patient endurance are the rightful products of manliness
since they provide the impetus to follow the teachings of Jesus—to turn the
other cheek, to give one's coat also to the thief who demands one's cloak.[142] This
passive refusal to fight back or to resist leads Clement into a discourse on distinctions between Christian women's ἄσκησις (training) and that of other
notable warrior and working women. "We do not train women like some Amazons in warlike exercises of manliness, since we wish even the men to be peace-
ful," writes Clement.[143] That said, the powerful capacity of "ethnographic" evidence of the lives of the women of "others" overtakes him.[144] Clement reports,
"I hear that the Sarmatian women practice war no less than the men; and the
women of the Sacae also, who shoot backwards, feigning flight as well as the
men. I am aware, too, that the women near Iberia practice manly work and toil,
not refraining from their tasks even though near their delivery; but even in the
very struggle of her pains, the woman, on being delivered, taking up the infant,
carries it home."[145] Clement links this ethnographic information to knowledge
he has of the natural world, pointing out that "female dogs no less than their
males watch over the house and hunt and guard the flocks."[146] Together, this
body of evidence provides Clement with a foundation to sustain his assertion
that "women should therefore philosophize equally with men," the assertion
undercut by the second assertion that males are still better in everything, unless
they are effeminate.[147] Leaving aside the rather unseemly comparison involving
the dogs, what Clement has to report about the Amazon, Sarmatian, Sacaean,
and Iberian women underwrites competing claims: cultural variations demonstrate the characteristic malleability of gender, and gender practices do not
always signify in the same ways.

Clement is, of course, not the only Christian writer to emphasize the role of
gender in discussions of martyrdom. Indeed, numerous scholars have traced the
influence of gender ideology in the emergent discourse of martyrdom in a wide
range of early Christian texts.[148] If women's capacity for "manliness" has been
amply documented in the Christian martyrological tradition, the potentially
contested character of men's masculinity has received rather less notice and discussion. Masculinity, it appears, inheres no more naturally in men than in
women. It must be exhorted, called into being, bolstered up, as has already been
seen in the example of *The Martyrdom of Polycarp*'s "Be strong, and play the
man."

But the positive value placed upon masculinity is not limited to lauding
those who display courage and emulate athletes and soldiers. Fatherhood—a

sort of spiritual fatherhood—is promised to the martyr who goes willingly to his death. Strikingly, this fatherhood emerges within a broader framing of martyrdom as sacrifice. In Origen's *Exhortation to Martyrdom*, one of the recurring arguments he makes concerning the impulse toward martyrdom as self-sacrifice is to press his most immediate addressees (Ambrose and Protoctetus) not to stay mired in the worldliness of human relationships and, in particular, to renounce family relationships. Presuming that his readers will worry about the fates of their children should they enter into the sacrifice of martyrdom, Origen seeks to reassure them:

> For this reason, if I become a martyr, I should wish also to leave behind children with lands and houses, so that from the God and Father of our Lord Jesus Christ, from whom every family in heaven and earth is named, I might be called the father of manifold, or to use the exact figure, a hundred-fold and holier children. And if there are fathers about whom it was said to Abraham, "You shall go to your fathers in peace when you have been buried in a good old age," someone might say (though I do not know whether he would be speaking the truth) that perhaps those fathers are those who were once martyrs and left children behind, in return for whom they have become fathers of the fathers, the patriarch Abraham and the other patriarchs. For in all likelihood those who have left children behind and become martyrs are fathers not of infants but of fathers.[149]

Partaking of the sacrificial act of martyrdom *may* (note Origen's unwillingness to embrace the truth of this claim wholeheartedly) produce a sort of hyperpaternity whereby ordinary fatherhood is supplanted by a grander form of masculine virility. The image is all the more striking insofar as the one who sacrifices himself does so with the promise that he will become the father of Israel's own patriarch, Abraham, the father who himself was willing to offer his own son in sacrifice—a story that becomes a critical intertext for Christian theories of martyrdom.

The emergent memories and constructions of Christian martyrdom simultaneously drew upon both sacrificial imagery and the culture's available repertoire of gendered metaphors and associations. Christian authors never excluded real, historical Christian women from the possibility of martyrdom, nor indeed did the persecutors of Christians entertain any qualms about making women their victims. It is striking, however, that women's historical participation in the experiences of persecution and martyrdom did not disrupt the metaphorical universe in which this historical experience was staged. When martyrdom was cast as typologically analogous to sacrifice and the martyr as an imitator of

Christ the "High Priest," it did not follow that the priestly functions associated with sacrifice transferred easily—or, indeed, at all—to Christian women. Origen, whose theology of martyrdom is the most sacrificial of any of the ancient Christian writers, emphasizes the way that martyrdom qua sacrifice engenders a heightened degree of generativity in its subjects. (Origen's rhetoric here operates at the level of metaphor. He did not exclude women from the ranks of potential martyrs.) In texts (such as Tertullian's *Ad Martyras*) where the sacrificial analogies are quite a bit looser, Christian women (and women as models of ethical fortitude) come more into view—but are still cast in masculine forms, perhaps as rhetorical figures to be used to shame men into more stalwart postures.[150]

Interpreters of early Christianity have debated for some time the broader question of whether the religious and cultural innovation that emergent Christianity represented in the Roman world included a fundamental challenge to the gender relations of the dominant society.[151] It may not be possible to draw definitive conclusions concerning the relationships among martyrdom, sacrifice, and gender. The complexity of the portrait as it emerges in this discussion, however, suggests that the available evidence cautions us against making any sweeping assumptions about the transgressive character of Christianity with respect to gender ideology. That women, too, could offer themselves in the most extreme and unalterable form of self-sacrifice—that they, too, could be tortured and killed—is a faint and, indeed, Pyrrhic victory in the struggle for gender equality.

CONCLUSION

This chapter has sought to provide a broad overview of the historical and ideological frameworks within which early Christian collective memory concerning persecution and martyrdom can be positioned. I have argued that the early Christian sources took up the legal, religious, and gender dynamics that were themselves part of the historical situation and the broader cultural context and then put them to use in the Christian commemorative project. The capriciousness that can be seen to result from the absence of strict and explicit anti-Christian legal formulations in the early period opened the door for Christian accusations of lawlessness or arbitrariness against imperial authorities. Even when explicit edicts came to be issued by emperors like Decius, Valerian, and Diocletian, these became in the hands of Christian writers simply occasions for challenging their authority and legality. The broader religious framework in which persecutions were carried out—particularly the sacrificial framework that governed Roman religious observance and that involved various manifestations of public violence from the games to public executions—came to be critiqued or, at times, appropriated by Christian theorists in the service of a counternarrative. As discourses of sacrifice served as root metaphors for figurations of martyrdom, they overlapped in significant ways with other socially foundational discourses, especially those related to gender and social status. In the contest over the meaning of what became "Christian martyrdom," law, religion, and gender each in its own way served as a disputed and multivalent category that could give way to a critical rereading of the character of the past. Together, these categories laid the groundwork for further Christian culture making in the elaboration of a memory of suffering. It is to this exploring some dimensions of this process of culture making that the next chapters are devoted.

3
THE MARTYR'S MEMORY
Autobiography and Self-Writing in Ignatius, Perpetua, and Pionius

THE GENESIS OF EARLY CHRISTIAN collective memory of martyrdom cannot be traced backward to a simple or singular parentage, as should be clear from the preceding discussion of the overlapping historical and ideological discourses that revolve around early Christian martyrdom. Nor does the genealogy of memory and martyrdom map straightforwardly onto a monolithic historical narrative. And yet, from the earliest examples of persecution and punishment, a generative impulse to record and remember these stories shaped the literary, liturgical, artistic, and architectural programs of Christian communities. From the discussion in the previous chapter, one can see how Christian theorists shaped the collective memory of martyrdom both narratively and rhetorically, using available concepts, practices, and tropes—of law, sacrifice and piety, and gender—to reframe Roman imperial domination as Christian martyrdom. Moreover, one sees how dimensions of Christians' usable past came to be mobilized in the ongoing generation and generativity of collective memory. This chapter shifts to a narrower aperture, one trained on some of the most compelling versions of the Christian impulse toward memory. These examples focus intensely on particular figures—the ordinary person turned extraordinary through the most trying of circumstances. If part of the point of remembering past suffering is retrieving exemplars for one's own project of living a Christian life, then the most valuable artifacts would be precisely those in which the martyr's self comes into most dramatic view. The three sources under discussion in this chapter are indeed such artifacts—texts that purport to record the martyrs' final days in letter or diary form, texts that seek to leave a trace of the askesis (that is, self-discipline and training) of the martyr's self-formation, texts of self-writing.[1]

THEORIZING SELF-WRITING

The literary practice of generating a self-portrait is, of course, not a Christian innovation. Although the term "autobiography" came into use only during the Enlightenment, the broader practice of leaving inscribed records of a life in order to assure its remembrance and commemoration has a much longer history.[2] If the term "autobiography" denotes a very particular genre in the modern context, the practice of writing about oneself in antiquity fell outside the boundaries of recognizable genres and therefore beyond the confines of rhetorical regulation.[3] I have chosen to designate the texts under discussion in this chapter as examples of self-writing—neither a genre nor a rhetorical form, but a literary activity by which a portrait of the self is generated, regardless of formal and generic varieties. Self-writing in antiquity was initially undertaken by public figures who were devoted to the project of preserving in memory their public lives. Hence, politicians, philosophers, emperors, and poets constituted the vast majority of autobiographers in antiquity. Yet, some interpreters of the literary history that survives from antiquity argue that what emerges over time is an increasingly private, self-disclosing dimension of the genres of self-writing, beginning in the Hellenistic period and reaching its apex in numerous late antique sources. This tendency toward self-revelation, they argue, is particularly visible in texts where philosophical self-analysis and religious experience are charted.[4]

The scholarship that argues for this turn toward interiority is unquestionably very suggestive. The texts I will analyze closely here, however, invite readers to problematize this set of simple binaries (public/private, exterior/interior). The textual production of the martyr's self through self-writing does not seem to emphasize interiority in opposition to exteriority but rather to draw attention to the production of the martyr's self within the context of a much more public, collective narrative. The authors/self-narrators of these texts are conscious of the potential readership for their writings, and they appear to see themselves contributing to their own memorializing.[5] In this way, these texts are generative of collective memory.

This chapter is then devoted to a close examination of three Christian examples of martyrological self-writing in the second and third centuries. The argument here is twofold: first, that self-writing contributes to a broader set of practices concerned with the generation and maintenance of Christian collective memory; and second, that the self-writing of martyrs operates as a process of self-crafting or self-formation. The discussion begins with a detour through some of the later writings of Foucault, whose explorations of "the technologies of the self" sparked my thinking about these Christian sources in terms of self-writing. My readings of the rhetorical character of three texts—Ignatius of Antioch's letter to the Roman church, Perpetua's prison diary, and Pionius's public speeches—ultimately serve to supplement and complicate Foucault's interpretive framework. Foucault traces a relatively straightforward path toward increasing interiority, culminating in the monastic confessions of the fourth and fifth centuries. In this chapter, I will argue that his failure to pay close attention to the martyrological tradition in its own right caused him to miss some critical, complicating features of the practice of self-writing in emergent Christianity. My readings of Ignatius, Perpetua, and Pionius will then both supplement Foucault's theory of self-writing in this period and contribute more substance and texture to the emergent portrait of Christian collective memory of martyrdom.

In the last few years of his life, Michel Foucault turned his attention systematically to what he called "the technologies of the self." This project, which included the second and third volumes of *The History of Sexuality*, augmented his earlier work on institutional technologies of power. Asking how the "self" comes to be produced, he sought to understand how self-regulation and askesis contribute to the process of subjectivation (*assujettissement*). During this period, Foucault focused his writing projects specifically on the techniques of self-transformation, and his increasing interest in early Christianity is manifest in many of these writings. Strikingly, Foucault focused his attention quite specifically on the traditionally construed ascetic tradition, especially in its full flowering in the fourth and fifth centuries. Paying close attention to the institutions and practices that came to represent askesis most dramatically, Foucault did not discuss at all second- and third-century Christian texts related to martyrdom, where techniques of self-formation were also very much on display. These techniques are, I will argue, foundational to Christian askesis, not simply foreground to it. Indeed, the martyrological tradition in early Christianity offers both a supplement to and a refinement of Foucault's analysis of askesis and self-formation. The readings offered here suggest how one might gloss Foucault's version of early Christianity, a portrait that never came to full articulation or completion.[6]

In a short essay entitled, "L'écriture de soi" or "Self Writing," that appeared in a 1983 issue of the French publication *Corps écrit*, Foucault turned his attention to a particular literary history of personal ethical writing. In Foucault's reading of it, this tradition began with the personal reading notebooks (ὑπομνήματα) and correspondence of philosophers of the Roman imperial period and ended with the emergence of self-conscious self-writing in fourth-century Christian asceticism and monasticism.[7] The trajectory Foucault sketched out in this short essay began with *hypomnēmata*, reading notebooks that functioned much like later commonplace books. "One wrote down quotes in them, extracts from books, examples, actions that one had witnessed or read about, reflections or reasonings that one had heard or that had come to mind. They constituted a record of things read, heard, or thought, thus offering them up as a kind of accumulated treasure for subsequent rereading and meditation. They also formed a raw material for the drafting of more systematic treatises."[8] For Foucault, they represented the products of a disciplined reading and writing life. Their contents could well be quite disparate, but they were brought together into an assemblage that ultimately had the potential to transform their collectors. Foucault emphasized that the *hypomnēmata*, although personal jottings, were distinct from the later spiritual memoirs generated by the early Christian monastic virtuosi. The notebooks collected and reorganized the discourse of others, becoming a record of the "already-said." Although one might consult these writings to think about one's own action in the world, they generally did not contain private self-assessments.

Hypomnēmata were certainly what Foucault described them to be, and yet the term is more broadly resonant than his discussion fully allows. The singular noun, "ὑπόμνημα," is both a reminder and a memorial—literally, something that goes underneath or undergirds the μνῆμα (memory or tomb). It can also mean reminder or mention, note or memorandum. In the plural, the term could refer to the minutes of a proceeding, the public records of an event, the officially recorded acts of a political body. It might also refer to dissertations or treatises written by philosophers or even commentaries—and so the commentary written upon a more systematic writing, a σύγγραμμα, which is what its ancient editor calls Pionius's text, which is discussed later in this chapter. The verb form of the word, "ὑπομνηματίζομαι," can mean "to note down for remembrance, to make a memorandum" or "to write memoirs" or "to explain or interpret."[9] *Hypomnēmata* are records that are linked to memory and memorializing as well as to interpretation and to public events. Yet *hypomnēmata* exceed both formal and generic categorization, even as classical authors used the term to name their varied efforts at self-writing.[10] For Foucault, *hypomnēmata* function primarily as commonplace books. Such a function invites the reader of early Christian literature to consider how the Bible comes to function as the *hypomnēmata* extraordinaire, on whose spiritual and ideological authority early Christian writers might seek to capitalize. For Foucault, *hypomnēmata* also function as one endpoint along a continuum of forms of self-writing.

The personal correspondence of philosophers that has been preserved from antiquity occupies the second place along Foucault's trajectory and is closely related to the first. Aimed at capturing the details of daily life for another (a fictive or actual audience), such correspondence acted upon both writer and reader, and it functioned as both a discipline (like the notebooks) and a way of manifesting the self to oneself and to others (unlike the notebooks). "To write is thus to 'show oneself,' to project oneself into view, to make one's own face appear in the other's presence. And by this it should be understood that the letter is both a gaze that one focuses on the addressee (through the missive he receives, he feels looked at) and a way of offering oneself to his gaze by what one tells him about oneself."[11] Whereas the personal notebooks functioned "to enable the formation of the self out of the collected discourse of others," the personal letters involved the generation of "a narrative of the self."[12]

On the far extreme of the trajectory of self-writing, Foucault locates the Christian anchorite spiritual memoir. No less disciplined than the other two forms of writing, this confessional form of writing turned the writer's own gaze back upon himself, creating a form of self-surveillance. Generated as a practice out of the solitude of ascetic withdrawal, "writing about oneself appears clearly in its relationship of complementarity with reclusion: it palliates the dangers of solitude; it offers what one has done or thought to a possible gaze; the fact of obliging oneself to write plays the role of a companion by giving rise to the fear of disapproval and to shame. . . . What others are to the ascetic in a community, the notebook is to the recluse. . . . Writing will exert [constraint] in the domain of the inner impulses of the soul."[13] Thus Foucault completes the trajectory that begins with the commonplace book, passes through personal correspondence, and culminates in confessional writing. This trajectory maps along another trajectory, one traveling from the realm of the "public" toward the realm of the "private."

In short, in this essay Foucault traced the contours of a genealogy of Christian solitary self-reflection along a trajectory that was increasingly self-referential and interiorized. Whereas the *hypomnēmata* functioned as records of the "already-said," personal correspondence that reflected on the details of ordinary life began to build toward the pinnacle of self-examination to be found in the ascetic spiritual exercise of self-writing.[14] The essay ends with a summary of the effects of these three sorts of personal writing:

> In this case—that of the *hypomnēmata*—it was a matter of constituting oneself as a subject of rational action through the appropriation, the unification, and the subjectivation of a fragmentary and selected already-said; in the case of the monastic notation of spiritual experiences, it will be a matter of dislodging the most hidden impulses from the inner recesses of the soul, thus enabling oneself to break free of them. In the case of the epis-

tolary account of oneself, it is a matter of bringing into congruence the gaze of the other and that gaze which one aims at oneself when one measures one's everyday actions according to the rules of a technique of living.[15]

In Foucault's view, as writing moves from citations and quotations of others' texts to shared epistolary self-reflection and on to a private record of inner experience, self-writing relocates the center of the ethical demand increasingly inward. In Foucault's description of the literary history here, shifts in practices of writing help to chart the changes over time in what drives ethics and subjectivity. Those who maintained *hypomnēmata* were interested in collecting advice that would help them to live well. Those who wrote personal letters recording the minutiae of daily existence sought to live well and to render their actions visible and legible—that is, to have others recognize the effort and its effects. But the writers of ascetical notebooks of spiritual development were not concerned merely with actions and their recognizability; they were interested, instead, in charting the motivations that drove the actions or impelled the practitioner toward action, even if he ultimately resisted it. The ascetic life that produced such texts insisted that the goal was not only mastery over action but also mastery over impulse. The increasingly interiorized ethical practice demanded an intensified self-examination and an ever more private form of writing.

The practice of self-examination and its relationship to different forms of interpretation and writing were also central themes in an essay Foucault wrote the previous year for the seminar he gave at the University of Vermont, "Technologies of the Self."[16] In this essay, Foucault began by pointing out the curious relationship between prohibitions and interdictions with respect to sexuality, on the one hand, and the obligation to speak the truth about oneself, on the other. Characterizing this problem as the question of "the relation between asceticism and truth," Foucault went on to articulate his question in this way: "What must one know about oneself in order to be willing to renounce anything?"[17] The study he went on to outline in this essay—a study of "the hermeneutics of technologies of the self in pagan and early Christian practice"—took its place within the broader framework for Foucault's interests in the four major technologies: technologies of production, technologies of sign systems, technologies of power, and technologies of the self. Observing that his own interest had been focused for a long time on technologies of domination (that is, technologies of power), he wondered whether "perhaps I've insisted too much on the technology of domination and power." The work that this essay and what followed in volumes 2 and 3 of *The History of Sexuality* represented was a turn toward a different interest—an interest "in the interaction between oneself and others, and in the technologies of individual domination, in the mode of action that an individual exercises upon himself by means of the technologies of the self."[18]

In this essay, Foucault charts the complex relationship between two ancient dicta on the self: "care for yourself" (ἐπιμέλεσθαι σεαυτοῦ) and "know your-self" (γνῶθι σαυτόν). Although self-knowledge eventually trumped self-care in the philosophical tradition, Foucault noted the important degree to which care for the self emerged in the Hellenistic and Roman periods as a pathway to knowledge of the self. Organizing his discussion as a comparison of Stoic ethi-cal practices and Christian monastic ones, Foucault distinguished different forms of askesis in these two contexts—different ways of disciplining and refin-ing the self.

There are different strains and emphases in Foucault's writing on the Graeco-Roman world and the emergence of early Christianity. At times, he emphasized the points of congruence between the two worlds, insisting (as specialists in the period would also do) that early Christianity should not be read simply or straightforwardly as a radical innovator in the Graeco-Roman world. Rather, it should be understood as a social and cultural development that drew upon diverse aspects of the cultures into which it was born, elaborating and intensify-ing some, reconfiguring others.[19] At other times, he strategically drew his readers' attention to striking differences between "pagan" and "Christian" in order to stress the development or refinement of a particular technology. As a conse-quence, the discussion of Stoic and Christian techniques of the self should not be read in simple, oppositional terms. What emerged out of Hellenistic and Roman cultures' grappling with the question of ethics and the problem of the self con-tributed to the particular early Christian engagement with the same problematic.

In Foucault's comparison in "Technologies of the Self," he drew attention in particular to four Stoic techniques of the self: letter-writing aimed at self-disclosure, self-examination, askesis, and dream interpretation. He argued that, for Christians, the techniques of the self emphasized both different forms of con-fession (he offers a lengthy discussion of the nuances of ἐξομολόγησις and ἐξαγόρευσις) and askesis as renunciation.[20] In Foucault's view, although both Stoics and Christians sought to answer the question of the ethics of the self, Christians negotiated inner and outer, public and private, in ways quite differ-ent from the Stoics.[21]

Because Foucault's larger project involved the emergence of askesis as the dominant and overarching technology of self, as this chapter demonstrates, he bypassed some intriguing, complicating, and perhaps reinforcing examples from the Christian tradition—in particular, texts emerging out of the martyro-logical tradition. He did evoke the martyrological tradition briefly but only, rather idiosyncratically, within the broader discussion of confession and penance, not in its own right:

> The most important model used to explain exomologesis ["a full confession, a public confession," *OED*] was the model of death, of torture, or of martyrdom. The theories and practices of penance were elaborated around the problem of the man who prefers to die rather than to compromise or abandon the faith; the way the martyr faces death is the model for the penitent. For the relapsed to be reintegrated into the Church, he must expose himself voluntarily to ritual martyrdom. Penance is the affect of change, of rupture with self, past, and world. It is a way to show that you are able to renounce life and self, to show that you can face and accept death. Penitence of sin does not have as its target the establishing of an identity but, instead, serves to mark the refusal of the self, the breaking away from self: *ego non sum, ego.* This formula is at the heart of *publicatio sui.* It represents a break with one's past identity. These ostentatious gestures have the function of showing the truth of the state of being of the sinner. Self-revelation is at the same time self-destruction.[22]

Two important critiques can be brought to bear here: First, the link between the public confession of Christian identity on the part of martyrs and the penitential practice of confession of one's sins represents a significant interpretive leap on Foucault's part. The ancient sources do not make this connection, nor generally speaking does the interpretive tradition based on these sources. Second, in his desire to trace a particular historical trajectory involving askesis, Foucault gave surprisingly short shrift to the critical period in Christian history when martyrdom was the central model for ideal Christian identity and, for some, a lived reality. Indeed, as this chapter will demonstrate, martyrdom was also a striking source of several important Christian texts of self-writing. This chapter seeks, then, to build on Foucault's insights and, in places, to critique them in the service of offering a broader supplement to his often suggestive arguments about early Christian self-writing.

It may be that Foucault did not attend to this historically intervening material because he was more interested in exploring Christian askesis in what seems to have been its full flowering, that is, fourth-century monasticism. It is certainly the case that he generally paid only cursory attention to Christian sources prior to the fourth century. The problem is not so much the partial character of the portrait—all discussions are, of course, partial (in both senses of the term). The problem is more the ideological effect of this particular focus. That is, in focusing on the fourth century's dramatic examples of askesis as an endpoint in a long process of development, Foucault inadvertently reinscribed a particular meta-narrative of early Christianity, a narrative that has been increasingly called into question in more contemporary scholarly discussion. This is a story in which "The Age of Monasticism," as an old-fashioned survey textbook might call it, emerged definitively in the fourth century out of what the same textbook might have called "The Age of Persecution."[23] In this narrative, early Christian asceticism appeared more or less full-grown in the period following the conversion of Constantine—and earlier ascetic impulses in the first three Christian centuries fade almost completely from view.[24]

The ascetic impulse, however, appeared in the earliest layers of the Christian sources from the first century on.[25] Monasticism was only one institutional form in which it was made manifest. Indeed, if, as Foucault himself held, askesis is not a narrow renunciation of pleasure but rather, "the work that one performs on oneself in order to transform oneself," then it becomes a much more overarching category.[26] As a consequence, religious experiences and practices that may not have ordinarily fallen under its reach now might well do so. I argue here that the ideal of martyrdom was not simply a historical precursor to askesis nor merely a retrospective analogy for it but rather, to some degree, a manifestation of it.[27]

Interestingly, all four of the technologies that Foucault lists in his "Technologies of the Self" as central to Stoic practice and ethics make their own particular appearances in the texts I will discuss here: letter writing, self-examination, askesis, and dream interpretation—though they are jumbled together in the Christian sources, overlapping each other significantly and not always easily separated. The relationship between Stoic and Christian ethics has been amply discussed by scholars, who emphasize the critical points of connection between Stoic and Christian ethics concerning responses to persecution and certain death.[28] My discussion here of the examples of self-writing that emerge out of the Christian martyrological tradition builds on this work and suggests how these examples supplement and complicate Foucault's account. Moreover, I also argue that where Foucault saw a clear trajectory, there is actually a more variegated terrain.

The three texts that I read closely here present themselves as having been written in the period just before representatives of the Roman government executed their writers. Ignatius of Antioch's *Letter to the Romans* is an early-second-century epistle written while Ignatius was on his way to his own execution at Rome. The third-century diary of the North African Christian matron Perpetua records her personal observations and visionary activity while she was awaiting execution in a Carthaginian prison.[29] The autobiographical text left by Pionius, a Christian presbyter in Smyrna (Asia Minor), is embedded in a text composed during the Decian persecution in the mid-third century. These three texts, differing in genre and place of origin, offer three powerful examples of self-conscious self-writing—and three critical additions to the literary history Foucault delineates in "Self Writing" and to the analysis of technologies of the self. The method that governs these readings is broadly rhetorical in nature. I am interested in the practice of persuasion in which each writer engages. Because I read these texts rhetorically, I assume that they are participating in some form of public discourse, that is, that the authors of these texts are seeking to persuade their reading audiences of their particular points of view. At the same time, I read these texts as examples of self-writing and as part of the broader trajectory that interpreters of ancient autobiography, including Foucault, are seeking to chart. That said, I also acknowledge the difficulties presented by the Perpetua and Pionius texts, although I would submit that the literary selves generated by these texts soon take on lives of their own in the collective memory of early Christians and their descendants. As a consequence, the rhetorical and the autobiographical work together to generate a useable past for the Christian communities that preserved and circulated these texts. As will become clear, these texts, each in its own way, attempt to create and control the memories they preserve. Rather than being writings devoted solely to the generation of a private self, they are self-writings that produce a public self—one shaped by askesis, preserved in language, and displayed for commemoration and remembrance.

"LEAVE NO TRACE OF MY BODY": IGNATIUS WRITES HIMSELF OUT OF MATERIAL EXISTENCE

Ignatius's *Letter to the Romans* is one of seven letters written by the third bishop of Antioch (Syria) as he was en route from his home city to Rome to face execution.[30] The details of his arrest are not known, but the letters indicate that he traveled as a captive from Antioch accompanied by an entourage of ten Roman soldiers to the capital city where he would be thrown to the beasts. Scholars are in consensus that Ignatius suffered martyrdom during the reign of Trajan (98–117), though they are split over the question of whether the events (and the letters) should be dated to the first or second decade of the second century.[31] Regardless of the precise dating of his death, Ignatius's letters are frequently used as one of the earliest sources for documenting both the historical experience of martyrdom and the emergent Christian theology of suffering and persecution. They are less often read as Ignatius's own self-portraiture, and when they are, one often encounters a discernible dose of scholarly queasiness. Consider perhaps the most famous passage from all of Ignatius's letters, the part of his *Letter to the Romans* in which he pleads with the Roman Christians not to intervene to spare his life:

> I am writing to all the Churches and I give injunctions to all people, that I am dying for God's sake, if you do not hinder it. I beseech you, be not "an unseasonable kindness" to me. Suffer me to be eaten by the beasts, through whom I can attain to God. I am God's wheat, and I am ground by the teeth of wild beasts that I may be found the pure bread of Christ. Rather entice the wild beasts that they may become my tomb, and leave no trace of my body, that when I fall asleep I be not burdensome to any. Then shall I be truly a disciple of Jesus Christ, when the world shall not even see my body. Beseech Christ on my behalf, that I may be found a sacrifice through these instruments.[32]

Many scholars have had an anxious and uncomfortable relationship to this famous paragraph, struggling with psychological language and diagnostic terminology in their attempts to cope with Ignatius's apparent zeal and psychic excess here. "The eager way in which he speaks of the tortures confronting him ... shows an abnormal mentality," writes one scholar.[33] Ignatius is "highly strung, even neurotic," according to one interpreter,[34] while another observes that "his language sometimes betrays an exuberance and wildness which could be interpreted as neurotic."[35] Yet another scholar diagnoses the bishop's state of mind as "exaltation bordering on mania."[36] Through the use of such language, writers have displayed their own ambivalence about the religious commitments that drive Ignatius, and they have distanced themselves from the self inscribed by the discourse of this soon-to-be martyr. But what is this famous paragraph by Ignatius about? Who is the "I" who speaks here?

Approaching the text naïvely, through its own syntactical operations and the predicates that are attached to Ignatius's "I," one finds in this short passage a rich and varied set of claims being made about who Ignatius is and who he might become. "I write to all the churches [ἐγὼ γράφω πάσαις ταῖς ἐκκλησίαις]," and "I command everyone [ἐντέλλομαι πᾶσιν] that I am dying on behalf of God." Ignatius fashions himself first of all as a writer of letters to churches and secondarily as a person who gives commands. In other terms, he is both an author and an authority.[37] The objective clause that follows these declarative verbs ("I write" and "I command") is curious—"that I am dying on behalf of God." In relation to the first verb, "I write," one might read this statement as a simple declaration: I am telling you what my experience is and what it means. But the second verb, "I command," suggests that the first declaration is perhaps too certain, or not certain enough: and now I am trying to insist upon a certain way of think-

ing about what my experience is and what it means. The second verb that underwrites Ignatius's self-understanding as an authority is also the one that suggests
to the reader that there is resistance to his way of controlling and interpreting his
experience. Absent his command, the events that Ignatius anticipates would
potentially be interrupted, hijacked by other historical agents—even the well-
meaning Christians of the church in Rome.

Ignatius's plea to the Roman church, replete with the ironies of obsequious
imperatives, ("permit me to be food for beasts"), tightly encapsulates his theory
of martyrdom even as the metaphors he uses are densely packed and not always
commensurate with one another. His is a self in the process of multiple transformations, some of which strain against logical credulity: his human flesh, torn
by the teeth of wild beasts, will become divine wheat ground into Christ's pure
bread. The image has inspired a range of interpretations by commentators.
Some hear eucharistic and sacrificial/sacramental resonances in the language of
wheat and "Christ's pure bread."[38] (If one reads this image as a reference to the
Eucharist, then the curious inversion of the conventional eucharistic associations is striking here: in Ignatius's formulation, bread does not become body,
but rather body becomes bread.) One commentator has sought to set the passage in the mundane material context of everyday life in the second century,
reading this image as drawing upon conventional bakery practices to mean that
"pure bread" stands for a quality product.[39] The image clearly implies transformation, as something must happen to ground grain before it can become
bread—though Ignatius leaves to the reader's imagination this question of how
the raw (dough) becomes the cooked (baked bread), as he does the question of
how flesh itself transforms into grain.

And yet it is not enough, however, that flesh should become grain and grain
be transformed into bread. For Ignatius, the highest manifestations of selfhood
(attainment to God, true discipleship) occur precisely when his body has been
obliterated, leaving no trace. Ignatius's physical disappearance is mentioned
twice in quick succession—once as a practical concern ("rather entice the wild
beasts that they may become my tomb, and leave no trace of my body, that when
I fall asleep I be not burdensome to any") and once as the necessary condition
for true discipleship ("then shall I be truly a disciple of Jesus Christ, when the
world shall not even see my body"). Visibility, remainders, physical presence are
all obstacles to Ignatius's achievement of a stable spiritual selfhood. In short, he
is laboring to write himself out of corporeal existence in the hopes of achieving
a transformed and wholly spiritual existence.

This confluence of language, selfhood, and the disappearing martyr's body
appear elsewhere in Ignatius's letter to the Roman churches. Indeed, there is a

deep-seated tension in Ignatius's letters between notions of presence and absence, visibility and identity, the body and language. At a critical point in his plea to the Roman church not to save his life, Ignatius suggests that the destruction of his own body will produce a form of intelligible discourse and that the silence of the Romans concerning his flesh will render him an incorporeal word of God:

> For neither shall I ever have such an opportunity of attaining to God; nor can you, if you be but silent, have any better deed ascribed to you. For if you are silent concerning me, I am a word of God, but if you love my flesh [ἐὰν δὲ ἐρασθῆτε τῆς σαρκός μου], I shall again be only a cry.[40]

On the other hand, Ignatius can only achieve the status of such a privileged utterance if the Roman Christians rein in both their passions and their tongues. Their silence is what will render Ignatius a word, but this is not enough: they must also renounce their love for him, a love that he characterizes as a passionate, impulsive, fleshly love (ἔρως). Whereas Ignatius had earlier on invoked the Roman Christians' ἀγάπη (a selfless kind of love that Ignatius nevertheless fears, since it might generate a well-intentioned but, in his view, disastrous intervention to save his life[41]), here he recasts their desire to help him escape his fate as a base passion for the flesh, an ἔρως τῆς σαρκός μου. As becomes evident a bit further on, the language of love and desire is a focal point for Ignatius's self-construction.

Later, Ignatius distinguishes between language, in its imperfect approximateness, and true reality, and between the compromising visibility of his body in the world and his true identity as a Christian. These distinctions will come into sharpest focus if the prayers, spoken on his behalf by the Romans, are successful:

> Only pray for me for strength, both inward and outward, that I may not merely *speak*, but also have the will; that I may not only be *called* a Christian, but may also be found to *be* one. For if I be found to be one, I can also be called one, and then be deemed faithful *when I no longer am visible in the world. Nothing visible is good*, for our God, Jesus Christ, being now in the Father, is the more plainly visible.[42]

This resident ambiguity in Ignatius' letter can also be seen in the description by Ignatius of the process of detachment from the physical self, a process described both in terms of the abandonment of materiality and desire and in terms of physical qualities that exceed the boundaries and fixedness of solidity. Ignatius writes of his own self, when it becomes uncoupled from its material framework, as a recipient of pure light. It is a self only then becoming human (ἄνθρωπος ἔσομαι),[43] a being in whom love has been crucified (ὁ ἐμὸς ἔρως ἐσταύρωται), a being filled with living and speaking water (ὕδωρ δὲ ζῶν καὶ λαλοῦν ἐν ἐμοί).[44]

Throughout his letter to the Romans, Ignatius emphasizes the degree to which his transformation is continuously in process. He writes repeatedly, for example, of "ἐπιτυχεῖν τοῦ θεοῦ [attaining God]" or "ἐπιτυχεῖν Ἰησοῦ Χριστοῦ [attaining Jesus Christ]" so frequently that the notion becomes a technical term in his writing.[45] He uses the future form of the Greek verb "εἰμί [to be] several times in reference to himself—"I will be," that is, "I am in the process of becoming." He writes of "beginning to be a disciple [νῦν ἄρχομαι μαθητὴς εἶναι]"[46] and "becoming more of a disciple [μᾶλλον μαθητεύομαι]"—discipleship is not an achieved state of being but a goal toward which Ignatius strives.[47] But perhaps nowhere is the notion of a self-in-process clearer than in the complex language of longing and desire in this letter. Ignatius's preparation for martyrdom is a spiritual exercise in focusing his wants and gaining control over his desires. It is, in essence, a form of askesis *avant le lettre*.

The verb "θελεῖν [to want]" appears many times in this letter, almost always in either the first-person singular or the second-person plural. Not as strong, perhaps, as the verb "ἐπιθυμεῖν [to desire]," *thelein* is a more generally applicable verb that nevertheless emphasizes that its motivations and its origin lie in the will, often the human will. It conveys a sense of voluntariness or deliberateness on the one hand, willfulness on the other. It can also mean "to take pleasure in" or "to like."[48] The nominal form of the verb, "θέλημα," is routinely translated, "will," as in "moral will," "free will" or, indeed, "God's will." Whereas Ignatius, as a disciple-in-process and a prisoner, is learning to desire nothing ("νῦν μανθάνω δεδεμένος μηδὲν ἐπιθυμεῖν"[49]), he nevertheless goes on in the letter to articulate his desire (and to attempt to influence the desire of the Roman Christians) repeatedly through the use of *thelein*.

Ignatius's desire is multilayered: he wants to die as a martyr and, as a consequence, to achieve discipleship, to imitate Christ, to attain God, to be rendered an acceptable sacrifice. This desire, focused on belonging to God or attaining God, is understood to be stronger than mere speech or rhetoric in Ignatius's world. "Pray that I will have the strength (both inward and outward) so that I may not only speak but also desire [ἵνα μὴ μόνον λέγω ἀλλὰ καὶ θέλω]."[50] And yet, as Ignatius's rhetoric builds, the language of want/will/desire intensifies: "Neither the ends of the earth nor the kingdoms of this age will profit me at all. It is better for me to die to Christ Jesus than to rule over the ends of the earth. I seek [ζητῶ] him who died on our behalf; I desire [θέλω] him who rose for us."[51] Not long after this repudiation of the world's powers will Ignatius assert the death of his desire for the things of the world, his abandonment of the world's power and values.

But already he distances himself from those values in his insistence that the Roman church's desire not stand in the way of his martyrdom. "Do not prevent me from living," Ignatius writes. "Do not desire that I die [μὴ θελήσητέ με ἀποθανεῖν]. Do not give to the world one who desires to belong to God [τὸν τοῦ θεοῦ θέλοντα εἶναι]."[52] Here, in reversing the ordinary meanings of "living" and "dying," Ignatius portrays his death as a martyr as the means by which he will be able to live and belong to God. He worries that the Roman Christians' desire to save him from execution (therefore, ironically, condemning him to death—understood as life in this world) will conflict with his own desire to belong to God. Ignatius describes this desire elsewhere in the letter as the Roman Christians' love (agapē) that he fears (at 1.2) and as their "passionate love for my flesh [ἐὰν δὲ ἐρασθῆτε τῆς σαρκός μου]," which, if indulged, would impede Ignatius's transformation from an inarticulate cry into a word of God.

Ignatius's greatest longing is to be separated from the world and united with God. A paradox resides in the expression of this longing in terms of the crucifixion of his love ("ὁ ἐμὸς ἔρως ἐσταύρωται").[53] Not only does his desire for God come to expression through the killing off of erōs, but Ignatius's ascendancy toward God is produced through radical debasements. And these debasements render him simultaneously worthy and unworthy of attaining God. Consider the passage that follows Ignatius's plea to the Romans that they not intervene to save his life. After making this strongly worded plea, Ignatius claims not to possess the authority with which to command the Roman church—and yet it is precisely his imprisoned and enslaved status that should both make his plea all the more urgent. Moreover, his status as one in bonds produces his position as a disciple. The language of bondage appears throughout this letter, and Ignatius uses this language not only to describe his actual legal and physical situation but also to describe a broader ontological status: "I do not command you as Peter and Paul did. They were apostles, I am a convict. They were free, I am even until now a slave. But if I suffer [πάθω], I will become a freedman of Jesus Christ and I will rise in him free. Now I am learning, in bondage, to desire nothing."[54]

As the rhetorical force of the letter builds, Ignatius casts himself in ever starker terms—bound to the ten soldiers who accompany him, who abuse him the more kindness is shown them, the prisoner "becomes ever more a disciple [μᾶλλον μαθητεύομαι]."[55] The chapter ends with a passage in which, according to one commentator, "he seems to have left all sobriety behind in [its] exultant tone."[56] "Let fire and cross and packs of wild beasts, mutilations, tearing apart, scatterings of bones, mangling of limbs, crushing of the whole body, evil tortures of the devil come upon me, only in order that I attain Jesus Christ."[57]

As the letter draws to a close, the language of humiliation, submission, and lowliness recurs. "I am not worthy," says Ignatius, "being the least of them [the bishops] and an abortion [ἔκτρωμα]."[58] Schoedel takes a psychologizing approach to this language of self-effacement, approaching it as a compelling sign of Ignatius's authentic state of mind.[59] But such self-effacement also has a profound rhetorical effect—the building up of Ignatius's own authority in his audience. An earlier Christian letter writer, Paul, made use of just such a rhetorical gesture frequently in his letters. Moreover, it is clear that the self that Ignatius is producing here is a self who—in imitation of Christ—is paradoxically lifted up through suffering.

This paradoxical language through which Ignatius describes how, through suffering and degradation, he will be elevated may be echoed in the language of sacrifice that also appears repeatedly in this text. The earliest reference in the letter comes in the second chapter, where Ignatius asks to be granted nothing more than the possibility of being poured out to God (σπονδισθῆναι θεῷ) "while an altar [θυσιαστήριον] is still ready."[60] The verb Ignatius uses here, "σπονδίζω/σπονδίζομαι," is a late form of the verb "σπένδω," which appears only twice in the New Testament—both times figuratively in the first-person voice of Paul describing his own fate.[61] In the logic of the text's argument, this strong sacrificial language follows directly on Ignatius's claim that if the Christians in Rome remain silent, he will become a word of God. Despite some commentators' reticence to hear strong cultic resonances in this language, they are hard to ignore.[62] When the language appears again, it is in the climax of Ignatius's insistence that he be completely consumed by the beasts. "Pray to Christ for me that I may be found a sacrifice [θυσία] by these instruments."[63]

Implied in this letter, though more explicit in other Ignatian letters, is the connection between this language of sacrifice and the idea of lowliness. The reigning theory of sacrifice that undergirds Ignatius's text involves the paradoxical status of the victim as simultaneously debased and pure. Thus, Ignatius describes himself in other letters with the word "περίψημα," a term that derives from sacrificial contexts and literally means "the offscouring," whose removal renders the thing or object to which it was attached newly pure.[64] It can then have the further sacrificial meaning of "scapegoat" or "ransom" and is linked to another term Ignatius uses frequently, "ἀντίψυχον," which means "ransom," as in something traded for someone's life. (This term is also used in 4 Maccabees, and some interpreters have linked Ignatius to the Maccabean tradition through the repetition of this term.[65])

The self that Ignatius crafts through his own language, the self that is crafted for him by the circumstances in which he finds himself, is not located only at the place where language and the body intersect. The story Ignatius tells of himself is no mere historical accounting but a narrative of cosmic proportions. This narrative can be seen in his repeated sacrificial language, in which his death will function as a piacular offering traversing the borders that separate the earthly world from the heavenly one, an explicit imitation of Christ. Moreover, Ignatius crafts himself through continued opposition to the world's powers, which are only apparently overarching and irresistible and are in fact ephemeral and progressively weakened by the deaths of the saints.[66] These powers are positioned in clear opposition to the power of God, and therefore Ignatius's battle takes place within this stark framework.

The resistance to the powers of this world, for Ignatius, is paradoxically an act of bodily compliance. The execution will, he hopes, leave no trace of his body. And yet his death ironically leaves all manner of significant material traces—his corpus of writings that continue to circulate; the authority reinscribed in the person of the bishop (a critical theme for Ignatius in his other letters); the investment of the earthly church with an ironic persistence and viability despite the destruction of the flesh of one of its bishops; and the tenacious ideological resolution that the certainty of life in the next world is most easily achieved through the physical sufferings endured in this one.

"SUDDENLY I BECAME A MAN": PERPETUA'S VISIONARY TRANSFORMATION

A century after Ignatius's ignominious death in a Roman arena, another Christian martyr prepared for an equally humiliating execution, this time in Carthage. Rather than writing letters to other Christians, this martyr narrated and reflected upon her experience in a diary. A well-born Roman wife when she was arrested, she was also a Christian catechumen given over to a visionary life. According to her diary, she repeatedly prayed for and received a series of dreams or visions in the days preceding her ordeal. These visions are recorded in the diary, itself preserved in a framing narrative written by someone else. This is the famous diary of Perpetua, preserved in the *Passion of Perpetua and Felicitas*.[67]

Numerous scholars have carefully situated the *Passion* historically and juridically in the religiopolitical circumstances of early third-century North Africa.[68] Others have focused more centrally on other aspects of the text: its genre and authorship,[69] its history-of-religions parallels,[70] its literary influences,[71] its imagery.[72] Perpetua's diary itself has been widely studied, interpreted, and glossed in recent years, both because of its status as a visionary text[73] and because of its importance as the earliest Christian text allegedly written by a woman.[74] Because the diary is contained within a framing narrative written by someone else, interpreters have sometimes sought to uncover points of tension between Perpetua's self-narration and the narrative of her redactor.[75] Questions of authority trouble the writer of the framing narrative from the very start; for Perpetua herself, these are not the pressing questions. For her, questions of identity—and the question of how to link identity (the truth of the self) with action (ethics)—are most urgent. Like Ignatius, she wishes to move beyond simply being *called* a Christian to really *being* a Christian.

So, in the diary, the question of identity—of Perpetua's true self—functions as a central driving force in the literary self-portrait. Moreover, the transformation of Perpetua from an upper-class *matrona* to a Christian heroine involves a series of struggles whereby she successively peels off worldly role after worldly role.[76] In this process, she consolidates her Christian identity through a combination of renunciations, disavowals, and actions by which she renders herself receptive to the various visions she receives. (It is nevertheless one of the ironies or paradoxes of the text that the final proof of her internal and external consistency can only be written by someone else—the narrator who recounts her martyrdom itself.) The narrative of Perpetua's preparatory process, preserved in the diary, charts a course of some ambivalence but one that is always focused in a forward-looking direction. The narrative is simultaneously straightforward and remarkable—sometimes tantalizingly imprecise in its descriptions, richly detailed in other ways. Unlike the Stoic letters Foucault discusses, in which the writer tends to the smallest routine details of daily life, Perpetua's diary is more episodic and partial. The self-writing in which Perpetua engages is not itself an ascetic practice. But her diary can be fruitfully read as a record of ascetic engagement, where disciplined practice and repetition generate a new identity and inaugurate a new symbolic reality.

Perpetua's diary contains two different sorts of accounts, organized around two very different kinds of experience. In her ordinary, earthly life, her attention and energy are fully focused upon extricating herself from her social (and especially familial) obligations—obligations that would have been considerable for a woman of her class and standing in third-century Roman society.[77] In these episodes, she engages in verbal and psychological battle with her father who seeks to convince her to recant her Christian confession. In the periods of time in between these earthly conflicts, she exercises her spiritual virtuosity to obtain visions that illuminate her destiny. The Perpetua who emerges from these different reports is at once willful and receptive, filled with intense conviction and yet fully open to the offerings of the spirit. Like Ignatius, driven by his intense longing for unity with God, a longing which requires his renunciation of all desire, Perpetua's commitment comes to be articulated most dramatically in her capacity to give way to a radical transformation.

Perpetua's diary opens without introduction in the midst of a debate with her father. Driven by his love for his daughter (*pro sua affectione*), he tries to persuade her to renounce her religious convictions. Her response is to shift the terms of the discussion away from the dangerous terrain of emotion and toward the safer ground of rationality and logic: she points to a vase ("or waterpot, or whatever") standing nearby and asks, "Could it be called by any other name than what it is?" When the father answers, "No," Perpetua then wins the argument by responding, "Well, so too I cannot be called anything other than what I am: a Christian." His anger almost manifests itself in violence, but then he leaves the prison, "beaten along with his diabolical arguments [*uictus cum argumentis diaboli*]."[78]

This opening scene provides the ground for an important part of Perpetua's self-portrait throughout the diary. She possesses a striking clarity about her identification as a Christian—this despite the fact that she is arrested only as a catechumen (one not yet baptized) and only after a few days in the prison does she undergo the transformative ritual with the others in the prison.[79] It is an identification, however, from which she never wavers. Yet, unlike Ignatius, whose attempts to persuade others not to intervene on his behalf display no ambivalence at all about the things of this world that he must renounce, Perpetua records the emotional and physical suffering that is the cost of her commitments. Indeed, she recognizes the potential fragility of her spiritual situation when she describes the days immediately following her baptism: "In that interval of a few days, we were baptized, and the Spirit prescribed to me not to strive after anything from the water except the endurance of the flesh."[80] She goes on to describe the hardships she and others suffer in the prison, characterizing herself as frightened (*expaui*) and mentally tormented with anxiety for her infant who was also there with her (*nouissime macerabar sollicitudine infantis ibi*).[81] When she gives her baby up to her mother and brother, she describes the pain she experiences knowing that they might suffer emotionally in their concern for her. Her relief when the baby has gone from the prison is double-edged—no longer required to claim the maternal role nor to worry over the well-being of the infant, she experiences the prison transformed for her into a palace (*factus est mihi carcer subito praetorium*).[82] Eventually, the renunciation of motherhood will liberate her, not only emotionally, but also physically from the ties that have bound her to family, society, and the world.

Perpetua's diary oscillates between these moments of conflict that are inevitably resolved through renunciation, on the one hand, and occasions of intense visionary experience, on the other. The next chapter records Perpetua's brother urging her to seek a vision that will clarify her fate. She records his precise words by which he names her "*Domina soror* [lady sister]," a title that emphasizes both their familial relationship and also Perpetua's social status and power—and even more, her close status with God, who is named in the next sentence, *Dominus*.[83] Perpetua accepts the suggestion with confidence and certainty that she has the ability to elicit a vision: "I knew that I could speak familiarly with the Lord [*ego quae me sciebam fabulari cum Domino*], whose great blessings I had come to experience."[84] By reporting the brother's vocative *Domina*, then asserting her own capacity to speak with her *Dominus*, Perpetua records her spiritual intimacy with the divine even as she situates herself in a different hierarchy from the social one in which she occupies a superordinate position. That she uses the verb "*fabulo*" (to speak familiarly) reinforces that sense of intimacy.[85]

The request for the vision is itself undocumented, although the word that Perpetua uses to describe the request itself is striking: "*postulaui*," she says. The verb "*postulo*" tends not to be used to signify a request that is made obsequiously or submissively. Rather, it implies a demand or a request for something to which someone is entitled.[86] Perpetua makes her request (for something to which she was entitled), and she immediately receives the first of her four visions.[87]

The account of this vision provides the first evidence of Perpetua's giftedness as a visionary. The vision is detailed and complex, borrowing from a range of religious and imaginative idioms. Perpetua sees an enormous ladder studded with sharp weapons that threaten the safety of the climber whose goal is heaven. At the foot of the ladder, there is a menacing dragon whose head Perpetua must use as a first step in her ascent. Another visionary, Saturus (whose experiences are documented later in the *Passion*), appears in the vision, ascending the ladder before Perpetua herself.

The vision of heaven evokes available imagery of the afterlife (a large and abundant garden) and conventional Christian symbolism of the main occupant of heaven as a shepherd. The thousands of white-clad people who surround the old shepherd represent the sainted dead. The shepherd gives Perpetua cheese to eat whose sweet flavor lingers in her mouth even after the vision has come to an end, perhaps as a proof of the reality of the vision. Some have suggested that, having now eaten food from heaven, Perpetua emerges from the vision a second Persephone, tied to heaven much as Persephone was tied to the underworld after swallowing pomegranate seeds she tasted there.[88]

Perpetua is not only a visionary but a straightforward interpreter of her own visions. In this case, as she reports the vision to her brother, they interpret it together: "*et intelleximus passionem esse futuram, et coepimus nullam iam spem in saeculo habere* [and we understood that suffering was imminent, and we began now to have no hope in this age]."[89] The vision is not only evidence of Perpetua's privileged status as a medium for the spirit, but her capacity to interpret it allows her to know the future with certainty.

In between this vision and the two that follow it, Perpetua records two more encounters with her increasingly desperate father. In the first of the two, he pleads with her to pay attention to all of her familial relationships and obligations—to have mercy on him, her aged father, and to give due consideration to her other relatives, whether her brothers or her mother or her aunt or her infant child. Frantic and disconsolate, her father throws himself at her feet, kissing her hands and crying. As Perpetua describes it, "he no longer called me 'daughter' [filia] but 'lady' [domina]." The power dynamics between father and daughter have shifted. Whereas he is consumed with grief and sorrow, she sees herself cast in the role of comforter, declaring, " 'It will happen on that [prisoners'] platform as God wills it' [Hoc fiet in illa catasta quod Deus uoluerit]."[90]

In the scene that follows, the stakes are raised as the Christians are brought before the governor and questioned. In front of a large crowd, the others who have been imprisoned with Perpetua are questioned and confess.[91] As for Perpetua, once again renouncing her obligations to both her family and the state in exchange for claiming a Christian identity, she refuses the governor's command that she show her father and her child consideration by sacrificing for the well-being of the emperors. Questioned directly, " 'Are you a Christian?' " Perpetua responds, " 'Christiana sum.' " This clear confession results in the further humiliation of her father who has arrived on the scene holding Perpetua's baby. He is thrown to the ground and beaten for persisting in his attempts to dissuade his daughter. Perpetua's confession, along with those of her companions, also results in the condemnation of the Christians as a group to death by the beasts (damnatio ad bestias). This episode ends with yet another brief allusion to Perpetua's ambivalent negotiation between two competing sets of demands—the worldly and the otherworldly. Returning to prison with the others, all of them in high spirits, Perpetua thinks again of her baby and how he has been used to breastfeeding and staying with his mother in prison. She sends for him, but her father refuses to turn him over. This is the last point at which concern for earthly relationships will trouble Perpetua, as God intervenes to wean the baby and miraculously dry up Perpetua's milk. The physical and psychological bonds between mother and infant are divinely severed, and Perpetua's renunciation of the world is complete. She can turn her attention more fully to the conclusion of her spiritual journey.

Perpetua's detachment from the world may account for the second and third of her visions in which she sees her brother Dinocrates, at first suffering in a very hot and dry place and then refreshed and healed after Perpetua's intervention by prayer. Interpreted by some as a "pagan" hold-over in Perpetua's imagination[92] and by others as an early attestation of a notion of Purgatory in Christian writings,[93] Perpetua's vision of her dead brother in a state of suffering comes upon her after some spiritual exercises—"I began to pray a good deal for him and to groan [*ingemescere*] to the Lord." The result of this intervention is another vision: "That very night, this is what was revealed to me [*continuo ipsa nocte ostensum est mihi hoc*]."[94] Seeing her brother suffering terribly, Perpetua intervenes with prayer and other spiritual practices (moaning and crying). As a demonstration of the efficacy of her practice, she receives her third vision (*ostensum est mihi hoc*)[95] in which her brother has been restored. Again, not only a recipient of visions but also an interpreter of them, she obverses, "I awoke, and I realized then that he had been delivered from pain [*et experrecta sum. Tunc intellexi translatum eum esse de poena*]."[96] Having detached herself from her worldly relationships and having confessed her Christian identity publicly, Perpetua increases her spiritual virtuosity: now, not only is she able to conjure visions, but she is able to transform the afterlife experience of her dead brother *and* to conjure a vision that confirms the efficacy of her intervention. The path toward the arena narrows for Perpetua, but her spiritual capacities develop and expand.

It is a small wonder, then, that her final encounter with her father is described only very briefly: he continues on his downward spiral of desperation, gesturing angrily and impotently, blaming his own existence and "saying such words as would move all of creation."[97] Perpetua's response is short and rather detached: "I felt sorry for his unhappy old age [*ego dolebam pro infelici senecta eius*]."[98] She turns her attention to what lies ahead: her final vision before her death.

The final vision is the most elaborate, and it has also inspired the most extensive commentary. In it, Perpetua is led by the deacon Pomponius to the arena where she knows she will meet the beasts. A huge crowd has gathered to watch the spectacle. Instead of beasts, an Egyptian appears with his seconds; the arena battle is transformed into the pancratium contest. Perpetua's own seconds ("handsome young men") appear, and as she is stripped of her clothing in preparation for the match, "I became a man [*facta sum masculus*]."[99] The potential for gender malleability and the masculine capacity for athletic victory intersect in this compressed statement, providing a dramatic crux where Perpetua's spiritual exercises achieve their apogee. In the narrative, the drama builds as Perpetua's seconds rub her down with oil and the Egyptian rolls in the dust. Then an enormous man, tall enough to tower over the arena itself, appears, wearing elaborate garb and carrying a baton and a green bough bearing golden apples. He calls for silence and announces, "If this Egyptian defeats her, he will kill her with a sword; if she defeats him, she will receive this bough." The battle ensues, a battle of fists and feet. Perpetua is deft and fleet-footed: "I felt lifted up in the air, and began to hit him as if I were not standing on the ground." Catching the Egyptian's head in her hands, she causes him to fall on his face, "and I trod upon his head." Having won the contest, Perpetua receives from the trainer (*lanista*) the green bough, a kiss, and the greeting, "Daughter, peace be with you." She walks triumphantly toward the *porta Sanavivaria*. Awaking from the vision, "I realized that it was not against beasts, but against the devil, that I would fight; but I knew that the victory would be mine."[100] It is here that the diary ends with the simple invitation: "This is what I did until the day before the contest; if anyone wants to write about what happened at the contest itself, let them write."[101]

The detail and drama of this vision have invited many interpreters to place Perpetua's dream in theological, psychological, and sociohistorical contexts. The self-portrait here is of a victorious athlete, a competitor with a competent and agile body, a combatant steeped in courage and raw nerve, the object of unambiguous display and spectacle, a woman who transcends the limits of gender as she abandons the confines of earthly existence. Set for victory against whatever opponent—beasts, Egyptian, father, devil—she moves unwaveringly toward the champion's gate, which stands, in the inverted logic of martyrdom, for her own martyr's death.

This vision testifies to Perpetua's askesis, her discipline, and her trading one set of identifications for another. Indeed, it returns us to the earliest uses of the term "askesis"—the arena of the athlete. The self-writing involved here turns increasingly inward, but it also continues to address an implied reader, an imagined audience. Where does Perpetua's text belong on Foucault's continuum or in the challenging terrain beyond the confines of genre and the rhetorical rules that govern it, a terrain where both ancient diaries and autobiographies reside?[102] Does our classification of it shape our reading, and is that classification gendered?[103] In concluding that the text we have as Perpetua's diary is a mediated text and the "character of Perpetua" is "a self that has deliberately been constructed," Heffernan reads the character and her textual remnant as figural and discursive bridges between two quite different alternatives: "The character of Perpetua . . . stands somewhere between the classical ideal of the individual householder, charged with a public responsibility to cultivate virtues that were outward-looking and designed to serve yet an even larger world, . . . and the nascent Christian ideal that viewed community not as the highest good, but as a necessary means to nurture an ethic that was inward-looking, private, and dedicated to serving the *civitas Dei*."[104] The focus of Perpetua's narrative shifts away from the world, with its familial attachments, and toward the metaphor-rich details of her spiritual struggle. The path to martyrdom is portrayed in striking detail, but the details eventually fade into the background as the figure of Perpetua the martyr emerges with a kind of shimmering clarity, separated from the "hope in this age" and poised inexorably on the verge of a different existence. Like Ignatius, whose love is crucified, who describes his own body as changing nature (becoming water and spirit) as he prepares for his ordeal, Perpetua narrates a process by which she peels away the things of this world and enters this fatal space unflinching, second thoughts banished, victorious.

PIONIUS, THE RHETOR AND STAGE MANAGER

No less complex than the *Passion of Perpetua and Felicitas* is *The Martyrdom of Pionius the Presbyter and his Companions*, a text that records the events leading up to the arrest of Pionius and several other Christians in Smyrna on the anniversary in the year 250 of the martyrdom of Polycarp, which had taken place some eighty years prior.[105] The Pionius text also includes accounts of the group's interrogation and imprisonment along with Pionius's eventual execution. This text puts itself forward explicitly as a memory-book, a σύγγραμμα (record) that provides its readers with a μνημοσύνη (memory), left behind by Pionius himself as a fortification for others.

The martyrdom opens with a striking appropriation of Romans 12:13. Where the biblical text reads, "ταῖς χρείαις τῶν ἁγίων κοινωνοῦντες [share in the needs of the saints]," *The Martyrdom of Pionius* begins: "The apostle exhorts [us] to share in the remembrances of the saints [Ταῖς μνείαις τῶν ἁγίων κοινωνεῖν ὁ ἀπόστολος παραινεῖ]" (1:1).[106] With this subtle adjustment of the textual tradition, the writer shifts attention away from the social imperative of Paul's letter to the Romans and toward a contemplative, even liturgical or ascetic imperative. By remembering the saints, those who "wish to imitate the higher things" will be elevated and fortified through their commemorative gestures. Yet Pionius's story is nevertheless understood here as a continuation of the apostolic imperative as, in the next sentence, Pionius is called an "apostolic man [ἀποστολικὸς ἀνήρ]. Following the model of the apostle before him, he converted many people and "left this writing [*to syngramma touto*] for our admonition so that even now we would have it as a memory [*mnēmosynē*] of his teaching" (1:2).[107]

Pionius's writings have not come down to us in their original form as a straightforward work of autobiographical writing. Like Perpetua's diary, Pionius's text has been domesticated by an editor's hand. Like the *Passion of Perpetua and Felicitas*, *The Martyrdom of Pionius the Presbyter and Those with Him* is a composite text. It comprises a version of Pionius's *autography*, two trial records, some prefatory and transitional additions by the editor, and of course the narrative of the passage of sentence and of the execution itself. In reworking the underlying text of Pionius, the editor has for the most part relegated the first-person voice to the dialogue and speeches in the text, rewriting the text in a third-person voice. Nevertheless, occasionally the point of view of the narrative shifts, fleetingly returning the perspective to the Smyrnean presbyter. Despite these textual complexities, such as shifts in voice, scholars agree almost unanimously that this martyrdom represents a remarkable occasion of self-writing by this early Christian witness.[108]

Scholarly commentators tend to emphasize the text's historical plausibility and specificity and to draw the attention of readers to those elements of the text that generate a sense of psychological authenticity. As a crucial witness to the Decian persecution, this text lends itself quite readily to readings that focus on the degree to which textual details can confirm or nuance reconstructions of this pivotal moment in the story of Christian relationships with Roman imperialism.[109] Moreover, the text's rhetorical immediacy has frequently invited a mode of reading that locates the force of the narrative in its psychological verisimilitude. Neither the historical nor the psychological effects of this text are minor or unimportant. Yet both strategies of reading render the text primarily an artifact to be mined for historical truth or psychological insight; both leave unexamined the ways in which the text works to generate a portrait of the martyr through his own rhetoric. Such an examination is the project of this reading.

Pionius's self-fashioning takes place in distinct discursive realms, the rhetorical and the theatrical/spectacular—both sites, it may be noted, of public performance. In all of his performances, Pionius works from his particular cultural and social location: he is a cultured, educated man, apparently accustomed to public life and its demands. It is quite sensible that his self-portrait would take the form of episodes in which his rhetorical skills are on display, whether in debate with others or in the context of delivering a carefully crafted speech. Moreover, he seems to be quite conscious of how his body and actions might be read, and he also seems anxious to maintain control over these appearances. As a martyr, one who bears witness and testifies, Pionius seeks to make a persuasive argument and to cut an impressive—even theatrical—figure.

Pionius's diary of captivity preserves a range of rhetorics, including two lengthy speeches given by Pionius, as well as several combative exchanges between the presbyter and those who seek to persuade him to offer sacrifice. The speeches repeatedly seek to define Christian identity in stark contrast to Jewish and "pagan" identities. They draw upon the literary and cultural legacies of these other religious worlds but emphasize the Christian (indeed, Catholic) appropriation of these inheritances as the correct one. Out of Pionius's rhetoric are generated clear claims to authority and a portrait of self-mastery. As it was for both Ignatius and Perpetua, the "name" is a crucial dimension of the self-portrait.

Pionius's self-portrait stresses his stature as a man of good education and high reputation, a public figure whose oratory generates rapt attention among his hearers and silence as a response. His *syngramma* includes the texts of two speeches Pionius delivered, one after his arrest and the other after his imprisonment. The first of these is addressed to "men who boast of the beauty of Smyrna" and to "those who are also present who are Jews."[110] The second speech is addressed primarily to "the many Christian brothers" who had come to the prison, disconsolate because of their own apostasy, having performed the required sacrifice after having been "dragged off by force [κατ' ἀνάγκην]."[111] Also present, however, are "many of the nations" who had come to the prison "wanting to persuade them [Pionius and his comrades]" but who end up "amazed hearing their answers."[112]

When Pionius begins his first speech, it is in response to the public challenge received from Polemon, the temple warden (νεωκόρος),[113] who addresses the presbyter publicly: "It is auspicious, Pionius, that you obey the ruler [πειϑαρχῆσαι] like everyone else and sacrifice [ἐπιϑῦσαι] in order that you may not be punished."[114] Pionius's response is that of an orator, gesturing with an outstretched hand, speaking in defense (ἀπολογέομαι) with his face glowing, illuminated.[115] The speech, then, is an apology (in the technical sense), an offering in which Pionius will seek to render his own position reasonable and intelligible for his audience. The line between theological apologia and a harsh rhetorical assault on one's opponents appears to be quite thin, however, and Pionius consistently maneuvers right at its cutting edge. Indeed, commentators have long recognized that Pionius's strategy for articulating Christian identity succeeds only at the expense of his Jewish neighbors. Although he also attacks the "pagan" community of Smyrna, Pionius reserves his starker and most venomous rhetoric for the Jews of the city. Indeed, the bulk of his first speech— ostensibly a speech in defense of his own refusal to sacrifice—is in fact a strident indictment of the Jews. This indictment draws upon scriptural references and interpretation, Pionius's own experience as a Christian pilgrim in the Holy Land, and an unmistakably deterministic and apocalyptic sensibility.

The speech opens with Pionius's observation that both Greeks and Jews have taken pleasure in the fact that some Christians have willingly offered sacrifice. The characterization of the Christian misstep is carefully framed and rendered. Pionius writes of the lapsed as those who have deserted (αὐτομολέω), and he calls their action a "missing of the mark," an error or a failure (ἀστόχημα). Both of these terms generate military associations. Pionius renders apostasy as a desertion of Christ's army; he figures the sinful failure to stand fast as the missing of a mark, as when one is aiming for and shooting at a target.[116] Both terms suggest soldierly activity and construe an identification with Christianity as enlistment in the *militia Christi*. But, of course, armies need enemies against whom they might close their ranks, and so it is not surprising that Pionius immediately invokes the notion and language of enemies. He admonishes the Greeks to pay attention to "your teacher [διδάσκαλος] Homer" who warns in his *Odyssey* against boasting over the imminent death of others.[117] For his Jewish audience, he cites Moses and Solomon, both of whom offer precise guidance concerning the proper response to one's enemy's suffering or misfortune.[118] This is subtle rhetoric since it appeals to the authorities that are recognized by his audience, and it shames Pionius's hearers by pointing out that they are not following the instructions of their own teachers. Pionius drives a wedge between his audience and their own traditions by suggesting that his hearers are themselves deserters and people who fail to succeed in hitting the mark. Moreover, Pionius places the onus on the Jews for construing the Christians as their enemies, leaving his Christian community innocent of such declarations.[119]

Meanwhile, Pionius sets himself up as the exemplar of consistency and non-contradiction. While the Greeks and the Jews enjoy, with amusement and pleasure, the shortcomings of others—and do so in violation of their own cultural, ethical, and religious traditions—Pionius, by contrast, is the picture of loyalty, rectitude, courage, and orthodox faithfulness. "For I, persuaded by [or, obedient to] my teacher [*didaskalos*], choose to die rather than to transgress his words, and I struggle [ἀγωνίζομαι] so as not to alter the things that first I learned and then I taught."[120] The language of struggle brings the argument into a different discursive realm. Whereas the world of the military is evoked earlier, here Pionius calls up a range of other public settings where struggle and competition reign—athletic or theatrical competitions, oratorical contests, and conflicts staged in courtrooms. Excellence in persuasion is at the heart of most of these settings where the victory is won through a public, virtuosic performance of skill and superiority. Like the earlier military metaphors, the metaphor of the *agōn* implies—indeed, requires—the presence of conflict, and its only possible resolution results when one solitary contestant is declared the victor. When used in the context of Pionius's commitment to preserving the integrity and authenticity of what he has learned and then transmitted to others, the term suggests an orthodox teaching both potentially under attack and victorious only when it remains the last one standing.[121] Whereas the Greeks do not obey their teacher, Homer, and the Jews refuse to listen to their teachers, Moses and Solomon, Pionius has by contrast thoroughly incorporated his own teacher's words in a radical way and declared himself prepared to sacrifice his own life rather than betray those teachings. The self-portrait is paradoxical—Pionius is drawn simultaneously as one porously receptive to the teaching of his master, as a vessel or a conduit for that teaching, but also as one engaged in the violent *agōn* required to protect the purity of that teaching. In this brief passage, then, the portrait of Pionius that emerges is as apologist, polemicist, dutiful disciple, faithful teacher, orator, actor, athlete, advocate—and presumed victor.

The next part of the speech is a rhetorically charged anti-Jewish polemic in which the humanity and the innocence of the Christians are underscored in explicit contrast with their opponents. Pionius repeatedly accuses the Jews of crimes against God and morality, his diatribe built upon a foundation of rhetorical questions, some of whose implied answers may be found in the biblical history of Israel.[122] The diatribe culminates in the claim that the moral and religious failures of his opponents are legible in the natural history of their lands and the natural disasters that have befallen them.[123] Such physical proof serves not only as evidence of divine wrath but also as an apocalyptic promise ("For judgment is suspended over the world, concerning which we have been fully assured by many things").[124] Pionius draws his evidence for this claim from his own lived experience as a pilgrim in Palestine.[125] He travelled to Palestine, crossed the Jordan River, and saw with his own eyes "land which even until now bears witness [μαρτυροῦσαν] to the anger from God against it because of the sins of those who occupy it—those who murdered foreigners, who banished foreigners, who did violence [against them]."[126] The biblical allusion here must certainly be to the story of Sodom and Gomorrah in Genesis 19, cities that are named explicitly in Pionius's later speech.[127] That Pionius can make such an oblique allusion suggests that his audience must be quite literate in the biblical sources. That he makes this particular connection also puts him in the company of other ancient Jewish and Christian writers who saw in the destruction of Sodom a precursor to and lasting exemplum for the final fiery punishment that would come from God.[128]

Pionius's speech closes with the threat of God's impending judgment to which he and his fellow Christians "bear witness [μαρτυρόμεθα]," a judgment that comes into the world through God's Logos, Jesus Christ. Situating Christian identity succinctly in opposition to both Jewish and "pagan" identities, Pionius concludes with the statement, "For this reason we do not serve [λατρεύομεν] your so-called gods nor do we fall down and worship [προσκυνοῦμεν] the golden idol."[129] This summary reminds the hearers not only that his intended audience is "pagan" but also that he has drawn an equation between "pagans" (those who serve so-called gods) and "Jews" (those who worship the golden calf). Both groups are aligned against Pionius and the other Christians (who serve and worship the one true God).[130]

In between the first and second speeches, Pionius continues to portray himself as a master orator whose arguments—whether before a whole crowd or directed at a specific interlocutor—are unmatched by those of his opponents. Indeed, the first speech has left Polemon, the temple warden, his companions, and the whole crowd in rapt attention and complete silence.[131] When they begin to plead with him again to sacrifice, it is not out of their commitment to the imperial cult but rather out of their love for Pionius himself and their admiration for his character: "Be persuaded by us, Pionius: we love you and on account of many things you are worthy to live—your manners and your reasonableness."[132] Yet when others debate with Pionius, each one in turn is outdone by the master's skill and steadfastness.

One commentator has characterized the whole text as "reminiscent of the baroque rhetoric of the late Cynic diatribe."[133] Although intended only to bolster an argument for the questionable historicity of Pionius's text, this commentator's observation nevertheless also points to the probable influence of certain Cynic styles in Pionius's argumentation. When Pionius is confronted with the arguments of the temple warden, the proconsul, or a member of the crowd, the scene often appears as a loose appropriation of the Cynic *chreia* form. In such stories, the philosopher-hero wins the day through the delivery of a clever retort to which his opponent has no response.[134] So, for example, Polemon the temple warden says to the Christian presbyter, "Be persuaded by us, Pionius," to which Pionius responds, "If only I were able to persuade you to become Christians." The crowd responds derisively to this wish, laughing at him and saying, "You do not have such power to cause us to burn alive." Pionius's response: "It is much worse to be burned when you are dead."[135] Pionius's retort must have been aimed at displaying his witty virtuosity. The text certainly registers the response by Sabina, the Christian woman who is part of Pionius's group. She smiles, a response that only earns her a special, gender-specific threat from these same men: "Those women who will not sacrifice are put in a brothel."[136] As becomes clearer as the text progresses, the opponents of the Christians cannot generate rhetorically persuasive responses to the Christians' arguments; they can only respond with clumsy violence or coercive threats. Much as Perpetua's father was reduced to a preverbal wailing, the opponents in this text degenerate into irrational brutality. Pionius and the others maintain dominance in the realm of language and argumentation. They remain the authors of their own identities, aligning themselves confidently with the order-generating realm of the Logos.

The second speech in this text is three times as long as the first and is delivered not in the public square but in the deep confines of the prison. If Pionius sought in the first speech to define Christian identity in contrast to Jewish and pagan examples, here he focuses his vitriolic rhetoric more completely on the Jewish tradition and community. Punctuated by pointed biblical quotations, Pionius's speech accuses the Jews of faithlessness toward God, of taking advantage of Christian fear of persecution, of false claims against Jesus that are made manifest through claims to have conjured his ghost through necromancy, and of betraying and crucifying Christ.

Pionius's rhetoric is largely a rhetoric of contrast and exclusion: the "Jews" are constituted by the litany of accusations he makes against them; the Christians are, by contrast, innocent of these crimes. Many readers of Pionius's speeches have sought to situate them quite concretely in the precise historical situation of relations between Christians and Jews in third-century Smyrna.[137] Such reconstructions tend to accept more or less at face value Pionius's rhetoric and accusations rather than reading his speech as a contributor to the relations in question. Insofar as Pionius seeks to change his community's relationship with Jews in Smyrna, he provides no straightforward description of either community but rather makes a polemical intervention into their interactions. The identity, "Christian," that Pionius seeks to consolidate in his self-portrait in this text is a rhetorical and interpretive construction, not a simple historical datum.

This second speech begins with a series of citations, quotations, and allusions to a wide range of biblical passages. It might, indeed, be read as an adaptation of the *hypomnēmata* to which Foucault refers in his discussion of ancient self-writing. In this case, the Bible is the sole source for helpful sayings, memorable passages, and excerpts preserved by a disciplined reader/writer who will return to what he has read in search of an apt turn of phrase or a fitting exemplum. Pionius mines the New Testament from Matthew to the Apocalypse for images that might graphically punctuate his argument. He also draws upon the Hebrew Bible, prophets as well as historians, and apocryphal writings. It is from these Jewish sources that the church comes to be imagined as a woman or city at risk— sometimes a virgin whose virtue is imperiled (Susanna), sometimes an honorably married and powerful woman (Esther), sometimes a collective in danger of profound moral failure (Sodom and Gomorrah).[138] Pionius, by implication, casts himself as the protector of God's honor against the prominent and omnipresent threat of feminine shame.

But Pionius is also the guardian of the church's borders and arbiter of what counts as legitimate religion. The problem he diagnoses in this speech concerns the fact that Jews have been inviting Christians into the synagogues. From this diagnosis, Pionius spins out a vitriolic critique of his Jewish neighbors, voluntary Christian alliance with whom Pionius views as far worse than coerced sacrifices to the Roman gods. The rhetoric is subtle and allusive. Pionius warns the Christians not to become "with them leaders of Sodom and people of Gomor-

rah, whose hands are polluted with blood [ὧν αἱ χεῖρες αἵματος πλήρεις]."¹³⁹
This last phrase is nearly a word-for-word quotation from Isaiah 1:15, part of a
longer passage in which Judah's sacrificial offerings are rejected by God (through
the prophet) since they have been presented within the broader context of sinfulness and iniquity.¹⁴⁰ In this context, the polluting blood on the hands of the
people of Judah is ambiguously unattributed. Is it the blood of sacrificial victims,
hypocritically offered and thus unacceptable to God, or the blood of the victims
of Judah's iniquity? Pionius makes use of this textual ambiguity, so that the murdered prophets and the crucified Christ can become simultaneously the victims
of the Jews' sinfulness *and* the innocent sacrificial victims. Pionius not only recognizes the crime but condemns it, making strategic use of the words of the
prophet in the process.

The stark contrasts that Pionius draws continue as he distinguishes between
the miraculous power of Jesus' name to cast out demons and the perverse necro-
mantic conjurings of the Jews who claim they can bring Jesus and his cross up
from hell.¹⁴¹ Detouring into a lengthy discussion of the story of the "witch" of
Endor in 1 Samuel, Pionius stakes a thoroughgoing claim to truth and authenticity against the disguises, delusions, and appearances available to those who
revolt against God.¹⁴² If all else fails in the argument, he suggests, then one must
simply assert that "however it may be, we are stronger than (or morally superior
to) you who without coercion committed fornication and served idols."¹⁴³

The self-portrait of Pionius that emerges from his speeches is one of an
authoritative apologist, a well-versed reader of the Scriptures, and a compelling
advocate for a Christian—indeed, Catholic—identity. But he is not only a
speaker but also an actor—much as Ignatius sought to link word and deed in a
harmonious and noncontradictory relation. From the opening of Pionius's text,
he knows that his spoken testimony must be supplemented by a bodily testimony—not only the ultimate visible testimony of martyrdom but also gestures
and performances that will unambiguously communicate the consistency of his
commitment. Hence, as the text opens, Pionius waits with Sabina the confessor
(ὁμολογήτρια) and Asclepiades in his house where the three of them are fasting.
Having come to realize through a dream that they will be seized, Pionius prepares himself and his companions for the arrest by placing woven cords around
their necks.¹⁴⁴ As his text explains it, "He did this so that when they were led
away no one would suspect that they were like the others led to eating defiled
meat, but in order that everyone see/know that they had chosen/decided to be
led directly to prison."¹⁴⁵ Later on, while the group is on display in the agora of
the city, Pionius provides an explicit explanation of the significance of the chains
when questioned by a wicked merchant named Alexander. Pionius articulates
three purposes for their voluntary self-chaining: first, in order that the group of

Christians not be suspected of having come to the city to eat defiled food; second, in order to teach the authorities that the group does not consent to questioning; third, in order to communicate that the group need not be taken coercively since the Christians are already in chains.[146] In other words, Pionius seeks simultaneously to control the perceptions and actions of others and to express Christian passive noncompliance with authority through this unlikely sartorial gesture. The rhetoric of Pionius's actions seems to be as winning as his oratory. According to the text, "and thus Alexander was silenced."[147]

Pionius's stage-managing of events is not limited to serving as the dresser for himself and his companions. Throughout his record of debate with the authorities, he presses them to act on the imperial decree, in order to force their hands. The exchanges he records are familiar ones in which "persecutors" are cast as pragmatic negotiators lacking in real conviction. By contrast, Pionius and his close companions, Christians who have not lapsed, are rigid and single-minded in their commitment, even if that commitment will lead to their deaths. Such contrasts may be seen especially in the dialogues Pionius records between himself and Polemon, the temple warden. Repeatedly, Polemon implores, "Be persuaded by us" or "Offer the sacrifice," and repeatedly Pionius refuses. At one point, Pionius clearly tries to move the conflict to its inevitable conclusion: " 'You have been commanded either to persuade or to punish. You do not persuade; punish.' "[148] Polemon's response, "Sacrifice, Pionius," only serves to generate Pionius's resistant declaration, "I am a Christian." Glossing this affirmation with a brief profession of faith in the creator God known through his Logos,[149] Pionius then rejects the apparent compromise that Polemon suggests: "Sacrifice, then, at least to the emperor." What must have struck the temple official as a reasonable alternative that might resolve the crisis reaches Pionius's ears as an impossible demand. "I do not sacrifice to a human being," Pionius responds. "For I am Christian."[150]

The religious and political conflict grows more heated as the presence of state authority becomes increasingly visible, and yet Pionius continues to direct the drama of his own witness. As soon as Pionius has completed his lengthy prison speech, Polemon appears on the scene, bringing with him the *hipparchos* Theophilus, a group of police (διωγμῖται), and a large crowd—all still seeking to persuade or coerce Pionius to offer sacrifice. In this attempt, they invoke the names of Euctemon, a Christian leader, and Lepidus, whom they report to be waiting for Pionius at the temple. (Euctemon has apparently already offered sacrifice, and indeed, a ridiculous portrait of his exuberant lapse emerges later on in the text.) In the face of this particular challenge, Pionius does not make a religious argument but a procedural one in response: " 'It is fitting that those who have been thrown in prison wait for the proconsul. Why do you rely on yourselves in this matter?' "[151] In essence, Pionius accuses those who seek to force him to sacrifice of violating their own juridical constraints. The refusal to cooperate with the imperial edict requires a judicial response from the appropriate quarters, not the haphazard and bullying coercion represented by the momentary coalition of a temple official, a military officer, some gendarmes, and a mob.[152] The ensuing exchange repeats a familiar pattern: the authorities seek to win Pionius's cooperation through sophistry, trickery, and lies, while Pionius's consistency and resistance reduce his opponents to flatfooted and self-authorizing declarations of their own authority and, finally, the rhetoric of brute force. When persuasion proves impossible, the *hipparchos* wordlessly grabs Pionius by a garment around his neck and, almost strangling him, hands him over to one of the policemen.[153]

The conflict and violence increase, as does the spectacle of coercion and resistance. Brought literally kicking and screaming before the altar in the temple of the Nemeseis, Pionius is confronted by the figure of Euctemon "standing idolatrously" and Lepidus demanding an explanation for the refusal to sacrifice. Here, Pionius combines a religious, almost creedal explanation with a challenge that blends religious, ethical, and judicial elements. Shouting, Pionius demands, " 'Respect piety, honor justice, have sympathy, be obedient to your own laws; you punish us since we do not obey, and you set yourselves free. You are commanded to punish, not to coerce.' "[154] As the conflict intensifies, Pionius continues to speak and behave simultaneously as a lawyer, a debater, and a theatrical director and actor. Confronted by the rhetor Rufinus who cajoles Pionius, urging him to abandon such vain ideas, Pionius responds by calling upon the rhetorical and philosophical traditions, citing famous examples of virtuous men unjustly persecuted by their city.[155] Were all these vainglorious because they exercised philosophy and justice and patient endurance?[156] But although Pionius continues to call upon familiar figures from the cultural world in which he continues to operate, however provisionally, what becomes increasingly amplified is the degree to which the arenas of rhetoric and worldly wisdom recede from Pionius's domain. Indeed, the contrast becomes starker and starker. In the wake of his debate with Rufinus (who is, now predictably, rendered silent by Pionius's rhetorical superiority), Pionius meets Lepidus with a man who has worldly authority and glory (ἐν ὑπεροχῇ καὶ δόξῃ κοσμικῇ), both admonishing him not to shout—that is, not to violate the conventions of social intercourse. Pionius responds: "Then don't coerce; light a fire and we will climb up to it ourselves."[157]

This willingness to be burned alive and the endurance of the taunts and blows of the crowds are set in stark contrast with the ludicrous spectacle of the lapsed Euctemon who had decided that it was fit that "we be coerced [ἀναγκασθῆναι ἡμᾶς]." Displaying himself in his crown, swearing by the genius of the emperor, eating a bit of the sacrificial meat and greedily taking the rest home with him, Euctemon makes his apostasy as complete as Pionius's continued faithfulness.[158] In the process, he makes a mockery of himself, rendering himself ridiculous with his exuberance. The accusation may be read as something of a paradox, since the Christians themselves are read by their opponents as violating decorum and, indeed, making a spectacle of themselves. But the reigning notions of self are becoming jumbled here as Pionius's self-portrait detaches itself ever more definitively from the values of worldly authority and glory and aligns itself decisively with a different ethos and value system.

The rest of the text consists of the final testimony of Pionius before Quintilian, the proconsul, and the execution Pionius endured, attached by nails through his flesh to a piece of wood and burned alive. The writer who completes Pionius's self-portrait, a purported eyewitness, reports the miraculous preservation of the martyr's body, a body restored to youth, athletic superiority, and health. This body, left as a remnant and a sign, mirrors back to those who observe it their own understanding of Pionius as he himself prepared it in his self-narration.

CONCLUSION

What, in the end, do these three accounts of self-writing provide us? Even as Ignatius is turning (variously) from flesh to grain to bread or from flesh to water, even as Perpetua is casting off the constraints of an upper-class Roman woman's life and even the confines of the female body, even as Pionius stage-manages his own arrest and trial—even as all are profoundly and sincerely anxious to abandon this transitory life for a lasting and eternal one, they still leave texts behind that others will read. Perpetua's closing line, "if anyone wants to write of the outcome, let them write," assumes that the story will be told. Pionius's editor repeatedly asserts that his *syngramma* has been left so that others will remember. Foucault's mapping of self-writing in antiquity as a process that culminates in late antique Christian expressions of heightened interiority is complicated and perhaps actually contradicted by these three examples where self-fashioning is enacted in the service of an imagined, implied, or even idealized audience. Even if one reads these examples of self-writing as evidence for a high degree of inward-looking self-absorption,[159] they are still material and textual remnants addressed to a readership that survives their authors.

Ignatius may well have imagined his own letters enjoying some of the public authority that those of Paul had already done by the time he wrote. Perpetua may not have imagined that her diary would be read in Augustine's church two hundred years later or that her text would have a much longer reception history, anthologized with medieval women's literature and in twenty-first-century collections of women's prison writings.[160] Pionius's intentions, meanwhile, are recorded only by his contemporary editor, who claims that the presbyter-martyr wrote explicitly for others. One can only speculate on the precise contours of these self-writers' anticipated audiences. Nevertheless, whatever else is going on in these texts, they are clearly texts written in order to be read. They imagine a future audience, one that survives the events that bring these martyrs to their earthly ends. They are texts that inspire memory, texts that seek to say something about the past in relation to a reading present. One of the most striking ironies of all of these self-portraits lies in the fact that even as the three writers give up the values and hopes of this life, they struggle narratively and rhetorically to continue to define the dimensions of their own annihilations. This is a commanding and, indeed, masterful attempt by each writer to maintain control over their own textual and interpretive destiny, even as they surrender themselves to the jaws of the beasts, the executioner's blow, the flames of the pyre, the will and love of God.

4

MARTYRDOM AND THE SPECTACLE
OF SUFFERING

In the preface to *The Martyrs of Palestine*, Eusebius of Caesarea situates his history of the martyrs of the Diocletianic persecution within the frame of the apostolic exhortation to remember the saints.[1] This memory is to be preserved, Eusebius avers, not in perishable images but in immortal words.

> So, for our part, we who need the help of their prayers and are commanded also in the book of the Apostles to *communicate in the commemoration of the saints*, let us also communicate with them, and let us begin to describe their contests against sin, contests whose fame is at all times on the lips of every believer who knew them. But their praises were declared, not by statues of stone, nor by pictures of mingled pigments, nor by colors or images of lifeless terrestrial things, but by the true word uttered before God. The deed which was seen by our eyes added its witness. Let us therefore tell the clear signs and glorious manifestations of the divine doctrine, and frame in writing an imperishable monument, and let us make their wondrous excellence a lasting vision before our eyes.[2]

Thus Eusebius opens his history of these Christian martyrdoms through a double rhetorical move, invoking "memory" as an analytic category and contrasting competing modes of representation. According to his argument, artistic representations—statuary or paintings or other passible images—are far from worthy containers for the memory of the martyred saints. Evoking the language with which Christian writers routinely criticized material representations as forms of idolatry ("images of lifeless terrestrial things"), Eusebius contrasts material reminders with the immaterial, immortal word, calling his own text a written, "imperishable monument" to the memory of the saints. This word, underwritten and intensified by his own eyewitness testimony, provides a lasting vision of the excellence of the saints. The memory of the saints will be a visual memory, but one distinct from human artistic creations that can tend toward the idolatrous. The memory of the martyrs, then, is a matter that privileges vision, but the vision is conjured through words and resides on a spiritual plane.

Meanwhile, several decades later, in one of his many preserved sermons, Augustine exhorts the Christians in his congregation to divert their friends from attending the still-popular spectacles and to bring them instead to church. What will the spectacle seekers find in church? Augustine promises dazzling and dramatic tableaux: to wit, the heroic stories of the Christian past embedded in accounts of the deaths of the martyrs. But how these Christian spectacles are interpreted depends fully on the character of the spectator, and Augustine declares that there are two kinds of people who look on—the materially minded and the spiritually minded. Here is how he distinguishes them:

> The materially-minded look on, and think how wretched and unfortunate those martyrs are, thrown to wild beasts, beheaded, burned with fire, and they are filled with detestation and horror. Others, however, look on, as do the holy angels also, and don't fix their attention on the mangling of bodies, but instead marvel at the completeness of faith. A splendid spectacle offered to the eyes of the mind is a spirit whole and unbroken while the body is torn to pieces. That is what you people gaze on with pleasure when the accounts of such things are read in church. After all, if you didn't form some sort of picture of what happened, it would mean you weren't listening at all.[3]

For Augustine in this sermon, those who look on with the eyes of the mind are akin to the gazing holy angels. They see beneath or beyond the somatic experience of the martyrs, beneath or beyond the surface of the image, focusing on a different spiritual scene where a splendid spectacle is visible and a different body of significations is available. Strikingly, the spiritual realm is also the realm of the visual, and the spectacular is both a Christian category and a practical feature of the liturgy aimed at drawing a crowd. Moreover, the capacity to form some sort of picture is a sign of good listening skills and proper attentiveness. The complex cultural and theological dynamics embedded in the formation of "some sort of picture" in the memory work of Christians around persecution and martyrdom is the topic of this chapter.

The work of forming a mental image or a picture on the part of Eusebius's readers or Augustine's congregation takes place within a much broader and more complex cultural and interpretive frame: the world of artistic representations and the world of Roman spectacle, both routinely critiqued by Christian writers as realms of idolatry. It was this world, where representation, idolatry, and spectacle overlapped, in which the persecution of Christians was staged (both historically by the Romans and imaginatively by the Christians). After all, martyrs need an audience, and the logic of spectacle that governed Christian martyrdom was not limited to the historical executions but extended into the generative work of Christian collective memory. The world of Roman spectacle could at one and the same time reassuringly reinscribe *and* dangerously trouble the culture's prevailing values concerning violence and the visual, gender and status, domination and death. Spectacle, here and elsewhere, was tied to a range of other elements within the performative and the practical: theater, ritual, violence, visuality, and the power of the gaze. The world of Roman spectacle was resoundingly critiqued by generations of Christian writers but also paradoxically appropriated by those who sought to preserve the memory of Christian suffering.

It might at first seem that early Christians unilaterally opposed spectacle: indeed, apologists like Athenagoras, Tatian, and Minucius Felix insisted that Christians were explicitly distinguished from others by their disinterest in the spectacles, while orators like John Chrysostom, polemicists like Tertullian and Lactantius, and rhetors like Augustine strongly cautioned against the seductions of the games and the spectacles.[4] At the same time, however, Christians also appropriated the logic of spectacle in order to preserve many of the stories of Christian martyrdom in collective memory—and martyrs in Christian narratives often display their virtue through their manipulations of the logic of the spectacular gaze. This chapter takes up the question of how Christian collective memory of martyrdom is constituted *as* spectacle—and how spectacle was variously manipulated, used, and resisted in the process. In particular, I want to explore the paradoxical relationship between Christian polemics against spectacle and Christian appropriations of spectacle when linked to the realm of persecution and martyrdom.

This chapter has four parts. It begins with the current scholarly discussion of the forms and meanings of Roman spectacle, a discussion that has flourished recently and has brought to the historical sources a salutary theoretical vocabulary and sensibility. It then turns to Christian critiques of spectacle and broader issues concerning the dangers involved in looking at all. Although these critiques may appear at first to be ubiquitous and monolithic, I locate some fissures in the systematic critique, places where Christian writers generate (as Augustine did in the sermon cited at the opening of this chapter) a sort of Christian counterspectacle. The final part considers the impact of Christian martyrdom reclaimed *as* spectacle. Given the traditional divisions of academic disciplines, Roman historians and historians of early Christianity have not collaborated frequently or substantively around the questions emerging from the Christian presence in the spectacles. This is as much as anything a result of the perspectival nature of primary sources on both sides of the disciplinary divide, but it is worth attempting to bring these two worlds into closer conversation with each other in order to understand how Roman spectacle became Christian memory.

ROMAN SPECTACLE IN OVERVIEW

The category "Roman spectacle" is a broad and expansive one. It comprises a wide range of public performances, including chariot races in the circus; athletic competitions in the palestra and the stadium; comedies, tragedies, mimes, and pantomimes in the theaters; military triumphs through the streets of Rome culminating on the Capitoline; and staged battles, mythological reenactments, gladiatorial contests, and executions in the amphitheater and the arena. These public displays served a number of different religious, political, social, and civic functions. They provided spatial, performative, and symbolic idioms for defining, articulating, and reinscribing social identities and hierarchies, power relations, and public allegiances.

As will become clear in the analysis of their rhetoric, Christian writers in their polemics against the spectacles tended to collapse this dazzling array of different kinds of performances, essentially viewing their remarkable variety as just so many particular manifestations of the same, more general, base, and idolatrous impulses. In spite of this rhetorical gesture to render all spectacles as simply particular manifestations or iterations of the same general problem, the amphitheater and the arena nevertheless clearly stood out, functioning as the most dramatic and compelling sites for the corruption these Christian authors sought to reveal. This was true both because of the stark violence that took place there and because of the arena's role within the judicial system as a privileged site of criminal executions. As a consequence, although the circus, the theater, and other spectacular venues endured their share of the Christian vituperation, the amphitheater and the arena became the privileged objects of Christian opprobrium and critique. It is because of this focus within the Christian sources that my discussion of Roman spectacle focuses on the religious, political, judicial, and ideological meanings that accrued to the arena.[5]

In the last century, scholars have carefully compiled and examined the literary, documentary, epigraphic, archaeological, and ideological remains of the Roman arena.[6] They have reconstructed its sight lines, its rituals, and its complex physical and ideological topography. More recent work has supplemented this foundation-building scholarship with theoretically inflected analyses of spectacle, public violence, the religious contexts of the games and public executions, and the role of representation in preserving this ancient cultural history.[7] Many questions arise in and from this scholarship—historical, cultural-critical, aesthetic, comparative, religious, and ethical questions. These questions range from the abstract, psychological, and ideological ("What are we to make of the paradoxical repugnance and allure of the arena's violence?"[8]) to the quite practical ("What did they do with all the dead bodies?"[9]).

The Roman arena was a public space in which the religious and political imaginary of the society was repeatedly constituted and acted out on the bodies of both animals and human beings. The person who entered the arena as a combatant or a condemned had already crossed over a symbolic line, his or her status radically diminished and his or her very claim to membership in human society denied. The people who populated the arena were prisoners of Rome's wars, criminals convicted of a range of possible crimes and condemned to torture and death, or enslaved people. All of them were marginal people marked by *infamia*, a status that attached to their person and rendered them legally, socially, and symbolically out of bounds, beyond the pale.[10] The ideology of the arena co-opted their struggles (whether real or staged), their courage (or its failure), their spilt blood (or their capacity to spill it), rendering them all part of a larger ideological drama in which state power and social relations were repeatedly contested, reconstituted, and reinscribed.

In the last two decades or so, interpreters of the arena have increasingly turned to the insights of various contemporary social and cultural theorists to make sense of the Roman use of social power and public violence to generate and inscribe the hegemony of the imperial institutions. In the 1980s, Monique Clavel-Lévêque drew upon anthropology, psychoanalysis, and Gramscian and Althusserian ideological critique to argue that the Roman games are not best understood as a "ludic phenomenon" with a generalized religious or cultural value, but rather that they need to be read in terms of their complex integration of religious, social, and "technico-economic" elements.[11] In her studies, Clavel-Lévêque sought to position the games in relation to other social institutions—the family and various other (civic, juridical, imperial) communities—in order to argue that the games functioned as "rituals of integration" serving as one critical element in the "apparatus of hegemony" that reinscribed social power.[12] Clavel-Lévêque argued against the view that the documentable increase in the frequency and complexity of the spectacles during the last two centuries of the republic provides incontrovertible evidence for the games having become detached from earlier ritual origins and having degenerated into "mere spectacle," mere entertainment in the imperial period.[13] In addition, she rejected the binarism implied in the "secularization" hypothesis ("game" vs. "everyday life," "imaginary" vs. "real"—and, I would suggest, implicitly, "religious" vs. "secular"), asserting that the games integrated these opposites more and more completely as the spectacles proliferated.[14] "The games were constituted fundamentally as a totalizing practical theology [of consent]," she wrote, and they were accompanied by rituals whose efficacy emerged through "recourse to a traditional religious imaginary, in Rome and in the provinces." The "ludic rituals [came] to represent an indispensable instrument in the conquest of power," beginning in the republic and extending through into the imperial period.[15]

More recently, Paul Plass's study of public violence in ancient Rome likewise reads the arena as a site replete with ritual and symbolic importance for the establishment and maintenance of social order.[16] Whereas Clavel-Lévêque built upon ideological critique in her analysis, Plass turns to the theory of sacrificial violence found in the work of literary critic René Girard to understand "the sociology of public violence." Drawing upon Girard's theory of sacrifice, in which he hypothesizes that controlled social violence serves as a mode of restoring order and collective sensibility, Plass emphasizes the salutary nature of public displays of violence.[17] For his part, Plass also views society as a corporate body, making use of medical metaphors throughout his discussion. Hence, the violence in the arena (and, concomitantly, political suicide) is a social form of immune response to the disease of social disequilibrium.[18] In this reading of the meanings of the violence in the arena, the deaths of gladiators and prisoners in the spectacles are transformed into a version of human sacrifice offered ritually in the service of restoring social balance, a healthy body politic. Plass's reconstruction and analysis emphasize the social-psychological dimensions of social violence, focusing on the productive character of this violence as it generates social solidarity through controlled and stylized expressions of disorder, which cycle back reassuringly into a version of restored order. Seeing "the need to process violence" as a "cultural universal," Plass emphasizes the necessity of aspects of the games that might well have seemed more contingent.[19] The dramatic (even fictional) character of the games, the displays of hypermasculine resoluteness and murderous rage, and so on were crucial to the workings of the violence that took place there. "The resolute performance from good gladiators is a direct corollary of their role as institutional transformers and conduits of violence. . . . Cowardly death is unseemly because it reveals that the victims were just that—cowards, perhaps, but mere victims, too."[20] Sharing with Clavel-Lévêque an interest in the ritual capacity of the arena, Plass seems to reject the more critically political rendering she offers, emphasizing the effectiveness of violent displays for staving off social crisis.

In an important recent study of the arena in the early decades of the empire, Erik Gunderson argues that "the arena plays an important role in the moralization and maintenance of Roman social roles and hierarchical relations."[21] Asking the question of how the arena came to be such an important site for the inscription and maintenance of roles and hierarchies, Gunderson turns to three distinct but interrelated theoretical frameworks. He begins with Michel Foucault's theoretical deployment of the Panopticon, the prison technology developed by Jeremy Bentham in the seventeenth century that allowed prison guards to observe the incarcerated without the prisoners being able to see whether or not they were being watched. This technology, as Foucault renders it in his study of the history of the prison, results in prisoners policing themselves since they can never be sure when they are unobserved.[22] In Gunderson's analysis, "the arena acts as a social organ of sight on the order of Foucault's Panopticon. The arena can thus be taken as an apparatus which not only looks in upon a spectacle, but one which in its organization and structure reproduces the relations subsisting between observer and observed."[23]

Supplementing Foucault's category of the Panopticon, with its emphasis on the role of looking, Gunderson then turns to Louis Althusser's analytic framework of the "Ideological State Apparatus."[24] Using Althusser, Gunderson argues that the arena functions as do other institutions in society (such as the family, churches, modes of communication, and schools) as "a vehicle for the reproduction of the relations of production." Moreover, "the arena serves to reproduce the Roman subject and thus acts as an instrument of the reproduction of Romanness as a variously lived experience."[25] Gunderson complements both Foucault and Althusser with the work of Florence Dupont, who emphasizes the theatrical and performative dimensions of public power embodied in the spectacles, drawing the analysis back to the importance of the visual for understanding how the public displays of political spectacle render the arena a privileged site for the production and maintenance of ideology.[26]

Using these three theoretical frameworks in tandem, Gunderson analyzes several different aspects of spectacle and arena culture. The physical arrangements of the arena, especially the seating, reinscribed and rendered highly visible the dominant social hierarchies. The emperor's public performance at the games made him and his power visible and available to the populace. The arena served to emphasize and naturalize Roman gender and sexual hierarchies. The physical arrangement of the arena symbolized Rome's imperial dominance by inverting its geography, positioning the hierarchically situated spectators in a ring around representatives of Rome's imperial conquest, whether captives of war or animals brought from the far reaches of the empire. As Gunderson argues it, "nearly every major theme of the Roman power structure was deployed in the spectacles: social stratification; political theater; crime and punishment; representations of civilization and the empire; repression of women and exaltation of bellicose masculinity."[27]

Whereas Gunderson uses Foucault, Althusser, and Dupont to emphasize the visual, ideological, and performative dimensions of the arena, Alison Futrell goes in a slightly different direction in her book *Blood in the Arena.* Invoking Durkheim's and Weber's functionalist definitions of religion as a social force, she argues that the arena, especially in the provinces, constantly reinscribed Roman political dominance through the carefully scripted mobilization of cultic practice and ritual action. Focusing on the gladiatorial contests and public executions that were staged in the arena, she goes further to argue that the spectacle of controlled violence was an "exercise in terror" and ultimately a form of human sacrifice.[28] Using a method of ethnographic analogy whereby she compares evidence for Sumerian, Carthaginian, Aztec, Incan, Chinese, and Dahomean human sacrifice with the Roman situation, Futrell argues that "the amphitheater was a politicized temple that housed the mythic reenactment of the cult of Roman statehood. . . . [The gladiator's] death served as a foundation sacrifice that answered the crisis of empire, validating the Roman struggle for power and offering a model for understanding the basis of Roman power."[29]

Each of these scholars approaches the arena from a slightly different theoretical vantage point, and each draws somewhat different conclusions about the meanings of violence in the arena. More importantly, what they agree on is that the bloodshed in the Roman arena—implicated as it was in the judicial, military, political, and religious institutions of the empire—must be read in terms of the logic of imperial interests. The blurring of lines between the games (as religious enterprise and public patronage) and execution (as gesture of judicial constraint and political containment) collapsed the religious, social, judicial, and political into the bloody theatrics of the arena. Staged as ritual performance and as public entertainment, the arena's spectacles were simultaneously acts of raw violence, gestures toward collective catharsis, and enactments of public power. Infrequently critiqued by the Roman elites whose literature is our primary record of this social world, the violence of the arena involved excess, conspicuous consumption, and impulses toward ever greater extravagance.[30] And although it is quite likely that the commonplace understanding of the Christian role in the arena is substantially overdrawn in both ancient Christian sources and their ongoing popular reception, the arena and related spectacles nevertheless occupy a major place in Christian apologetic, polemic, and martyrology. And, as will become apparent, the overlap between the judicial, political, and religious domains in the arena will give Christian critics added rhetorical ammunition for their critiques of the violence that was staged there.

CHRISTIAN POLEMICS AGAINST SPECTACLE

The first Christian polemics against spectacle appear in the second-century apologists who defend the Christian community against criticism and accusation by portraying Christians as ascetic, violence deploring, and deeply moral. Defending against the common accusation that Christians are murderers and cannibals, for example, Athenagoras of Athens decries the slander with a two-pronged argument. First, he points out that Christian-owned slaves would most certainly be witness to such outrageous behavior and would as a consequence readily testify against their owners. The fact that not a single slave of a Christian has been produced to provide (or, in Athenagoras's terms, to invent) such testimony is compelling evidence of the charge's absurdity. (Slave owning, it should be noted, is meanwhile apparently not incongruous with Christian asceticism, the renunciation of violence, and a self-congratulatory morality.[31]) Second, Athenagoras emphasizes Christian opposition to all forms of murder, including capital punishment: "For when they [the slaves of Christians] know that we cannot endure even to see a man put to death, though justly, who of them can accuse us of murder or cannibalism?" he asks. "We, deeming that to see a man put to death is much the same as killing him, have abjured such spectacles."[32]

Athenagoras's peer and fellow apologist Theophilus of Antioch makes a similar argument, defending Christians against the accusations of incest and cannibalism by asking how Christians could be guilty of such crimes "when we are forbidden even to witness gladiatorial shows lest we should become participants and accomplices in murders."[33] As other Christian critics will do as well, Theophilus connects the dangers of witnessing violence in the arena to the threats embodied in other forms of spectacle: "And we are not allowed to witness other spectacles, lest our eyes and ears should be defiled."[34] Like other apologists, Theophilus distinguishes Christians from their critics with a double rhetorical move: Christians are guilt-free, they argue, and their innocence stands in stark contrast to the murderous guilt (and, by the way, sexual excess) of their opponents.

Tatian, a contemporary of both Athenagoras and Theophilus, makes a similar rhetorical gesture when he polemicizes against public shows of all sorts, lumping together acting, dancing, mime, gladiatorial shows, drama, and music. In Tatian's assessment of the cultural scene, all of these performances involve superstition, idolatry, doubleness, madness, perversion, and unnaturalness. His critique opens with a riveting description of an actor, a certain man whom Tatian had seen, interestingly enough, "on many occasions." The man's offense has many layers: "he was one man in himself, but quite another in the outward mask he assumed: very affected and putting on all sorts of delicate airs, now with flashing eyes, now wringing his hands and expressing madness with a clay make-up; sometimes appearing as Aphrodite, and sometimes as Apollo; a one-man accuser of all the gods, epitome of superstition, disparager of heroism, actor of murder, demonstrator of adultery, repository of madness, teacher of perverts, instigator of condemned criminals."[35] Linking the religious practices he deplores with the bloodlust of the audiences and the gender deviance of the performers, Tatian constitutes Christian identity as the precise opposite: where the "Greeks" engage in ridiculous and demonic festivals in which men shame themselves with effeminate affectation or debase themselves through hypermasculine violence, Christians (by implication) devote themselves to solemn, single-minded, and consistent lives of religious piety characterized by the embrace of "natural" gender and sexuality.[36] In this short passage, Tatian offers a rhetorical and interpretive framework that will be repeated by numerous other Christian critics of spectacle: the spectacles are collapsed into a single category of evildoing, and they collectively represent the mirror opposite of Christian moral ideals. Superstition, idolatry, changeability, madness, and perversion are the elements of spectacle.[37] Piety, singleness of identity, sanity, and naturalness by contrast are the characteristics of the Christian.

Tertullian also draws upon notions of "the natural" and natural law to polemicize against the shows. In a short treatise he wrote against the wearing of a garland (a sign of victory in military, athletic, or dramatic contests), Tertullian links the unnatural moral depravity of the spectacles to two particular biblical passages: 1 Corinthians 11 (on the veiling of prophesying women) and Romans 1 (on homoeroticism as a punishment for idolatry). In the first passage, Paul writes, "Does not even Nature teach you that for a man to wear long hair is degrading to him, but if a woman has long hair, it is her pride?" (1 Cor. 11:14–15). The broader context of this passage concerns Paul's insistence that women be veiled during worship services in order to maintain clear gender distinctions in the Corinthian community. In the second passage, Paul writes of idolaters who "exchanged the truth about God for a lie and worshipped and served the creature rather than the creator." "For this reason," Paul writes, "God gave them up to dishonorable passions. Their women exchanged natural relations for unnatural, and the men likewise gave up natural relations with women and were consumed with passion for one another, men committing shameless acts with men and receiving in their own persons the due penalty for their error" (Rom. 1:25–27). Both passages invoke "nature" as the standard by which proper gender and sexual categories should be judged and maintained.[38] Tertullian then links these two passages and their celebration of "both natural law and a law-revealing nature" to his own argument about spectacles. "It is thus, accordingly, in the pleasures of the shows, that the creature is dishonored by those who by nature indeed perceive that all the materials of which shows are got up belong to God, but lack the knowledge to perceive as well that they have all been changed by the devil."[39] In other words, the pleasures of the shows are analogous to the sexual and gender confusion embodied in women's refusal to wear veils while prophesying and in the unnatural exchanges of passion and lust among idolaters. According to Tertullian, idolatry, the blurring or refusal of gender differences, homoeroticism, and the spectacles all involve the dishonoring of the creature. And all of them should consequently be condemned as violations of both nature and natural law. Tertullian closes his discussion with a gesture toward his own, more substantive polemic against all of these public performances, *De spectaculis*.

It is in this more substantive text that Tertullian lays out the most sustained Christian critique of spectacles.[40] Spectacles, he proclaims, are forbidden to Christians by faith, by truth, and by discipline.[41] Christian faith requires a renunciation of idolatry, and since the spectacles are by definition idolatrous (linked to pagan religion, devoted to pagan deities, and focused on the creature rather than the creator), spectacles must be renounced.[42] Christian devotion to truth requires a renunciation of falsehood, and since the spectacles are devoted to illusion and the turning of created things away from their proper goals, they are false and must be rejected.[43] Christian teaching, moreover, forbids participation in the spectacles since it forbids concupiscence and passion. Hence Christian discipline requires that the faithful avoid the frenzy of the circus, the immodesty of the theater, the vanity of the stadium, and the cruelty of the amphitheater.[44] Tertullian proceeds to elaborate each of these points in considerable detail, going on to argue that the devil himself is behind the falsehoods and deceptions of the spectacles.[45] Tertullian's conclusion, a quintessential example of the Christian rhetoric of counterspectacle, promises a dramatic turning of the tables.[46]

Many Christian writers worry particularly about the impact of the spectacles as a broader problem of the gaze, as the apologists have already demonstrated.[47] Tertullian is not alone here, but he provides a compelling argument about the brutalizing impact of looking upon violence, embedding this argument within the broader claim that the spectacles are damaging because they disrupt stable notions of how things are and what constitutes the right and the true. He writes,

> The Gentiles have not truth in its completeness, because their teacher of truth is not God; so they construe evil and good to square with their own judgment and pleasure; sometimes a thing is good that at other times is bad, and the same with evil, now evil now good. So it comes about that a man who will scarcely lift his tunic in public for the necessities of nature,

will take it off in the circus in such a way as to make a full display of himself before all; . . . that the man who when he sees a quarrel on the streets coming to blows will try to quiet it or expresses his strong disapproval, will in the stadium applaud fights far more dangerous; that he who shudders at the body of a man who died by nature's law the common death of all, will, in the amphitheatre, gaze down with most tolerant eyes on the bodies of men mangled, torn in pieces, defiled with their own blood; yes, and that he who comes to the spectacle to signify his approval of murder being punished, will have a reluctant gladiator hounded on with lash and rod to do murder; that the man who calls for the lion as the punishment for some notorious murderer, will call for the rod of discharge for the savage gladiator and give him the cap of liberty as a reward, yes! And the other man who was killed in the fight he will have fetched back to take a look at his face, with more delight inspecting under his eyes the man he wished killed at a distance; and, if he did not wish it, so much the crueller he![48]

Tertullian was hardly alone among Christian writers in being troubled by the impact of looking. A century later, Lactantius worried that being a spectator to even the most deserved execution would result in the defilement of the conscience of the one who watches.[49] And in his *Confessions*, Augustine tells the story of his friend Alypius who went unwillingly to the games in Rome with friends but who ultimately was compelled by his own irrational and passionate response to the roar of the crowd to open his eyes and to look at the violence taking place in the center of the arena. In what amounts to a quintessential deconversion story, Alypius experienced his downfall because of the seductions of the spectacular. Once forced to open his eyes by the cries of the crowd, Alypius was thereafter hooked on the drama and violence of the games.[50]

But the dangers of the gaze exceed the action in the arena and on the stage. What the crowd can see of itself is also an impulse toward vice. In the third century, Clement of Alexandria assured his readers that "the Pedagogue" (Christ) would not lead Christians to the public spectacles, the racecourse, or the theater. "These assemblies, indeed, are full of confusion and iniquity; and these pretexts for assembling are the cause of disorder—men and women assembling promiscuously for the sight of one another. In this respect the assembly has already shown itself bad: for when the eye is lascivious, the desires grow warm; and the eyes that are accustomed to look impudently at one's neighbors during the leisure granted to them, inflame the amatory desires."[51] Over a century later, John Chrysostom polemicizes strongly against all forms of spectacle, urging a discipline of chastity of the eyes, an ascetical practice he articulates as one of metaphorical fasting: "Let the feet fast, by ceasing from running to the unlawful spectacles," he preaches. "Let the eyes fast, being taught never to fix themselves rudely upon handsome countenances, or to busy themselves with strange beauties. For looking is the food of the eyes."[52]

But Tertullian would be the one who predictably puts the argument in the starkest terms. Arguing against those who claim that the Scriptures do not forbid one from attending spectacles, he cites what he calls "a novel defense" of the practice. " 'The sun,' says [the spectacle lover], 'yes, and God Himself from heaven look on, and are not defiled.' Why, yes," Tertullian responds, "the sun sends his rays into the sewer and is not polluted. . . . God looks on at brigandage, God looks at cheating, adultery, fraud, idolatry, yes, and the spectacles, too. And that is why we will not look at them, that we may not be seen by Him who looks on everything. Man! You are putting defendant and judge on one level!—the defendant who is a defendant because he is seen, the judge who because he sees is judge."[53]

Another North African Christian writer invokes the view from nowhere that also inspires Tertullian, though toward a slightly different rhetorical end. In his moral epistle/treatise *Ad Donatum*, Cyprian, bishop of Carthage, conjures the power and danger of the sense of vision, at first complimenting Donatus for holding the pleasures of vision in contempt and instead fixing his gaze upon Cyprian himself.[54] As the argument unfolds, Cyprian urges his correspondent to encounter divine truth by envisioning himself transported to a high peak from which he will be able to gaze on the whole world while thankfully being no longer part of it.[55] Cyprian begins with a broad critique of human violence and depravity: "The whole world is soaked with the blood of both sides, and homicide, which is admitted to be a crime when carried out by an individual, when it is committed on behalf of the state, is called a virtue."[56] But almost immediately, his argument turns to a narrower range of human activities—the gladiatorial games, the theater, and private sexual practices undertaken in secret places. Throughout his critique of the games and of the theater, Cyprian emphasizes the scandal and depravity nurtured by the act of looking. "The gladiatorial game is prepared so that blood might entertain the desire of cruel eyes."[57] Family members watch as their kin perform in the arena, so caught up in the impious spectacles that they seem to be unaware that they are "parricides by means of the eyes."[58] The critique of theater that follows mirrors others that one encounters in Christian polemics. By attending the theater, one imbibes immoral lessons, especially of the sexual sort because adultery and incest are so frequently the subjects of performances. The theater emasculates men and rewards with highest praise those who are most effeminate.[59] Throughout his entire critique of spectacles, games, and theater, Cyprian emphasizes the perilousness of the look. Even as he has urged Donatus to visualize himself as possessing the perspective of the view from nowhere, he condemns those who look upon the worldly spectacles in the arena and on the stage.

For all these writers, the eyes were a powerful and dangerous portal into the soul. The spectacles were the quintessential threat to Christian well-being because, through the power of the gaze, they incited feelings of desire and bloodlust. Because of the power of the images one encountered in the arena or at other spectacles, the soul became brutalized, coarsened, and assimilated to the violence and duplicity of the performances. And yet, as will also become clear, the idiom and logic of the spectacles were clearly too compelling or persuasive to be avoided altogether. And, as if engaged in a late ancient version of a competitive marketing plan, Christian writers recognized the appeal of the spectacular and sought to lay claim to it in asserting that Christians had athletes, heroic gladiators, and daring spectacles of all sorts to compete with the more quotidian offerings found in urban amphitheaters and on stages.[60]

SPECTACULA CHRISTIANA

Despite these many examples of Christian polemic against spectacles—and one could produce many, many more—there exists a striking counterdiscourse in these texts devoted to a more positive rendering of spectacle—Christian spectacle, that is. Clement of Alexandria, for example, elaborates the Pauline image of the Christian as athlete by figuring the Christian true gnostic as the athlete in the stadium (standing in allegorically for the world) crowned "for the true victory over all the passions." The spectators are angels and gods, the contest sponsor and trainer is God, the one who awards the prizes is the Son of God. This Christian athlete endures pain that "is found beneficial in the healing art, and in discipline, and in punishment." Because of his endurance and triumph over all circumstances, he "appears truly a man [ἀνήρ] among the rest of human beings."[61]

Some Christian writers use Paul even more explicitly, either as an exemplar or as an authority. In the latter case, they often cite 1 Corinthians 4:9: "For I think that God has exhibited us apostles as last of all, like men sentenced to death; because we have become a spectacle to the world, to angels and to human beings [δοκῶ γάρ, ὁ θεὸς ἡμᾶς τοὺς ἀποστόλους ἐσχάτους ἀπέδειξεν ὡς ἐπιθανατίους, ὅτι θέατρον ἐγενήθημεν τῷ κόσμῳ καὶ ἀγγέλοις καὶ ἀνθρώποις]."[62] Augustine, for example, holds up Paul as a model of Christ's athlete and performer in the theater of the world. "The citizens of God's City are happy to gaze at this hero with the eyes of faith."[63] In one sermon, Augustine quotes the line from 1 Cor. 4:9 in the broader context of discussing Christ as himself "a spectacle to be gaped at." He then distinguishes between two sorts of spectators—the materially minded and the spiritually minded—in the quotation with which this chapter began.

But, almost two centuries before Augustine, Tertullian, in the midst of exhorting Christians not to flee persecution, argues that public infamy and the gaze of others is a boon for the Christian who will undergo punishment and execution.[64] "If you are exposed to public infamy, says he [the Spirit], it is for your good; for he who is not exposed to dishonor among men is sure to be so before the Lord. Do not be ashamed; righteousness brings you forth into the public gaze. Why should you be ashamed of gaining glory? The opportunity is given you when you are before the eyes of men. So also elsewhere, seek not to die on bridal beds, nor in miscarriages, nor in soft fevers, but to die the martyr's death, that he may be glorified who has suffered for you."[65] An easy death in private figures in Tertullian's discussion as a feminine (and hence less worthy) enterprise. A difficult, public death as a martyr, by contrast, brings glory and takes on masculine coloring. As has been seen repeatedly in the earlier discussion of the ideologies of martyrdom, the ordinary values of honor and shame, glory and dishonor are disrupted, inverted, and overturned by the logic of martyrdom.

But Tertullian's most intense explication of his idea of Christian spectacle can be found at the end of his text *De spectaculis*. Here, he makes a series of arguments that seem to undermine his earlier complete dismissal of the logic of spectacle. Do you like the races in the circus? he asks. Well, Christians have "the race of time" to follow with giddy anticipation, the passing of the seasons until the expected end of history. Do you prefer theatrical literature? Christians have books, poems, aphorisms, and songs aplenty. Or is it the fights in the arena that attract you? Christians have an abundance of battles: "See impurity overthrown by chastity," Tertullian writes, "perfidy slain by faith, cruelty crushed by pity, impudence thrown into the shade by modesty." And remarkably, the question and answer: "Have you a mind for blood? You have the blood of Christ."[66] At this point, the rhetorical structure of the argument nearly collapses under the weight of Tertullian's enthusiasm as the final chapter spins into apocalyptic fervor. After twenty-eight chapters all indicting the spectacles and a lone twenty-ninth chapter offering up the rather anemic prospect of Christian counterspectacles, the closing chapter of Tertullian's polemic promises a last act that will literally bring down the house: the second coming, the resurrection of the saints, the establishment of the New Jerusalem, and the day of judgment.

> How vast the spectacle that day, and how wide! What sight shall wake my wonder, what my laughter, my joy and exaltation? As I see all those kings . . . groaning in the depths of darkness! And the magistrates who per-

secuted the name of Jesus, liquefying in fiercer flames than they kindled in their rage against the Christians! Those sages, too, the philosophers blushing before their disciples as they blaze together.... . And then there will be the tragic actors to be heard, more vocal in their own tragedy; and the players to be seen, lither of limb by far in the fire; and then the charioteer to watch, red all over in the wheel of flame; and, next, the athletes to be gazed upon, not in their gymnasiums but hurled in the fire—unless it be that not even then would I wish to see them, in my desire rather to turn an insatiable gaze on them who vented their rage and fury on the Lord. . . . Such sights, such exultation—what praetor, consul, quaestor, priest, will ever give you of his bounty? And yet all these, in some sort, are ours, pictured through faith in the imagination of the spirit.[67]

In other words, one might indulge in watching or participating in the spectacles now, but one does so at one's peril since the fiery punishments that will accompany Jesus' return in the end times will provide the long-deferred entertainment for Christians who have been promised Paradise and eternal life.[68]

MARTYRDOM AS SPECTACLE

Set in the context of Roman arena spectacles both historically and imaginatively, the executions of Christians could not help but assimilate characteristics of the setting in their commemorative retelling. The condemned criminal became a participant in the dramatic and violent spectacles of the arena, and Christian sources preserve an eloquent ambivalence toward the power and danger of the spectacular. At the levels of both lived reality and symbolic citation, executions in imperial Rome, as in virtually every premodern society, were events designed to be seen, and they were staged for maximum impact.[69] As the earlier discussion of the power dynamics of the arena made clear, whatever was performed in that space served to reinscribe imperial authority, the conventions of social order and hierarchy, and a wide range of dominant values. The dramatic staging of events that ended in death, often accompanied with theatrical flourishes and elaborate costuming, sought to produce a legible and intelligible narrative that entertained as it inculcated social, political, ethical, and religious values.[70] Moreover, as David Potter observes in his essay "Martyrdom as Spectacle," such events were scripted rituals in which an audience well versed in the script had grown accustomed to the drama unfolding in a predictable fashion and following carefully proscribed patterns of practice.[71] It was within the constraints of this sort of practical and ideological framing that (a few) Christians experienced the spectacular form of the arena and (a good many more) Christians produced their own counterscript of what happened before the audience's eyes.

Christian critics of the spectacles in the arena focused, as we have seen, on the brutalizing impact of violence on the viewer. But what is equally striking is the degree to which Christian accounts of martyrdom nevertheless highlight the spectacular nature of the events they recount. Of course, they do so with rhetorical and didactic goals in mind, attempting both to shame the fictive audience for its bloodlust and to offer up exemplars of courage and virtue in the figures of the martyrs. But these rhetorical and didactic goals require graphic descriptions to assure their achievement. At the same time, the Christian sources thematize alternative renderings of both debasement and spectacle within the narratives themselves, thereby attempting to subvert the meanings imposed by the physical arrangements of the arena or other public execution space. The audience itself becomes a complex topos in Christian narratives, and it performs a variety of narrative functions. In some texts, the audience is the diabolical engine driving the event, as it does in the *Martyrdom of Polycarp* when the crowd shouts for Polycarp's immolation or in the letter describing the mob-inspired violence and persecution against Christians in Lyon and Vienne in 177.[72] Elsewhere, the audience appears as a single body whose shamelessness occasionally finds its own limits when the extreme cruelties of the torturers engender horror and resistance. For example, the audience objects when, in the *Passion of Perpetua and Felicitas*, the two women are brought naked into the arena, Perpetua, "a delicate girl," and Felicitas, "having just recently given birth with dripping breasts."[73] As a consequence, the two women are taken away and returned to the arena in simple tunics. The audience can also serve narratively as the audience for the martyr's testimony—a testimony so persuasive that some who watch the martyr's suffering are so moved by it that some of them are themselves converted (and martyred) on the spot.

The audience for Christian martyrdom is not, however, limited to historical spectators or the characters of martyrological narrative. In his rhetorically elegant *Octavius*, the second-century Christian apologist and lawyer Minucius Felix offers an intriguing argument concerning the pleasure that resides for God in the vision of Christian suffering. "How beautiful is the spectacle to God when a Christian does battle with pain; when he is drawn up against threats, and punishments, and tortures; when, mocking the noise of death, he treads under foot the horror of the executioner; when he raises up his liberty against kings and princes, and yields to God alone, whose he is; when, triumphant and victorious, he tramples upon the very man who has pronounced sentence against him!"[74] He goes on to argue that the difference between the Christian's miserable appearance and his actual exalted state is a difference between seeming and being. Whereas the actor in a spectacle is critiqued, by Minucius and other Christians, for his enactment of something that he is not, the Christian martyr's spectacular suffering is a different sort of illusion, one to be embraced and celebrated. For the martyr, according to Minucius, does not embody an illusion that seeks to pass itself off as the truth of the matter. Instead, the suffering that the martyr undergoes produces an illusory appearance whose truth can only be read by a person of proper discernment and understanding.[75]

In his *Exhortation to Martyrdom*, Origen makes a slightly different argument. In his portrait of the spectacle of martyrdom, the earthly arena is not the true setting of the contest. Instead, he posits the existence of a great theater (μέγα θέατρον) divided in starkly dualistic terms: "Thus the whole world and all the angels, right and left, and all human beings, those from God's measure and those from the rest, listen to us contesting the contest concerning Christianity." Meanwhile, the angels in heaven and the powers from below constitute the cosmic audience, each side cheering for a different outcome. Those to whom Origen addresses his exhortation will, no less than Paul, utter proudly and defiantly the words recorded in 1 Corinthians 4:9: "We have become a spectacle to the world, to angels, and to human beings."[76] Here, the display is not a shameful reality to be resignified in other terms, whether by Christian narrators who retell the tale or by onlookers who reinterpret it by means of careful discernment. In Origen's account, the spectacle is itself the very point of the experience, an experience addressed to "the whole world," both mortal and supernatural.

Many readers have observed that as the past of Christian suffering recedes, the spectacular quality of martyrdom intensifies. The more distant the events being narrated, the more gruesome and detailed the accounts and the more blood-saturated the representations seem to become. The bodies of the martyrs are increasingly on display, not only for the audience in the narrative, but for the readers/hearers of the narratives as well.[77] And this spectacle borrows from the broader culture's repertoire of ideas about gender, honor, shame, and the power of the gaze. There are various elements of the Christian appropriation of spectacle that I want to stress in particular here. First, the narrative elements of performance, theatricality, and stage-managing that emerge out of various martyrological texts invite readers to understand the contest that is staged to have multiple layers of resonance and signification—and to begin to see the performative as itself a source of Christian commemorative counterscripts. Second, this negotiation with spectacle often involves a troubling of the received cultural conventions of gender in at least two ways. The masculine ideal of stoic fortitude dominates the arena, and it is so crucial to Christian claims to virtue that women can provisionally embody it—sometimes quite literally. And when this happens,

Christian polemics against gender confusion—in the liturgy, certainly, but all the more in the spectacles—dissolve into praise for the woman who has managed to transcend superficial elements of sexual difference. Third, in the polemics against the spectacles, Christian writers emphasize the brutalizing impact of looking upon acts of violence, whether real or staged. But when Christian writers take over the logic of spectacle, they contradict this critique—again, in two ways. Some argue that the Christian spectator, looking on in the proper spirit (like Augustine's spiritually minded spectator), will see past the surfaces of the violent display to the truer, more spiritually uplifting narrative that underlies the bloody spectacle. Others argue that the very image of violence can have a salutary and edifying impact on the viewer and that the failure to look on such violence can limit one's spiritual development.

Performance and Counterscripts

Whatever else it was, the arena was a performance space. Recent scholarship on Roman spectacle has emphasized, among other things, the degree to which arena events involved conscious staging and fictive reenactment.[78] The blurring of the lines between the real and the fictional, the "true" and the "false" produced the excitement and emotional charge of all sorts of performances, whether staged in the arena or in the theater. It is precisely this power that causes Roland Auguet to characterize such spectacles as "perverse," since the blurring collapses the ambiguity between the imaginary and the real, "making the imaginary one with reality" in the spectators' minds.[79] This blurring was also a major object of Christian critique. What one encounters in the Christian texts concerning martyrdom is a series of attempts to wrest control of the spectacle from the hands of the producers and to put it in the hands either of the performers, the narrators, or the Christian audience ex post facto. For the characters in the narratives, controlling the spectacle means acting out of turn, upsetting expectations, even stage-managing the events. For the narrators of these stories, it means providing a counternarrative so that the scene cannot be misread. For the later audiences, it means placing whatever martyrological memory text that comes their way within a recognizable interpretive frame. In this way, the later Christian audiences take on an uncanny resemblance to the earlier Roman audiences described by Potter. The Christian counterscript eventually becomes as rote as the earlier Roman script, and audiences grow impatient when the action or narrative diverges from the formula. But in the meantime, the counterscript offers a powerful alternative version of events and a way for the spectacle to work toward Christian advantage.[80]

The performative dimension of Christian martyrology can be traced through almost every conceivable example. Ignatius, Perpetua, and Pionius, whose texts were discussed at length in the last chapter, each in his or her own way engages in attempts to overturn the dynamics of domination that frame their arrests, captivity, trials, and executions. They do this not through physical escape but through gestures and words that seek to resignify the events taking place. Allen Brent has made a compelling case for understanding Ignatius's journey from Syria to Rome to be executed as a "counterpart" to the religious processions undertaken to the imperial altar.[81] One might take the argument even a step further and suggest that Ignatius's procession is almost parodic in its relationship to the imperial spectacle, with Ignatius refusing the role of prisoner precisely by embracing it so exuberantly.[82]

The text that provides an account of Perpetua in the arena offers a quite different example of the struggle on the part of Christian writers to cope with the arena's spectacular and performative dimensions.[83] When Perpetua and the rest of the group of condemned Christians are brought from the prison to the amphitheater, they are the objects of curious and scrutinizing gazes. But the narrator emphasizes that Perpetua carries herself self-consciously, playing Christ's wife and God's lover ("*ut matrona Christi ut Dei delicata*"), staring down those who look at her with her own powerful gaze.[84] When the Christians are compelled to dress in costumes that will make them appear as priests and priestesses of Roman cults, Perpetua explicitly resists the attire and the role being forced upon her.[85] Her resistance results in Felicitas and her being brought naked into the arena itself, whereupon the narrator emphasizes how the nakedness of Perpetua and Felicitas stuns and shocks the crowd. The effect of the text's narration is ambivalent, since the description lingers over the physical details of their nakedness much as the eyes of the spectators might have done, at once repelled and drawn to the sight.[86] As the scene plays out, Perpetua and the others perform resistance through compliance, draining the event of its bloody thrills by presenting themselves as willing participants. Meanwhile, Perpetua's death scene renders her a heroic gladiatorial figure, baring her neck and ultimately guiding the weapon in the hand of an unsteady young gladiator to her own throat.[87] Perpetua appears consistently in this narrative as a performer acting out a counter-script, deeply committed to her version of the story. What renders her performance more complex is the narrator's role, which, at critical junctures, places the reader in the role of voyeuristic spectator, reminding the reader of the instability of any performance and its openness to multiple interpretations.

Pionius's performance comes across as even more self-conscious and explicit, beginning early in the narrative when he and his comrades sit at home awaiting arrest, draped in chains so that everyone who sees them will know immediately that they are in captivity and not on the way to perform sacrifices. The figure of the martyr as rhetor in the Pionius text further emphasizes the performative character of the portrait.[88] The sharp exchanges that characterize Pionius's debates with his opponents, whether the temple warden, the proconsul, or a member of the crowd, inevitably end with Pionius's winning the rhetorical point. As Pionius's rhetorical performance achieves ever greater heights of cleverness and virtuosity, his interlocutors become increasingly unable to reply and are reduced to threats and violence. Meanwhile, his rhetoric serves by turns to delimit the range of options available to his persecutors; in essence, his performance forces their hands. In this fashion, the text implies that it is Pionius who controls the events as they unfold, that the spectacle is Pionius's show.

Examples could be multiplied here from the early martyr acts to demonstrate the repeated narrative enactment of the same move that Tertullian, Minucius, Origen, Cyprian, and other theorists of martyrdom also make, resituating martyrdom as a form of spectacle pleasing to God and potentially transformative of spectators/readers. The move becomes increasingly important over time as the memory work of martyrology becomes ever more distant from its historical anchoring. The performance is detached from the arena as a historical setting and begins to travel more freely in the imaginations of later readers and hearers. The spectacle of Christian suffering becomes, in the commemorative repetitions in the liturgy and devotional texts, its own genre of performance.

The spectacular character of Perpetua's last moments in the arena becomes itself part of the ongoing collective memory of the event in liturgical context. Two centuries later, for example, Augustine preached on the feast day of Perpetua and Felicitas, drawing his congregation into the position of the spectators, but reconfiguring the quality and character of their spectatorship in order to distinguish it from that of the historical audience. After reminding his audience that they have just heard the story read, and after characterizing Perpetua and Felicitas as women "whom men can admire more easily than imitate," Augustine turns his homiletic acumen to the problem of the spectacular in the story and to its capacity to implicate those engaged in this commemorative project.[89] Indeed, the congregation is simultaneously connected to the original spectators and yet different from them. Moreover, the original spectators are themselves objects of a mocking divine gaze: "At that time, when the holy bodies of the martyrs were exposed to the wild beasts, *the nations were roaring* throughout the amphitheater, *and peoples meditating vain things. But the one who dwells in the heavens was laughing at them, and the Lord was mocking them* [Ps. 2:1, 4]. Now, however, at this time, the descendants of those whose voices were impiously raging against the flesh of the martyrs are raising their voices in pious praise of the martyrs' merits."[90] The genealogical connection between the spectators and the congregants, the link between then and now, is disrupted by a shift of attention and intention. Where the spectators in the past saw suffering flesh, those who participate in the commemorative liturgy in the present see moral triumph.

The spectacle is transformed not only because of a difference between past and present, but also because of a series of other differences: a singular historical moment recapitulated through liturgical repetition, fleshly eyes replaced by eyes of the heart, rejoicing and mourning transposed by a shift in orientation and affect. Augustine preaches:

> Nor at that time was the theater of cruelty filled with as great a throng of people to see them killed, as the one that now at this times fills the Church of family piety to do them honor. Every year loving-kindness watches in a religious service what ungodliness committed on one day in an act of sacrilege. They too watched, but with a vastly different intention and attitude. They achieved by their shouts what the wild beasts did not complete with their bites. We, on the other hand, both deplore what was done by the godless, and venerate what was suffered by the godly. They saw with the eyes of flesh sights with which to glut the monstrous inhumanity of their hearts; we behold with the eyes of the heart sights which they were not permitted to see. They rejoiced over the martyrs' dead bodies, we grieve over their own dead minds. They, lacking the light of faith, thought the martyrs liquidated; we, with the clear sight of faith, perceive them crowned. Finally, their shouts of abuse and mockery have been turned into our shouts of admiration and joy. And these indeed are religious and everlasting; while those were impious then, and are of course non-existent now.[91]

In the process of commemoration, the dynamics of the spectacle are reframed by a new generation of Christian spectators who, with their claim to immortality, displace and replace the impious audience that is no more. The memory of martyrdom becomes a pious and uplifting spectacle because those who saw in the wrong ways have disappeared; those who remain, Augustine's congregation, see with eyes of the heart.

Critiquing and Celebrating Gender-Bending

The Christian critiques of theatrical performances emphasize the falsity and unnaturalness of the theater, especially the tendency of actors to enact and embody disorderly gender ambiguities. That Christian writers felt compelled to polemicize so strongly against the theater and its gender-bending suggests that both were sufficiently attractive to Christian audiences that they required strong rhetorical obstacles as impediments to their lures.[92] But if gender-bending was the object of near-universal opprobrium when Christians critiqued the theater and other spectacles, it was less clear that gender transformation was a problem in the spectacle of martyrdom. One thinks, for example, of Perpetua's transformation into a male body in her final prison vision as she engages in the athletic contest with the giant Egyptian.[93] The literalism of the gender transformation here is striking: Perpetua's piety and virtue are figured in the graphically physical transformation of her body into a man's body. Of course, the literalism I ascribe to this transformation is offset by the fact that the image is part of a vision and not part of "history." But such a distinction imposes an unfair standard on the text itself, a text in which visions are not at all divorced from "the real" but are themselves manifestations of the hyperreal. Within the narrative and visionary logic of the text, Perpetua's achievement of the Christian masculine ideal is written on her body and put on display for the readers to consume.

Or one thinks of the slave girl Blandina and the famous account of her crucifixion and transformation in the eyes of those with her into the figure of Christ himself.[94] In this account, Blandina simultaneously interrupts the dominant script while also shape-shifting into the body of Christ. According to the text, Blandina's spiritual practice in the midst of this humiliating and gratuitous violence manages to conjure a remarkable form of counterspectacle. It is not that the faithful turn their eyes away in horror: it is that they keep looking, but what they see is transformed—no longer a suffering slave girl, but now Christ crucified.

As the memory work of Christian martyrology unfolds, the capacity of Christian women to be transformed into masculine heroes becomes almost a cliché, and this cliché translates eventually onto a new type of spiritual virtuosity when asceticism supplants martyrdom as the privileged form of Christian suffering.[95] What is useful to notice in this context is the way in which the near-unilateral critique of gender-bending in the context of theater and spectacle gives way in the memory work of Christian martyrology to a radically different valuation of the capacity of the martyr to transcend nature's bounds. Gender-bending, then, becomes one of the critical aspects of the paradoxical appropriation of Roman spectacle in the midst of Christian critique.

LOOKING AT VIOLENCE

The commemorative martyrological traditions generated and sustained by early Christians consciously engaged the power dynamics of spectacular suffering, as the preceding discussion has demonstrated. Moreover, Christian theorists of the memorializing processes at work knew the power of vision to brutalize and corrupt even as they also privileged the realm of the visual for its capacity to engage the viewer in seeing below the surfaces of representation. When Augustine describes congregants listening to the stories of the martyrs and conjuring pictures of their suffering, he creates a connection between the words of the liturgical reading and the personal reception and translation of those words into mental images, images that are supposed to supplant the popular civic spectacles and provide material for spiritual reflection and advancement.[96] In addition, Christian writers who emphasized the positive aspects of the spectacle of Christian martyrdom understood the power of visuality, the emotional and affective charges embedded in representations of violence, and the capacity for images to work in the service of both Christian piety and Christian conversion. One particularly intriguing example of how the commemorative and the martyrological intersect with the theorization of the ethical impact of visual representations of violence may be found in the traditions surrounding the fourth-century martyr Euphemia.

A century after the death of Perpetua in North Africa, another young Christian woman, Euphemia, is remembered for having suffered torture and persecution in the midst of Diocletian's "Great Persecution." The *Acta Sanctorum* places the feast of Euphemia on the sixteenth of September and provides a collection of texts narrating her martyrdom, the translation of her relics, and the geographical extent of her cult.[97] Meanwhile, the *Fasti Vindobonenses*, a liturgical document compiled during the fourth through the sixth centuries, provides only the barest record of her martyrdom: "In the consulships of Diocletian VII and Maximian V, churches were destroyed, holy books burned, and Saint Euphemia died on the sixteenth of October."[98] With only a collection of liturgical calendar mentionings, and absent concrete historical evidence concerning the conditions and details of Euphemia's death, there nevertheless emerged an important cult devoted to her in late antiquity and the Middle Ages, as the *Acta Sanctorum* and other sources amply attest. Egeria, the Christian pilgrim whose travels are recorded in a surviving diary, mentions the martyrium dedicated to Euphemia in the city of Chalcedon.[99] Melania the Younger is reported by her biographer Gerontius to have taken courage from a visit to Euphemia's shrine when she was about to leave the rigors of the ascetic life behind and reenter society in Constantinople.[100] The medieval *Golden Legend* by Jacobus de Voragine records a detailed and imaginative account of her suffering and death.[101] Perhaps most importantly for the history of Christian theology, the basilica named for her in the city of Chalcedon was the site for the fourth ecumenical council in 451, which produced the orthodox formulations on the dual nature of Christ.[102]

Three distinct textual traditions preserve three different accounts of the suffering and death of Euphemia, each related to different commemorative traditions. The most well-known tradition is the passion thought to have been composed right around the time of the Council of Chalcedon in 451.[103] In this detail-rich account of Euphemia's death, she suffers numerous tortures (the wheel, beatings with a variety of weapons) and is ultimately cast into the arena where she succumbs to the attacks of wild beasts. Just prior to her death, a voice resounds from heaven, an earthquake erupts, and the saint herself calls down divine vengeance upon the proconsul who condemns her. Because of its exuberance and hyperbolic indulgences, and because it was likely written in such close proximity to the Council of Chalcedon (approximately 150 years after the events that are being narrated), most scholarly assessments of this version of Euphemia's death judge it "a legend."[104]

A second, less well-known tradition is connected with a diffuse set of texts and images in Rouen and Milan and with the translation of Euphemia's relics in the latter part of the fourth century.[105] The texts associated with this tradition include a brief mention in Victor of Rouen's *De laude sanctorum*, a work composed on the occasion of the introduction of relics of several saints to the new church at Rouen in 395.[106] They also include a short passage from one of Paulinus of Nola's poems[107] and the preface to the Milanese rite for St. Euphemia.[108] This latter text dates to the sixth century and claims that Euphemia died having been stabbed with a sword (rather than having died *ad bestias* in the arena). In his discussion of this diffuse tradition, Schrier connects these diverse sources to a twelfth-century passion-book, which also portrays Euphemia dying by the sword.[109]

The third narrative tradition concerning Euphemia's martyrdom claims that she was burned to death; this tradition is preserved in a brief sermon by the fourth-century bishop Asterius of Amasea.[110] Scholars have debated extensively the question of the historical details of Euphemia's death, especially over the means by which it was achieved. This is not the question that interests me here. Rather, I am interested in the spectacular aspects of its description. Because Asterius's sermon focuses on an artistic representation of Euphemia's torture and martyrdom, I will focus my discussion on his description of the violence portrayed there and the claims made concerning the salutary character of looking on the spectacle of that violence. I will also consider the later reception of Asterius's sermon as another piece of evidence for the ongoing legacy of martyrdom as spectacle.

Asterius' sermon is an *ekphrasis* on the martyrdom of Saint Euphemia—that is, a carefully crafted description of a painting of the martyrdom of Euphemia which Asterius claims that he has seen in a church near her tomb.[111] According to Asterius, the painting comprises a series of panels in which the story of Euphemia's death is recounted in a vivid graphic idiom. In one scene, scantily clad torturers pull Euphemia's teeth while court reporters holding their wax tablets lean forward to make sure not to miss a word of her testimony and the judge scowls hostilely at Euphemia from his high throne. In a second scene, Euphemia is at prayer in her prison cell, and the sign of the cross makes an ethereal appearance over her head, presaging the tortures and rewards that lie ahead. In the final image, Euphemia appears in the midst of the flames with her arms reached heavenward.

Asterius's text generates a whole series of questions: Did the painting really exist, or was Asterius just experimenting and practicing with the rhetorical form of *ekphrasis*? If the painting did exist, was it based on an historical account of the martyrdom of Euphemia, an account now lost but to which the painter had access? Or did the artist simply engage in a form of visual rhetoric, drawing upon the available visual idioms of the day in portraying the death of this virgin saint?

As pressing and important as these questions are, they are not the questions that concern me here. Rather, I am interested in the intense visuality embodied in Asterius's description of the painting. I am also interested in the values that he and later readers of his text will attribute to the images contained in the painting as he describes it. Even bracketing the historical problem of whether the painting actually existed, one can still pursue the question of the impact of the painting's rhetorical materiality and visuality. For Asterius's sermon makes this painting its own text, and it aligns the graphic representation of the suffering and execution of Euphemia with the verbal portraits offered by the priests to honor her memory. Thus, unlike Eusebius, who makes a clear ethical distinction between passible artistic representations and immortal verbal portraits, Asterius claims that the painting provides a visual memory that parallels the words spoken in liturgies of commemoration.

Ekphrasis emphasizes the critical relationship between rhetoric and representation, between language and image. Indeed, an especially successful verbal description can effectively supplant the artistic representation.[112] The *progymnasmata* (rhetorical handbooks) offer consistent definitions of *ekphrasis* as "a descriptive speech bringing the thing shown vividly before the eyes [λόγος περιηγηματικὸς ὑπ' ὄψιν ἄγων ἐναργῶς τὸ δηλούμενον]."[113] According to James and Webb, the rhetorical masters understood *ekphrasis* as "performing a similar function to visual art: it is a vivid visual passage describing the subject so clearly that anyone hearing the words would seem to see it. Indeed, the authors of the progymnasmata refer to this paradox, saying that the language of *ekphra-*

sis should bring about sight through sound, or that it should turn listeners into spectators."[114] The emphasis in the project of *ekphrasis* is to bring images to life and thereby to stir the hearers'/viewers' emotions and affections.[115]

Asterius's sermon begins with his taking a walk in order to enjoy some leisure after spending time reading a debate between Demosthenes and Aischines. He comes upon the painting quite by accident, and it overwhelms him.[116] As he undertakes to describe the picture in considerable detail, he explicitly situates the visual elements within a narrative framework concerning both the bravery of Euphemia and the ongoing commemorative practice of those who remember her. Drawing attention simultaneously to the liturgical practice of honoring her memory in an annual ceremony and to the painting, Asterius links the visual, the verbal, and the ritual. As a consequence, he also makes a connection between the past he narrates and the present in which he seeks to persuade his audience, thereby collapsing time.

The description of the painting focuses on both the material details of the scene, complimenting the artist's capacity to render them vividly, and the emotional intensity of the painting's impact. The first vignette includes the dramatis personae of the trial and torture: the judge, the bodyguards, the soldiers, the scribes, and the virgin. The tools of writing are displayed as prominently as the tools of torture, and the figure of Euphemia is strikingly clothed in the dark tunic and cloak of a philosopher. Asterius focuses on the paradoxical emotional tenor of the scene, repeatedly emphasizing that the portrait brings out ambiguities: Euphemia is the simultaneous embodiment of both modesty and strength. In a somewhat surprising analogy, given their incommensurate stories, Asterius comments that the portrait of Euphemia in this first vignette calls to mind for him the performance of the tragic character Medea, who succeeds in performing both pity and anger simultaneously.[117] Asterius credits the artist's technique for bringing to the surface of the canvas a balance between modesty and courage in the portrait of Euphemia, virtues which, he observes, are "by their nature contrary to one another."[118]

The next scene is a scene of torture in which two men knock out Euphemia's teeth, one holding her head steady and the other making use of the very visible hammer and chisel. Asterius emphasizes the lifelike quality of the painter's representation of Euphemia's physical suffering.[119] Instead of writing of the paint looking like blood, Asterius says the painter has smeared drops of blood on the canvas. Looking upon this graphic portrait causes Asterius to weep and cut short his discourse on the image, claiming that the viewer would feel called upon to sing a dirge when seeing it. Asterius's description of the painting's vibrancy suggests not a series of fixed images, but rather images in motion—a staged drama rather than a still portrait. And just so, the images evoke strong emotional responses, grief and weeping, as Asterius and the viewer are drawn into proximity with the events being visually narrated.

The next scene is Euphemia at prayer in the prison, her arms stretched toward heaven and the sign of the cross appearing over her head. Asterius evokes the immediacy of the scene by narrating in the present tense: Euphemia sits in prison; she prays; the cross appears. The visual immediacy is paired with a sense of unfolding action. Asterius then glosses the scene, observing, "I imagine it [e.g., the cross] to be the symbol of the very suffering that awaited her."[120] The final scene focuses on her death itself, Euphemia with her arms raised amidst the ubiquitous red flames. The paradox of martyrdom is written on Euphemia's rapturous countenance: her face, Asterius writes, displays no burden but instead shows the virgin rejoicing over her journey toward bodilessness and holiness. The sermon then ends quickly, the painter's hand and the preacher's tongue stopping at the same moment. Asterius closes with an invitation to his listeners to finish the inscription ("γραφή," both writing and graphic representation, that is, painting) in order to judge the worthiness of his interpretation.[121]

Asterius's homily emphasizes the dramatic quality of Euphemia's story and draws attention to elements of performance, spectacle, and visuality. He emphasizes details of her appearance—her clothing being like that of a philosopher, her refined appearance, her modest blushing when she was the object of the male gaze (literally, "she blushed before the eyes of males"),[122] her capacity to embody both modesty (αἰδώς) and courage (ἀνδρεία) visibly and simultaneously, her bleeding under torture, her prayerfulness, her rejoicing amidst the flames. When Asterius compares her emotional range to that of Medea on the verge of murdering her children, he calls up a canonical scene from the mythological and theatrical heritage of Greek culture and positions Euphemia in paradoxical relation to the tragic tradition. He also emphasizes both the visuality and the theatricality of the comparison, describing himself "as if I were contemplating [or looking at] the drama of that Colchian woman [Medea]."[123] The visual immediacy of Euphemia's suffering and the transparency of her rejoicing at her death recalls the familiar trope of the martyr whose performance answers back to the spectators in an audience-disappointing (or -transforming) refusal of the more conventional script of execution. Of course, this familiar trope has become its own conventional script, one which the martyrs' actions in story after story repeatedly embody. Asterius's sermon, though mediating his audience's experience of the visual representation by means of his own words, ends up advising his hearers to see for themselves whether his account was sufficient. Indeed, the text implies that hearing the violence portrayed in the painting described or, better yet, seeing it for oneself will have a salutary effect. Here, the spectacle of martyr-dom goes a step further beyond the earlier idea of *spectacula Christiana* and toward the use of these violent images in the service of teaching, contemplation, and commemorative piety.

Asterius's homily did not enjoy a wide audience after it was written, and, indeed, there is no testimony to its reception for several hundred years. When it reappears in the written history of the Christian church, however, it does so in a remarkable place: in the official records of the Seventh Ecumenical Council of Nicea in 787, in a theological debate over the religious use of images.[124] During this session, a series of biblical and patristic texts were mobilized in the service of legitimizing the cult of images. Carefully distinguishing between religiously legitimate images and idolatry, the testimony presented in this session mobilized a series of examples from the church fathers arguing that images—especially those of violence and suffering—have the capacity to move the viewer emotion-ally and to inspire conversion. A long series of texts were pulled into service of the broader argument, including several concerning representations of the sac-rifice of Isaac and several more involving saints and martyrs. Among these texts was a long fragment from Asterius's sermon. In this context, Asterius's graphic description of Euphemia's suffering served as testimony to the fact that images—even images of violence—hold the promise of a positive effect on their viewers. In this way, the spectacle that Asterius celebrated in his homily—even as it made him weep and grieve—became part of a broader argument concern-ing visuality and representation.

CONCLUSION

That Christians could and did appropriate the logic of spectacle for their own ends was diagnosed early on in the process by some critics, most notably by the Stoic emperor Marcus Aurelius. It might be all quite noble to face one's inevitable death with courage and fortitude, Marcus argues, "But the readiness must spring from a man's inner judgment, and not be the result of mere oppo-sition [as is the case with the Christians]. It must be associated with deliberation and dignity and, if others too are to be convinced, with nothing like stage-heroics."[125] Of course, for Christians, the performances that were staged by mar-tyrs were persuasive precisely because they did not *seem* to be true (as in the case of a mere stage performance) but rather *enacted* a far-reaching truth. The spec-tacle, when read properly, offered a compelling and memorable portrait worthy even of God's eyes.

The texts and practices surrounding martyrdom and commemoration call up a wide array of associations with the power and anxiety associated with the experience of seeing and being seen, with the social practices associated with both the theatre and the arena, and with the complex semantic possibilities embedded in the term "martyr" itself. Deriving from a courtroom context where the "martyr" is the "witness" who testifies to what he has seen, the cultural production of Christian martyrdom as performance and spectacle transforms the seer into the seen, the testifier into the testimony. And it transforms the readers and consumers of this tradition into uneasy voyeurs of the suffering of others even as it calls them into identification with that suffering. As one considers the memory work embedded in the ongoing Christian spectacularization of martyrdom, the paradoxes and ambivalence embedded in that commemoration require particularly cautious attention.[126] At the same time, the Christian appropriation of spectacle is a potentially illuminating example of what Simon Goldhill describes in this fashion: "Contests around cultural dominance take place not merely within a matrix of domination and resistance (the imperial gaze and the subaltern text) but with a more complex dynamic of local and central knowledge, practices of displacement and marginalization, imagined forces and unrecognized collusiveness. There are many, interlocking strategies by which the Empire writes back."[127]

5

LAYERS OF VERBAL AND VISUAL MEMORY
Commemorating Thecla the Protomartyr

If I wanted to say more, I would be able to find [more miracles], I who have brought them together with toil and pain, running around collecting and compiling them, as if gathering the miracles up out of some abyss of expansive time and of forgetfulness. . . .

—*The Miracles of Saint and [Proto-]Martyr Thecla*

NEAR THE END OF HIS two-volume work on the life and miracles of the early Christian saint, apostle, and martyr Thecla, an anonymous fifth-century Christian writer claims that the memory work of his hagiography has involved the arduous labor of rescue and retrieval, ransoming the past from the inexorable passage of time and the yawning abyss of oblivion.[1] He has been working on his writing project for a long time by this point, between thirty and forty years according to his modern editor.[2] As the work comes to a conclusion, the hagiographer describes his intense commemorative labor as a painful contest against the gaping maw of temporality and forgetfulness.

This eloquent expression of the motivations that have driven his work stands in some tension with what the author wrote at the opening of the first volume of his magnum opus. In that prologue, he articulates his singular goal: to assure that no one be ignorant of the entirety of the words and acts of the apostle and martyr. At the same time, he insists that he has *not* written out of concern that Thecla's acts will be lost to oblivion (ἐξίτηλα) or obscurity (ἄδηλα). Indeed, he argues that the actions of the saints are, by their very nature, immune from being haunted or threatened by forgetfulness. Rather, it is their character to remain steadfast, solid, and immortal, guarded by God in the service of his own perpetual fame (κλέος) and as a form of solace for human beings who still live on earth.[3] Surely this formulation is an ironic citation of Herodotus, whose *Histories* begin with his commitment to assure that things created by human beings not be forgotten (μήτε . . . ἐξίτηλα) nor marvelous works be deprived of fame (μήτε . . . ἀκλέα).[4] Indeed, this Christian author explicitly contrasts his motives with those of Herodotus, Thucydides, and those who have followed them in writing histories. Where they write spontaneously in response to their own wills, Thecla's hagiographer writes because he has repeatedly heard a divine voice tell him to do so and because an "excellent and very wise Achaios" has also advised him to undertake the project.[5]

What are we to make of this apparent contradiction between the beginning and the end of this hagiographic work, a contradiction that hinges on the problems of memory and forgetfulness, fame and oblivion, the apparent solidity of saintly actions and their potentially fragile legacies? Should the writer's insistence upon his difference from the classical historians be taken at face value? Or should it be read as a rhetorical convention by which ancient historians clear ground for their own endeavors in an archaic version of the anxiety of influence? If his modern editor and commentator is correct in suggesting that the work in question was thirty or forty years in the writing, is the writer simply changing his mind about the degree to which forgetfulness constitutes a threat against which literary commemoration affords a bulwark? Or has he himself merely forgotten the claim he made at the beginning? Or, yet again, has the issue of memory asserted itself differently at a late stage in the life of a writer who has dedicated several decades to devotional, commemorative writing? Although these questions cannot be answered with any certainty, the contradiction that frames his text nevertheless provides a fruitful occasion for thinking about the perceived need for commemoration over time. It invites one to think anew about the flourishing and proliferation of memory as the person and events commemorated recede inexorably backwards into the past.

This writer's two-volume work narrates Thecla's life and documents the emergence of a healing cult organized around the witness and divine power of this martyr who, paradoxically, did not die a martyr's death—indeed, according to some sources, did not die at all. The *Life and Miracles of Saint Thecla* documents the emergence of a particular piety devoted to Thecla's intercessionary power, but it also offers compelling testimony to the role of collective memory in generating a useable past for Christians out of a story that incorporates compelling episodes of innocent suffering and eventual vindication. Meanwhile, numerous other early Christian texts recall the story and example of Thecla, emphasizing variously her averted martyrdom, her ascetic fervor, and her role as healer, traveling evangelist, and apostle. Together with the visual testimony of artistic representations—some produced contemporaneously but most in later periods—these texts amplify and transform earlier traditions about Thecla, creating a new set of memories through processes of association, displacement, consolidation, and expansion. In the hagiographic elaboration of the founding narrative, the diegetical scaffolding remains largely in place, while the discursive elements of the story broaden and take on more responsibility for bearing the increasing weight of the account's theological message. In other written sources, Thecla functions most often as a placeholder for a touted virtue or ideal, as an object of shared memory in the service of a contemporary institutional or ideological interest. In the artistic representations, specific scenes are captured and recapitulated, much like snapshots, simultaneously evoking the remembered narrative and offering a visual exegesis of the precursor text. But both the literary and the artistic remnants stage different modes of memory work, reframing and reformulating the Thecla story in terms that render it into a useable past. In important ways, the scholarly debate over the character of the Thecla memory preserved in these remnants makes analogous gestures.

Thecla is an especially apt example for exploring the culture-making dimensions of martyrdom and memory, especially the culture-making dimensions that depend upon repetition and the dynamics of recognition. The later literary records that preserve Thecla's story are unabashedly citational, and even at times derivative of earlier written sources, in terms of both content and genre. The artistic remnants, meanwhile, are stylized, conventional, and, in some cases, even mass produced. Both the literary and the artistic remains of Thecla depend upon familiar genres, media, conventions, stereotypes, and the recognizability of the component narrative and thematic elements. Both raise the question of the past and its function as a meaningful resource for the present. Both raise the question of the past—and, in some important senses, leave it hanging. Indeed, one cannot definitively answer even the most elementary question that one might pose—was Thecla a historical figure or a persuasive fictional invention? But neither can one dismiss the impact of Thecla's commemoration in text and image, whether or not she ever actually lived and whatever formidable obstacles might lie in the way of any attempt at historical reconstruction. The commemorative narratives and representations take on lives of their own in rereadings, retellings, reinscriptions. As a consequence, the question of historicity seems to recede just as the apparent contradiction embodied in a martyr who does not die is effectively neutralized by adaptations in representation and imagination.

The preceding chapters have shown how the memory work of martyrdom among early Christians consists of complex layers and multiple manifestations. As we have seen, a foundational concern for collective memory animates the historiographical and hermeneutical activity of the ancient theorists of martyrdom.

These writers made sense of political and religious pressure against Christian individuals and communities by drawing upon the resources of tradition (e.g., law and sacrifice) even as they engaged in cultural critique and contestation with discourses and interpretations of power, value, and difference. What constitutes a social, political, religious, or relational norm? What constitutes deviance? How are contemporary debates over identity mapped backwards onto a shared past, out of which exemplars and models might be generated? Memory is at the heart of answering these questions in the context of martyrological writing, and guaranteeing the survival of a memorial trace is one impulse that drove the autobiographical efforts of Ignatius, Perpetua, and Pionius. As the last chapter showed, collectively generated and sustained memories of spectacular death, with their stress on the visual dimension of memory, significantly complicated the broader practice of Christian cultural critique. Contestations over law, religion, status, and norms; practices of life writing that preserve the story of an individual while mapping it onto a larger, even epic, narrative about the past and localizing that memory in space; the exploitation of the spectacular dimensions of martyrdom and miracle through the creation of visual, material memories—all of these aspects of culture making also emerge in the different layers of the textual and artistic artifacts by which Thecla came to be commemorated. The history of martyrdom and memory resides here, a history that oscillates and adapts itself over time, sacrificing none of its authority in its changing focus, its amplification of details, and its transformation of its object.

One of the paradoxical dimensions of collective memory, as we have seen, lies in its capacity to become fixed and formulaic, on the one hand, and its malleability or openness to change, on the other. In the traditions surrounding of Thecla, both the fixity and the malleability of memory characterize the textual and material remains of her commemoration. In these remains, memory tends to be formed and sustained through quotation, citation, and allusion (both verbal and visual). In the process, certain aspects of Thecla's tradition become reinscribed, some dimensions of Thecla's identity become more stable and entrenched, while others seem to disappear altogether. The traditions surrounding Thecla, meanwhile, also eventually serve other purposes: to underwrite the increasingly institutionalized ascetic life, to retrofit orthodox theological claims for an earlier historical period (creating a useable past for the orthodox present), to participate in a burgeoning exegetical practice, and to provide an epic past for the liturgical life at her shrines. As a consequence, aspects of Thecla's story are emphasized and highlighted while other parts of the shared memory of Paul's purported early companion fade away. This chapter is devoted to an exploration of these complex dynamics of memory and memorializing as Thecla comes to be produced as the quintessential figure of the woman martyr, overshadowing her status in earlier layers of tradition and memory as an itinerant ascetic evangelist and apostle.[6]

THE FOUNDING NARRATIVE:
THE ACTS OF PAUL AND THECLA

The *Acts of Paul and Thecla* provide the earliest literary testimony for the Thecla story.[7] In recent years, this text and other Apocryphal Acts have been the focus of considerable scholarly scrutiny.[8] Among other questions, some of this scholarly debate focuses on the question of memory, specifically, of what are the stories of women in the Apocryphal Acts a textual memory?[9] For some, the *Acts of Paul and Thecla* (and the other Apocryphal Acts) consist of historical remnants of early Christian women's piety and provide a specific and salutary witness for the spiritual autonomy available to Christian women who embraced the ascetic life.[10] For others, the stories of Thecla and other women deploy early Christian women as rhetorical figures in a theological and polemical debate among elite men over their own status as men.

The most sustained argument for this latter view may be found in Kate Cooper's *The Virgin and the Bride*, an exploration of the literary representation of female virtue in narrative literature from the Roman imperial period.[11] In this reading of the literature where women protagonists enjoy an especially important narrative place, Cooper argues that women characters serve to refract images of men's character and perform a thoroughly rhetorical (and hence not historical) function.[12] In her reading of the *Acts of Paul and Thecla*, the story is therefore not really about Thecla's emergence as an autonomous Christian itinerant teacher, and even less about Thecla as an emblem for Christian women's religious autonomy *tout court*. Rather, the text concerns the contest staged between Paul, as the representative of the Christian ethical ideal of virginity, and Thamyris, Thecla's fiancé, as the representative of the dominant social order as it is symbolized by conventional and socially sanctioned marriage. That is, the *Acts of Paul and Thecla* provides readers with an account of a contest between two men who are (in Lévi-Strauss's formulation) using women to think with, and not with the straightforwardly recoverable story of the spiritual virtuosity of a remarkable woman.[13]

This position has been critiqued by authors concerned about the resulting potential erasure of the history of early Christian women. In her essay on this controversy in the scholarship on Thecla, for example, Shelly Matthews formulates the question in this way: "How is it conceivable that in the early church, which was never an exclusively male sect, questions about authority and social order could have *nothing do to with women*?"[14] She goes on to critique the interpretive appropriation of Lévi-Strauss's "using women to think with" for its suppression of Lévi-Strauss's own complicating caveat: "For words do not speak, while women do; as producers of signs, women can never be reduced to the status of symbols or tokens."[15] Matthews suggests that the scholarly question should not be approached in binary, oppositional, either/or terms, and argues for a feminist historiography that focuses on both the critical history of gender and the reconstructive history of women.[16] Meanwhile, in his monograph on the cult of Thecla, Stephen J. Davis has argued that the position represented by Cooper (and others) "may be a bit too pessimistic about the historian's ability to read ancient narratives for insight into the social roles of early Christian women."[17] Davis argues that the *Acts of Paul and Thecla* may not offer an unvarnished historical portrait of women's lives, but that the text may nevertheless provide a window onto the world of social roles and values concerning women. As such, the *Acts* may offer a useable portrait of the historical experiences of asceticism and itinerancy that characterized the lives of Thecla's followers.[18]

For the purposes of my argument concerning the commemorative aspects of the Thecla traditions, it is not necessary to resolve this scholarly debate concerning rhetoricity and historicity in a definitive fashion. Indeed, it is part of my argument that the martyrological past *tout court* is as much (if not more) a discursively generated and sustained memory as a lived historical reality. It derives its authority, not from definitive answers to the question "What really happened?" but from its ongoing capacity to persuade and to create continuity between the commemorated past and the lived present. Whatever the original ideological function of the *Acts*, their reception history within a longer Christian legacy effectively (if paradoxically) evades the problems inherent in any attempted quest of the historical Thecla, much as the literary Thecla repeatedly escapes martyrdom and yet is remembered and revered as a martyr. As the invocations of Thecla in a wide range of hagiographic and ethical literature, the retelling in the fifth-century *Life* and *Miracles* of Thecla, and the artistic legacy of representations of Thecla demonstrate, the figure of Thecla emerges as the divine woman/heroine of her own hagiographic and martyrological representation, and the contest between men that may well be a part of the earlier text comes to be supplanted by other claims about the virgin martyr.[19] Moreover, regardless of how one settles the question of the historical/rhetorical character of the founding text, the commemorative and ideological aspects of its reception history provide a critical ground for the emergent culture-making project represented by the Thecla cult.

The undecidability of Thecla's historicity is foregrounded in the earliest literary attestation of her story by its author's very choice of genre. *The Acts of Paul and Thecla*, after all, echoes the genre of the ancient romantic novel, though explicitly in the service of a religiously infused ethical project.[20] The standard novel form involves the meeting of the paired lovers; their subsequent separation by circumstance, whether hardship or adventure; and their eventual restoration to each other by the end of the story, a restoration often symbolized by marriage and generally predicated upon mutual fidelity and trust in the divine.[21] The Christian novel takes up this formulaic narrative framework and adjusts it to the interests of personal piety. In particular, the *Acts of Paul and Thecla* emphasizes the ascetic imperative that they affirm resides at the heart of Christian commitment. The desire of the lover for the beloved transforms itself in the Apocryphal Acts into the desire of the Christian for unity with God.[22]

The contents of the *Acts of Paul and Thecla* are well known and require only a brief, not detailed, exposition here. Following the romance formula, Thecla "meets" Paul by hearing him preach from the window of her house. The two "lovers" repeatedly encounter each other, suffer separations, and overcome a series of obstacles. A cycle of episodes recurs, first in Iconium, Thecla's home city, and then in Syrian Antioch, where Thecla has traveled with Paul: Paul and Thecla are temporarily reunited, separated by circumstance and hardship, then reunited again. Thecla is twice threatened with spectacular violence but escapes thanks to divine intervention; her faithfulness to God and her desire to stay with Paul are unwavering. The figure of the mother is also doubled in the narrative: first, Thecla's biological mother, who condemns her to the authorities, and then Tryphaena, a rich woman who offers Thecla protection in Antioch and seeks to have Thecla replace her recently deceased daughter.[23] The *Acts* records several other occasions of female solidarity, beyond the bond established between Thecla and Tryphaena, in the figures of female animals who protect Thecla and female spectators who use the conventional feminine tools at their disposal to intervene on Thecla's behalf. Meanwhile, Thecla makes several displays of autonomy and persistence, including acts that radically undermine the gender norms of her context: cutting her hair, putting on men's clothing, and baptizing herself. Finally reunited with Paul, he gives her the apostolic command, "Go and teach the word of God," and Thecla travels on her own, first back to her own city and then on to Seleucia. Her story ends with her teaching and ultimately with her death, "a noble sleep."[24]

The *Acts of Paul and Thecla* includes stories about Thecla's trials—stories that will eventually earn her the title "martyr"—but it is worth noticing the absence of the term itself from the text.[25] The *Acts* documents Thecla's struggles with her opponents, but it especially emphasizes the ascetic impulse as the driving force behind the action in the narrative and, indeed, Thecla's own actions. Martyrdom and asceticism overlap in significant ways in this text, as they do also in the autobiographical writings examined in chapter 3. And, like other texts examined thus far, this text also pays attention to questions of law and social convention, piety and power, madness and rationality, and the inversion of conventional values and categories that constitutes the Christian project. Here, as elsewhere, gender serves as a shorthand and a code for signifying certain social and power relations and their transgression.

The central message of the *Acts and Paul and Thecla* focuses on the need for asceticism, especially the renunciation of marriage, sexual activity, and "the world" as a whole. The centrality of askesis first comes to expression in Paul's preaching, where he articulates a series of macarisms, or beatitudes, echoing in form but not in substance the beatitudes of Jesus' Sermon on the Mount (or plain) in Matthew and Luke. As the Paul of this text would have it, blessed are the clean (οἱ καθαροί) of heart, those who have kept the flesh pure (οἱ ἁγνὴν τὴν σάρκα τηρήσαντες), the continent (οἱ ἐγκρατεῖς), those who have set themselves apart (οἱ ἀποταξάμενοι) from this world, the ones who have wives as if they did not have them, and the bodies of the virgins.[26] For making these claims, Paul is called a stranger (ὁ ξένος),[27] a person of unknown provenance (ὁ ἄνθρωπος οὗτος οὐκ οἴδαμεν πόθεν ἐστίν),[28] and a magician (ὁ μάγος).[29] When asked to explain himself to the proconsul, Paul defines himself as the instrument of God's desire for human salvation, to be brought about by Paul's leading people away from corruption and uncleanness (φθορά καὶ ἀκαθαρσία) and pleasure and death (ἡδονὴ καὶ θάνατος) and toward sinlessness.[30]

A contest of worldviews and forms of power ensues, as Paul's message disrupts the social order, family relationships, and households. At one point, this contest is characterized as a full-blown battle. The language Thecla's mother uses to describe her daughter's state portrays her as the vanquished in a military campaign, a campaign for the affections of the young woman: "she is conquered by a new desire and a fearful passion. . . . the virgin is taken captive."[31] Meanwhile, Theokleia and Thamyris join forces in their attempt to persuade Thecla to abandon her attachment to Paul; they characterize Thecla's problem as one of deviant passion, diagnosing her with an affective ailment. "What is this passion that oppresses you, terror-stricken?" asks Thamyris. "Child, why do you sit this way looking down and not answering but as one frenzy-stricken/mad?" demands Theokleia.[32] There is no question but that the battle staged here is a life-and-death struggle: when Thecla persists in ignoring their pleas, the entire household goes into mourning, and Thecla is essentially declared as good as dead.

The contest preserved in this framing of events involves competing values, associations, and identifications. Paul indicts marriage as the bearer of corruption, uncleanness, pleasure, and death. The logic of Theokleia's and Thamyris's world, meanwhile, renders this refusal of marriage a symptom of disturbed passion and madness, pointing toward a social death whereby Thecla as daughter, fiancée, and mistress is understood by her mother, her betrothed, and her slaves to have gone astray.[33] Theokleia later calls for her daughter's burning, displaying the logic of her stance with striking verbal economy in demanding the execution of the lawless one (ἄνομος) for insisting upon remaining the unmarried one (ἄνυμφος).[34] According to the logic of the world, which sees marriage as a fulfillment of law and legacy, remaining unmarried cannot help but be associated with criminality and death. The text expresses this by calling the death by fire that Thecla faces "the *necessity* of the spectacle [ἡ ἀνάγκη τῆς θεωρίας],"[35] a spectacle miraculously interrupted by violent divine intervention in the form of an earthquake and a murderous storm of rain and hail that extinguishes the flames, kills many spectators, and rescues Thecla.[36]

Paul's message and Thecla's conviction are, from the point of view of Theokleia and Thamyris, manifestations of deviancy on several different levels: the religious, the emotional, the legal, and the sexual. Such deviancies are thematized in the narrative in its emphasis on the out-of-placeness of the characters. The problem of straying from one's proper place is not only metaphorical but also literal. The text links ascetic qualities to bodies unanchored by conventional identities, bodies in transit and physically unclassifiable and out of place. Paul is repeatedly figured as a stranger whose origins are obscure and therefore suspect. Thecla is portrayed as a wellborn woman who rejects the expectations that constitute her proper social role and who is repeatedly and literally "out of place," not where she ought to be. When she ought to be at home, she is instead scandalously discovered in Paul's presence in the prison, bound with him in what the text calls "affection" (συνδεδεμένην τῇ στοργῇ),[37] a term sufficiently ambiguous to draw attention to the purportedly disreputable character of Thecla's actions while also emphasizing the overarching innocence of Thecla's emotional attachment to Paul.[38] Moreover, Thecla herself embraces identities that signal her rejection of the social position to which she is entitled ("Of the Iconians, I am first [Ἰκονιέων εἰμὶ πρώτη]") but which she can no longer claim since her refusal of marriage has resulted in her literal displacement, being cast out of the city. As a consequence, she adopts new titles, calling herself "the stranger [ἡ ξένη]" and "the slave of God [ἡ δούλη τοῦ θεοῦ]."[39] Both figures, the foreigner and the slave, are quintessential outsiders to civic identity, having no claim to the legal status accorded citizens and free persons, being in essence ἄτοποι, physically and socially perennially out of place.[40] When she finally finds a place, it is in a different city and, indeed, in a different physical realm—the city of Seleucia and, according to the longer endings of *The Acts of Paul and Thecla*, no longer in the visible world at all but rather in residence beneath it as she is absorbed alive into the earth through a narrow passageway.[41] Physically out of reach, Thecla remains in the world as an authority and an evoked memory—or, better, a series of memories that multiply and disperse.

THE LEGACY OF *THE ACTS OF PAUL AND THECLA*

The *Acts of Paul and Thecla* was written before either "asceticism" or "martyrdom" had been generated as coherent and comprehensive categories in Christian discourse or practice; indeed, the *Acts* contributes alongside many other texts to the emergence and eventual ideological stabilization of these categories. It does so in significant part by providing a crucial memory for later Christians whose experiences and spiritual identifications with both asceticism and martyrdom would be framed with reference to the life and legacy of Thecla. Even a writer like Tertullian, who sought to undermine the authority of this text by declaring its spurious authorship and denouncing its purportedly heretical warrant for women's evangelical and liturgical practice, clearly understood the influential character of the memory it preserved for interpreting and sanctioning contemporary Christian life.[42] Other Christian writers were far less suspicious of Thecla's story, and she was widely remembered and celebrated by hagiographers of other early Christian female saints, by ascetic theorists, and by preachers who celebrated her martyrdom.[43] Appealing to the collective memory of Thecla's asceticism and her suffering under persecution, these Christian writers called upon the authority of the Thecla narrative to underwrite and create warrants for contemporary practices and teachings. By means of narrative condensation, expansion, citation, and allusion, these authors created lines of transmission and continuity between the commemorated past (Thecla's apostolic experience) and their contemporary situations.

Intriguingly, one of the first elements of the story to disappear in these processes of condensation and citation is the figure of Paul, who essentially falls away from Thecla's story altogether in some (though not all) later sources, both literary and artistic. Thecla, meanwhile, remains to stand alone as an exemplar of endurance and ascetic rigor. What one is to make of this particular form of memory loss, forgetfulness, or occlusion is unclear. Detaching the figure of Thecla from the genre of romance may render the figure of Paul less crucial to her commemoration; that is, when the story is deracinated from its narrative origin in the Christian romance novel and restaged in other genres, elements that were once formally quite necessary may now have become dispensable. The symptom of forgetting Paul, however, may have a theologically and institutionally interested drive behind it. That is, the erasure of Paul may also suggest an increasing anxiety over the link between Thecla and the apostolic era as a whole and a desire to disrupt that link, domesticating Thecla in the process. The anxieties that Tertullian expressed around the year 200 concerning women's evangelical and liturgical authority were, after all, not unique to this North African presbyter despite the particular vitriol of his misogynist rhetoric. Moreover, the emergence of institutionalized forms of asceticism for both men and women seemed to demand increasingly regulated forms of religious life, and Thecla emerged as a critical exemplar in this context—an exemplar whose authority was grounded in her devotion to virginity, not in the audacious and out-of-place behavior attributed to her by the *Acts of Paul and Thecla.* Finally, this occlusion of the figure of Paul may contribute to the process by which Thecla's figuration as a "martyr" intensifies in textual and artistic representations and evocations of her. Even in *The Acts of Paul and Thecla,* when Thecla encounters the threat of physical violence, whether in the arena or at the hands of Alexander in Antioch, Paul is elusive, unhelpful, doubting, or absent altogether.[44] His elusiveness, skepticism, and absence serve narratively to elevate the portrait of Thecla's persistence in the face of torment—to the point, perhaps, that eventually she comes to be represented as a lone heroine engaged in solitary battle.

This memory of Thecla's martyrdom is emphasized in two rather different ways in two important works deriving from the Egyptian ascetic movements of the fourth century: the *Peri Parthenias* of Athanasius, bishop of Alexandria, and the *Life* of St. Syncletica (spuriously attributed to Athanasius). In the first work, in which Athanasius offers advice to virgins, he includes Thecla in a long list of biblical figures whose commemoration and imitation will aid in the spiritual formation of those to whom he writes, emphasizing the figure of Thecla by including a whole paragraph devoted to a summary of her story.[45] Davis's recent study of the Thecla cult emphasizes the importance of this text for his reconstruction of the social history of women's devotions in fourth-century Egypt. In particular, he argues that Athanasius conjures Thecla not as a novel exemplar but "as a model *already actively embraced by his audience.*"[46] Moreover, he demonstrates how Athanasius's argument in this text draws attention to the interpretation of the *Acts of Paul and Thecla* that this particular group of Egyptian Christian virgins had adopted, an interpretation that places special emphasis on the Pauline beatitude preserved there, "Blessed are they who have preserved their own bodies by means of purity."[47] As Davis explicates the treatise, Athanasius's argument links this beatitude to those preserved in the gospel of Matthew (5:3–11) and to Matthew's parable of the wise and foolish virgins (Matt. 25), emphasizing the need for both internal and external forms of purity. Thecla functions as an idealized exemplar within this framework of Athanasian ascetic theory, addressed to a specific group of female monks in Alexandria.[48]

Memory plays an explicit role in Athanasius's invocation of Thecla and the other exemplars. Davis notes the role played by memory in the project of moral exhortation, a project that linked memory (ὑπομιμνησκεῖν) with imitation (μίμησις), and he emphasizes that the exhortation to remember the prophets and to remain with Thecla suggests that Athanasius's audience is already well acquainted with these exemplars.[49] Athanasius's exhortation to the virgins of Alexandria invokes an eclectic list of privileged exemplars, a list that culminates with Thecla. Although the biblical figures are collectively praised for their function as models of chastity, they suggest several other significant associations that are relevant to a consideration of Thecla as a martyr.

The list includes Elijah, Elishah, Daniel, Ananias and his companions (the three youths cast in the furnace in Daniel 3), Jeremiah, Miriam, Zipporah (Sepphora), John the Baptist, John the Evangelist, Paul—and, finally, Thecla. The logic of this list is not completely self-evident: The prophetic powers of Elijah, Elishah, Jeremiah, Miriam, and Zipporah/Sepphora (according to the text, "she was a prophetess and judged Israel for a long time"[50]) are emphasized, as are those of John the Baptist. Daniel and the three youths are frequently linked to early Christian martyrs, especially in artistic representations (see below), although the textual traditions commemorating them emphasize their escape from the threat of martyrdom, and the text in which their stories are preserved also presents itself in a prophetic/apocalyptic genre. Daniel's encounter with the lions and the three youths' experience of the fiery furnace connect narratively with some of the torments to which Thecla is said to have been subjected. Moreover, traditions concerning the violent deaths of the two Johns and Paul were well known to early Christians. The eclecticism of this list, its overlapping sets of associations with different modes of religious experience and piety, and its inclusion of Thecla as the sole nonbiblical exemplar are all open to multiple interpretations. The memory work of moral exhortation in this case seems to be both citational and situational, the naming of each example meant to recall already familiar aspects of their stories. Thecla is privileged, both as the only nonbiblical example and as the only example warranting a lengthy gloss, an interpretation that emphasizes the martyrological dimensions of her story even as she is held up as a model for the life of chastity. In this example, the memory of Thecla's sufferings serves as an authorizing touchstone for the elaboration of an ethical model.

But this is not the only way in which Thecla's memory as a martyr serves the interests of later interpreters. Her memory is evoked somewhat differently in a fifth-century hagiographic text of unknown authorship devoted to praising and commemorating the ascetic precocity and virtuosity of Syncletica, the fourth-century desert mother.[51] In the introductory chapters to this vita, Syncletica is called "the true disciple of Thecla," and their spiritual lives are compared by the author. According to this writer, these two spiritual exemplars share the same suitor (Christ), the same guide to the bridegroom (Paul), the same bridal chamber (the Church), the same sacred serenades (from David and Miriam), the same bridal garment (Christ), the same love, the same wedding gifts, and the same contests against the same opponent (Satan). The only distinction between the teacher and her disciple lies in the sufferings each undertook, for, as this hagiographer would have it, Syncletica's ascetic torment was more extreme than was Thecla's martyrological one. Thecla suffered physical torture from the outside; Syncletica suffered the internal torture of oppositional and destructive thoughts.[52]

In making the comparison between Thecla and Syncletica, the writer aligns the two figures as teacher and disciple (implicitly as model and copy), emphasizing the many things they have in common. At the same time, however, the distinction he or she draws between Thecla and Syncletica ultimately portrays the disciple upstaging the teacher; it is, moreover, a distinction organized around the experience and memory of martyrdom. "For no one was ignorant of the martyrdoms of the blessed Thecla, as she struggled bravely through fire and wild beasts," this author writes, effectively eliding Thecla's own ascetic rigors and focusing on the martyrological aspects of her story. The shared knowledge of Thecla's martyrdoms does not keep the writer from speculating that Syncletica's torments were in fact more intense, Syncletica's ascetic prowess displacing Thecla's capacity for physical endurance.

These examples illustrate how the memory of Thecla's martyrdom contributed to the emergence of theories, models, and institutions of asceticism and monasticism. They could be augmented by others—the lives of Olympias and Macrina, for example, or a variety of treatises on virginity and chastity. In these different examples, one would encounter an ongoing tension around the relationship between two forms of Christian piety—martyrdom and asceticism. In some cases, the memory of Thecla's martyrdom serves as a more or less straightforward analogy for asceticism or, indeed, the foundation upon which successful asceticism could be staged. In others, the two kinds of piety are pitted against each other in a contest of nerve and endurance.[53] The memory of Thecla's martyrdom, in both kinds of examples, contributes to the reification and institutionalization of the ascetic impulse in early Christian life.

THEOLOGICAL ELABORATION IN THE LIFE OF THECLA

The fifth-century Life of Thecla is in essence an extended narrative palimpsest inscribed over a version of the Acts of Paul and Thecla.[54] The Life follows the narrative and chronological contours of the *Acts*, concealing aspects of the earlier text and allowing other dimensions of the original to peek through while also elaborating important elements in the record. The author calls his text "a story [ἱστορία]," "a prose work [σύγγραμμα] and narrative [διήγησις] of the ancient acts accomplished by the blessed Thecla apostle and martyr."[55] He admits borrowing freely from the earlier document, his faithfulness to the original functioning as partial testimony to the seriousness with which he takes all of the elements that propel his own work: divine inspiration (ἡ θεία ὀμφή), the urgings of a most virtuous man (τὰ δὲ καὶ ὑπὸ συμβουλῆς ἀνδρὸς ἀρίστου προτραπείς), and a personal vow (ἡ εὐχή).[56] The goal of the rewriting is to leave no word or deed of the apostle and martyr unknown—to preserve, in other words, a complete and comprehensive memory.[57] Curiously, as we noted at the beginning of this chapter, the writer also makes the point that the actions of the saints actually do not require memory work, insofar as they are by nature everlasting and eternal. Nevertheless, the writer exuberantly undertakes his somewhat paradoxical task of preserving a comprehensive memory that does not require preservation. The comprehensiveness of this memory includes discourses that exceed and supplement those found in the Apocryphal Acts, each speech crafted (the author assures the reader) to cleave closely to the character of the speaker.[58] It is in these speeches that one encounters the smooth theological overlay, discourses that amplify the theological orthodoxy of Thecla and Paul and that draw attention to the heightened stakes involved in the embrace of Christian belief and practice.

The *Life* does, indeed, follow the general narrative outline of the *Acts*, picking up on themes and elaborating on them in significant ways. The *Life* emphasizes the character of the conflict between Paul and Thecla, on the one hand, and those who oppose their teachings and commitments, on the other, as a conflict over interpretations of law, custom, and nature. Moreover, the *Life* picks up on a theme expressed embryonically in the *Acts*, where newness is contrasted with tradition and the foreign and strange are contrasted with those whose identities and affiliations are uncontroversial, well established, and of good repute. Marriage is figured by the representatives of the dominant society as the foundation of social order and as the root cause of all of human civilization and culture. The Christian attempts to undermine this institution, embodied in Paul's and Thecla's refusals to be interpellated by the representatives of social authority, generate a violence that the text calls demonic, mad, and bestial. Chastity and martyrdom come to be linked in this text much more explicitly than in the *Acts*, where, although the connection is made narratively, Thecla significantly is never explicitly named as a martyr.

The *Life* emphasizes the complex and overlapping conflict between the values embodied by Paul and Thecla and those of the dominant culture. Where the

Acts recorded the claim that Paul generated anxiety in Iconium and Antioch by being a foreigner of uncertain origins and by preaching something new and strange, the *Life* extends the portrait of newness and foreignness and links it more explicitly to the broader concerns over law, custom, nature, reputation, provenance, and identity. From the point of view of Paul's and Thecla's opponents, the contest is between tradition and innovation, between those who are rooted in the accepted patterns of social life and those restless wanderers who seek to disrupt them, between culture and barbarism, between those whose status and behavior cohere into a unified subjectivity and those whose identities are disordered and questionable. The text plays with the ambiguity between "foreignness" and "strangeness," and it repeatedly has Paul's opponents link his foreignness to deceitfulness and to rootlessness, calling him a stranger (ὁ ξένος), a cheat (ὁ ἀπατεών), and a wanderer (ὁ πλάνος).[59] Good reputation and social standing belong to those who live according to society's laws and occupy their proper places. Hence Theokleia urges Thamyris to intervene lest "we become [the subject of] a shameful story [ὁ μῦθος αἰσχρός] and the worst narrative of the human race [τὸ διήγημα κάκιστον τῷ τῶν ἀνθρώπων γένει]" and seeks to have her daughter condemned in this text for her lawless (ἄθεσμος) and eccentric, out-of-place (ἄτοπος) actions.[60] Likewise, Thamyris pleads with Thecla to abandon her infatuation with Paul, observing that her current behavior does not correspond with either her character or custom, her sense of shame or her reverence. "It is, I believe, the spiteful abuse of a sinister and evil demon, trying to pervert you from proper reason, to upset the ancient happiness of the household, and to attach shameful abuse to all of us against our excellent reputation [εὐφημίας καλλίστης]."[61]

While Thecla's mother and fiancé and later public officials all worry over the threat to status and reputation, Thecla freely manipulates these categories, sometimes turning the critique back against the critic, other times overturning their dominant values and embracing their opposites. In her encounter with the lustful and maniacal Alexander, she pelts him with accusations: "O violence! O transgression of the law [παρανομία]! O unreasonable tyranny [ἀλόγιστος τυραννίς]! O licentiousness shameless and beyond blushing [ἀναίσχυντος καὶ ἀπηρυθριασμένη ἀκολασία]!"[62] Simultaneously claiming her status as a stranger (ξενή) and an unknown (ἄγνωστος) and making reference to her class and social standing in Iconium, Thecla proclaims her love for chastity and virginity (ὁ ἔρως σωφροσύνης καὶ παρθενίας) and her enslavement to Christ, an enslavement (ἡ δουλεία) superior to any liberty.[63] She begs not to be shamed before God, her patron (μηδὲ οὕτω καταισχυναίμην τὸν προστάτην μου Θεόν), and closes with the line familiar from the *Acts*: "Do not do violence to the stranger; do not do violence to the slave of God."[64] Embracing the roles of stranger and slave, she nevertheless retains a claim upon the categories of lawfulness, reason, and honor. As a stranger and a slave, she is paradoxically relieved of the demands required of a proper young woman of high standing, all the while laying claim to the virtues lauded by the dominant culture and generally accorded to the free male adult citizen.

The ideological character and the high stakes of the conflict between the ascetic project promoted by Paul and Thecla, on the one hand, and the dominant culture with which it finds itself in opposition, on the other, become apparent in the set of speeches staged when Paul is brought before the proconsul by Thamyris. Thamyris's accusatory speech comes first, in which he indicts Paul, "this guilty cheat," of undermining civilization by his critique of marriage. According to Thamyris, Paul's critique threatens to subvert the entire social, political, and religious order since it is from marriage that all institutions and cultural practices emerge. Thamyris introduces his formal charges against Paul with the apparently already damning statement, "The man is a stranger and unknown to us."[65] The indictment proceeds in this way:

As you have seen, under the false disguise of virtue, he offers some new and foreign teaching against the common race of humans (καινήν τινα καὶ ἀλλόκοτον κατὰ τοῦ κοινοῦ γένους τῶν ἀνθρώπων ποιεῖται διδασκαλίαν), censuring marriage which is—one might say—the beginning, the root, and the source of our nature (τὴν ἀρχὴν καὶ ῥίζαν καὶ πηγὴν τῆς ἡμετέρας φύσεως), from which came into being fathers and mothers and children and families (τὰ γένη) and cities and estates and villages; from which [came into being] navigation and agriculture and all the arts of the earth; from which [came into being] the empire (ἡ βασιλεία) and government (ἡ πολιτεία) and laws and administrations and jurisdictions and military campaigns (αἱ στρατεῖαι) and military commands (αἱ στρατηγίαι), from which [came into being] philosophy and rhetoric and the entire swarm of arguments (ὁ σύμπας τῶν λόγων ἑσμός) and, even greater, from which [came into being] temples and sanctuaries and sacrifices and initiations and mysteries and vows and prayers. For all these things . . . are accomplished and enacted by human beings, and the human being is the cultivated crop of marriage.[66]

Condemning Paul's critique of marriage and promotion of celibacy, Thamyris observes, "For if all human beings were persuaded by this, soon the human race would die out."[67] As Thamyris goes on to praise marriage, it becomes clear that marriage is not only the source of social, political, cultural, and religious institutions, but that it also assures human beings access to immortality through the reproduction of children.

Paul's response to Thamyris's dramatic speech functions in some important respects as a corrective to the ascetic theory articulated in the *Acts of Paul and Thecla*. First, Paul situates his promotion of purity and virginity as a cure for the illness (νόσος) that has plagued human beings from their origins: to wit, idolatry. Turning Thamyris's list of the salutary religious fruits of marriage back upon itself, Paul lists "initiations, mysteries, animal sacrifices, and human murders" as the products of human diversion from the one true God.[68] What has such apparent religious deviancy to do with marriage? Commitment to these religious practices and the stories (μῦθοι) that ground them, Paul argues, causes people to worship and serve "adultery and prostitution and paederasty and incest and the corruption of boys."[69] Marriage, meanwhile, was given by God as a remedy (φάρμακον) and a cure (βοήθεια) for the human race, an antidote against sexual immorality (πορνείας τε ἀλεξιφάρμακον).[70] In other words, marriage functions in this argument as a cure for sexual impropriety, itself a symptom of the disease of idolatry.

The linkage between idolatry (religious deviance) and nonnormative sexual practices (sexual deviance) is no innovation on the part of this text, nor is the view that marriage can function as a form of prophylaxis. Indeed, both views can be traced back to the letters of the historical Paul, in particular, Romans 1 and 1 Corinthians 7, and back further yet to the Hebrew Bible.[71] That religious and sexual deviance are interwoven in the Christian imaginary was apparent in the literature on the spectacles considered in the last chapter. In addition, the use of vituperative sexual slander by Christians defending themselves against their opponents both outside and inside the church was an increasingly common rhetorical move.[72] Moreover, when non-Christians criticize Christians in this text (and elsewhere), the critique also both depends upon religious and social/sexual norms and involves accusations of religious deviance (magic) and sexual deviance (the refusal of marriage). Just so, later on the story, Thecla's continued refusal to be interpellated into the dominant culture's view of her proper place will cause her very identity to be radically called into question. Alexander, the Antiochene who sought unsuccessfully to force himself on Thecla, complains of her assault on him to the governor, testifying that he does not know whether she is a woman, a demon, or an evil genius (κακδαίμων) since he does not know what name to give this "foreign and strange beast [τὸ ξένον τοῦτο καὶ ἀλλόκοτον θηρίον] who shows herself to be more reckless than all the beasts."[73] He maligns her power as being a form of magic (μαγγανεία) or some even stronger art (τέκνη) or initiation (τελετή) by which she exercises over others the effects of a strange and novel nature (ἡ οὕτω ξένη καὶ καινοτέρα φύσις).[74] The arguments of each side against the other become mirror images.

A crucial difference between this text and the *Acts* on which it is narratively and structurally based is that the *Life* blunts the ascetic drive that pulses so sharply through the earlier narrative, reframing the promotion of celibacy in terms that do not condemn marriage altogether. Marriage, according to Paul in this text, is a temporary good that produces more human beings for salvation and resurrection.[75] Such a claim stands in critical contrast to the ascetic arguments found in the *Acts*, where sexual renunciation was the sine qua non of Christian identity. It is striking, however, that the author chooses the word "*pharmakon*" to describe marriage's role, since the word itself is deeply ambiguous, meaning both "remedy" and "poison." Perhaps the choice of this word betrays an ambivalence or a less than wholehearted embrace of the emergent orthodox theology of marriage?

The later text commemorates Thecla as a "martyr" in a way that the earlier text never came close to achieving. The first chapter of the *Life* frames Thecla's story with two different sets of claims and descriptions. On the one hand, the author seeks to position the story of Thecla within a historical lineage that establishes her continuity with a divine history and with acceptable theological norms. The author situates the story of Thecla within an epic lineage that stretches back to the origin of creation with language that recalls the prologue of the Gospel of John. He also emphasizes the doctrine of the incarnation as a critical framework for the story, drawing upon creedal language to cast the story in a rigorously orthodox theological setting.[76] This move will be replicated at other points in the text, where later orthodox theological formulations will be anachronistically placed in the mouths of the story's characters. On the other hand, the writer goes out of his way both to situate Thecla in the historical lineage of the martyrs and to place her at the front of the historical line. "Many, innumerable herds of martyrs sprouted up and poured down as rain after the ascension of Christ into the heavens," and Thecla appeared at this time, "not after many [masc.] martyrs or many [fem.] ones, but second immediately after the apostles and Stephen the martyr who was the first to see the word of truth, the first [fem.] of all women, just as Stephen led the men who struggled for Christ and on Christ's behalf, Thecla led the women, contending earnestly like the athletes [masc.]."[77]

The portrait in this text of Thecla as the first woman martyr is painted on a canvas stretched across the frame of the familiar narrative structure of the *Acts of Paul and Thecla*. While the *Life* follows the broad contours of the *Acts*, the discourse of martyrdom is elaborated in a number of striking ways. For example, in the *Acts*, Thecla bribes her way into the prison to be in Paul's company, but the text says nothing about what was spoken between the two characters. In the *Life*, Paul gives a long speech in prison in which Thecla appears as a Christian athlete and soldier, roles available to her because of her abandonment of her family, wealth, city, and impending marriage. Thecla's renunciation of wealth, sex, and social connections are evidence for her having "already taken up the cross" and "prepared the evangelical race course."[78] Already transformed by the renunciatory process, having entered into a realm where fear has fallen away from her, Thecla still faces further struggles. Her transformation is not yet complete—a transformation that involves both ascetic commitments and martyrological suffering, a transformation that is figured in the familiar terms of gender. "Think no more of the feminine and the unmanly,"[79] Paul exhorts her, implying that the absence of virility might be her downfall, just as it is for Christians who love life more than they love God.[80] Against such people, the enemy arrays a vast and menacing machinery of war—that is, the pleasures and the passions.[81] But against those who comport themselves with stalwartness and virility, high-mindedness and pride, fortified by the weapons of faith, the enemy tries yet other weapons: flattery, fawning, and trickery by magic.[82] When these do not work, then come the physical threats of persecution and public torture: the sword, the fire, the judges, the crowd, the executioners, the beasts.[83] Paul's speech spills over with military metaphors at this point: the faithful soldier of Christ holds the line even until death and slaughter, weakening the enemy and causing him to give up, to become insensible, to fall down, to run away, to hold his hands up in the air conceding defeat.[84] And the martyr, *whether living or dead*, is the more formidable opponent.[85] From here, Paul predicts Thecla's future in a compressed prophecy in which the language of military victory, political sovereignty, marital intimacy, and evangelism mesh: With Christ as her king, her comrade in arms, and her bridegroom, Thecla will herself reign as a sovereign against all the arms arrayed against her and will win the military victory against the tyrant. Like Peter and John, she will bring many other disciples to the bridegroom, disciples too numerous for her to count.[86]

When Thecla is first condemned in this text to die by the flames for refusing marriage, her fortune, and her class standing and for "deliberately choosing the life of a prostitute and shameful servant . . . running after the wanderer and stranger,"[87] the author punctuates the narrative with a series of comments, citations, and associations that simultaneously intensify the portrait of martyrdom and situate Thecla within broader cosmic and theological frameworks and more expansive historical legacies. The condemnation of Thecla is not simply the result of collusion between her mother, her fiancé, and Kestellius, the representative of Roman authority, according to the text. Rather, the events unfold so

that Christ's power might be made visible, so that the grace of the martyr (Thecla) might shine forth hereafter, and so that Paul's suffering might not be fruit-
less.[88] The cosmic intentionality of Thecla's predicament serves propagandistic
and commemorative ends—to say nothing of saving Paul's missionary excur-
sion from failure. Strikingly for Thecla's own legacy, the events take place precisely so that they might be remembered.

Meanwhile, in the fiery scene itself, the simpler narrative preserved in the
Acts is amplified in several striking ways. Thecla, who has been silent during her
trial, suddenly comes to speech, addressing Paul (who is, the text tells us, actually Christ appearing in Paul's form), simultaneously reassuring him of her commitment and requesting his prayers. In the Acts, she makes the sign of the cross;
here, her whole body takes on the form of the cross as she extends her arms. As
a consequence and out of "fear of the cross," the fire "utterly forgetting its own
nature," became more a "bridal-chamber" than a "furnace."[89] The author notes
that the scene recalls the miracle of the three youths in the Babylonian furnace
recorded in Daniel 3 (a story frequently associated with Christian martyrdom).[90]
The deadly miracle that extinguishes the flames, a miracle recorded briefly in the
Acts, is now glossed by this author as a penalty exacted from the Iconians for
their recklessness in subjecting Thecla to the fire.[91]

All of these elaborating details serve to situate Thecla and her story within a
broader network of associations. Her body becomes the cross itself, simultaneously a visual imitation or reenactment of the crucifixion and a textual moment
whereby the martyr's body itself becomes the legible message, where body and
conviction occupy the identical space.[92] Meanwhile, nature is repeatedly
thwarted, overcome, and undone. The opposite of "natural" here is not "unnatural" but rather "supernatural," and nature's subversion or undoing assures the
ascendancy of the supernatural. Just so, Thecla calls upon the spirit to support
"the weakness of my nature" while the fire, fearing the cross, "utterly forgets its
own nature" and transforms itself into a sheltering site.[93] That it does so allows
for Thecla to be written into a historical lineage of interrupted martyrdoms with
the three Hebrew youths in Daniel, an association that establishes a continuity
between the texts that commemorate them both and between the divine forces
that have saved them all from almost certain death. In Thecla's case, her physical liberation from the flames is then mapped onto a divine ethical plan of retri-
bution and reward, further linking her to a mode of apocalyptic sensibility
whereby the tables of persecution are turned, the wicked punished, and the
righteous vindicated.

In the second scene of persecution and threatened martyrdom, the stakes are
raised in a number of important ways. Thecla has resisted the violent advances

of Alexander, humiliating him in public by tearing his cloak and grabbing his crown from his head. This struggle took place, according to the author, on the precise site where a sanctuary has been built to proclaim and testify (μαρτυρέω) to Thecla's victory over her oppressor. Moreover, a relic of the garment, the author interjects, is preserved as a souvenir (μνήμη) in Thecla's temple so that people can see Thecla victorious and Alexander naked, vanquished, and laughed at.[94] Thecla's humiliation of Alexander, who has earlier been described as enflamed with passion like an enraged dog or a daemoniac,[95] only renders her opponent yet more savage. She is handed over to "justice," a move that she interprets as "a victory and an addition of martyrological struggles."[96] Thecla's encounters with the beasts in this episode mirror those from the *Acts*, but with some significant amplifications of the story. Whereas in the *Acts* the lioness sent out against Thecla simply sits down at her feet, in this text the scene is fleshed out with important details. Here, the beast "neglected her own nature [τῆς μὲν οἰκείας ἀπημέλει φύσεως]" and behaved like "a servant [θεραπαινίς] who had grown up from the beginning with the girl," sitting down next to her and caressing her feet, protecting her lest "the evangelical feet of the martyr [τοὺς εὐαγγελικοὺς πόδας τῆς μάρτυρος] be wounded or attacked."[97] Much as the fire in the earlier scene violated its own nature, the lioness here abandons her nature and takes on the role of a loyal servant and protector. Thecla, meanwhile, bears the title "martyr," and her feet—feet that will ultimately carry her on her itinerant mission—are "evangelical."[98]

A second encounter with the beasts also results in Thecla's miraculous escape from physical harm; two things are striking about this narrative's account of the event. In the first place, "nature" again is invoked and supplanted. In the second place, Thecla is again compared with Daniel and the three Hebrew youths in the Babylonian furnace, though here Thecla's delivery from danger is judged superior to theirs. "Nature" serves here as a limit beyond which change cannot occur, apart from divine intervention. The fact that Thecla escapes from beasts and flames goes against the nature of both animals and fire; only God has the power to transform their impulses. "For beasts are always beasts, and they have the nature that they have," the author writes. God can cause them to be pliable in relation to the saints while retaining their savage and inhuman impulses toward others.[99] Likewise, the fire was a true fire, hot, all-consuming, deadly— "for this is the nature of fire."[100] Its nature can be transformed only through the command of God. Meanwhile, the shared character of the miraculous in Thecla's story and in the book of Daniel nevertheless itself has its limits: where Daniel is delivered from the lions' den and his life is saved, in Thecla's story a battle among the beasts over Thecla ensues. "Therefore, how superior is our miracle," the author opines.[101]

Distinguishing the natural from the supernatural and comparing the quality and character of miracles are not random amplifications and elaborations of the earlier Thecla narrative. They serve a particular purpose within the setting of this author's own context by positioning the memory of Thecla's threatened martyrdom within the framework of the ongoing miraculous activity taking place in her name at the Hagia Thekla shrine near Seleucia. The emphasis on the difference between the natural and the miraculous is mirrored in the narrative that surrounds Thecla's self-explanation to the governor when he questions the source of her ability to overcome the beasts. Here the author expounds upon the difference between miracle and magic. The memory of Thecla's miraculous escapes from persecution and torture undergirds the author's theory of the miraculous and his polemic against a wide range of magical arts.

"Magic" is a capacious and slippery concept, signified in this text (as elsewhere) by several different terms ("μαγγανεία," "μαγικὴ τέχνη," "γοητεία"), all of which function as malleable terms for the Other of "miracle" or "religion." Linked in the characterization of Paul to the category "*xenos* [foreign/strange]," magic functions as a shorthand for the illegitimate religion of others. Hence, Paul is accused of being a *magos*. The governor worries about Thecla's identity and the source of her ability to overcome the beasts. The author of this text seeks to distinguish Thecla's miraculous abilities from the miasma of sorcery represented by figures like Apollonius of Tyana, the gymnosophists of Egypt and India, Julian the theurgist, Simon Magus, and "that throng of evil ones." Moreover, the author cites various miracles brought about by prayer, including Moses parting the sea by enjoining it to go against its nature and Peter's resuscitation of a dead person by means of prayer and "speaking in a foreign/barbarous voice [βαρβαριζούσης φωνῆς]." It is by prayers of this sort, the author argues, that Thecla liberates herself—by prayers that produce miracles, not by acts that are magical.[102]

But these are not the only places where the amplification and intensification of memory produce significantly different portraits of the past. In the most explicit example of this phenomenon, when Thecla finds Paul again in Myra after her persecution at Antioch, she praises him as her teacher (διδάσκαλος), to whom she owes a great debt. In the speech that follows, she summarizes what she has learned from Paul: sophisticated theological formulations concerning God, his only begotten son, and the trinity. The language is the product of the Christological and especially the Trinitarian controversies staged among Christian theologians long after the first century, when Thecla purportedly lived. "For I knew through you God the king over all, and his only begotten Son [τὸν Υἱον αὐτοῦ τὸν μονογενῆ] the one ruling with the Father and creator (δημιουργόν) of all, and the holy Spirit who rules with the Father and the Son and sanctifies and perfects all, the Trinity which is of the same substance and equal in honor and status [τὴν ὁμοούσιον καὶ ἰσότιμον καὶ ἰσοστάσιον Τριάδα]."[103] The speech goes on at some length, making use of formulaic and theologically loaded language and vocabulary. It retrojects the theological innovations of the fourth and fifth centuries backward into the first, reframing the Christian past as singular, monolithic, and always already theologically complete. Ironically, the manuscript tradition for this speech includes a significant number of variants, and the editor observes that "it is not always easy to distinguish what is an omission and what an addition" in the speech.[104] The text commemorates Thecla as a rescued martyr and as a *porte-parole* for orthodox Trinitarian theology with a refined and sophisticated grasp of the technical vocabulary required. As a result of Thecla's orthodox proclamation, Paul declares her ready to undertake apostolic pains and racecourses (οἱ ἀποστόλικοι πόνοι καὶ δρόμοι), lacking nothing to become apostle and successor to the divine proclamation (μηδὲν ἐνδεῖν ἔτι σοι πρὸς ἀποστολὴν καὶ διαδοχὴν τοῦ θείου κηρύγματος).[105] Paul sends her out with these words, "Go and teach the word, complete the apostolic racecourse, and share with me the zeal for Christ," declaring her his intermediary chosen by Christ for the apostolate to pursue teaching in cities not yet catechized.[106] Having traveled through her ordeals to arrive at this place, Thecla is remembered as the bearer of orthodox theology, sharing Paul's status as one chosen by Christ to be an apostle. Meanwhile, the text's theological anachronism establishes a continuity between the apostolic times commemorated in the text and the contemporary time in which the author writes.

The closing chapter of the *Life* also expands significantly on the memory of Thecla recorded in the *Acts*, portraying Thecla as evangelist, teacher, baptizer, recruiter for the army of Christ, miracle worker, virgin, martyr, and apostle.[107] Moreover, in contrast with the conventional ending of the *Acts* in which Thecla "slept with a noble sleep," this text argues that "the widespread and truer discourse [ὁ πολὺς καὶ ἀληθέστερος λόγος]" is that she did not die at all. Instead, she sank alive into the earth, entering it secretly right at the place where an altar was erected for liturgical celebrations and from which many healings emerged.[108] Hence, the Thecla commemorated in this text emerges as a many-faceted figure whose martyrdom simultaneously testifies to her spiritual prowess and provides a ground for her miraculous powers of healing. But although her martyrdom is amplified in this text, it is balanced by the other claims about her work in the world as an evangelist, Christian teacher, apostle, and virgin. As the portrait of Thecla makes the transition from text to artistic representation, many of the dimensions of the figure will be stripped away, ambiguities rationalized, portraiture stylized, and multiplicities reduced. It is to some of the examples of this artistic memory to which we now turn.

THE MATERIALITY OF MEMORY:
THE ART OF REPRESENTING THECLA

The textual representation of Thecla included the romance account of her life after Paul, hagiographic elaborations of this life in light of contemporary interests and theological concerns, and frequent citations in ancient ascetic theory, whether treatises on virginity, lives of other early Christian female ascetics (e.g., Syncletica, Olympias, Macrina), or sermons and panegyrics. But Thecla is remembered not only through such textual traces in narratives, sermons, and parenetic exhortations to mimesis. She is also widely remembered in early Christian art, and her artistic commemoration tends to emphasize the parts of her story that involve the threat of martyrdom and the miraculous rescue from it. Rarely are other dimensions of her textual portraiture preserved. That is, when Thecla comes to be represented artistically, her status as virgin, apostle, disciple, miracle worker, and evangelist, so emphasized in her written legacy, gives way to her visual figuration as (an often unambiguously feminized) martyr. The remainder of this chapter explores some examples of this commemorative move and some of the possible reasons for this shift in portraiture.

Before examining some of the rich and diverse artistic evidence associated with Thecla, it is important to make a few preliminary observations about the uses of artistic evidence in the intellectual and cultural history of early Christianity. There have traditionally been strong disciplinary divisions between the students of early Christianity who interpret texts and those who read images and material artifacts. These divisions are the result of training, shaped interests, and important differences in the history of scholarship over the last centuries. As Robin Jensen has recently and persuasively argued, however, the omission of the artistic, visual, and material evidence from critical examination leaves out crucial elements of the portrait of early Christian culture.[109]

Rather than using ancient art as mere gloss or illustration, Jensen urges an interdisciplinary project that brings texts, on the one hand, and visual artifacts, on the other, under the same critical interpretive gaze. Joining with Mary Charles Murray who, a quarter century ago, challenged the received scholarly wisdom concerning the negative status accorded to representational art in the early church,[110] Jensen has issued a challenge to historians of the early church to take seriously the artistic legacy found in frescoes, sculpture, mosaics, objects, and other material remnants of Christian artistic imagination. As Jensen demonstrates in her history of the scholarship, the separation of art from texts has often had to do with preformed judgments about the character of the early church as a whole—whether the emergence of early Christian art is seen as a capitulation to retrograde religious impulses among illiterate "pagan" converts or as a surrender to the cultural and political demands of an empire turned Christian. As Jensen shows, both sets of assumptions position early Christian art in opposition to early Christian texts, whether the art is understood to domesticate and simplify the complex theological claims found in texts or whether the art is understood to engage in the suspicious work of propaganda.[111] Arguing against those who would characterize early Christian art as the vernacular of the unlettered common people (against a literate elite), Jensen insists that the artistic remains of the early church—remains that cost money to produce and that were part and parcel of a communal, liturgical life involving Christians of all classes and social standings—need to be read and interpreted within a more complex frame. This frame situates the artwork of early Christians in close relationship with the textual remains of early Christians, and it sets the two bodies of cultural work in balance and synoptic comparison. As she articulates the contours of her own project:

> Rather than beginning with the presumption that visual art and literary texts represent divergent belief systems, theological sophistication, or the varying taste of different social groups, this study proceeds from the proposition that written documents and art objects emerge from the same or similar communities, and have common purposes and outlooks. This proposition does not mean that images and texts will always be in complete accord, or that they will present aspects of religious faith in parallel form, but rather that one mode of discourse may help to elucidate another and give historians a better understanding of ancient symbol systems.[112]

The discussion of representations of Thecla in early Christian art that follows takes up Jensen's challenge to engage in a synoptic practice that places artistic representations and literary portraits on the same field, using both as resources for understanding the development of religious ideas and practices and avoiding reducing the artistic to the merely decorative or illustrative. It is beyond the scope of this chapter to discuss every example in which Thecla appears.[113] I have chosen examples that are significant and representative, both in terms of their genres (whether paintings, sculpture, or portable objects) and in terms of their content (which overwhelmingly represents Thecla in her role as martyr). There is some critical tension between the literary and artistic evidence on this latter point, and this tension points to the malleability of collective memory in the service of different sorts of institutional and personal religious needs. Jensen properly cautions against assuming that literary sources are normative expressions while artistic sources are religiously deviant ones. In a related way, she warns interpreters not to presuppose that literary sources are the products of a learned elite while artistic sources are the products of the simple and illiterate. These cautions are well taken. My observations concerning the shift in focus between the literary and artistic sources commemorating Thecla do not presume that one version of the memory is normative and the other eccentric nor that the literary and artistic reminders of Thecla are divided or bound by class or status. Nevertheless, there are important differences between the literary and the material commemorations of Thecla, and these differences invite exploration and explanation.[114]

One of the earliest artistic artifacts commemorating Thecla is found on the west wall of a hypogeum (burial chamber) in Thessaloniki which dates to the reign of Constantine or his successor (mid-fourth century).[115] The frescoes are not in a good state of preservation, but interpretation is aided by the fact that many of the figures bear inscriptions indicating the identity of the person or element represented. On the north wall, there are two scenes: Daniel in the lions' den and (perhaps) Noah.[116] The west wall bears a badly damaged portrait of Thecla, veiled, in a praying position, standing next to a furnace or altar where a fire—inscribed with the Greek word "ΠΥΡ [fire]"—burns. Above her head is the partial inscription "ΘΕΚ," which should most likely be completed with the letters "ΛΑ". To her right stands another figure whose face is not preserved, but who is identified by the inscription, "ΧΡΙΣΤΟ".[117] The south wall mirrors the north wall in bearing two scenes: Abraham sacrificing Isaac (the image inscribed with their names and the words "ΘΥΣΙΑ [sacrifice]" and "ΦΩΝΗ [voice (of God)]"), and Adam and Eve in Paradise.[118] The east wall is very badly damaged, but the portrait has been identified as likely one of the Good Shepherd.[119]

The very presence of a portrait of Thecla in this hypogeum is itself quite striking, as is the fact that Thecla is unusually portrayed here sharing the frame with the figure of Christ. The frescoes together constitute a collection of evocations of narratives and images familiar (except, of course, for Thecla) from biblical sources.[120] Daniel is a commonplace in Christian funereal art; thirty-nine portraits of him have been identified from the catacombs,[121] and he appears on Christian sarcophagi and in other genres as well.[122] Abraham offering his son Isaac in sacrifice—here, being stilled by the hand of God—which is marked in the fresco by the inscriptional gloss, "ΦΩΝΗ [voice]"—was also a popular iconographic figure in early Christian art, offering both a story of divine intervention interrupting violence and death and a typological reference to the crucifixion of Jesus as a father's sacrifice of his son.[123] Noah, Adam and Eve, and the Good Shepherd are all popular representations in early Christian funereal art from the earliest (e.g., third-century) examples of catacomb frescoes and other genres.[124] But if the program of this hypogeum draws otherwise exclusively on biblical narratives and symbols, what is Thecla doing positioned between Daniel and Noah, on one side, Abraham and Isaac and Adam and Eve, on the other, and opposite a representation of the Good Shepherd?

The interpretation of the portrait of Thecla here relies on a number of different elements, but context is probably the most important of these—both the physical and the symbolic and ideological contexts. The fresco appears in a burial chamber and therefore likely invites interpretation in light of Christian ideas about death and its aftermath.[125] Moreover, Thecla's portrait is framed by others all deriving from biblical narratives, implicitly elevating the importance of her story by association. Finally, the images each call to mind specific narratives and set these narratives in intertextual relationships. The images thereby imply and implicate one another, encouraging interpretations that read the images together as part of a unified program of representation, symbolism, and significance. Drawing on the literary narrative traditions associated with each figure, the fresco paintings would seem to be exegetical in orientation, simultaneously calling the narratives to mind and interpreting them through citation and visual commentary.

In distinguishing various functions of early Christian art, Robin Jensen has argued that religious art can do a wide variety of work in the articulation and elaboration of a religious tradition. She names seven possible types of function: decorative, illustrative, didactic, exegetical, symbolic, liturgical, and iconic.[126] Moreover, she makes a distinction between what she calls "narrative and iconic expression," the former functioning in relation to memory and the latter serving as a form of mediation between the human and divine realms.[127] Obviously, the exegetical, symbolic, liturgical, and iconic functions of early Christian art are the more theologically complex and generative. The exegetical function in particular serves as a mode of scriptural/narrative interpretation, a form of theological engagement with a longstanding privilege of place among early Christians. The frescoes of the hypogeum in Thessaloniki can be read as examples of this exegetical work, since each image contained in the burial chamber can be paired with a textual source and recalls the narrative to which the image refers. Moreover, the exegetical function of early Christian art is also a form of cultural memory work, evoking and generating not only more abstracted theological associations (e.g., the escape from death thanks to divine intervention) but also the narratives themselves on which the images are based.

No matter how narrative these images are, they are also heavily condensed, episodic, and citational. That is, they depend upon a small number of visual quotations to call up a memory of the story that lies behind them. (Indeed, the reconstructive work of scholars that allows a portrait of Noah to be retrieved in this particular fresco from the positioning of a single bird at the edge of the image testifies to the capacity of these largely conventionalized images to generate meaning out of the most minimalist or fragmentary representations.) More importantly, these images assume an audience familiar enough with the stories in question to be able to recognize the narrative from a small number of visual (and, in this case, verbal) cues. This familiarity is especially important for considering the presence of Thecla in this hypogeum's artistic program. All of the other figures represented in this burial chamber appear routinely in other early Christian funereal art, whether in catacomb paintings or in sarcophagus carvings, and their stories are well-known biblical narratives.[128] Thecla, on the other hand, is otherwise absent from the catacombs and sarcophagi—apart from this remarkable example and one other (possible but quite unlikely) example, a third- or fourth-century sarcophagus carving in Saint-Just de Valcabrère.[129] But in addition to the uniqueness of Thecla's presence in a funereal context, the representation here of Thecla with Christ next to her is also unattested elsewhere among representations of the martyr. The image is probably an ironic (or mistaken) citation of the *Acts of Paul and Thecla*, where Thecla has been condemned to be burned and Christ appears to her in the form of Paul before disappearing into the heavens.[130]

Thecla's inclusion in this funereal artistic program suggests that her story was sufficiently well known and well regarded in the Christian community at Thessaloniki to be included alongside the canonical images and narratives. It also suggests that her story was understood to reinforce, reiterate, and amplify the meanings generated by the other images in the burial chamber. Three of the four Hebrew Bible narratives exegeted in this fresco are stories of violence diverted and death avoided, thanks to divine intervention—Noah, Abraham and Isaac, and Daniel in the lions' den. The fourth—Adam and Eve in Paradise—evokes associations of immortality and eternal life. The episode of the Thecla narrative portrayed here—her trial by fire in Iconium—is also a story of violence diverted and death avoided, the miraculous result of divine intervention. In later representations, Thecla is far more likely to be portrayed in the second episode of physical trial—being thrown to the beasts—and in these images, as will be seen, she is sometimes paired with Daniel, both figures flanked by lions and each bearing a striking resemblance to the other. All of these images link physical suffering and the threat of death with miraculous, divinely inspired escape. These associations will be rendered even more strongly when Thecla appears on the pilgrimage ampullae that were carried away from her shrines by devotees of her healing cult, objects that I discuss below.

It is likely that the hypogeum fresco at Thessaloniki is the earliest surviving artistic representation of Thecla. In addition to the important intertextual associations that help to interpret its presence in this burial chamber, it is worth noticing the focus on Thecla's experiences as a potential martyr in the painting, an emphasis that will dominate future artistic representations of her. The narratives that such representations recall and exegete preserve a range of roles for Thecla and emphasize her countercultural resistance to all sorts of social norms, including the constraints of conventionalized gender. The artistic representations, on the other hand, tend to focalize on her martyrological status, most often the Antiochene encounter with the beasts, and to reposition her within the recognized framework of the idealized feminine. Indeed, as later portraits emerge, they will overwhelmingly preserve an image of Thecla as a bound and sexualized condemned prisoner.

A well-preserved example of this iconography is the fifth-century Egyptian round relief in which Thecla appears with her hands tied behind her back and with the binding ropes attached to the lions that flank her on each side (see fig. 1).[131] She is clothed, but the drapery of the robe she wears and its belting accentuate her breasts and her hips and pelvic area; her hair appears to be elaborately braided. The two lions, one male (marked by its ample mane) and one female (signaled by the absence of a mane and the presence of swollen teats on its belly), are nearly completely symmetrical in their carved execution. Some scholars read their presence as heraldic animals resembling those on a dynastic coat of arms.[132] On either side of the figure of Thecla, two winged angels appear wearing necklaces bearing crosses and stretching their arms and open palms toward the front of the relief. A laurel wreath encircles the entire scene, marking the moment as one of athletic, military, and now spiritual victory.

The earlier narrative elements from the *Acts of Paul and Thecla* that emphasize Thecla's rejection of gender conventions in the service of her ascetic project (especially her transvestitism and her renunciatory cutting of her beautiful hair) are strikingly absent and, indeed, replaced by clothing and coiffure that emphasize the conventional, upper-class femininity of the figure. Moreover, the artist has chosen to capture in limestone a particular narrative moment in a portrait that points to Thecla's physical struggle, her experience in the arena in Antioch. This is a portrait whose clear reference to violence amplifies Thecla's femininity even as its implied brutality is offset by the apparently placid aspect of Thecla's face, by the presence of the two framing angels, and by the border of laurel wreath.[133]

Since the relief survives independent of its original setting, it is difficult to reconstruct its range of meanings either intertextually or in the context of a broader devotional practice.[134] It is clear, however, that representations of this sort may be understood to function as a kind of visual or material quotation, a condensed snapshot that refers back to another text and that sparks the viewer's memory of a familiar story. The quotation here is inexact, however, insofar as

FIGURE 1 *Saint Thecla with Wild Beasts and Angels*
Egyptian/Coptic, fifth century. Limestone; 25.5 x 3.75 inches (64.8 x 9.5 cm).
The Nelson-Atkins Museum of Art, Kansas City, Missouri (Purchased by the Nelson Trust), 48–10.

the *Acts of Paul and Thecla* portrays the lion and lioness as formidable enemies of each other. In the narrative, the lioness at first obsequiously displays her loyalty to Thecla by lying down and licking the potential martyr's feet and then later loses her life in her fierce and fatal attempt to protect Thecla from the male lion's threatened harm.[135] In this later relief carving, the lions are paired and symmetrical. The detail and nuance of the narrative conflict between the protective lioness and the attacking lion—detail and nuance that recapitulate the narrative's subtheme of female solidarity against male aggression—recede from the material memory, and the viewer is left with symmetrically arranged lions in an abbreviated citational form. Meanwhile, the image simultaneously quotes the Thecla narrative (albeit imprecisely) and makes an intertextual reference to a different narrative cycle in which martyrdom is both threatened and thwarted. That is, the visual representation of Thecla here is also almost certainly a quotation of the figure of the biblical Daniel, who is conventionally, even stereotypically, represented flanked by two lions.[136]

The imaginative pairing of Thecla with Daniel is not limited to the apparent intertextual reference on the Kansas City round relief, but is made explicit in another object, a fourth-century wooden comb found in Panopolis.[137] The comb has a central panel on both the front and the back, each panel featuring a representation of a human figure in a praying position with arms upraised. Crouching animals, usually interpreted to be lions, flank both figures. The images are both framed by diagonally striated columns on the two sides and some sort of canopy roof stretching over the top of the scene. The male figure wears a short tunic that ends just above his knees. The female figure wears a veil and a long gown that is cinched at the waist, draped in such a way as to draw attention to the hips and lower half of the body. Although one scholar has identified the female figure to be the biblical Susanna,[138] the more general consensus contends that the figure is Thecla.[139]

The pairing of Thecla and Daniel links two stories that share certain important structural elements: a saintly figure persists in following a religious course opposed by the dominant powers; as a consequence, he or she is placed in mortal danger, is threatened by the lions/beasts, and escapes through some form of divine intervention. Both stories, in other words, commemorate an impending martyrdom that is foiled by supernatural interference. The story of Daniel, along with that of the three Hebrew youths whose story is also preserved in the biblical book of Daniel, occupies an important place in the early Christian memory of martyrdom, as these biblical figures come to be seen as precursors to later Christian martyrs.[140] As the story comes to be represented artistically, many complicating details and dimensions of the literary narrative—such as Daniel's graphic and prophetic visions, for example—disappear while the artist zeroes in on an iconic representation of Daniel-as-martyr.[141] Likewise, as in the context of the Thecla medallion, when it comes to be captured in these visual snapshots, the Thecla story sheds its gender-bending complexities and its emphasis on Thecla's literary role as itinerant teacher, apostle, and evangelist. In the process, the artistic representation intensifies its focus on the arena episodes from the literary narrative and represents Thecla primarily by recourse to an increasingly standardized martyrological iconography, an iconography that is itself dependent upon visual models deriving from the arena. Daniel and Thecla appear almost as mirror images of each other as the portraits of these two divine figures nearly merge in a stylized portrait of the martyr, surrounded by the things of the world but untouched by them. Although it is likely that the representation of

Thecla is in some measure citational or derivative of the Daniel portrait, once the images have been condensed in this way, the overlapping iconography functions as a repetitive, oscillating, and mutually referential quotation.[142]

Thecla is represented in a wide array of other artwork from late antiquity and the middle ages, in a range of media including gold glass, textiles, manuscript illuminations, painted icons, ivory plaques, metal objects (a reliquary and an inscribed cross), and even jewelry. Many of these representations and objects are unique, one-of-a-kind remnants of Thecla commemoration. In addition to these representations, however, a significant number of portable objects—terra-cotta ampullae—that bear the image of Thecla and that functioned as memory objects (souvenirs) for early Christian pilgrims also remain.

There are sixteen published examples of Egyptian pilgrimage ampullae that bear Thecla's image.[143] The objects themselves resemble one another in size, mode of production, and iconography. They are round and flat, and some surviving examples still retain the necks and arms that were attached to them after the two sides of the body were joined together. Both sides of the body bear the imprint of a saint, in these cases, Thecla on one side and the Egyptian saint Menas on the other.[144] The representations of both figures are stylized and formulaic, and many are not well preserved, having given way to the passage of time and their repeated handling and use by their owners. The objects were mass-produced by workshops catering to the burgeoning market for pilgrimage souvenirs.

A typical, moderately well-preserved example of such ampullae can be found in the collection of the British Museum (fig. 2).[145] On one side of the flask, which is about six inches in diameter, Thecla appears bound to a stake, her upper arms visible and her lower arms disappearing behind her back. She is flanked by beasts: lions, bears, and bulls. Her hair frames her face and drapes down onto her shoulders. She wears an apron attached by a fillet around her waist, but her upper body is exposed. The scene recalls the narrative in the *Acts of Paul and Thecla* where, as punishment for resisting Alexander's advances in Antioch, Thecla is condemned to the beasts.[146] Like the relief and the portraiture on the Daniel-Thecla comb, the emphasis in the ampulla image is on Thecla's physical exposure, her vulnerability, and her femininity. Her hair, nude upper body, and bondage all work together in the image to draw attention to both her gender identity and the presence of overpowering physical threats and constraints. Nowhere in the image is there an explicit suggestion of the miraculous escape that is to come in the narrative.[147]

Another striking element in this portrait of Thecla among the beasts is the fact that Thecla is bound with her arms tied behind her back. This visual element certainly adds to the drama of the scene. It also represents a significant difference

FIGURE 2 *Pilgrim Ampulla (reverse), Saint Thecla's Martyrdom*
Date uncertain. Terra-cotta, h. 14 cm.
London: British Museum, EC 882 (© British Museum).

from the textual version of the narrative. In the *Acts of Paul and Thecla*, Thecla was cast into the stadium to face the beasts and, after the lioness is killed trying to protect Thecla from the bears and the male lion and still more beasts are let loose upon her, Thecla "stood and stretched out her hands and prayed."[148] Later, when the bulls are brought against Thecla, her feet are tied.[149] But nowhere in the story are her hands or arms bound. The portrait on the ampullae (and the relief and the comb) is both an interpretation and an innovation. Images like this, where the condemned person is bound to a stake and exposed to beasts, are found elsewhere in the Roman and late ancient Mediterranean world, specifically on terra-cotta dishes in North Africa.[150] The portraiture of Thecla here, itself a visual exegesis and commentary on the textual tradition concerning the saint, may be borrowing from the available repertoires of visual idioms for portraying arena violence and connecting it to the Thecla narrative. The visuality of the arena was a central aspect of its cultural impact, and hence the importation of artistic representations drawing upon the arena in this context may have to do with making a connection between the Thecla story in particular and the vulnerabilities of the arena more generally.

The majority of the ampullae that bear Thecla's stamp on one side and that of Menas (flanked by camels) on the other seem to have followed the same iconographic pattern. There are minor, incidental differences among these objects—differences, for example, in the presence or absence of decorative borders or their character—but the main features of their iconography are strikingly similar. One somewhat different example is an ampulla in the Louvre collection (fig. 3).[151] This flask is slightly larger than the other examples, and the images of the two saints are bordered by Greek inscriptions that make the object's function within the context of pilgrimage piety more explicit. The side of the flask with the image of Thecla has two inscriptions, one bordering the image and reading "ΕΥΛΟΓΙΑ ΤΟΥ ΑΓΙΟΥ ΜΗΝΑ ΑΜΗ(Ν) [Blessing of Saint Menas Amen]," and the other inside the image itself, reading "Η ΑΓΙΑ ΘΕΚΛ [Α] [Saint Thecla]." The other side, on which an image of a male orant (presumably Saint Menas) appears, bears the inscription "ΕΥΛΟ + ΓΙΑ ΤΟΥ ΑΓΙ(ΟΥ) ΜΗΝΑ ΑΜΗ(Ν)." The figure of Thecla is flanked by two animals, one of which is generally agreed to be a lion and the other of which has been variously identified as a lioness, a bear, a tiger, or a panther.[152]

The character of this representation of Thecla is similar to the British Museum ampulla, where Thecla is portrayed with her arms bound behind her back, flanked by animals in a scene recalling other representations of convicts condemned *ad bestias*. Nauerth and Warns interpret the image as an exegetical image that is simultaneously illustrative and symbolic. They read the indeterminate animal on the right side of the image as the lioness who protected The-

FIGURE 3 *Ampulla, Saint Thecla Between Two Beasts*
Sixth–seventh century. Terra-cotta, 27 x 17 cm.
*Louvre, Paris, France, MNC 1926. Photo: Hervé Lewandowski. Photo Credit: Réunion des Musées
Nationaux/Art Resource, N.Y.*

cla from the lion in the arena in the narrative, so that the image functions in part simply as an illustration of the narrative scene. Indeed, they consider the possibility that a manuscript illumination could lie in the background of this the highly condensed image.[153] They go beyond the more literal, illustrative dimensions of the image, however, suggesting that the positioning of the different figures in the image is intentional, aimed at evoking a second, more symbolic level of meaning underlying the more literal visual quotation from the text. "That the lion in the ampulla image approaches the lioness from behind is certainly no accident," they argue. "Thecla's animal battle signifies a battle for the sake of the virtue of virginity, a battle against the beastly vices."[154] In other words, they interpret the story of Thecla's condemnation *ad bestias* and her triumph over the beasts allegorically, so that this representation of her physical constraint and trial symbolizes her ascetic struggles and her victory over fleshly passions.

Other interpreters have focused less on the particular images and iconography preserved on these ampullae than on the juxtaposition of the portraits of Thecla with those of Menas and the possible significance of the connection between the two saints.[155] In his recent study of the cult of Saint Thecla, Stephen Davis has focused his discussion of the artistic evidence associated with Thecla (and, in the case of the ampullae, Thecla and Menas) in order to reconstruct the history of Christian piety associated with the saint and, in particular, the dispersion and reach of her cult.[156] Situating the ampullae within the broader context of pilgrimage piety, Davis suggests that the linking of Thecla and Menas imagery provided pilgrims with gender-specific religious models *and* may offer evidence of competition for devotees between the two cults, including the appropriation of Thecla traditions by the Menas cult.[157] Both cults were healing cults, and both generated collections of miracle stories eulogizing the capacity of the saints to protect devotees from danger and return them to health. The iconography of these paired saints shares important formal features, most significantly the central position of the saint flanked by animals. But their differences are also significant: Thecla always appears on these ampullae with her hands bound in the prisoner's or martyr's position, and the animals that flank her are linked specifically to the story of her condemnation *ad bestias*. Menas, meanwhile, appears in the orant position—his arms and hands free and raised up in prayer—and flanked by two camels, animals that play a range of roles in stories about the saint. The representation of Thecla is unmistakably that of a martyr, and the image preserved on the pilgrims' flasks iconographically recalls the portion of her story that links martyrdom and the miraculous.

The importance of these sorts of visual images for conveying memory cannot be underestimated in a world that remained extensively illiterate. Jaś Elsner has argued that Christian art was essential to the dissemination of scripture and the spread of theologically defensible modes of exegesis and interpretation.

> The deep Christian project of fostering a cohesive sense of identity related to Scripture was thus made accessible even to those without the ability to read Scripture. Moreover, such exegetic cycles of images were used to decorate not only churches but all kinds of boxes, ampullae, pilgrimage relics and the like. Such images apparently adorned holy matter (water, dust or oil from holy places, or a martyr's bone, for instance) with appropriate themes. But in fact they gave that matter its meaning by placing it visually at the heart of complex programmes of Christian doctrine. In this way, Christian art worked—perhaps harder than any other aspect of Christianization—towards what has been described as draining the secular from society, towards eliminating non-exegetic ways of viewing.[158]

In her Sather Lectures on the rhetoric of empire in the process of Christianization, Averil Cameron also argues for the critical importance of the visual in the spread of Christian ideas and cultural forms. She emphasizes the "figural quality" of Christian writing, especially as it concerns the lives of spiritual exemplars, and points ahead toward the emergence of an iconic Christian culture. She observes that the translation of the literary into the visual was not a difficult move for Christian cultural workers to make. Verbal images were often superior in their capacity to convey theological meanings, and the transition from the verbal to the visual image was a simple shift in medium. Moreover, the visual did not merely respond to the practical problem of illiteracy in the transmission of a religion that privileged texts and writing. It also created a form of intimacy between the viewer and the image that generated sustainable relationships between the believer and the biblical figure or the saint. "What the pictures showed was people; they constituted narrative art—that is, they told stories about people. . . . Christians were presented with a pictorial world thickly populated by holy people. It would not be long before they became as familiar and as beloved as living friends."[159]

The growing emphasis on the exegetical as a lens for looking at and interpreting Christian art and the visual as a medium for the transmission of doctrine and religious sentiments is noteworthy in relation to Thecla images for at least two reasons. First, it is significant that texts like the *Acts of Paul and Thecla* and the *Life and Miracles of Thecla* proved sufficiently influential that they took on a quasi-scriptural cast, becoming worthy themselves of recirculation and exegesis in the context of visual art. Second, as one considers which dimensions of the Thecla narrative are preserved, interpreted, and disseminated artistically, Thecla is represented overwhelmingly by a bound, exposed, and explicitly female body. The memory preserved in these images emphasizes Thecla's vulnerability and femininity, even while doing so, in the case of the pilgrimage ampullae, to evoke the connection between Thecla's suffering and her power to stage the miraculous. The exegetical and the spectacular intersect in these images to preserve a memory of Thecla that occludes important elements of the literary traditions surrounding her and emphasizes the martyrological. The iconography applied to the walls of a burial chamber and inscribed on the surface of objects imbued their materiality with a refined and transformed set of meanings—and, indeed, with a new set of memories.

6

RELIGION AS A CHAIN OF MEMORY
Cassie Bernall of Columbine High and the American Legacy of Early Christian Martyrdom

The witnesses thank God. The witnesses share what they have seen and fit their perspectives into one narrative through a system of sobbing barter. In these first few minutes a thousand different stories collide; this making of truth is violence too, out of which facts are formed.
—COLSON WHITEHEAD, *John Henry Days*

ON APRIL 20, 1999, two students at Columbine High School in Littleton, Colorado, brought an arsenal of bombs and guns to school. They proceeded on a murderous shooting spree that left two dozen students wounded and twelve other students and a teacher dead. They brought their attack to an end with their own suicides. The aftermath of this tragedy was, in many respects, predictable: journalists, commentators, and advocates sought to uncover the motivations of the two killers, whom *Time* Magazine featured menacingly on its cover as "The Monsters Next Door."[1] Many people interpreted the events in Littleton in light of a wide range of political, social, and cultural concerns from gun control to popular music, from religion in the public schools to adolescent social cruelty.[2] Moreover, almost immediately, out of this stark act of calculated violence and mass killing emerged narratives of Christian martyrdom. Through narrative retelling, the monstrous took on meaning.

Why turn to a discussion of a near-millennial twentieth-century American example in the context of this exploration of early Christian martyrdom and culture making? What, in other words, has Carthage to do with Columbine?[3] There are, after all, obviously many important historical and contextual differences between these two settings. When Christians were the victims of persecution, torture, and execution in the Roman period, they suffered primarily at the hands of imperial authorities and in a context in which they were a distinct social, political, and religious minority—perceived to be or rhetorically constructed as dangerous cultural outsiders, *xenoi, barbaroi.* The two students who came to be identified as martyrs at Columbine High School, meanwhile, were part of the mainstream of their society with respect to their (white) race, (middle-) class status, and, most importantly, (Protestant Christian) religious identification. Their killers were not representatives of state authority but were rather their disaffected and deeply alienated peers. In the Columbine case, the killers—not the Christians—were repeatedly identified as the dangerous cultural outsiders. The primary shared feature of the two examples is the narrative of the spoken confession, and, as we will see, the Columbine case erupted into unresolved controversy precisely at this point. With all of these differences between the ancient and contemporary narratives, why read the story of Columbine alongside the many early Christian examples?

There are several reasons for turning to a contemporary American example, distant in time, place, and circumstance from the late ancient Roman Empire. First of all, the majority of this book has been devoted to exploring the legacies of early Christian martyrdom, the ways in which the *memory* of past suffering came to serve as a foundation for a wide range of Christian cultural projects and theological interventions. Focusing on early Christian sources, I have argued that there is a critical link between the memory of suffering, on the one hand, and Christian culture making on the other. This link has to do with what happens to stories and traditions as they are transmitted, repackaged, and deployed into new situations, making meaning as they go. The reception histories of early Christian martyrdom do not stop in the late ancient or medieval periods; they continue into modernity and, as it turns out, into postmodernity. The Columbine story preserves dimensions of this ancient narrative formula while at the same time framing it in contemporary terms and in response to current cultural and religious circumstances. That is does so within the context of Protestant evangelicalism—a form of Christianity markedly devoid of anything approximating the Catholic cult of saints—invites a more detailed exploration.

A second reason to pursue this epoch-bridging comparison is the question of martyrdom as a product of discourse rather than a matter of unmediated experience. I have argued throughout this book that martyrdom is not simply an action but rather the product of interpretation and retelling. Martyrdom is, as we have seen over and over again, rhetorically constituted and discursively sustained. The rhetorical and discursive character of martyrdom has challenged the scholarly focus on questions of "what really happened" and obsessions with separating the historical kernel from the chaff of legend. But it is one thing to reach the limits of the question of historicity when one is concerned with very distant events for which there are fragmentary and competing sources of information. It is quite another to be immersed in the moment itself—surrounded by newspapers, magazines, videotape, and eyewitness testimony—and still to have the question of "the real" emerge almost immediately. In the example of Columbine High, one encounters an interpretive dynamic and debate that offer insight into the dynamics and debates of earlier ages. The processes by which the tragedy of Columbine transmogrified into Christian martyrdom, appropriating an ideological prototype from the ancient Roman past and mapping it imaginatively onto the current American scene, are illuminating manifestations of the dynamics of collective memory.

The Columbine story evoked the problem of memory almost immediately in at least two different ways. First, journalists and commentators turned to the commemorative past of early Christian martyrdom in search of historical precursors. Alongside a laundry list of other early Christian women martyrs, Perpetua appears repeatedly as an illustrative example and parallel case in several major articles concerning the Columbine shootings and the subsequent elevation of Cassie Bernall to the status of martyr.[4] Moreover, participants in the emergent cult of Cassie also sought historical analogies in a range of Christian (and, indeed, non-Christian) examples. Second, the controversy that erupted in the media over the multiplicity and veracity of eyewitness accounts—over "the facts" and "what really happened?"—turned on the pivot of memory and meaning making. The events of Columbine High School emerged in both the mass media and Protestant evangelical literature and popular culture as a moment of cultural contest and as a striking example of Christians' making culture out of the memory of suffering. As one journalist in the conservative magazine edited by William Kristol, *The Weekly Standard*, summed it up, "it's like something from the famous account of the martyrdom of Perpetua and Felicity or the tales of the thousands of early Christians who went joyously to their deaths in the Roman coliseums [*sic*]."[5] The analogy speaks for itself somehow, even if there may be so many ways in which the Columbine story is *not* like something from the martyrdom of Perpetua and Felicitas and even if the writer has engaged in a commonplace practice of numerical exaggeration here, inflating the numbers of early Christian martyrs *and* multiplying the lone Colosseum at Rome into many. As we have seen repeatedly, the question here does not concern the historically verifiable. It is rather about what this same journalist in another context approvingly characterized as the "archetypal" quality of Cassie's death the "adolescent's *fantasy* of martyrdom."[6] Archetype or fantasy, the story of martyrdom that emerged out of Columbine fed a strong and nostalgic hunger and became a shared memory whose meanings radiated out in many directions from its receding and contested source.

Cassie Bernall died in the shootings at Columbine High School in Littleton, Colorado, on April 20, 1999. Within days of her death, journalistic reports emerged recounting her exchange with Dylan Klebold, one of the two killers, in the high school library. According to these reports, Cassie was hiding under a table when Dylan looked underneath it and challenged Cassie with a taunting question: "Do you believe in God?" The news stories reported that Cassie responded, "Yes," and Dylan then shot and killed her. This story, which came to be condensed succinctly into the slogan, "She said yes," engendered an enormous response. Almost immediately, Cassie was crowned a martyr in the press and in her evangelical Christian community.[7] "Now she's in heaven," one of the members of her Bible study is reported to have said. "She's so much better off than any of us."[8] Meanwhile, at her funeral, her pastor proclaimed, "Cassie died a martyr's death. She went to the martyr's Hall of Fame."[9] News magazines and other media reported that Cassie's death sparked a wave of evangelism among teenagers, including 73,000 who turned out for a Teen Mania rally in Pontiac, Michigan, in the weeks following her death.[10] One commentator in the conservative Christian publication *First Things* saw her death as a spiritual reactant with the potential to usher in a victory in the American culture wars: "If the fourth Great Awakening that people have been predicting since the 1970s actually occurs," he wrote, "it will have begun on April 20, 1999, and Cassie Bernall will be its martyr, its catalyst, and its patron saint. . . . It's an ever-widening faith that the whole pornographic, violent, anarchic disaster of popular American culture will soon be swept away . . . the national change of heart . . . is, after Littleton, trembling on the cusp of breaking forth."[11]

Like the early Christian martyrologies that provide the narrative framework on which the story of Cassie came to be suspended, from the start the story of Columbine included starkly differentiated elements of good and evil, inclusion and exclusion. Like the early Christian martyrologies, these oppositions were constructed around the values of the prevailing culture and involved claims about the character of both normalcy and deviance. From the earliest news accounts and opinion pieces published on the tragedy, the two killers, Eric Harris and Dylan Klebold, were identified with a whole range of religious, ideological, and personal positions that, by means of a chilly shorthand—racism, Nazism, and Satanism—rendered them outsiders and beyond the pale. Rumors circulated that they were gay and that the killings were a reversed hate crime, "striking back at the homophobic culture of Colorado."[12] *Time* magazine called them "monsters" while other commentators, especially (though by no means exclusively) from the political right, characterized them as "evil" or "mad."[13]

The explanatory power of neuroscience was brought to bear on the matter, bestowing on the demonizing quality of the accusation of "madness" a cooler, more dispassionate veneer. Emblematic of such rhetorical moves was an article entitled "Why the Young Kill," which appeared in *Newsweek* two weeks after the shootings and offered a scientific explanation and reassurance: "Science has a new understanding of the roots of violence that promises to explain why not *every* child with access to guns becomes an Eric Harris or a Dylan Klebold, and why not *every* child who feels ostracized, or who embraces the Goth esthetic, goes on a murderous rampage. The bottom line: you need a particular environment imposed on a particular biology to turn a child into a killer." The article was accompanied by a graphic illustration, "The Science of Teen Violence," claiming that "scans of the brain of a 16-year-old who assaulted another teen show several abnormalities compared with a normal brain" and displaying the corresponding images bearing the stark labels, "Normal" and "Violent."[14] Although a surprising number of young people who had suffered ostracism and bullying in junior high and high schools across America articulated some form of recognition and understanding of the pressures that erupted in these murderous acts,[15] the adult members of the commentating classes quickly quarantined Harris and Klebold as the embodiments of otherness.

Some analysts of the events at Columbine interpreted what happened less as evidence for the psychological, moral, or ontological deviance of the two assailants than as uncompromising testimony for the cultural corruption of American society as a whole. One commentator condemned "the backwash of so much of what passes as 'teen culture,'" asserting that "we must not avert our eyes from the foulness into which young people in America may be plunged."[16] Others identified the sources of this corruption more specifically: "dark comic books," the animated cable television show *South Park* (set in a fictional Rocky Mountain town not far from Littleton),[17] the music of Marilyn Manson[18]—and continental philosophy. "This is what the hip nihilism of the French philosophy professors looks like after twenty years of commercialization have sanded it down to something vulgar enough to fit in the minds of middling teenagers," this writer opined.[19] Yet another laid the crime at modernity's doorstep, a doorstep ominously constructed by the likes of Machiavelli: "And wasn't it the 'absolutely intolerant' killers who were thoroughly modern, who disbelieved in moral absolutes, who denied that any truth bound them? . . . There you have it: the culmination, the end, of modernity."[20]

In addition, journalists, commentators, and individuals who experienced the Columbine tragedy repeatedly used the language of "blackness" and "darkness" to describe the worldview of the killers (and of Cassie prior to her conversion). The killers were known to have connections with "Goth" culture, and the trademark black clothing of these disaffected adolescents was a self-selected marker of outsider status that then became a powerful signifier of deviance. Jean Bethke Elshtain's review of Misty Bernall's book about her daughter's death was entitled, "Heartland of Darkness," a (most certainly conscious) play on the title of the novel by Joseph Conrad.[21] Cassie was reported by her youth pastor to have been "into black magic, the dark stuff." One friend reported that she wrote "these really dark, suicidal poems," and Cassie herself wrote, "throughout this time I hated my parents and God with the deepest, darkest hatred. There are no words that can accurately describe the blackness I felt."[22] The language of darkness and blackness was of course metaphorical, but it was also explicitly linked to an interpretive framework that understood what was happening in Columbine as fundamentally a spiritual matter, a cosmic battle between good and evil. This mythic framework elevated the ideological force of the imagery associated with it, including the language of darkness and blackness.

Spiritual warfare was the structuring framework for the first, most sustained treatment of Cassie's death as a martyrdom, which appeared in print within five months of the shootings—a book written by her mother, Misty Bernall: *She Said Yes: The Unlikely Martyrdom of Cassie Bernall.*[23] The cover of the book bears two versions of the same photograph of Cassie, one superimposed upon the other. The smaller photo is set in a circle that has four lines at ninety-degree angles to one another extending outside its circumference. The image simultaneously evokes a gunsight and a crucifix. This double vision of the crosshairs and the cross serves as the interpretive crux, as it were, for the narrative as a whole. Relatively short—140 small pages with well-spaced typography and numerous photographs interspersed—*She Said Yes* is the story of Cassie's conversion and death, made tentatively meaningful through the interpretive framework of verbal testimony.

Although it is not simply a book devoted to the elevation of Cassie's memory and martyrdom, *She Said Yes* in many important respects follows the conventional narrative structure of hagiography. In the story, the reader encounters the radical and unpredicted transformation of a lost and fallen girl into an upright Christian heroine. Foregrounded are Cassie's adolescent struggles against drugs, alcohol, homicidal fantasies, self-mutilation, and popular culture (in the form of Marilyn Manson's music)—all set firmly within the larger framework of a spiritual struggle against Satan. Chance events in her life appear in retrospect less accidental, functioning narratively more like premonitions and foretellings of her ultimate fate and sometimes explicitly glossed in this way.[24] One sees Cassie's saintliness manifest in her own transformed life and in the ongoing effects of her life and death. Despite her mother's explicit ambivalence toward framing Cassie's story in terms of sainthood and martyrdom, the narrative structure of the story nevertheless affirms the hagiographic project. Moreover, the reader is invited to situate Cassie's story in relation to other stories—of martyrs and heroes—and thereby to make her story meaningful.

The reader is also invited into a program of interpretation by the epigraphs that begin each chapter. The principle of selection governing the choice of authors represented is not immediately apparent, with writers representing a range of historical periods, geographical settings, genres, and sensibilities. Canonical writers like Shakespeare and Emily Dickinson appear alongside figures of Christian devotional writing: the well known, such as Simone Weil and Francis of Assisi, accompanied by the less well known, such as Sundar Singh. George MacDonald, the nineteenth-century Scottish poet, novelist, and author of allegorical fairy tales provides one epigraph; Tom Petty's lyrics offer another. The eclectic collection of epigraphs also rather intriguingly includes a quotation from Gabriela Mistral, the Chilean winner of the Nobel Prize for literature, a mythic figure in the nationalist narrative of Chile and, as she has been christened in a recent scholarly study, "a queer mother for the nation." It may be more than incidental that Mistral also lost a child to an untimely death, a death that she also interpreted religiously. Mistral's adopted son Juan Miguel committed suicide in 1943, which Mistral later explained in a letter as God's punishment for her own sin of idolatry (for "I was guilty of this sin in respect to Juan Miguel").[25] And although there may have been no systematic method for selecting the authors whose words would appear as epigraphs in this book, it is striking that all three women quoted (Weil, Dickinson, Mistral) lived in one way or another outside the dominant social conventions of their times—none married, each struggling in different fashions with inherited religious traditions and constraints, each producing a body of work whose importance would register most profoundly only after her death.

The structure of the narrative presented in *She Said Yes* recalls the ancient genre of the saint's life in striking ways. In a traditional Christian hagiography, the childhood and youth of the saint tends to follow one of two predictable patterns. In one version of the model for narrating the saint's childhood, the story will emphasize the precocious piety of the child. According to this model, the saint avoids childish games, preaches at a very young age, and/or appears to have an unnatural knowingness about the world. These qualities serve in the hagiographic tradition as signs pointing to an uncommon destiny for the saint.[26] The other version of the saint's childhood and youth narrates, often in considerable detail, what amounts to the total abjection of the fallen subject. This radical debasement serves narratively as the dark backdrop against which the bright light of conversion may be projected.[27]

In hagiographical terms, Cassie's story follows this second pattern. In the narrative, Bernall presents her daughter in adolescence as a miserable misfit who drank and smoked and used drugs, who "was obsessed with death rock and vampires and self-mutilation,"[28] and who planned with her friend Mona to kill her own parents. In response to finding letters from Mona in Cassie's room in which Mona chillingly extolled the virtues of murder as a solution to Cassie's conflicts with her parents, Cassie's parents immediately contacted their pastor, the sheriff's department, and Mona's parents. (It is worth noticing the institutions to which the parents turned in this crisis—the church and the police, rather than the medical profession—even though *She Said Yes* includes many references to Cassie's self-destructive impulses, suicidal thoughts, and acts of self-mutilation. Cassie's distress was interpreted from the beginning as a spiritual and law-enforcement, but not a medical, matter.) Dave McPherson, the youth pastor who will figure prominently in the story as it unfolds appears at this stage of the narrative, offering Cassie's parents a starkly binary choice of how to proceed: "I told them they had two alternatives: either you lock her in the house and cut the phone cords and all that till things are going in the right direction again, or you let things slide—hang in there till she's an adult and hope she survives."[29] This either/or reasoning is not limited to this occasion in the book but seems to mirror a sort of reductive dualism that emerged in a wide range of episodes in Bernall's account. It also seems to have provided an important part of the interpretive context in which these events took place and out of which the story of Cassie's martyrdom emerges. It is as a consequence of Dave McPherson's advice that Cassie's parents intervened in their daughter's life by enrolling her in the Christian Fellowship School, carefully monitoring her every activity, and compelling her to attend the youth group at West Bowles Community Church where McPherson served as youth pastor.[30] While on a retreat with a school friend's church group, Cassie had a conversion experience and took on the identity of a Christian girl, born again.

Cassie's preconversion personality and character are framed in terms that are familiar from the traditional hagiographic model. Misty Bernall reports that Cassie's troubled character prior to her conversion was more than ordinary teenaged angst. Bernall situates Cassie's suffering in cosmic, almost apocalyptic terms: "She had felt gripped by a very real power of darkness, and it had taken her months to break free. Part of it was that she had apparently given her soul to Satan. . . . Unfashionable as it might be to suggest it, I felt that we were engaged in a spiritual battle."[31] Cassie's conversion, meanwhile, produces a form of discourse conventionally associated with American evangelicalism—"giving it all up to Christ," "growing in God," wondering "what God is going to do with my life."[32] The emphasis in Cassie's conversion falls on a highly personal relationship with God. Following the hagiographic pattern, the differences between "before" and "after" are starkly drawn in the text.

Cassie's story includes occasions that the narrator of her story recognizes as moments of prescient foresight. Early on in the book, Bernall reflects on "the good dreams" she had for her daughter—"Cassie graduating, Cassie walking down the aisle in a bridal veil, Cassie looking forward to her own children."[33] This reflection contrasts with Cassie's own dream of going to Cambridge University and becoming an obstetrician, a dream that her mother discouraged her from nurturing as unrealistic given the financial costs involved. Bernall then returns to "our dreams of her marrying and raising a family" and to the memory of her husband repeatedly teasing Cassie about his wanting grandchildren and of Cassie's inevitable response: "I'm never going to get married. I'll never have kids."[34] One cannot know why Cassie repeatedly insisted on this point, though one could interpret the response in a number of different ways. She may have thought that her desire to pursue higher education and a demanding career would render marriage and motherhood out of reach. She may have projected her adolescent loneliness and social self-doubts into the future. She may have not wanted to replicate the model of the nuclear family in which she herself had struggled so desperately to find her way. But whatever the impulse behind the answer she consistently gave to the question, the response performs a particular rhetorical function in both this specific passage and, indeed, in the broader hagiographic form in which it is framed. Coming at the end of this "dream" sequence and bringing the passage to a conclusion, Cassie's words become prophetic and prescient. Read from the point of view of her untimely death, the statement becomes poignantly and irrevocably true. Read within the framework of female martyrologies and hagiographies, it echoes the familiar topos of these genres which mourns the lost motherhood of holy women.

Such passing comments were not the only clues pointing toward the future, according to Cassie's mother. Books that Cassie had read, notes and letters she left behind all provide the narrative with yet more potential evidence for foreknowledge of her fate. Toward the end of the book, Bernall quotes passages from youth group readings Cassie had been doing, noting the passages Cassie had underlined or highlighted. In a particular chapter of one book whose other chapters Cassie had marked and annotated heavily, Bernall reports, "Cassie underlined only a solitary sentence: 'All of us should live life so as to be able to face eternity at any time.' "[35] The reading for the youth group meeting on April 20, the day of Cassie's murder, included a passage quoting a 1963 speech by Martin Luther King Jr.: "I submit to you that if a man hasn't discovered something that he will die for, he isn't fit to live."[36] Both quotations situate Cassie's life in a broader framework of Christian ideas about the ethical charge of death and immortality. They draw upon familiar Christian martyrological language and are used rhetorically in this context to suggest a bittersweet prescience on the part of Cassie, the unlikely martyr.[37]

And yet it is not the case that Misty Bernall makes unequivocal claims about her daughter's martyrdom, and a close reader of her text will find tensions and ambivalence embedded in the portrait of Cassie's status in life and in death. Bernall reports her own initial uncertainty about the claim that her daughter was a martyr: "Cassie is my daughter, I thought. You can't turn her into Joan of Arc. . . . But even if Cassie's death is a martyrdom, it is an unlikely one. I say that because before she was a martyr, she was a teen."[38] Indeed, the rhetoric of *She Said Yes* oscillates back and forth between two different sorts of claims about Cassie—either she was just a normal teenager or she was specially chosen all along for her fate. "People say that nothing happens without a purpose—that perhaps Cassie was fulfilling a divine plan, or that in standing up for her beliefs, she was being used by God to further his kingdom. At a certain level, I take comfort in these thoughts. . . . At another level, though, I get weary of the explanations and interpretations, of hearing about the lessons to be learned."[39] Yet, if Cassie was chosen, her chosenness might somehow be legible through her behavior. Hence, the book preserves a detail that also appeared in news reports and on commemorative Internet sites dedicated to Cassie: that she was planning on cutting her long blond hair very short so that it could be made into wigs for children undergoing chemotherapy for leukemia.[40]

In spite of her hesitancy to see her daughter as a martyr instead of simply as a girl, Bernall nevertheless mobilizes some dramatic comparisons in making sense of her daughter's death.[41] Toward the end of the book, as we have seen, Bernall records Cassie's highlighting of a passage in which Martin Luther King Jr. declares the unfitness of a person to live who has not discovered a cause worth dying for. King's iconic status in U.S. culture renders him a national saint whose death has most certainly taken on both mythic and martyrological proportions in this country's history and beyond its borders.[42] The citation of King makes a rhetorical connection between his words and Cassie's death, linking their two narratives together. An even more striking comparison is the one which closes *She Said Yes*, in which Cassie's death is read synchronously with those of all the dead of the Israeli defense forces. Misty Bernall writes:

A few days after my daughter's death, I learned that on April 20, while bullets wreaked havoc in the halls of Columbine High, friends of ours traveling in Israel were attending a service to remember fallen soldiers. As the choir chanted in Hebrew, an interpreter explained. It was a tribute to the country's martyrs, and the translation ran something like this: "My death is not my own, but yours, and its significance depends on what you do with it."

    If there is anything I would like to leave you, the reader, it is the same thought: Cassie's story is not only mine and Brad's. It is yours, and what you do with it now will give it meaning.[43]

Bernall is not the only writer to link Cassie's death to those of others. In *The Weekly Standard*, a conservative publication edited by William Kristol, J. Bottum's article about Cassie's martyrdom compared her to the early Christian martyrs Perpetua and Felicitas, Eulalia of Mérida, Catherine of Alexandria, and Crispina.[44] When reviewing *She Said Yes* for *The New Republic*, Jean Bethke Elshtain opened her essay with a discussion of early Christian martyrdom, retelling the Perpetua story and then making reference to other youthful women martyrs from the history of the church—Eulalia, Agnes, Joan of Arc, and Maria Goretti.[45] In an intriguing example of associative interpretation, enabled by postmodern high-tech tools, the page at Amazon.com dedicated to *She Said Yes* provided readers with a link to another book about martyrs: Foxe's *Book of Martyrs*, the sixteenth-century anti-Catholic martyrology of Protestant reformers. Thus, Cassie's story has repeatedly been set in direct relationship to various highly charged martyrological traditions: originating in American, Israeli, early Christian, medieval, Reformation, and contemporary Christian contexts. And lest one need to be reminded that these analogies are being drawn in the broader context of the formation of collective memory, one need only turn to the "Customers' Responses" to Foxe's *Book of Martyrs* to see the force of the desire for a useable past. One respondent praises Foxe's martyrology but observes that the book would have been better had it included an account of the Columbine shootings, something of a trick for a sixteenth-century work to perform. At least one publisher, however, seems to have shared the view that this historic work could use a contemporary revision. An edition of Foxe's *Book of Martyrs* released since then has been "updated" to include Christian martyrs through 1996.[46] Meanwhile, an upsurge in mass culture representations of martyrdom was also taking place during this period. A group of "the world's top comics artists" produced *The Big Book of Martyrs*, containing "amazing-but-true tales of faith in the face of certain death!" in comic-book form in 1997.[47] Soon afterwards, in 1999, a popular book devoted to Christian martyrs across the centuries and addressed to a teen audience entitled *Jesus Freaks* appeared in print; its seventh printing claims there are 450,000 copies in print.[48]

In addition to being positioned within this broad historical frame of martyr-dom, both in *She Said Yes* and in other media coverage, Cassie is also credited with having a far broader influence over the lives of others—not only in life, but more dramatically in death. Josh Lapp, one of the students who claims to have witnessed Cassie's exchange with her killer, credits her death with transforming his outlook on life. This transformation is expressed in terms drawing on the middle-class suburban values that resound through *She Said Yes*:

> Until that day, I just took everything for granted. I pitch for the baseball team at school, and I took playing for granted. Even hiding under the desk that day, I was thinking, "Where do I want to get shot, if I get shot, so that I can still play ball, or walk around." Because I lived for those games. But now I look at it completely different. I still live for baseball, but now I look at it as a privilege to be able to play.[49]

Meanwhile, Cassie's youth minister Dave McPherson followed in the tradition of many survivors of saints and martyrs by receiving a vision of Cassie after her death. While ministering to the Bernall family, he reports, "I saw Cassie, and I saw Jesus, hand in hand. And they had just gotten married. They had just celebrated their marriage ceremony. And Cassie kind of winked over at me like, 'Dave, I'd like to talk, but I'm so much in love.' Her greatest prayer was to find the right guy. Don't you think she did?"[50] Interestingly, the link between Cassie and marriage is crucial to the youth pastor's vision of the martyred girl. From Misty Bernall's account in the "dream" section, the reader knows that Cassie repeatedly insisted that she would never marry and have children. In *She Said Yes*, however, Dave McPherson recalls Cassie's participation in the church youth group, remarking, "we were all studying this one book, *Discipleship*, and she went straight to the chapter on marriage. She was normal, all right."[51]

But if Cassie's story is situated in the broader hagiographic and martyrological framework of Christian storytelling, it is also set firmly within the framework of American, middle-class, largely Protestant suburbia. At one point, Bernall expresses her frustration with Cassie's preconversion inability to appreciate her parents' sacrifices on her behalf: "Wasn't it for you, I wanted to ask her . . . that we moved out of the old house in the first place? That we left the neighborhood that I loved? That I stopped working for four months and gave up what I considered an ideal house in exchange for a less-than-perfect one? How many more sacrifices did she expect us to make for her?"[52] Meanwhile, fitting in and embodying the ideals of "normalcy" and "realness" were highly valued goals in this social world. Moreover, this is a world in which appearances are privileged pathways into "the normal" and "the real," even as both "the normal" and "the real" remain on a still-unachieved plane of existence. Bernall expresses her nervousness about Cassie's new friend at the Christian school where Cassie was enrolled before transferring to Columbine: "Jamie had a short, bleached-blond haircut, and big chains and metal beads around her neck, and she was wearing the sort of grungy attire that alternative types buy from places like Goodwill. Definitely not my idea of a nice Christian girl."[53] When deciding whether to allow Cassie to transfer to Columbine, Bernall narrates how she and her husband "talked to other parents, and . . . *looked at the kids.*"[54] While parents' talk is important, the kids are simply there to be visually evaluated—as though their appearances were sufficiently transparent for the observer to form a judgment. Considering the post mortem recognition that appearances governed Columbine's culture to a disturbing extent—and that appearances could be deceiving—this emphasis on the apparent legibility of the kids in this story is haunting.

The broader framework of Cassie's martyrdom is a postmodern one that allows for the instantaneous transmission, fragmentation, and recombination of information and images. Cassie's martyrdom depended much less on the historicity of the events that unfolded so tragically in the high school library than on the media's role in disseminating the story about it. The resulting frenzy of accusation and anxiety that eventually surrounded the question of whether or not Cassie had *really* said yes is telling. The possibility that both witnesses and reporters might well have been caught up in the processes by which martyrologies have been generated for centuries seems to have taken almost everyone by surprise.

And yet, just as *She Said Yes* was about to be released five months after the shootings at Columbine High School, a heated controversy about the Cassie Bernall story emerged. According to some witnesses, Cassie Bernall had *not* been asked by a gun-toting classmate at Columbine High in Littleton, Colorado, if she believed in God. She had *not* said yes. Instead, according to a new round of news stories, Emily Wyant, the girl who was hiding under a library table with Cassie, insisted that the famed exchange between Cassie and Dylan Klebold never took place. According to Emily, Cassie was crouched under the library table next to her. "Cassie was praying, 'Dear God. Dear God. Why is this happening? I just want to go home.' Dylan Klebold suddenly slammed his hand on the table, yelled, 'Peekaboo,' and looked underneath. He shot Cassie without exchanging a word."[55] Meanwhile, another girl named Valeen Schnurr claimed that, in another part of the school library and after having been shot numerous times, *she* had been asked if she believed in God *after* she was shot, and that *she* said yes. Her assailants asked "why?" but then just walked away, leaving her alone.[56] Despite her multiple shotgun wounds, Valeen survived. Members of Christian youth group audiences to whom she subsequently told her story accused her of trying to appropriate Cassie's story. Misty Bernall meanwhile defended her own version of the story as it appears in *She Said Yes*, despite "slight discrepancies" in witness accounts. The debate raged in the print and broadcast media and on the Internet.[57]

Questions about the "truth" of *She Said Yes* and the broader martyrological narrative of which it was a part were answered in a variety of interesting ways. For some people, the conflicting testimony called the whole narrative thoroughly into question. Some people accused the publisher of the book or Cassie's parents of trying to take advantage of the situation and profit off the story.[58] Meanwhile, the original publisher of the book (Plough Publishers, a small publishing house affiliated with the Anabaptist community, the Bruderhof) defended the narrative, observing, "Questions about the particulars of what transpired in the library do not detract from the crux of Bernall's book, which is Cassie's transformation from a troubled teen who at one time entertained murderous fantasies to a young woman ready to face both life and death with confidence."[59] Moreover, the publisher of *She Said Yes* already knew there would be controversy concerning the book's title and claims prior to the book's appearance. In a note published at the front of the volume, the publisher argued, "Though the precise chronology of the murderous rampage that took place at Columbine High on April 20, 1999—including the exact details of Cassie's death—may never be known, the author's description in this book is based on the reports of numerous survivors of the library (the main scene of the massacre) and takes into account their varying recollections."[60]

The mothers of the various girls whose testimony was under scrutiny were fully involved in the debate. Defending her own daughter's testimony (that Cassie and Dylan never exchanged any words), Cindie Wyant (Emily's mother) offered, "That's her memory. That's her truth. She doesn't want to stir anything up, but that's how she remembers it."[61] Valeen Schnurr's mother also defended her daughter's counterclaim of having been the one who was asked if she believed in God by suggesting that perhaps both girls were asked the question and answered it affirmatively.[62]

Meanwhile, journalists, commentators, and religious leaders lined up on different sides of the debate. Dave Cullen, the *Salon.com* reporter who first broke the story of the controversy concerning what had really happened in the library and what Cassie had really said,[63] ultimately published a book provocatively entitled, *Cloud Over Columbine: How the Press Got It Wrong and the Police Let It Happen*, arguing that Cassie never gave the testimony attributed to her.[64] *Brill's Content*, the purported "independent voice of the information age," early on compared the *Time* and *Newsweek* coverage of the events in its August 1999 issue and tagged the martyrdom story with the label, "accurate,"[65] but reversed itself in a subsequent issue. Wendy Murray Zoba, a reporter covering the Columbine story for *Christianity Today*, in contrast to Cullen and others, concluded from her assessment of the evidence that the martyrdom story was true.[66]

Others straddled the fence, like Jean Bethke Elshtain in her review of *She Said Yes* for the *New Republic*. Elshtain summarized several witness accounts and then wrote, "Whatever the exact words, there seems little doubt that Cassie was challenged and that she refused to deny her faith." She then went on to admit, "No, that's not quite right. There is some doubt in some recent journalistic reports about what exactly happened and who said exactly what." *Some* doubt in *some* journalistic reports about the *exact* events and words spoken, however, did not give Elshtain much pause, as she continued with a statement of faith: "I happen to believe that the doomed young woman did say 'yes.'" But then she immediately changed the focus of analysis: "But what is more interesting, I think, is the reaction from various quarters to the prospect of any kind of martyr in our midst. The United States . . . is a country that has not seen systemic religious persecution with a high body count. It has been dominated by forms of Protestantism that, at least by the turn of the [twentieth] century, frequently took pride in its 'reasonableness' when compared with Catholicism or Anabaptists or other extremists. Such a polity will not kindle to the phenomenon of martyrdom."[67]

Whether they should be characterized in Elshtain's terms as "reasonable" or "extremist," and although some religious leaders urged caution in relation to the martyr story,[68] many Protestant leaders apparently *did* kindle to the phenomenon of martyrdom and, indeed, caught fire. At the same time, they found themselves needing to respond to the problem of the contested character of the story, and they did so, sometimes in remarkable ways. For example, the president of the North American Missions Board of the Southern Baptist Convention told the Baptist Press that "regardless of who said yes, two things are true. The first is that some young person under terrifying circumstances testified to their faith. Praise God for that. Secondly, whether it was Cassie Bernall or not, Cassie's life and words prior to the shooting testified to the change in her life that came from knowing Jesus Christ."[69] What is particularly remarkable about this response is its willingness to bracket questions of literalism and historicity—long the centerpieces of the evangelical hermeneutic—and to embrace a broader, more symbolic version of the truth concerning Cassie Bernall.[70]

The controversy over the historicity and veracity of the Cassie story did not hinder the emergence of a kind of martyr cult surrounding the murdered girl. Commemorative Web sites soon appeared where one could, for example, take "The Cassie Pledge" and make a contribution toward the Cassie Bernall Youth

Center and Gymnasium[71] or simply reflect on "Seeing Christ at Columbine."[72] Christian musician Michael W. Smith released a CD entitled, *This is Your Time*, described on the Christian Book Distributors Web site as "inspired by stories of tragedy and heroism at Columbine High School."[73] Evangelical churches around the country, using a kit marketed by the Abundant Life Christian Center in Arvada, Colorado, restaged the shootings at Columbine—with Cassie declaring her faith, Jesus leading her to heaven, and demons dragging her killers away to damnation—as part of their yearly Halloween "Hell House" activities.[74] The congregation of a Baptist church in Denver performed a play entitled, "Crossroads at Columbine," six months after the incident.[75] Teenagers in suburban New Orleans produced weekly Friday-evening performances of "Beyond the Grave: The Class of 2000," featuring the Columbine shootings, Cassie's confession, and an altar call inviting audience members to respond positively to the invitation to give their lives to Jesus.[76] Less than a month after the killings at Columbine, and before the controversy over the veracity of the martyrdom story, a fifteen-year-old girl decided to take "Cassie" as her confirmation name because she was so moved by the story.[77]

The Bernall family itself authorized a Web site called "yesibelieve.com" to market a range of *She Said Yes* products: the book, the video, the Bible study guide as well as a whole line of "Yes I Believe" products including bracelets, baseball caps, key chains, necklaces, t-shirts, and Web site banners. An electronic tagline on the Web site announces that "Yes, I Believe" is "the cry of the new millennium."[78] One can subscribe to the "Yes, I Believe" online newsletter. The sign-up form asks the subscriber to "please select the following: 'Yes, I Believe in God!' and 'Yes, I want to receive the YIB Newsletter and occasional information regarding updates to the services and products at YesIbelieve.com.'"[79] The site invites visitors to "Make a Statement of Faith" by enrolling to receive a free e-mail address, yourname@yesibelieve.com. Meanwhile, a small-print notice on the Web site assures the consumer that, "a portion of the proceeds from all Yes, I Believe products will be given to the Cassie Bernall Foundation. All YIB! Products have been approved and endorsed by the Bernall family as the official line of products relating to their daughter's life and testimony."[80] But if one finds this sales pitch a bit too crass, Yes, I Believe, Inc. has also established a page on its Web site dedicated to the Cassie Bernall Foundation so that "you will be able to donate online without purchasing anything."[81]

Although the commemoration of Cassie's death as a martyrdom has received much wider coverage in the mainstream media, this memory work needs to be interpreted in relationship to other, sometimes contested commemorative acts staged around the Columbine events. Almost immediately after the shootings, a makeshift memorial appeared, consisting of banners with written messages, stuffed animals, flowers, and fifteen crosses—four pink (for the female students who were murdered), nine blue (for the eight male students and one male teacher killed), and two black (for the two killers).[82] Later, having been contacted by people in Littleton and invited to come, Greg Zanis, an Illinois carpenter, constructed a set of fifteen eight-foot-high plain pine crosses and placed them on a hilltop in Clement Park overlooking the school in commemoration of both the victims and the killers. Almost immediately, the scene became a pilgrimage site where visitors waited in line to stand near the crosses, write messages on them, and leave flowers and notes and commemorative objects. The crosses also became a source of conflict and enmity, with some visitors draping the crosses for the two killers in black trash bags and others inscribing these crosses with hostile or obscene messages.[83] Brian Rohrbough, the father of one of the victims, cut down the crosses for the two killers, angered that they were being memorialized alongside their victims. For all the controversy, the crosses nevertheless became a centerpiece in the community's grief, anger, and commemorative practice and have subsequently been displayed around the country. Various institutions ranging from the Smithsonian to the Vatican have inquired about the possibility of acquiring them for their collections.[84] The crosses continued to be displayed and to generate controversy when their builder sued in order to be able to place them in their original setting in Clement Park across from the school for the second anniversary of the shootings.[85]

But these crosses were not the only commemorative objects subject to contest and challenge. Controversy over commemoration extended to a tree-planting at West Bowles Community Church, Cassie's family's church, where fifteen trees were planted "to honor the families that have been hurt." Brian Rohrbough and the family and friends of another student who had been killed cut down two of the trees, again because they represented the killers, while church members claimed that one of the trees that was destroyed was (or would be) dedicated to Cassie Bernall.[86] Moreover, just months after the tragedy, friends and relatives of the victims of the shootings filed a federal lawsuit against the school district for its refusal to allow religious symbols in a memorial project composed of tiles to be displayed above the lockers in the hallways at Columbine High.[87]

In the wake of Columbine, then, the pressing questions became what to remember, who to remember, and how to remember. They were questions involving the politics of both martyrdom and memory. It seemed, in some cases, that they were also questions of taste and opportunism, generating worry by some that the memory of Columbine did not have sufficient substance and gravitas but rather was tilting in the direction of vulgarity and crassness.[88] Praising what she called Misty Bernall's "restraint," Jean Bethke Elshtain, for example, contrasted it with Cassie's ascendancy to martyrdom, which she characterized as "the vulgar beatification that one found in other quarters." She went on to dismiss the saccharine and clichéd images present on the different Cassie Web sites as "too insubstantial to provide a perdurable message of spiritual formation."[89] Underlying much of this concern seemed to be an anxiety over the enthusiasms generated by the notion of martyrdom itself and the worry that this exuberance might exceed an easily managed and institutionally constrained framework. Indeed, as Elshtain put it in a negative comparison with the memory of early Christian martyrdom: "The early martyrs were taken up, over the span of centuries, and made part of a highly complicated intellectual and institutional framework. Such traditions require above all a capacity that we lack: attention over time. But nothing durable will come from all the pink-tinged websites. . . . Absent the sustaining forms of spiritual discipline, of *any* discipline, Cassie Bernall's death has become just the latest splash in the stream of American spiritual self-help."[90]

There is an earnest and unselfconscious quality to the commemoration of Cassie Bernall, Rachel Scott, and the other Columbine dead that draws upon the images and idioms of mainstream American middle-class culture. The teddy bears left at the feet of the Columbine crosses, the pastel-colored portraits of Cassie and Jesus on the memorial Web sites, the messages written on Cassie's casket in thick black magic marker before it was lowered into the ground, the paraphernalia (key chains, baseball caps, t-shirts) one could purchase from the "Yes I Believe!" Web site—all of these material manifestations of grief and memory strike some observers as lacking the grandeur and theological embeddedness of the commemorations of early martyrs. There is something makeshift and deeply ordinary about these expressions, generated out of the emotional, spiritual, and material resources that lie closest to hand.[91] Yet, it is not clear that they differ in significance or substance from their counterparts generated centuries ago in the late ancient workshops that churned out pilgrim souvenirs bearing images of Thecla and Menas, for example. Were there critics in antiquity who called into question the "tastefulness" of pilgrim flasks bearing images of a half-naked Thecla surrounded by wild and hungry beasts? Were there not controversies over the pieties undertaken by pilgrims, especially over the generation and dissemination of relics? Are the worries over "taste" and "vulgarity" in the current American situation similar sorts of controversies, translated into a new idiom of cultural value?

The Columbine commemoration can be assessed in relation to a number of different interpretive frameworks—evangelical Protestantism, the Americanization of the figure of "the martyr," and broader contemporary appropriations of the discourse and politics of persecution and martyrdom, especially the use of "early Christian martyrdom" as an authorizing trope. Each of these elements invites a lengthy investigation that is beyond the scope of this current project. What follows is a brief set of observations concerning these frameworks and some consideration of the implications of the language of martyrdom in these different settings.

One of the most striking features of the elevation of Cassie Bernall to the status of a martyr in the wake of the Columbine shootings was the fact that this canonization took place in the context of American evangelical Protestantism, a version of Christianity with very particular relationships to the practice of interpretation and to history and with a distinct aversion to forms of piety such as the veneration of saints. Evangelical approaches to interpretation favor literalism—a focus on the semantic rather than the rhetorical, a privileging of "plain" and "commonsense" meaning over against the figural or allegorical, and a belief in the transparency and decidability of language.[92] History tends to be read in such contexts in terms of a linear "salvation history" that is, down to its most (apparently) insignificant details, coherent and meaningful—even when a significant amount of ambiguity in detail can be tolerated in the process. When a contemporary evangelical community seeks to position itself in relation to Christian history, it tends to privilege Christian origins and the apostolic age over against subsequent periods of Christian (that is, Catholic) history and thus to downplay or ignore precisely the sorts of stories and traditions that preserve the martyrological background against which the Cassie Bernall story would come to be projected. Where Catholicism has a long history of the veneration of saints (including martyrs, whose intercessionary powers have an ancient lineage), evangelicals tend to look upon such pieties with at least a measure of caution and suspicion, if not outright alarm.

At the same time, however, evangelical Protestant churches have been the leaders in recent public policy initiatives in the United States, including the passage of legislation by Congress, that capitalize on concerns over the religious persecution of Christians around the world.[93] Responding to pressure from evangelicals and others, the State Department established an Advisory Committee on Religious Freedom Abroad in 1996.[94] A year later, evangelicals lobbied for and Congress mandated a State Department report on the treatment of Christians around the world.[95] In May 1998, the House of Representatives passed the Freedom From Religious Persecution Act of 1998 by a large margin (375 to 41), a bill that would restrict U.S. exports, ban nonhumanitarian aid, and oppose development loans and subsidies to governments found responsible for religious persecution.[96] In October 1998, the Senate passed its own version of the bill, the International Religious Freedom Act, and when the House conceded to this version of the bill, President Clinton signed it into law.[97] The enacted version of the law requires the State Department to monitor the violation of religious rights in other countries and the president to sanction economically the countries judged guilty of such abuses. Linked rhetorically by their supporters to the fiftieth anniversary of the Universal Declaration of Human Rights, the bills passed in large measure because of the lobbying efforts of evangelicals who organized themselves into a broad movement of solidarity with what they call "the persecuted church." Comparing the contemporary situation of Christians around the world to the circumstances of European Jews during the Shoah, evangelical activists in this political movement use the words of Jewish writers such as Anne Frank and Elie Wiesel to frame their message. They also view the message of persecution and martyrdom as a tool for both evangelization and shoring up the church in America. "Blood is spilled, that's when we grow," as Steve Haas, the president of Prayer for the Persecuted Church, put it.[98]

More generally, the language of persecution often serves in American evangelical circles as a source of moral authority, and evangelicals frequently express the view that they are a religious minority serving as a hearty but always threatened bulwark against secularist mainstream culture. Yet, claiming the privileged position as the inheritors of the legacy of early Christian martyrs is not limited to the evangelical religious right. When the Christian Coalition met in 1996 for its national convention, a fledging left-leaning evangelical social justice movement, the Call to Renewal, included members who called themselves the " 'catacomb' Christians of the underground," explicitly contrasting themselves with the more well-heeled members of the Christian Coalition.[99]

Although evangelical Christianity does not share with Catholicism a centuries-long tradition of saint and martyr veneration, the ground may nevertheless have been especially ripe for the planting of the seeds of a martyr cult in the evangelical heartland in the spring of 1999, given the increased focus among American evangelicals on the problem of the persecution of Christians in the late 1990s. What remains remarkable about the emergence of the Columbine martyr cult in this context is the relative ease with which the controversies over "what really happened" were so summarily dismissed by evangelicals themselves. Meanwhile, outsiders to the evangelical tradition (journalists, primarily) were placed in the ironic position of literalists, seeking the "plain truth" while people like the president of the Southern Baptist Convention's North American Missions Board expeditiously dispatched the controversy with a sentence that began, "Regardless of who said yes. . . ." This is a remarkable turn of interpretive events. Even as evangelicals used Cassie Bernall's death to parse and narrate America's current "crisis" around "values" and situated the events of Columbine in their own version of salvation history, they remarkably embraced an interpretive framework that focused—not on literal truth, but—on analogy, figuration, and deferral. In this, the story of Cassie entered into the long and venerable tradition of martyrology, a tradition that has always embodied the tensions of narrative proliferation and multiplicity. That a postmodern Protestant martyr's story should do so is both highly appropriate and appropriately ironic. Like all ritualized repetitions of commemorative martyrological narratives, the truth of Cassie's story cannot help but reside elsewhere and be a truth that refuses to be pinned down.

But there are other frames in which to situate the martyrdom of Cassie Bernall since, of course, interpreting the American experience of violence in martyrological—and oftentimes redemptive—terms is by no means an innovation in the Columbine tragedy.[100] It is, however, worthy of notice that it has been far more likely in the past that martyrological imagery would emerge within frameworks that are only partially concerned with religious identity and commitment. American martyrdom has historically had far more to do with political conflicts and especially with race, though both political and racial contests and confrontations—and different responses to them—have often been inflected in religious terms. When, in 1838, Harriet Martineau wrote her important essay on the emergent abolitionist movement in the United States, for example, she saw this religiously inspired political movement that opposed the violence of slavery as emblematic of an era that she called "A Martyr Age in the United States."[101] Martyrdom in America has almost always been connected to the pressing political issues of the day and to the violence through which those political issues have sometimes been engaged, rather than isolated within the framework of religious identity narrowly construed. Hence, one can generate a long list of political assassinations (Abraham Lincoln, Martin Luther King Jr., Malcolm X, John and Robert Kennedy); lynchings, political murders, and racist killings (the Klan killings of James Earl Chaney, Andrew Goodman, and Michael Schwerner, to choose just one of the more well documented examples); as well as state-sponsored executions for treason (John Brown, Ethel and Julius Rosenberg) where the language of martyrdom emerged as the dominant mode by which many people extracted meaning from fatal violence and untimely death.

In recent American history, acts of violence that travel under the name of "hate crimes" have seen the language of martyrdom emerge as a meaning-making discourse. The 1998 killing of Matthew Shepard, a gay University of Wyoming undergraduate, by two men who beat him and left him for dead, tied to a fence in a field outside Laramie, immediately took on the aura of the martyrological, and not only because of the position in which his body was left by his assailants, suggestive of a crucifixion.[102] Meanwhile, the brutal murder of Teena Brandon/Brandon Teena, the transgendered teenager who was killed in rural Nebraska in 1993 by two acquaintances after they discovered that Brandon was passing as a boy and became worried that Brandon would report having been raped by them, has also been framed in martyrological terms.[103] In both cases, the murder victims were singled out for brutal violence because of their sexual and gender "outsider" status, and the use of the term "martyr" to describe them served both metaphorically rich and politically potent ends.

That martyrdom resides in the eye of the beholder in circumstances involving hate crime violence may be seen in the competing responses to two different examples of racist violence in the summer of 1999, just months after the Columbine shootings. Over the July 4th weekend that summer, Benjamin Nathaniel Smith, a member of the racist World Church of the Creator, targeted African Americans, Jews, and Asians in a shooting spree spanning two Midwestern states, killing two people and injuring twelve before committing suicide. In the aftermath, Matthew Hale, the leader of the World Church of the Creator, said that he only felt compassion for Smith and his family, not for Smith's victims, and called Smith "a martyr for free speech for white people."[104] A month later, Buford Furrow Jr., a member of the Aryan Nations, shot and killed Joseph Santos Ileto, a Filipino postal worker in Los Angeles, reportedly because Mr. Ileto was not white and because he worked for the federal government. At Ileto's funeral, Congressman Brad Sherman, who represents the district where Ileto worked, described the murdered postal worker as "a martyr to the cause of us just living together."[105]

The language of martyrdom serves in these different examples as a way of assigning a broader symbolic meaning to an event that might otherwise be interpreted as senseless and capricious violence. Behind this usage resides the authorizing and foundational archetype of martyrdom embodied in the early Christian example. Indeed, if we return our attention to Cassie Bernall, we can see how, in the midst of all the different kinds of controversies concerning the martyrdom at Columbine and the proper modes of commemoration and remembrance, the early Christian example floats in the background uncannily, as a distant analogy, a narrative resource, and an object of ambivalent nostalgia. Most often when early Christian martyrdom was evoked in the Columbine story, there was a tendency to conflate different examples preserved in different genres into multiple manifestations of a repeated historical truth. Elshtain paraphrases the *Martyrdom of Perpetua and Felicitas* in her review of *She Said Yes*, presenting it as a historical example that is "shockingly, uncompromisingly extreme," and yet, Elshtain argues, "in the context of persecution, and in the understanding of faith, there was no acceptable alternative except the radical one."[106] Later on, she calls up the examples of Eulalia and Agnes, quoting from unnamed ancient sources (though perhaps Prudentius) to describe the youth and celebrated status of these two "historical martyrs."[107] The rhetorical move here collapses and conflates early Christian collective memory with contemporary notions of history and renders the image generated out of commemorative, devotional literature both a reliable portrait of the past and an apt analogy for the present.

The images that came readily to mind among commentators seem to have been inspired and augmented, whether consciously or not, by Hollywood epic restagings of Roman cruelties and Christian pieties. In his article "The Making of a Martyr" in *The Weekly Standard,* J. Bottum observed, "It's like something from the famous account of the martyrdom of Perpetua and Felicity, or the tales of the thousands of early Christians who went joyously to their deaths in the Roman coliseums [sic]."[108] Bottum's vague and unglossed analogy ("it's *like something* from . . .") and his lack of specific historical knowledge about the Roman period are not unique. *Newsweek,* for example, when covering the Columbine martyrdom phenomenon, called evangelical Web sites places "where pious adolescents meet like Christians in the catacombs," recirculating the commonplace (if also incorrect) view that the catacombs were secret hiding places used by persecuted Christians rather than funereal spaces where the living openly buried and commemorated their dead.[109]

This nostalgic appropriation of early Christian martyrdom works precisely because of the power of the images involved, none more powerful than the grand ruin of the Colosseum in Rome itself. Revered as a shrine to early Christian martyrs by present-day right-wing religious groups in Italy, the Colosseum performs ideological work in the defense of socially conservative, even neofascist political programs. Claimed at the same time as a symbol for the international campaign against capital punishment, the Colosseum comes to stand for the improper arrogation of the power to take human life by governments and for state oppression *tout court.* These two interpretations of the meaning of the Colosseum came into direct conflict in the summer of 2000 when, in the middle of the Catholic Church's Jubilee Year celebrations, participants in the World Pride Roma 2000 gay-pride parade promised to surround the Colosseum in defiance of the city's refusal to provide a parade permit that included the streets encircling the monumental symbol. Meanwhile, at a counterdemonstration sponsored by neofascists, participants displayed banners that read, "Gays at the Colosseum? Only with Lions!"[110]

More generally, early Christian martyrdom has been called upon in a wide range of contemporary debates, used always as a resource for authorizing a particular point of view and silencing criticism and debate. An especially egregious version of this rhetorical move occurred in the summer of 2002, when Cardinal Oscar Rodriguez Maradiaga, the Archbishop of Tegucigalpa, Honduras, and one of the men whose names have been floated as possible successors to Pope John Paul II, attacked the U.S. media's coverage of the sex scandals that had erupted in the Roman Catholic church earlier that year. In his attack, he compared the media to Hitler, Stalin, and the Roman emperors Nero and Diocletian. The cardinal characterized the questioning of Cardinal Bernard Law of Boston in a legal deposition as using "methods that recall the dark days of Stalinist trials of churchmen of eastern Europe." The media's actions displayed, he continued, "a fury which reminds me of the times of Diocletian and Nero and more recently, Stalin and Hitler." Attempting to delegitimize any form of critique, he further argued that the coverage was simply an anti-Catholic backlash against the Church's support for a Palestinian homeland and against the Church's teachings on abortion, euthanasia, and capital punishment.[111] The citational references to Diocletian and Nero alongside Stalin and Hitler served to demonize any person who would critique the Catholic hierarchy's handling of the sex scandal, attempting to divert attention away from the violence inflicted by the clergy and the bishops by evoking the persecutory violence of Roman emperors and twentieth-century dictators. One sees in such examples both the power and danger embedded in the rhetoric of martyrdom.

This chapter began by quoting a text that is as distant from the early Christian martyrological tradition as is the example of Cassie Bernall of Columbine High: an epigraph taken from Colson Whitehead's *John Henry Days*, a contemporary American novel that explores the kaleidoscopic character of an American legend, a martyr to the machine age. The passage describes most immediately, not the life of John Henry himself, but the aftermath of violent events that take place at a celebration staged by an economically depressed town seeking to revitalize its tourist industry by capitalizing on the memory of the famed steel driver. But of course, the passage also describes more generally the work of eyewitnesses, of the bearers of memory, of those who have been capriciously spared violence and feel compelled by many different motivations to generate a useable narrative out of traumatic experience. The participation in this "system of sobbing barter" is simultaneously the "making of truth" and "violence." One cannot, Colson Whitehead implies, have the one without the other.

Such a claim leaves me uneasy, even though I suspect that it also represents some kind of profound if also deeply unsettling truth about the relationship between martyrdom and memory and about the production of culture and meaning out of suffering. Having spent such a long time in this academic engagement with the Christian story of martyrdom, both in its ancient articulations and its contemporary manifestations, I find myself still deeply ambivalent about the work that it does and the legacy that it has helped to create and sustain. What are the consequences, intended and unintended, I find myself asking, of repetitiously reinscribing this link between "violence" and "truth"? What sorts of identifications and alliances are formed by celebrating this conjunction? What forms of violence are underwritten, authorized, and romanticized in the process? One does not need to look far, after all, to encounter horrific examples wherein the willingness to sacrifice the self has morphed seamlessly into the willingness to sacrifice the other.[112] It may be a difficult, even impossible task to decouple "violence" and "truth." I sometimes think that they are irrevocably hardwired together into the circuitry of our culture. But even if they cannot be simply decoupled, their relationship to each other can still most certainly be analyzed more subtly rather than being simply taken for granted.

As I discussed the reception of the Cassie Bernall martyrdom story, I highlighted some examples where commentators felt queasy about the purported kitsch quality of the commemoration of the Columbine martyr, privileging instead a more ancient and perduring martyrological tradition grounded in a respectable, time-tested history and an institutionally situated spiritual discipline. As I reflect upon the ambivalence inspired by the traditions traced here, I wonder whether this comparison and contrast are quite apt. For if the emergence of Cassie Bernall as an American martyr is indeed no more than a flash in the pan of superficial, quick-fix American self-help, then it is simply of no consequence; it does not require analysis, interpretation, or engagement. But just so, if it is so ephemeral, then it is not the potential source of danger that the more institutionally grounded version of martyrdom is—and so one should hardly expend energy defending the staid, venerable, and ancient tradition against the potential influence of the kitschiness of Cassie. One should rather worry about the staid, venerable, and ancient tradition that insists that death is a meaning-producing event, that truth and violence inexorably imply each other—and that, indeed, the first requires the second. My argument, in contrast to those who would marginalize or trivialize the Cassie Bernall example, is that the two examples are actually profoundly linked, and that this link invites—demands—careful and ongoing ethical analysis and exploration. The memory of martyrdom, I have argued, lies at the heart of a certain practice of culture making, and it remains an urgent task to continue to engage the complex and multifaceted effects by which meaning is generated out of suffering.

EPILOGUE

To participate in the preservation of the memory of martyrdom is to enter into a discourse that lionizes suffering in its most extreme forms: suffering endured in the service of an idea and/or a communal identity; suffering undertaken willingly or, perhaps more accurately, through the sublimation of the will to that of another; suffering that requires an audience and an interpretation.[1] The discourse of martyrdom is also a discourse of power, which is why anxieties emerge about the creation of martyrs in contemporary political situations, particularly when the state exercises its power to take life, whether through capital punishment or through military engagement. I write these words in the early twenty-first century in the United States, a nation especially attuned to the power of the martyr's narrative, a nation that has made the martyr's story a cornerstone in the edifice of its own social formation.[2] I made some notes for this framing of the problem of "the martyr" in the summer of 2001, in the days following the execution of Timothy McVeigh for the April 1995 bombing of the federal building in Oklahoma City, an execution that, commentators were at great pains to reassure the public (and, perhaps, themselves), did not constitute a martyrdom. At almost the same time, a federal jury became deadlocked over a death sentence for a man convicted of participating in the 1998 bombing of the U.S. embassy in Nairobi, Kenya, resulting in a penalty of life imprisonment. In court, the jury's forewoman explained that ten of the jurors believed that "executing [Mohamed Rashed Daoud] al-'Owhali could make him a martyr."[3] In both cases, the power dynamics of state-sponsored violence and the question of how that violence and resulting death come to be narrated and interpreted and *remembered* are at the heart of the public discussion. Whether one insists that one execution *is not* a martyrdom or whether one worries that another execution *might become* a martyrdom, both gestures are concerned with containing and controlling the potentially unruly and multiple meanings of violence.

Several months after the execution of McVeigh and the sentencing of al-'Owhali came a Tuesday morning whose unfolding events would place the ambivalent figure of "the martyr" at center stage: September 11, 2001. On that day, nineteen men who understood themselves to be soldier-martyrs commandeered four commercial airliners and crashed two of them into the World Trade Center in New York City, my home; the other two also crashed, one into the Pentagon and the other in the Pennsylvania countryside. In the wake of these events, the language of heroism, of selfless giving of one's own life for others, entered our daily discourse in New York as the city mourned the deaths of more than three hundred fire fighters and police officers engaged in acts of rescue. In the weeks and months afterwards, I found myself incapable of complete ironic distance from this language. Like so many residents of New York City, I too was drawn into the particularity of loss and the attempts to render suffering meaningful, attempts materialized in makeshift handmade shrines in front of firehouses and in other public spaces around the city. At the same time, having worked on the double-edged character of martyrological language and commemoration for such a long time, I was also struck by the ease with which the language of heroism and cowardice (with all their gendered qualities intact) had come to frame the situation. I am in a state of heightened awareness concerning the powers and dangers of the discourse of martyrdom and the degree to which the contestation over martyrological identities can slip so easily into paralyzing absolutes. I am also deeply conscious of my country's capacity to commemorate its own losses and suffering, an ability nearly always paired with its ethically challenged correlate: the inability to put a human face on the loss and suffering of others. I do not pretend that my current project on early Christian martyrdom and collective memory will (or should) have a direct impact on the contemporary situation, but I remain very aware of both the contemporary global discourses of "martyrdom" and of the particular Americanization of this category. Both of these dimensions of the current situation function as part of the broad context within which I do my work. And, as the last chapter of this book showed, the critical links between early Christian antiquity and contemporary American discourses of martyrdom compel one to grapple with the ongoing legacy of what might otherwise seem to be a remote past.

The discourse of martyrdom is never merely a simple assertion of subjectivity nor the easily charted redemptive and meaning-generating interpretation of the raw data of innocent suffering. Martyrdom generates its own self-authorizing claims to a privileged status in relation to truth and public authority. One could generate multiple historical and contemporary examples. With the rise of politicized Christianity in the United States in the latter part of the twentieth century came a wellspring of martyr language. The politically right-wing Christian Coalition mastered the use of the language of religious persecution and martyrdom to deflect and defuse virtually any critique lodged by any opponents of its theocratic political project. During his campaign for the Republican nomination for the presidency in 1996, Pat Buchanan and his family often had recourse to the silencing accusation of "anti-Catholicism" and "persecution of Christians" as a kind of blanket protection against critique. Meanwhile, during that same year, a *New York Times* article on the fledgling left-leaning Christian social justice movement, Call to Renewal, reported that members of this group had taken to referring to themselves as the " 'catacomb' Christians of the underground" in conscious contrast to the Christian Coalition.[4] Here, the figure of "the martyr" conjures a heightened sense of certainty about the righteousness of one's cause and the favor that God bestows on one's earthly projects.

But the discourse of martyrdom can also be a discourse of deep-seated ambivalence. To call someone a martyr, in this sense, is to accuse them of suffering *too much* or *in the wrong ways*, to accuse them of histrionics, self-absorption, or manipulation. "My habit is to drag myself imperiously through a world that owes me unpayable debts," thinks Adah, the mute daughter in a fictional American missionary family in Barbara Kingsolver's novel about mid-twentieth-century Congo, *The Poisonwood Bible*. "I have long relied on the comforts of martyrdom."[5] Or consider the response I hear frequently in social situations when I say that I am writing a book about martyrs. "Oh," some dry-witted person will quip, "you're writing about my mother."

Martyrs are, then, objects of awe and reverence at some moments, of suspicion and derision at others. They can inspire loyalty and conversion, scorn and contempt. Martyrs inspire anxiety, fear, and loathing precisely because of their refusal of dominant systems of rationality and meaning, whatever they may be. They claim by word and by action allegiance to another realm of signification, one whose provenance is superior and all-encompassing. From the insider's point of view, the martyr is a powerful and irreducible figure, an exemplar and an ideal. The martyr's death promises or threatens a hypernatural generativity: as Tertullian, the early Christian church father put it, the blood of the martyrs constitutes the seeds of the church. From the outsider's point of view, this generativity is a source of anxiety, fear, even loathing. One worries about "making a martyr" of someone and, as a consequence, inspiring devotion and imitation, encouraging extremism and absolutism, and in doing so ultimately producing more martyrs.

In the context of early Christian martyrdom and the broader Roman society in which this idea of martyrdom emerged, the pattern of oscillating perspectives becomes numbing in its repetitiveness. Christians saw the martyrs as a sort of spiritual avant-garde. Romans saw them as annoyingly stubborn refuseniks. In the end, however, the scripts of persecution and martyrdom that were written and enacted in the early Christian centuries and that became the material of Christian collective memory produced versions of Christian identity that would be formative even into the current moment. Such is the combined power of the discourses of martyrdom and memory.

Martyrs inspire ambivalence, anxiety, fear, and loathing because of their radical refusal of the dominant systems of rationality, meaning, and value, which they oppose, but also—and perhaps more tellingly—because of their compulsion to align themselves with power through the paradoxical repudiation of self and will. Hence Kierkegaard can make a haunting and provocative comparison between the tyrant and the martyr, finding their point of commonality in this sense:

> The first form of rulers in the world were "the tyrants," the last will be "the martyrs." In the world's evolution this is the movement . . . from worldliness to religiousness. No doubt there is an infinite difference between a tyrant and martyr, yet they have one thing in common: compulsion. The tyrant, himself with a craving for power, compels by force; the martyr, in himself unconditionally obedient to God, compels through his own sufferings. So the tyrant dies and his rule is over; the martyr dies and his rule begins.[6]

Martyrs' allegiance to their superior realm of signification eclipses the divide between the ideal and the real, between thought and the body. As Françoise Meltzer argues in her recent exploration of the legacy of Joan of Arc in relation to current philosophies of subjectivity, the fascination with martyrs on the part of certain contemporary philosophers involves the apparent promise that they represent: the possibility of the recuperation of the metaphysics and experience of a seamlessness between body and idea.[7]

The people who hijacked the planes on September 11 apparently saw themselves as martyrs, dying for their cause. We are unsettled by this claim both because it undermines the sacrosanct character of the category of "martyrdom" and because we want to argue that theirs is not a martyr's death since they killed themselves and others in the pursuit of this sacred status. Their claim to a martyr's death, we want to argue, is both illegitimate and perverse. But if the nineteen hijackers were simply mass murderers and not martyrs, their perversion of the term "martyr" nevertheless points to the ethical danger embedded in the category itself. For the willingness to sacrifice the self can all too easily morph into the willingness to sacrifice the other. As Talal Asad puts it in a rather different rhetorical context, writing of the role of European Christianity in the colonial project, "in a tradition that connects pain with achievement, the inflicting of suffering on others is not in itself reprehensible: it is to be condemned only when it is gratuitous—where the pain as means is out of proportion to an objective end."[8] *In a tradition that connects pain with achievement, the inflicting of suffering on others is not in itself reprehensible.* Here is one critical place where the double-edged logic of martyrdom comes chillingly into view, and no tradition that makes such a connection should be exempt from the critical scrutiny that the ethical implications and material effects of such a claim demand.

But there are other ways in which the figure of the martyr raises ethical questions and dilemmas.[9] The elevation of the martyr, his or her idealization, can have the disarming effect of rendering the victim of suffering him- or herself beyond the human while at the same time calling the suffering and ontological value of others facilely into question. The "martyr"—and her cousin, "the hero"—emerge sometimes too easily as romanticized, sentimentalized figures impervious to the painful realities of human frailty and ambivalence, indemnified against critique, immune to notions of the tragic or the accidental, invulnerable to the meaninglessness that dogs the very notion of death. The violence suffered by the martyr comes to be glorified and spectacularized, rendering suffering itself a necessary component of their stories—and undermining sustainable critiques of the fact of suffering itself and the conditions that generate and nurture that suffering. The lionizing of the martyr's suffering, codified in the attributions of "innocence" and "guilt," magnifies that suffering to such an extent that those who are charged with responsibility for engendering it lose their claim to their own humanness. In conventional early Christian martyr stories, the inhumanity of the human persecutors is a narrative trope in a melodrama in which moral choice is infinitely displaced, where the abstracted compulsion to good or evil effaces the will in all the dramatic players, and where those who inflict violence become simply placeholders for demonic forces, narrative embodiments of "the enemy," the devil himself. The other side of the elevation of the martyr to a level beyond the human is, in other words, the degradation of the one responsible for her suffering to a level below the human. Such an imaginative move allows us to focus on the glamorized suffering of the martyr and simultaneously rationalize the inhuman treatment suffered by those thought to be responsible for her fate. In the current U.S. situation, post–September 11, the discourse of martyrdom allows us to turn our gaze away from the people of Afghanistan; the prisoners incarcerated at Camp X-Ray in Guantánamo Bay, Cuba; the people of Iraq; and countless others whose deaths and suffering are rendered invisible or illegible to us. We must ask what kind of ethical narrative of suffering is being written here.[10]

I want to be very clear about the claims I am making here. In no way do I mean to minimize the terrible losses of life that occurred in New York, in Washington, and in Pennsylvania on September 11th, nor to dishonor the world-shattering grief that thousands have experienced as a result. Nor do I intend to call into question the many acts of solidarity and bravery that most certainly took place on that day. But what I want to suggest is that we have some choices about how we craft the stories that we tell about those losses, that suffering, and the fortitude and fierceness by which some people negotiated their ideas about self and other on that day. We also have some choices about how to acknowledge those who experienced fear, who fell apart, who died unawares and instantaneously. And we have some choices about how we frame our ethical response to these terrible losses and about how we rationalize, deny, or numb ourselves to the violence that intensifies around us daily, using the narrative of suffering on September 11th as its touchstone and its justification.

It is out of this line of thinking that I want to pursue the notion that a reconceptualization of the very category of "religion"—a set of performances that interrupts the everyday and seeks to create occasions for paying attention—can function generatively in the current situation precisely because "religion" can serve as a critical theory of suffering. Hent de Vries opens his book, *Religion and Violence*, with this argument:

> "Religion" is the relation between the self (or some selves) and the other—some Other—a relation that, as Levinas has suggested, does not close itself off in a conceptual totality (or does so only arbitrarily, i.e., violently) and thus at least in part escapes human autonomy, voluntary decision, and so on. By the same token, "religion" also stands for the other—*the* Other—of violence. It evokes its counterimage, its opposite, redemption, and critique.[11]

I would supplement this paradoxical articulation of the figure of "religion" by suggesting that it might be useful to consider the ways in which "religion" serves—among other things—as a critical theory of suffering. As such, it generates a range of responses to suffering—urging its endurance, providing practices for its elimination, creating frameworks for its interpretation. Putting it this way keeps in view two competing aspects of the relationship between religion, violence, and suffering: on the one hand, religion's capacity to illuminate suffering, to focus our attention on it, to provide practices for tending to it and for critiquing the conditions that bring it into being—on the other hand, religion's capacity to rationalize suffering, to inscribe it with divine sanctions, to blunt the impulse to alleviate it.[12]

Likewise, the figure of the "martyr" might also be reconfigured in light of the ethical problematics I've already raised. What if, for example, we retrieved an older resonance of the term "martyr" and chose not to focus on the willful, the willing, the will-sublimating sacrifice of self (a sacrifice that can too easily, in its logic, enable a sacrifice of the other); what if we chose not to privilege this particular dimension of the semantic field for the term? What if, instead, we retrieved and critically engaged the dimension of the term that emphasizes a different range of ethical options: witnessing, truth-telling, testimony? What I want to suggest is that the overprivileging of the self-sacrificial dimensions of the "martyr" results in a flattening out, the dangerous eclipsing of the possibility of recognizing the suffering of others. Focusing on "the martyrs" as those who willingly give up their lives keeps our attention converged on the narrowest category of victims, and may keep us from seeing those who do not give their lives willingly—those who just showed up for work one day; those who do not die in the spectacle of a terrorist attack but nevertheless are just as dead when caught in the systemic violence and routinized everydayness of grinding poverty, in the searing crossfire of political conflict riddling the bodies of the refugee or the ethnically cleansed, in the ordinary and terrible violence that both characterizes the lives of so much of the world and overwhelms our capacity to apprehend and assimilate its scope and its depth. Perhaps the figure of "the martyr" that we need to mobilize here is not the one who sacrifices him- or herself but the one whose compulsion is to witness and to provide testimony. Such a figure of martyrdom calls all of us into its service, demanding that we see and testify to the real losses and suffering that took place on September 11th, but that we do not do so at the cost of rendering ourselves unable to recognize and witness to suffering elsewhere. For our September 11th is not the only September 11th (we must also think of Chile, 1973), nor is this particular date the only one stained with the blood of thousands (we must think of other dates and other places: Srebrenica, July 1995; Rwanda, April–June 1994). The list could expand infinitely.

Neither of the gestures of reimagination that I suggest here—reimagining religion as a critical theory of suffering or martyrdom as a program of witnessing and providing testimony—is offered as anything but a provisional and partial response to the ethical challenges of our current situation. Yet both terms have the capacity to serve as powerful elements in a working lexicon, representing some ways by which we might make provisional and generative meaning out of losses that exceed our capacity to narrate them completely and our ability to absorb them fully.

NOTES

INTRODUCTION

1. Michel de Certeau, *The Writing of History*, trans. Tom Conley (New York: Columbia University Press, 1988), 85, writes of history as the impossibility of this bridging, "the means of representing a difference." For historiography as "the touch across time," see Carolyn Dinshaw, *Getting Medieval: Sexualities and Communities, Pre- and Postmodern* (Durham, N.C.: Duke University Press, 1999).

2. See, for example, Peter Brown, *The Cult of the Saints: Its Rise and Function in Latin Christianity* (Chicago: University of Chicago Press, 1981); and, more recently, Robin Darling Young, *In Procession Before the World: Martyrdom as Public Liturgy in Early Christianity*, The Père Marquette Lecture in Theology, 2001 (Milwaukee, Wis.: Marquette University Press, 2001).

3. The intersections of gender and collective memory have recently been explored with theoretical sophistication and subtlety in Marianne Hirsch and Valerie Smith, eds., "Gender and Cultural Memory," special issue of *Signs* 28, no. 1 (Autumn 2002): 1–479.

4. Joan Wallach Scott, *Gender and the Politics of History* (New York: Columbia University Press, 1988), 28–50, quotation at 42.

5. Important works from the last decade or so include: Jan Willem van Henten, Boudewijn Dehandschutter, and J. W. van der Klaauw, eds., *Die Entstehung der jüdischen Martyrologie*, Studia post-Biblica 38 (Leiden: Brill, 1989); Paul-Albert Février, "Martyre et sainteté," in *Les fonctions des saints dans le monde occidental (IIIe–XIIIe siècle): Actes du colloque organisé par l'École Française de Rome avec le concours de l'Université de Rome "La Sapienza", 27–29 octobre 1988* (Rome: École Française de Rome, 1991), 51–80; Maureen A. Tilley, "The Ascetic Body and the (Un)Making of the World of the Martyr," *JAAR* 59 (1991): 467–79; Arthur J. Droge and James D. Tabor, *A Noble Death: Suicide and Martyrdom Among Christians and Jews in Antiquity* (San Francisco: HarperSan Francisco, 1992); Everett Ferguson, "Early Christian Martyrdom and Civil Disobedience," *JECS* 1 (1993): 73–83; Carlin A. Barton, "Savage Miracles: Redemption

of Lost Honor in Roman Society and the Sacrament of the Gladiator and the Martyr," *Representations* 45 (1994): 41–71; G. W. Bowersock, *Martyrdom and Rome* (Cambridge: Cambridge University Press, 1995); Virginia Burrus, "Reading Agnes: The Rhetoric of Gender in Ambrose and Prudentius," *JECS* 3 (1995): 25–46; David Goodblatt, "Suicide in the Sanctuary: Traditions on Priestly Martyrdom," *JJS* 46 (1995): 10–29; M. Lamberigts and P. van Deun, eds., *Martyrium in Multidisciplinary Perspective: Memorial Louis Reekmans* (Leuven: Leuven University Press/Peeters, 1995); Judith Perkins, *The Suffering Self: Pain and Narrative Representation in the Early Christian Era* (New York: Routledge, 1995); Brent D. Shaw, "Body/Power/Identity: Passions of the Martyrs," *JECS* 4 (1996): 269–312; Gillian Clark, "Bodies and Blood: Late Antique Debate on Martyrdom, Virginity, and Resurrection," in *Changing Bodies, Changing Meanings: Studies on the Human Body in Antiquity*, ed. Dominic Montserrat (New York: Routledge, 1997), 99–115; Jan Willem van Henten, *The Maccabean Martyrs as Saviours of the Jewish People: A Study of 2 and 4 Maccabees*, Supplements to the Journal for the Study of Judaism 57 (Leiden: Brill, 1997); Tessa Rajak, "Dying for the Law: The Martyr's Portrait in Jewish-Greek Literature," in *Portraits: Biographical Representation in the Greek and Latin Literature of the Roman Empire*, ed. M. J. Edwards and Simon Swain (Oxford: Clarendon Press, 1997), 39–67; Aryeh Cohen, "Toward an Erotics of Martyrdom," *Journal of Jewish Thought and Philosophy* 7 (1998): 227–56; Daniel Boyarin, *Dying for God: Martyrdom and the Making of Christianity and Judaism* (Stanford: Stanford University Press, 1999).

6. See, for example, Susan L. Mizruchi, ed., *Religion and Cultural Studies* (Princeton, N.J.: Princeton University Press, 2001).

1. COLLECTIVE MEMORY AND THE MEANINGS OF THE PAST

1. Elaine Scarry, *The Body in Pain: The Making and Unmaking of the World* (New York: Oxford University Press, 1985).

2. The bibliography here is quite extensive. See the recent survey article by Jeffrey K. Olick and Joyce Robbins, "Social Memory Studies: From 'Collective Memory' to the Historical Sociology of Mnemonic Practices," *Annual Review of Sociology* 24 (1998): 105–40. Also see Barbie Zelizer, "Reading the Past Against the Grain: The Shape of Memory Studies," *Studies in Mass Communication* 12 (1995): 214–39. For a suggestive study of religion as a particularly apt setting for collective memory, see Danièle Hervieu-Léger, *La religion pour mémoire* (Paris: Editions du Cerf, 1993), trans. Simon Lee as *Religion as a Chain of Memory* (New Brunswick: Rutgers University Press, 2000).

3. Halbwachs is certainly not completely alone in exploring such ideas. Cultural and art historian Aby Warburg, for example, worked with a notion of *soziales Gedächtnis* (social memory), though he did not present a systematic explication of his ideas. A brief treatment of his ideas may be found in Kurt W. Forster, "Aby Warburg's History of Art: Collective Memory and the Social Mediation of Images," *Daedalus* 105, no.1 (Winter 1976): 169–76. For further bibliography on Warburg, see Alon Confino, "Collective Memory and Cultural History: Problems of Method," *AHR* 102 (1997): 1390n11.

4. The relationship between individual and collective consciousness and psychology is addressed specifically in two essays by Halbwachs: "Individual Psychology and

Collective Psychology," *American Sociological Review* 3 (1938): 615–23; and "Individual Consciousness and Collective Mind," *American Journal of Sociology* 44 (1939): 812–22. See also Patrick H. Hutton, "Collective Memory and Collective Mentalities: The Halbwachs-Ariès Connection," *Historical Reflections/Réflexions Historiques* 15, no. 2 (1988): 311–22.

5. Maurice Halbwachs, *Les cadres sociaux de la mémoire* (Paris: Librairie Félix Alcan, 1925; new ed., Paris: Presses Universitaires de France, 1952; repr., Paris: Mouton, 1975). Portions of this text have been translated into English and appear in Maurice Halbwachs, *On Collective Memory*, ed. and trans. Lewis A. Coser (Chicago: University of Chicago Press, 1992), 37–189.

6. Maurice Halbwachs, *La topographie légendaire des évangiles en terre sainte: Étude de mémoire collective* (Paris: Presses Universitaires de France, 1941). The conclusion appears in English translation in Halbwachs, *On Collective Memory*, 193–235.

7. Maurice Halbwachs, *La mémoire collective* (Paris: Presses Universitaires de France, 1950; 2nd rev. aug. ed., 1968), trans. Francis J. Ditter, Jr. and Vida Yazdi Ditter as *The Collective Memory* (New York: Harper & Row, 1980).

8. Halbwachs, *Cadres sociaux*, 144; *On Collective Memory*, 53. Paul Connerton picks up on the embodied (ritual and performative) dimensions of social memory in his *How Societies Remember* (New York: Cambridge University Press, 1989). One could make more explicit here the point that language might be visual as well as verbal. That is, memory can be preserved in/as narrative, but that narrative can be evoked in images or recalled in a linguistic/literary mode. On image as a privileged mode of premodern memory—albeit images organized in order to be "read" in what Dante called "the book of memory"—see Mary Carruthers, *The Book of Memory: A Study of Memory in Medieval Culture*, Cambridge Studies in Medieval Literature 10 (New York: Cambridge University Press, 1990), esp. 16–45.

9. This emphasis on tradition appears in a range of related works. See especially Eric J. Hobsbawm and Terence O. Ranger, eds., *The Invention of Tradition* (Cambridge: Cambridge University Press, 1983); David Lowenthal, *The Past is a Foreign Country* (Cambridge: Cambridge University Press, 1985); and works on oral history (cited below in note 56).

10. In this study, I tend to use "collective memory" and "social memory" interchangeably. For a discussion of the terminology, see Olick and Robbins, "Social Memory Studies."

11. Henri Bergson, *Matter and Memory*, trans. N. M. Paul and W. S. Palmer (New York: Zone Books, 1988).

12. Halbwachs, *On Collective Memory*, 84; *Cadres sociaux*, 178.

13. Halbwachs, *On Collective Memory*, 86; *Cadres sociaux*, 186.

14. Karl Galinsky, *Augustan Culture* (Princeton, N.J.: Princeton University Press, 1996), 288–331; Paul Zanker, *The Power of Images in the Age of Augustus*, trans. Alan Shapiro (Ann Arbor: University of Michigan Press, 1990), esp. 101–238; Alexandre Grandazzi, *The Foundation of Rome: Myth and History*, trans. Jane Marie Todd (Ithaca, N.Y.: Cornell University Press, 1997), esp. part 3 ("And Rome Became a City . . ."), 125–211; Catherine Edwards, *Writing Rome: Textual Approaches to the City* (New York: Cambridge University Press, 1996).

208 1. COLLECTIVE MEMORY AND THE MEANINGS OF THE PAST

15. The rabbis, for example, associated rabbinic authority with the Sinai revelation through the "chain of tradition." See *'Abot* 1:1; *'Abot R. Nat.* a1; Elias Bickermann, "La chaîne de la tradition pharisienne," *RB* 59 (1952): 44–54. For general overview, also see Anthony J. Saldarini, *Scholastic Rabbinism: A Literary Study of the Fathers According to Rabbi Nathan,* BJS 14 (Chico, Calif.: Scholars Press, 1982), 9–10, 67–78; Steven D. Fraade, *From Tradition to Commentary: Torah and Its Interpretation in the Midrash Sifre to Deuteronomy* (Albany, N.Y.: SUNY Press, 1991), 70–75; Shaye J. D. Cohen, *The Beginnings of Judaism: Boundaries, Varieties, Uncertainties* (Berkeley: University of California Press, 1999). On collective memory and its authorizing return to origins, also see Yosef Hayim Yerushalmi, *Zakhor: Jewish History and Jewish Memory* (Seattle: University of Washington Press, 1982).

16. Burton L. Mack, *A Myth of Innocence: Mark and Christian Origins* (Philadelphia: Fortress Press, 1988); and Burton L. Mack, *Who Wrote the New Testament? The Making of the Christian Myth* (San Francisco: Harper, 1995); Elizabeth A. Castelli and Hal Taussig, eds., *Reimagining Christian Origins: A Colloquium Honoring Burton L. Mack* (Valley Forge, Penn.: Trinity Press International, 1996); Averil Cameron, *Christianity and the Rhetoric of Empire: The Development of Christian Discourse,* Sather Classical Lectures 55 (Berkeley: University of California Press, 1991).

17. The literature on Christian apologetic is extensive. Two important, recent contributions are: Bernard Pouderon and Joseph Doré, eds., *Les apologistes chrétiens et la culture grecque,* ThH 105 (Paris: Beauchesne, 1998); Mark J. Edwards, Martin Goodman, S. R. F. Price, and Christopher Rowland, eds., *Apologetics in the Roman Empire: Pagans, Jews, and Christians* (Oxford: Clarendon Press, 1999).

18. Peter Brown, *The Cult of the Saints: Its Rise and Function in Latin Christianity* (Chicago: University of Chicago Press, 1981), 81, refers to a related version of this collapsing of time in the narrative and liturgical repetitions within the martyr cults as a concertina effect. See also Elizabeth A. Castelli, "Visions and Voyeurism: Holy Women and the Politics of Sight in Early Christianity," in *Protocol of the Colloquy of the Center for Hermeneutical Studies,* n.s., 2, ed. Christopher Ocker (Berkeley: Center for Hermeneutical Studies, 1994), 9; Daniel Boyarin, *Dying for God: Martyrdom and the Making of Christianity and Judaism* (Stanford: Stanford University Press, 1999), 111. In a similar characterization, Yerushalmi observes, "Unlike the biblical writers the rabbis seem to play with time as though with an accordion, expanding and collapsing it at will" (17).

19. Halbwachs, *On Collective Memory,* 90; *Cadres sociaux,* 190.

20. Halbwachs, *On Collective Memory,* 91; *Cadres sociaux,* 191.

21. Halbwachs, *On Collective Memory,* 91; *Cadres sociaux,* 191; emphasis mine.

22. Halbwachs, *Cadres sociaux,* 114–45; pages 143–45 are translated in Halbwachs, *On Collective Memory,* 52–53 (note error in editor's citation at the bottom of 52).

23. Ernest Renan, *Vie de Jesus,* Histoire des origines du christianisme 1 (Paris: M. Levy frères, 1863), 22nd ed., rev. and aug. (Paris: Calmann Levy, 1893). See also Ernest Renan, *Oeuvres complètes,* 7th ed., ed. Henriette Psichari, vol. 4 (Paris: Calmann-Levy, 1947). Renan's work, it should be noted, also contributed to racializing discourses that played a critical role in nineteenth century scholarship on biblical history. See Maurice Olender, *The Languages of Paradise: Race, Religion, and Philology in the Nineteenth*

Century, trans. Arthur Goldhammer (Cambridge, Mass.: Harvard University Press, 1992), 51–81. See now Shawn Kelley, *Racializing Jesus: Race, Ideology, and the Formation of Modern Biblical Scholarship* (New York: Routledge, 2002), 82–87.

24. Ever since Albert Schweitzer, *The Quest of the Historical Jesus: A Critical Study of Its Progress from Reimarus to Wrede*, trans. W. Montgomery (New York: Macmillan, 1961), originally published in German, 1906.

25. Halbwachs, *On Collective Memory*, 194; *Topographie légendaire*, 150.

26. Halbwachs, *On Collective Memory*, 214; *Topographie légendaire*, 177.

27. Halbwachs, *On Collective Memory*, 199; *Topographie légendaire*, 156–57.

28. Mitchell B. Merback, *The Thief, the Cross, and the Wheel: Pain and the Spectacle of Punishment in Medieval and Renaissance Europe* (Chicago: University of Chicago Press, 1998), 54, notes a similar kind of temporal and geographical displacement for medieval viewers of art representing the passion of Jesus, as if they, as viewers, were on pilgrimage. For nineteenth- and twentieth-century American versions of this imaginative displacement, see Burke O. Long, *Imagining the Holy Land: Maps, Models, and Fantasy Travels* (Bloomington: Indiana University Press, 2003).

29. Halbwachs, *On Collective Memory*, 216; *Topographie légendaire*, 180.

30. Halbwachs, *On Collective Memory*, 94–95; *Cadres sociaux*, 194–95.

31. Pierre Nora, ed., *Les lieux de mémoire*, 3 vols. (Paris: Gallimard, 1984–1992); see also Pierre Nora, "Between Memory and History: *Les lieux de mémoire*," *Representations* 26 (1989): 7–25.

32. Halbwachs, *On Collective Memory*, 204–5; *Topographie légendaire*, 164.

33. Halbwachs, *On Collective Memory*, 205; *Topographie légendaire*, 165.

34. Halbwachs, *On Collective Memory*, 106; *Cadres sociaux*, 207.

35. The image of "natural selection" (drawn from the theory of evolution) to which collective memory is subject may also be found in Yerushalmi, *Zakhor*, 95: "Certain memories live on; the rest are winnowed out, repressed, or simply discarded by a process of natural selection which the historian, uninvited, disturbs and reverses."

36. Halbwachs, *On Collective Memory*, 95; *Cadres sociaux*, 195.

37. Halbwachs, *La mémoire collective*, 35–79; *The Collective Memory*, 50–87.

38. Halbwachs, *The Collective Memory*, 84; *La mémoire collective*, 75.

39. Marc Bloch, "Mémoire collective, tradition et coutume," *Revue de Synthèse Historique* 40 (1925): 73–83. For the importance of Strasbourg as an institutional home for Halbwachs's work, see John E. Craig, "Maurice Halbwachs à Strasbourg," *Revue française de sociologie* 20 (1979): 273–92.

40. Roger Bastide, "Mémoire collective et sociologie du bricolage," *L'année sociologique*, 3rd ser., 21 (1970): 82–83, translation mine.

41. James Fentress and Chris Wickham, *Social Memory* (Cambridge: Blackwell, 1992), ix. This passage is also quoted in Olick and Robbins, "Social Memory Studies," 111. See also a similar critique levelled by Noa Gedi and Yigal Elam, "Collective Memory—What Is It?" *History and Memory* 8 (Spring/Summer 1996): 30–50.

42. Assmann, *Das kulturelle Gedächtnis: Schrift, Erinnerung und politische Identität in frühen Hochkulturen* (Munich: C. H. Beck, 1992). See also Jan Assmann, "Collective Memory and Cultural Identity," trans. John Czaplicka, *New German Critique* 65 (Spring/Summer 1995): 125–33, originally published as: "Kollektives Gedächtnis und

kulturelle Identität," in *Kultur und Gedächtnis*, ed. Jan Assmann and Tonio Hölscher (Frankfurt am Main: Suhrkamp, 1988), 9–19. On memory and culture more generally, see Otto Gerhard Oexle, ed., *Memoria als Kultur*, Veröffentlichungen des Max-Planck-Instituts für Geschichte 121 (Göttingen: Vandenhoeck & Ruprecht, 1995), esp. Oexle's introduction, "Memoria als Kultur," 9–78. Sociologists Jeffrey Olick and Joyce Robbins, meanwhile, propose "social memory" and resist the potential difficulties of reification embodied in the term "collective memory" through a focus on memory performances or, as they term them, "mnemonic practices." See their "Social Memory Studies," cited above. The problem of reification is engaged and helpfully disrupted by sociologist Peter Hejl in his "Wie Gesellschaften Erfahrungen machen, oder: Was Gesellschaftstheorie zum Verständnis des Gedächtnisproblems beitragen kann," in *Gedächtnis: Probleme und Perspektiven der interdisziplinären Gedächtnisforschung*, ed. Siegfried J. Schmidt (Frankfurt: Suhrkamp, 1991), 293–336. For a brief discussion of Hejl's project, see Gerdien Jonker, *The Topography of Remembrance: The Dead, Tradition, and Collective Memory in Mesopotamia*, SHR 68 (Leiden: Brill, 1995), 22–23.

43. Olick and Robbins, "Social Memory Studies," 112.

44. The literature concerning memory and historic events in the twentieth century is wide-ranging. For general theoretical treatments, see James W. Pennebaker, Darío Páez, and Bernard Rimé, *Collective Memory of Political Events: Social Psychological Perspectives* (Mahwah, N.J.: Lawrence Erlbaum Associates, 1997); Theodore Plantinga, *How Memory Shapes Narratives: A Philosophical Essay on Redeeming the Past* (Lewiston, N.Y.: Edwin Mellen Press, 1992); Marea C. Teski and Jacob J. Climo, eds., *The Labyrinth of Memory: Ethnographic Journeys* (Westport, Conn.: Bergin & Garvey, 1995); Iwona Irwin-Zarecka, *Frames of Remembrance: The Dynamics of Collective Memory* (New Brunswick, N.J.: Transaction Publishers, 1994); Thomas Butler, ed., *Memory: History, Culture, and the Mind* (New York: Basil Blackwell, 1989). On World War I, see Paul Fussell, *The Great War and Modern Memory* (New York: Oxford University Press, 1975); Jay Winter, *Sites of Memory, Sites of Mourning: The Great War in European Cultural History* (New York: Cambridge University Press, 1995); George L. Mosse, *Fallen Soldiers: Reshaping the Memory of the World Wars* (New York: Oxford University Press, 1990). On the Spanish Civil War, see Paloma Aguilar, *Collective Memory of the Spanish Civil War: The Case of the Political Amnesty in the Spanish Transition to Democracy* (Madrid: Centro de Estudios Avanzados en Ciencias Sociales, Instituto Juan March de Estudios e Investigaciones, 1996). On the Shoah as a point of entry, see the important work of James E. Young, *Writing and Rewriting the Holocaust: Narrative and the Consequences of Interpretation* (Bloomington: Indiana University Press, 1988); *The Texture of Memory: Holocaust Memorials and Meaning* (New Haven, Conn.: Yale University Press, 1993); *The Art of Memory: Holocaust Memorials in History* (New York: Prestel, 1994); *At Memory's Edge: After-Images of the Holocaust in Contemporary Art and Architecture* (New Haven, Conn.: Yale University Press, 2000). See also Jeffrey Olick and Daniel Levy, "Collective Memory and Cultural Constraint: Holocaust Myth and Rationality in German Politics," *American Sociological Review* 62 (1997): 921–36; Mark Osiel, *Mass Atrocity, Collective Memory, and the Law* (New Brunswick, N.J.: Transaction Publishers, 1997); Lawrence L. Langer, *Holocaust Testimonies: The Ruins of Memory* (New Haven, Conn.: Yale University Press, 1991); Ronald J. Berger, *Constructing a Collective*

Memory of the Holocaust: A Life History of Two Brothers' Survival (Boulder: University Press of Colorado, 1995); Yael Zerubavel, "The 'Death of Memory' and the Memory of Death: Masada and the Holocaust as Historical Metaphors," *Representations* 45 (1994): 72–100; and several contributions in Mieke Bal, Jonathan Crewe, and Leo Spitzer, eds., *Acts of Memory: Cultural Recall in the Present* (Hanover, N.H.: Dartmouth College/University Press of New England, 1999). On World War II, see Ian Buruma, *The Wages of Guilt: Memories of War in Germany and Japan* (New York: Farrar, Straus, Giroux, 1994). On the dropping of the atomic bomb in 1945, see Lisa Yoneyama, *Hiroshima Traces: Time, Space, and the Dialectics of Memory* (Berkeley: University of California Press, 1999); J. W. Dower, "The Bombed: Hiroshimas and Nagasakis in Japanese Memory," *Diplomatic History* 19 (1995): 275–95; J. Samuel Walker, "History, Collective Memory, and the Decision to Use the Bomb," *Diplomatic History* 19 (1995): 319–28; Laura Hein and Mark Selden, "Commemoration and Silence: Fifty Years of Remembering the Bomb in America and Japan," in *Living with the Bomb: American and Japanese Cultural Conflict in the Nuclear Age*, ed. Laura Hein and Mark Selden (Armonk, N.Y.: M. E. Sharpe, 1997), 3–34; Michael Perlman, *Imaginal Memory and the Place of Hiroshima* (Albany, N.Y.: SUNY Press, 1988). On Vietnam, see Thomas D. Beamish, Harvey Molotch, and Richard Flacks, "Who Supports the Troops? Vietnam, the Gulf War, and the Making of Collective Memory," *Social Problems* 42 (1995): 344–60; Marita Sturken, "The Wall, the Screen, and the Image: The Vietnam Veterans Memorial," *Representations* 35 (1991): 118–42; Marita Sturken, *Tangled Memories: The Vietnam War, the AIDS Epidemic, and the Politics of Remembering* (Berkeley: University of California Press, 1997); and Kristin Ann Hass, *Carried to the Wall: American Memory and the Vietnam Veterans Memorial* (Berkeley: University of California Press, 1998). On twentieth-century American history, see Arthur G. Neal, *National Trauma and Collective Memory: Major Events in the American Century* (Armonk, N.Y.: M. E. Sharpe, 1998); Barbie Zelizer, *Covering the Body: The Kennedy Assassination, the Media, and the Shaping of Collective Memory* (Chicago: University of Chicago Press, 1992); Thomas J. Johnson, *The Rehabilitation of Richard Nixon: The Media's Effect on Collective Memory* (New York: Garland, 1995); Michael Schudson, *Watergate in American Memory: How We Remember, Forget, and Reconstruct the Past* (New York: Basic Books, 1992); David Thelen, "Memory and American History," *Journal of American History* 75 (1989): 1117–29.

45. Again, the literature is wide-ranging here. See, for some examples: Nora, *Les lieux de mémoire*; Riki van Boeschoten, *From Armatolik to People's Rule: Investigation into the Collective Memory of Rural Greece, 1750–1949* (Amsterdam: A.M. Hakkert, 1991); Barry Schwartz, Yael Zerubavel, and Bernice M. Barnett, "The Recovery of Masada: A Study in Collective Memory," *Sociological Quarterly* 27 (1986): 147–64; Yael Zerubavel, *Recovered Roots: Collective Memory and the Making of Israeli National Tradition* (Chicago: University of Chicago Press, 1995); Nachman Ben-Yehuda, *The Masada Myth: Collective Memory and Mythmaking in Israel* (Madison: University of Wisconsin Press, 1995); Edward M. Bruner and Phyllis Gorfain, "Dialogic Narration and the Paradoxes of Masada," in *Text, Play, and Story: The Construction and Reconstruction of the Self and Society*, ed. Stuart Plattner and Edward M. Bruner (Washington, D.C.: American Ethnological Society, 1984), 56–75; Jonathan Boyarin, *Storm from*

Paradise: The Politics of Jewish Memory (Minneapolis: University of Minnesota Press, 1992); Jonathan Boyarin, ed., *Remapping Memory: The Politics of TimeSpace* (Minneapolis: University of Minnesota Press, 1994); Jean Halperin and Georges Levitte, eds., *Mémoire et histoire: données et debats: Actes du XXVe Colloque des intellectuels juifs de langue française* (Paris: Denoël, 1986); Charles S. Maier, *The Unmasterable Past: History, Holocaust, and the German National Identity* (Cambridge, Mass.: Harvard University Press, 1988); Mahmoud Darwish, *Memory for Forgetfulness: August, Beirut, 1982*, trans. Ibrahim Muhawi (Berkeley: University of California Press, 1982); Ted Swedenburg, *Memories of Revolt: The 1936–1939 Rebellion and the Palestinian National Past* (Minneapolis: University of Minnesota Press, 1995); Michael Kammen, *Mystic Chords of Memory: The Transformation of Tradition in American Culture* (New York: Alfred A. Knopf, 1991); John Bodnar, *Remaking America: Public Memory, Commemoration, and Patriotism in the Twentieth Century* (Princeton, N.J.: Princeton University Press, 1992).

46. Diane L. Barthel, *Historic Preservation: Collective Memory and Historical Identity* (New Brunswick, N.J.: Rutgers University Press, 1996); Michael S. Roth, *The Ironist's Cage: Memory, Trauma, and the Construction of History* (New York: Columbia University Press, 1995); Jaclyn Jeffrey and Glenace Edwall, eds., *Memory and History: Essays on Recalling and Interpreting Experience* (Lanham, Md.: University Press of America, 1994); Geoffrey H. Hartmann, "Public Memory and Modern Experience," *Yale Journal of Criticism* 6 (1993): 239–47; Patrick H. Hutton, *History as an Art of Memory* (Hanover, N.H.: University Press of New England, 1993); Richard Terdiman, *Present Past: Modernity and the Memory Crisis* (Ithaca, N.Y.: Cornell University Press, 1993); Jacques LeGoff, *History and Memory*, trans. Steven Rendall and Elizabeth Claman (New York: Columbia University Press, 1992); Michel de Certeau, *The Writing of History*, trans. Tom Conley (New York: Columbia University Press, 1988); Amos Funkenstein, "Collective Memory and Historical Consciousness," *History and Memory* 1 (1989): 5–26; Jacques LeGoff and Pierre Nora, eds., *Constructing the Past: Essays in Historical Methodology* (New York: Cambridge University Press, 1985).

47. One dramatic example of this can be found in the controversy around the memoir by the Mayan Rigoberta Menchù: *I, Rigoberta Menchù: An Indian Woman in Guatemala* (London: Verso, 1984), a memoir that was challenged by the research of anthropologist David Stoll in his *Rigoberta Menchù and the Story of All Poor Guatemalans* (Boulder, Colo.: Westview, 1999). See an anthology chronicling the controversy in Arturo Arias, ed., *The Rigoberta Menchù Controversy* (Minneapolis: University of Minnesota Press, 2001).

48. Joseph R. Roach, *Cities of the Dead: Circum-Atlantic Performance* (New York: Columbia University Press, 1996); Amritjit Singh, Joseph T. Skerrett Jr., and Robert E. Hogan, eds., *Memory and Cultural Politics: New Approaches to American Ethnic Literatures* (Boston: Northeastern University Press, 1996); Lynne Cooke, Bice Curiger, Greg Hilty, Lynne Richards, and Hayward Gallery, *Doubletake: Collective Memory and Current Art* (London: South Bank Centre, 1992); Philip Kuberski, *The Persistence of Memory: Organism, Myth, Text* (Berkeley: University of California Press, 1992); Susanne Kuchler and Walter Melion, eds., *Images of Memory: On Remembering and Representation* (Washington, D.C.: Smithsonian Institution Press, 1991); William Rowe and Vivian Shelling, *Memory and Modernity: Popular Culture in Latin America* (New York:

Verso, 1991); Eric L. Santner, *Stranded Objects: Mourning, Memory, and Film in Post-war Germany* (Ithaca, N.Y.: Cornell University Press, 1990); David Farrell Krell, *Of Memory, Reminiscence, and Writing: On the Verge* (Bloomington: Indiana University Press, 1990); George Lipsitz, *Time Passages: Collective Memory and American Popular Culture* (Minneapolis: University of Minnesota Press, 1990); Michael M. J. Fischer, "Ethnicity and the Post-Modern Arts of Memory," in *Writing Culture: The Poetics and Politics of Ethnography*, ed. James Clifford and George E. Marcus (Berkeley: University of California Press, 1986), 194–233; Frigga Haug, *Female Sexualization: A Collective Work of Memory* (London: Verso, 1987); William Haver, *The Body of this Death: Historicity and Sociality in the Time of AIDS* (Stanford, Calif.: Stanford University Press, 1996); Andreas Huyssen, *Twilight Memories: Marking Time in a Culture of Amnesia* (New York: Routledge, 1995).

49. See Jonathan Crary's discussion of Bergson's *Matter and Memory* and the problematic of memory as simulacrum in "Spectacle, Attention, Counter-Memory," *October* 50 (1989): 103–4.

50. See Peter Burke, "History as Social Memory," in *Memory: History, Culture and the Mind*, ed. Thomas Butler (New York: Basil Blackwell, 1989), 97–113, esp. 98–99, reprinted in Peter Burke, *Varieties of Cultural History* (Ithaca: Cornell University Press, 1997), 43–59; Patrick H. Hutton, "Halbwachs as Historian of Collective Memory," in *History as an Art of Memory*, 73–90, esp. 75–77; Brian Fay, Philip Pomper, and Richard T. Vann, eds., *History and Theory: Contemporary Readings* (Malden, Mass.: Blackwell, 1998).

51. LeGoff, *History and Memory*.

52. See the discussion in Confino, "Collective Memory and Cultural History," along with (for example) ongoing debates in the journal *History and Memory*.

53. Susan A. Crane, "Writing the Individual Back into Collective Memory," *AHR* 102 (1997): 1372.

54. See, for example, *Index on Censorship*, special issue, "Memory and Forgetting," *Index on Censorship* 30:1, no. 198 (January/February 2001).

55. For recent examples, see John R. Gillis, ed., *Commemorations: The Politics of National Identity* (Princeton, N.J.: Princeton University Press, 1994); Winter, *Sites of Memory, Sites of Mourning*; the work of James E. Young (cited above in note 44); and Barry Schwartz, "The Social Context of Commemoration: A Study in Collective Memory," *Social Forces* 61 (1982): 374–402. Notice the privileged status of memory and the political danger implied in its displacement or erasure in Pierre Vidal-Naquet, *Assassins of Memory: Essays on the Denial of the Holocaust*, trans. Jeffrey Mehlman (New York: Columbia University Press, 1992).

56. Marie Noëlle Bourguet, Lucette Valensi, and Nathan Wachtel, eds. "Between Memory and History," Special issue of *History and Anthropology* 2, no. 2 (October 1986): 1–400; "Archives orales: Une autre histoire?" Special section on oral history and collective memory in *Annales: Économies Sociétés Civilisations* 35 (1980): 124–99; Alistair Thomson, "Unreliable Memories? The Use and Abuse of Oral History," in *Historical Controversies and Historians*, ed. William Lamont (London: UCL Press, 1998), 23–34, esp. the bibliography at 33–34; Ruth Finnegan, "Tradition, but What Tradition and for Whom?" *Oral Tradition* 6 (1991): 104–24.

57. Michel Foucault, *Language, Counter-Memory, Practice: Selected Essays and Interviews*, ed. Donald Bouchard, trans. Donald Bouchard and Sherry Simon (Ithaca, N.Y.: Cornell University Press, 1977). See also Natalie Zemon Davis and Randolph Starns, eds., "Collective Memory and Countermemory," special issue of *Representations* 26 (Spring 1989).

58. Just one example, Ana Maria Alonso, "The Effects of Truth: Re-Presentations of the Past and the Imagining of Community," *Journal of Historical Sociology* 1 (1988): 33–57, looks at these dynamics in the context of competing official and popular social memory in Mexico.

59. Zerubavel's *Recovered Roots* is an excellent example of this process in the emergence of the modern state of Israel.

60. Ian Hacking, *Rewriting the Soul: Multiple Personality and the Sciences of Memory* (Princeton, N.J.: Princeton University Press, 1995); Cathy Caruth, ed., *Trauma: Explorations in Memory* (Baltimore: Johns Hopkins University Press, 1995); Paul Antze and Michael Lambek, eds., *Tense Past: Cultural Essays in Trauma and Memory* (New York: Routledge, 1996); Janice Haaken, *Pillar of Salt: Gender, Memory, and the Perils of Looking Back* (New Brunswick, N.J.: Rutgers University Press, 1998).

61. See Stanley Cohen, *States of Denial* (London: Polity Press, 2001), 222–48, especially the discussion of truth commissions at 227–28. Citing the report of the South African Truth and Reconciliation Commission, Cohen describes how "the 'life of the Commission' revealed four notions of truth: factual or forensic; personal or narrative; social or 'dialogue'; healing and restorative" (227), whose contours Cohen goes on to characterize (227–28), providing at 323n8 the citation to the commission's report: Archbishop Desmond Tutu, *Truth and Reconciliation Commission of South Africa Report*, vol. 1 (London: Macmillan, 1999), 103–34. The complex dynamics of memory and truth in the South African situation are represented in a compelling fashion in a recently published novel by the daughter of anti-apartheid activists Ruth First and Joe Slovo; see Gillian Slovo, *Red Dust* (London: Virago, 2001). See now Allen Feldman, "Strange Fruit: The South African Truth Commission and the Demonic Economics of Violence," *Social Analysis* 46, no. 3 (2002): 234–65.

62. Crane, "Writing the Individual," 1375, points out this danger, using the 1994–95 Smithsonian Institution exhibition of the Enola Gay as an example of the stakes involved in a debate over collective memory. See also Vidal-Naquet, *Assassins of Memory*. On the category of experience, see Joan W. Scott, " 'Experience,' " in *Feminists Theorize the Political*, ed. Judith Butler and Joan W. Scott (New York: Routledge, 1992), 22–40.

63. Gabriel Josipovici, "Rethinking Memory: Too Much/Too Little," *Judaism* 47 (1998): 232–39.

64. Josipovici, "Rethinking Memory," 236.

65. Josipovici, "Rethinking Memory," 238.

66. Confino, "Collective Memory and Cultural History."

67. Confino, "Collective Memory and Cultural History," 1389n8.

68. Confino, "Collective Memory and Cultural History," 1392–1402.

69. For discussion of the role of theologically inflected metanarratives in other Christian (and also Jewish) sources, see Michael A. Signer, ed., *Memory and History in*

Christianity and Judaism (Notre Dame, Ind.: University of Notre Dame Press, 2001). See also Jean-Daniel Kaestli, "Mémoire et pseudépigraphie dans le christianisme de l'âge post-apostolique," *RTP* 125 (1993): 41–63.

70. For a helpful discussion of the dynamics of early Christian historiography in cultural context, see Arnaldo Momigliano, "Pagan and Christian Historiography in the Fourth Century A.D.," in his *Essays in Ancient and Modern Historiography* (Oxford: Blackwell, 1977), 107–26, reprinted from Arnaldo Momigliano, *The Conflict Between Paganism and Christianity in the Fourth Century* (Oxford: Clarendon Press, 1963), 79–99.

71. Momigliano, "Pagan and Christian Historiography," 116–17.

72. Personal communication from Beth Berkowitz, September 2002, who offered the rabbis as a compelling counterexample to the early Christians here.

73. Personal communication with James B. Rives, August 2001.

74. For an etymological investigation of the terminology, see Gerald A. Press, *The Development of the Idea of History in Antiquity*, McGill-Queen's Studies in the History of Ideas 2 (Kingston/Montreal: McGill-Queen's University Press, 1982).

75. This idea of ancient Christian sources as "texts" rather than as "documents" comes from Elizabeth A. Clark, "Women, Gender, and the Study of Christian History," *CH* 70 (2001): 424. Also see A. J. Woodman, *Rhetoric in Classical Historiography: Four Studies* (London: Croom Helm, 1988); Averil Cameron, ed., *History as Text: The Writing of Ancient History* (London: Duckworth, 1989); and David S. Potter, *Literary Texts and the Roman Historian* (New York: Routledge, 1999).

76. Herodotus, *Hist.* 1.1 (in Godley's LCL translation) . See also Charles W. Fornara, *The Nature of History in Ancient Greece and Rome* (Berkeley: University of California Press, 1983), 92: "Herodotus . . . defined his subject as the memorable deeds of men, and this definition, with some expansions relating to the treatment of notable individuals, remained standard thereafter."

77. Rosalind Thomas, *Herodotus in Context: Ethnography, Science, and the Art of Persuasion* (Cambridge: Cambridge University Press, 2000). Also see James A. Arieti, *Discourses on the First Book of Herodotus* (London: Littlefield Adams Books, 1995); J. L. Moles, "Truth and Untruth in Herodotus and Thucydides," in *Lies and Fiction in the Ancient World*, ed. Christopher Gill and T. P. Wiseman (Austin: University of Texas Press, 1993), 88–121; and T. P. Wiseman, "Lying Historians: Seven Types of Mendacity," in *Lies and Fiction in the Ancient World*, ed. Christopher Gill and T. P. Wiseman (Austin: University of Texas Press, 1993), 122–46.

78. Diodorus Siculus, 1.1.3 (in Oldfather's LCL translation). On the prefaces in Diodorus, see Kenneth S. Sacks, *Diodorus Siculus and the First Century* (Princeton, N.J.: Princeton University Press, 1990), 9–22.

79. Diodorus Siculus, 1.2.1. See Sacks, *Diodorus Siculus and the First Century*, 205: "Without patrons or recourse to political action, Diodorus constructs the *Bibliotheke* around a program for moral living. Again and again, he judges individuals and nations by how benevolently they act while enjoying good fortune and awards special praise to benefactors, mythological and historical, who contributed civilizing gifts in the arts and sciences and in politics."

80. Diodorus Siculus, 1.2.4.

81. Diodorus Siculus, 1.2.7–8.

82. Livy, bk. 1, Praef., 3 (LCL translation): "Yet, however this shall be, it will be a satisfaction to have done myself as much as lies in me to commemorate the deeds of the foremost people of the world [*rerum gestarum memoriae principis terrarum populi pro virili parte*]." bk. 1, Praef., 5: "I myself, on the contrary, shall seek in this an additional reward for my toil, that I may avert my gaze from the troubles which our age has been witnessing for so many years, so long at least as I am absorbed in the recollection of the brave days of old, free from every care which, even if it could not divert the historian's mind from the truth, might nevertheless cause it anxiety."

83. Livy, bk. 1, Praef., 9.

84. Paul Veyne, *Did the Greeks Believe in Their Myths? An Essay on the Constitutive Imagination*, trans. Paula Wissing (Chicago: University of Chicago Press, 1988), 5.

85. See, for example, Raoul Mortley, "The Hellenistic Foundations of Ecclesiastical Historiography," in *Reading the Past in Late Antiquity*, ed. Graeme Clarke with Brian Croke, Raoul Mortley, and Alanna Emmett Nobbs (Rushcutters Bay, New South Wales: Australian National University Press, 1990), 225–50.

86. Press, *The Development of the Idea of History in Antiquity*, 134: "Such changes as were made in the idea of history under the impact of Judaeo-Christianity, then, were rhetorical, and it would be appropriate to say that the idea, so altered, is a rhetorical idea."

87. G. W. Bowersock, *Martyrdom and Rome* (New York: Cambridge University Press, 1995), argues explicitly that these documents are, in fact, documentary. Many other scholars routinely privilege these documents as "historical" rather than "legendary."

88. The relationship among these three elements is widely discussed. In the field of ancient history, see especially M. I. Finley, "Myth, Memory, and History," in his *The Use and Abuse of History* (New York: Viking Press, 1971), 11–33; expanded reprint of "Myth, Memory, and History," *History and Theory* 4 (1965): 281–302. More recently, see John Marincola, *Authority and Tradition in Ancient Historiography* (New York: Cambridge University Press, 1997), 117–27.

89. Wendy Doniger O'Flaherty, *Other Peoples' Myths* (New York: Macmillan, 1988).

90. These categories are adapted from Zerubavel, *Recovered Roots*, esp. part 1, "History, Collective Memory, and Countermemory," 3–36.

91. This work remains controversial because it challenges the adequacy of theologically grounded accounts of the origins of Christianity. See Burton L. Mack, *A Myth of Innocence*; Mack, *Who Wrote the New Testament?*; and Mack, *The Christian Myth: Origins, Logic, and Legacy* (New York: Continuum, 2001). Mack's work should be distinguished from the critical founding work of Rudolf Bultmann, whose existentialist approach to the mythologizing aspects of the New Testament texts sought to retrieve a theological core message hidden behind the veils of myth. Mack's project is to demonstrate that the mythic quality of the text is not to be found only in the passages that strain the credulity of rationalist, post-Enlightenment readers but in the very structure of the gospel narratives.

92. Bruce Lincoln, *Theorizing Myth: Narrative, Ideology, and Scholarship* (Chicago: University of Chicago Press, 1999).

2. PERFORMING PERSECUTION, THEORIZING MARTYRDOM

1. Lacey Baldwin Smith, *Fools, Martyrs, Traitors: The Story of Martyrdom in the Western World* (New York: Knopf, 1997).

2. Jas Elsner, "Cultural Resistance and the Visual Image: The Case of Dura Europos," *CPh* 96 (2001): 269–304, shows how religious association provided a potent form of cultural identity, one that could also offer access to effective (if often oblique) modes of social resistance. Thanks to Jennifer Glancy for bringing this article to my attention.

3. Paul Allard, *Histoire des persécutions* (1903–1908), 3rd ed., rev. and aug. (Rome: "L'Erma" di Bretschneider, 1971); Norbert Brox, *Zeuge und Märtyrer: Untersuchungen zur frühchristlichen Zeugnis-Terminologie*, SANT 5 (Munich: Kösel, 1961); Hans von Campenhausen, *Die Idee des Martyriums in der alten Kirche*, 2nd ed. (Göttingen: Vandenhoeck & Ruprecht, 1964); W. H. C. Frend, *Martyrdom and Persecution in the Early Church: A Study of a Conflict from the Maccabees to Donatus* (Oxford: Basil Blackwell, 1965); Antonius J. Brekelmans, *Martyrerkranz: Eine symbolgeschichtliche Untersuchung im frühchristlichen Schrifttum*, Analecta Gregoriana 150 (Rome: Libreria Editrice dell' Università Gregoriana, 1965); Herbert B. Workman, *Persecution in the Early Church* (New York: Oxford University Press, 1980); Theofried Baumeister, *Die Anfänge der Theologie des Martyriums* (Münster: Aschendorff, 1980); Theofried Baumeister, *Genese und Entfaltung der altkirchlichen Theologie des Martyriums* (New York: Peter Lang, 1991); Gerhard Besier, "Bekenntis—Widerstand—Martyrium als historisch-theologische Kategorien," in *Bekenntnis, Widerstand, Martyrium*, ed. Gerhard Besier and Gerhard Ringshausen (Göttingen: Vandenhoeck & Ruprecht, 1986), 126–47; Pierre Maraval, *Les persécutions des chrétiens durant les quatres premiers siècles*, Bibliothèque d'histoire du christianisme 30 (Paris: Desclée, 1992); Arthur J. Droge and James D. Tabor, *A Noble Death: Suicide and Marytrdom Among the Christians and Jews in Antiquity* (San Francisco: HarperSan Francisco, 1992); Everett Ferguson, "Early Christian Martyrdom and Civil Disobedience" *JECS* 1 (1993): 73–83; Everett Ferguson, ed., *Church and State in the Early Church* (New York: Garland, 1993); Christel Butterweck, *"Martyriumssucht" in der Alten Kirche? Studien zur Darstellung und Deutung frühchristlicher Martyrien* (Tübingen: Mohr [Siebeck], 1995).

4. William Horbury and Brian McNeil, eds., *Suffering and Martyrdom in the New Testament: Studies Presented to G. M. Styler by the Cambridge New Testament Seminar* (Cambridge: Cambridge University Press, 1981); Richard J. Cassidy, *Christians and Roman Rule in the New Testament: New Perspectives* (New York: Crossroad, 2001).

5. Sam K. Williams, *Jesus' Death as Saving Event: The Origin of a Concept*, HDR 2 (Missoula, Mont.: Scholars Press, 1975); David Seeley, *The Noble Death: Graeco-Roman Martyrology and Paul's Concept of Salvation*, JSNTSup 28 (Sheffield: JSOT Press, 1990).

6. John S. Pobee, *Persecution and Martyrdom in the Theology of Paul*, JSNTSup 6 (Sheffield: JSOT Press, 1985); Saviero Xeres, "La 'bella morte' del cristiano: La metafora agonistica in Paolo e nei primi atti dei martiri," in *Dulce et decorum est pro patria mori:*

La morte in combattimento nell'antichità, ed. Marta Sordi (Milan: Vita e Pensiero, 1990), 281–93; Richard J. Cassidy, *Paul in Chains: Roman Imprisonment and the Letters of St. Paul* (New York: Crossroad, 2001). On later traditions concerning Paul's martyrdom, see H. W. Tajra, *The Trial of St. Paul: A Juridical Exegesis of the Second Half of the Acts of the Apostles*, WUNT 2, Reihe 35 (Tübingen: Mohr [Siebeck], 1989); H. W. Tajra, *The Martyrdom of St. Paul: Historical and Judicial Context, Traditions, and Legends*, WUNT 2, Reihe 67 (Tübingen: Mohr [Siebeck], 1994).

7. Mack, *A Myth of Innocence*. On the ongoing influence of the Passion of Jesus on early Christians' interpretations of their own experiences, see Elaine Pagels, "Gnostic and Orthodox Views of Christ's Passion: Paradigms for the Christian's Response to Persecution?" in *Rediscovery of Gnosticism*, ed. Bentley Layton (Leiden: Brill, 1980), 1:262–88; and Jan Bremmer, " 'Christianus sum': The Early Christian Martyrs and Christ," in *Eulogia: Mélanges offerts à Antoon A. R. Bastiaensen à l'occasion de son soix-ante-cinquième anniversaire*, ed. G. J. M. Bartelink, A. Hilhorst, and C. H. Kneepkens (Steenbrugge: in Abbatia S. Petri; The Hague: Nijhoff, 1991), 11–20.

8. Charles H. Talbert, "Martyrdom in Luke-Acts and the Lukan Social Ethic," in *Political Issues in Luke-Acts*, ed. Richard Cassidy and Philip J. Scharper (Maryknoll, N.Y.: Orbis, 1983), 99–110; Scott Cunningham, *"Through Many Tribulations": The Theology of Persecution in Luke-Acts*, JSNTSup 142 (Sheffield: Sheffield Academic Press, 1997).

9. Adela Yarbro Collins, *Crisis and Catharsis: The Power of the Apocalypse* (Philadelphia: Westminster, 1984); Leonard L. Thompson, *The Book of Revelation: Apocalypse and Empire* (New York: Oxford University Press, 1990). See also Mitchell Glenn Reddish, "The Theme of Martyrdom in the Book of Revelation," Ph.D. diss., Southern Baptist Theological Seminary, 1982.

10. Keith Hopkins, *A World Full of Gods: Pagans, Jews, and Christians in the Roman Empire* (London: Weidenfeld and Nicolson, 1999), 84: "No precise figures survive, but best estimates suggest that there were considerably fewer than 10,000 Christians in 100 CE, and only about 200,000 Christians in 200 CE, dispersed among several hundred towns. The late second-century figure equals only 0.3 percent of the total population of the Roman empire (c. sixty million)." Also see the more substantive treatment of the demographic question in Keith Hopkins, "Early Christian Number and Its Implications," *JECS* 6 (1998): 185–226.

11. Hopkins, *A World Full of Gods*, 85–86.

12. Roman sources include primarily brief references: Tacitus, *Ann.* 15.44; Suetonius, *Ner.* 16.2; Pliny, *Ep.* 10.96–97. Pliny's correspondence with the emperor Trajan is the most substantive piece of evidence.

13. The Christian sources for this period include the letters of Ignatius (in *The sApostolic Fathers: Greek Texts and English Translations of Their Writings*, 2nd ed., trans. J. B. Lightfoot and J. R. Harmer, ed. and rev. Michael W. Holmes [Grand Rapids, Mich.: Baker Book House, 1992], 129–201); and martyrological texts collected by different editors. The two standard collections that will be consulted throughout this book are: A. A. R. Bastiaensen et al., eds., *Atti e passioni dei martiri*, 4th ed. (Milan: Mondadori, 1998 [1987]); and Herbert Musurillo, ed. and trans., *The Acts of the Christian Martyrs* (Oxford: Clarendon Press, 1972). Specific documents for this period

include the *Martyrdom of Polycarp* (Musurillo, 2–21; Bastiaensen et al., 3–31); *Acts of Carpus, Papylus, and Agathonicê* (Musurillo, 22–37; Bastiaensen et al., 33–45); *Martyrdom of Ptolemaeus and Lucius* (Musurillo, 38–41); *Acts of Justin and his Companions* (Musurillo, 42–61; Bastiaensen et al., 47–57); *Martyrs of Lyon* (Eusebius, *Hist. Eccl.* 5.1.3–5.2.8; Musurillo, 62–85; Bastiaensen et al., 59–95); *Acts of the Scillitan Martyrs* (Musurillo, 86–89; Bastiaensen et al., 97–105); *Acts of Apollonius* (Musurillo, 90–105); *Passion of Perpetua and Felicitas* (Musurillo, 106–31; Bastiaensen et al., 107–47; discussed below in detail in chapter 3, where the significant bibliography is collected); *Martyrdom of Potamiaena and Basilides* (Musurillo, 132–35). Of these nine, the second, seventh, and ninth are generally considered furthest removed from historical accuracy. For a critical review of these sources, see Gary A. Bisbee, *Pre-Decian Acts of the Martyrs and Commentarii*, HDR 22 (Philadelphia: Fortress Press, 1988). See also the review essays by Jan den Boeft and Jan Bremmer: "*Notiunculae Martyrologicae*," VC 35 (1981): 43–56; "*Notiunculae Martyrologicae* II," VC 36 (1982): 383–402; "*Notiunculae Martyrologicae* III: Some Observations on the *Martyria* of Polycarp and Pionius," VC 39 (1985): 110–30; "*Notiunculae Martyrologicae* IV," VC 45 (1991): 105–22; and "*Notiunculae Martyrologicae* V," VC 36 (1992): 146–64.

14. The Christian sources for the Decian persecution are: Cyprian, *Epistolae*, ed. Wilhelm August Hartel, CSEL 3.2 (Vienna: Geroldi, 1871); English translation in G. W. Clarke, trans., *The Letters of St. Cyprian of Carthage*, 4 vols., ACW 43, 44, 46, 47 (New York: Newman Press, 1984–89) and Cyprian's treatise *De lapsis*, in Cyprian, *De Lapsis and De Ecclesiae Catholicae Unitate*, ed. and trans. Maurice Bévenot, S.J. (Oxford: Clarendon Press, 1971), 2–55; Eusebius, *Hist. Eccl.* 6.39.1–6.42.6; and the *Passio Pionii* (found in Musurillo, 136–67; Bastiaensen et al., 149–91). See chapter 3 for a close reading of the Pionius text as one of several examples of Christian martyrological self-portraiture (and for corresponding bibliography). In addition to these sources, a significant number of papyrus receipts attesting to the performance of individual sacrifices have been preserved from Egypt. Texts and translations of forty-one of these may be found in J. R. Knipfing, "The *Libelli* of the Decian Persecution," HTR 16 (1923): 345–90.

15. J. B. Rives, "The Decree of Decius and the Religion of Empire," JRS 89 (1999): 135–54. This article also includes extensive bibliographic citations for the scholarship on the Decian decree.

16. Christian sources concerning the Great Persecution include several passions and *acta* of the martyrs, including *The Martyrdom of Julius the Veteran* (Musurillo, 260–65); *The Martyrdom of Felix the Bishop* (Musurillo, 266–71); *The Martyrdom of the Saintly Dasius* (Musurillo, 272–79); *The Martyrdoms of Agapê, Irenê, and Chionê at Saloniki* (Musurillo, 280–93); *The Martyrdom of Saint Irenaeus Bishop of Sirmium* (Musurillo, 294–301); *Martyrdom of Saint Crispina* (Musurillo, 302–9). Eusebius, *The Martyrs of Palestine*: the Greek text with French translation may be found in Eusèbe de Césarée, *Histoire Ecclésiastique, livres VIII–X et Les Martyrs en Palestine*, ed., trans. and annot. Gustave Bardy, SC 55 (Paris: Éditions du Cerf, 1958), 121–74; English translation in Eusebius, *The Ecclesiastical History and the Martyrs of Palestine*, trans. Hugh Jackson Lawlor and John Ernest Leonard Oulton, 2 vols. (London: Society for Promoting Christian Knowledge, 1927), 1:329–400. Lactantius, *De Mortibus Persecutorum*, ed. and trans. J. L. Creed (Oxford: Clarendon Press, 1984).

17. For discussions of these historical circumstances, see Averil Cameron, *The Later Roman Empire* (Cambridge, Mass.: Harvard University Press, 1993), 30–46; Stephen Williams, *Diocletian and the Roman Recovery* (New York: Routledge, 1985), esp. 153–85. On Christian response to Diocletian, see Elizabeth DePalma Digeser, *The Making of a Christian Empire: Lactantius and Rome* (Ithaca, N.Y.: Cornell University Press, 2000).

18. Stephen Williams, *Diocletian*, 174.

19. G. E. M. de Ste. Croix, "Aspects of the 'Great' Persecution," *HTR* 47 (1954): 106.

20. Henri Leclercq, "Martyr," *DACL* 10.2 (1932): 2375.

21. Ramsay MacMullen, "Judicial Savagery in the Roman Empire," *Chiron* 16 (1986): 152.

22. The classic discussion of Roman criminal law is to be found in Theodor Mommsen, *Römisches Strafrecht*, Systematisches Handbuch der deutschen Rectswissenschaft, 1 Abt., 4 vols. (Leipzig: Duncker & Humblot, 1899). More recently, see O. F. Robinson, *The Criminal Law of Ancient Rome* (Baltimore: Johns Hopkins University Press, 1995) and Richard A. Bauman, *Crime and Punishment in Ancient Rome* (New York: Routledge, 1996). On capital punishment in particular, see Denise Grodzynski, "Tortures mortelles et catégories sociales: Les *Summa Supplicia* dans le droit romain aux IIIe et IVe siècles," in *Du châtiment du corps dans la cité: Supplices corporels et peine du morte dans le monde antique: Table ronde, Rome, 1982*, Collection École française de Rome 79 (Rome: École Française de Rome, 1984), 361–403; Eva Cantarella, *I supplizi capitali in Grecia e a Roma: Origini e funzioni delle pene di morte nell'antichità classica* (Milan: Rizzoli, 1991; reprint, 1996); MacMullen, "Judicial Savagery in the Roman Empire"; J. Vergote, "Les principaux modes de supplice chez les anciens et dans les textes chrétiens," *Bulletin de l'Institut historique belge de Rome* 20 (1939): 141–63; J.-L. Voisin, "Pendus, crucifiés, *oscilla* dans la Rome païenne," *Latomus* 38 (1979): 442–50. Also see Toivo Viljamaa, Asko Timonen, and Christian Krötze, eds., *Crudelitas: The Politics of Cruelty in the Ancient and Medieval World* (Krems: Medium Aevum Quotidianum, 1992).

23. Robinson, *Criminal Law of Ancient Rome*, 5.

24. *Digesta Iustiniani* (hereafter, *Dig.*) 48.19.9.11, cited in Bauman, *Crime and Punishment*, 129.

25. Modestinus, *De poenis* 4 (*Dig.* 49.16.3.1), cited in Bauman, *Crime and Punishment*, 131.

26. Menander, *De re militari* 3 (*Dig.* 49.18.1), cited in Bauman, *Crime and Punishment*, 130.

27. Pliny, *Ep.* 4.11; Plutarch, *Vit. Num.* 10.4–7. See "Domitian and the Vestals," in Bauman, *Crime and Punishment*, 92–97, for contextual discussion. On the broader issue of the ritualized status of vestal virgins, see Ariadne Staples, *From Good Goddess to Vestal Virgins: Sex and Category in Roman Religion* (London: Routledge, 1998), 127–56.

28. Bauman, *Crime and Punishment*, 93.

29. Cyprian, *Ep.* 10.5.1–2: "Now should the mercy of God chance to bring peace before the day of your combat, your resolve remains still unsullied, your conscience ever glorious: no-one among you should feel downcast believing that he is inferior to

those who, ahead of you, have spurned and vanquished this world, have endured their tortures to the end, and so have gone to the Lord by the paths of glory. . . . Either course, therefore, my dearly beloved brothers, equally confers nobility and glory."

30. Cyprian, *Ep.* 12.1.2–3. See also *Passio Perpetuae et Felicitatis* (hereafter, *Pass. Perp.*) 11.9, 14, where those who died in prison were to receive the title "martyr," and *Mart. Lyon //* Eusebius, *Hist. Eccl.* 5.2.3 for a similar point. Also *Acta Montani et Lucii* 2.

31. Fergus Millar, "Condemnation to Hard Labour in the Roman Empire, from the Julio-Claudians to Constantine," *Papers of the British School at Rome* 52 (1984): 138. On condemnation to the mines as a penalty, also see Mark Gustafson, "Condemnation to the Mines in the Later Roman Empire," *HTR* 87 (1994): 421–33.

32. A. N. Sherwin-White, "The Early Persecutions and Roman Law Again," *JTS*, n.s., 3, pt. 2 (1952): 199–213, and see also the updated version of this paper, published as an appendix to his *The Letters of Pliny* (Oxford: Oxford University Press, 1966), 772–87; G. E. M. Ste. Croix, "Why Were the Early Christians Persecuted?" *Past and Present* 26 (1963): 6–38; A. N. Sherwin-White, "Why Were the Early Christians Persecuted?—An Amendment," *Past and Present* 27 (1964): 23–7; G. E. M. Ste. Croix, "Why Were the Early Christians Persecuted?—A Rejoinder," *Past and Present* 27 (1964): 28–33; T. D. Barnes, "Legislation Against the Christians," *JRS* 58 (1968): 32–50. An excellent summary of the evidence and the debate may be found in O. F. Robinson, "The Repression of Christians in the Pre-Decian Period: A Legal Problem Still," *Irish Jurist* 25–27 (1990–1992): 269–92. See also Olivia F. Robinson, "Repressionen gegen Christen in der Zeit vor Decius—noch immer ein Rechtsproblem," *Zeitschrift der Savigny-Stiftung für Rechtsgeschichte* 112 (1995): 352–69. Against the consensus that there was little legislative activism against Christians, see (as representatives of a broader view shared by many French and Italian scholars) Henri Grégoire, with P. Orgels, J. Moreau and A. Maricq, *Les persécutions dans l'empire romain*, 2nd ed., Academie Royale de Belgique, Mémoires de la Classe des lettres et des sciences morales et politiques 47.1 (Brussels: Academie Royale de Belgique, 1964); and Marta Sordi, *The Christians and the Roman Empire*, trans. Annabel Bedini (Norman: University of Oklahoma Press, 1986).

33. The correspondence between Pliny, the newly appointed governor of Bithynia, and the emperor Trajan provides the precedent. See Pliny, *Ep.* 10.96–97.

34. For one example, see James Rives, "The Piety of a Persecutor," *JECS* 4 (1996): 1–25, which makes this point in relation to P. Aelius Hilarianus, the religiously conservative governor who is likely the persecutor whose actions are preserved in the *Passion of Perpetua and Felicitas*.

35. Famously recorded in Tacitus, *Ann.* 15.44.

36. On *imperium*, see Andrew Lintott, *Imperium Romanum: Politics and Administration* (London: Routledge, 1993).

37. Sherwin-White, "The Early Persecutions," 199, discussing Mommsen's theory of *coercitio*: "The grounds for such magisterial suppression, in Mommsen, is that the Christians offended against a canon of government in introducing an alien cult which induced 'natural apostasy.' "

38. The accusations and apologia are well known. See Robert Wilken, *The Christians as the Romans Saw Them* (New Haven, Conn.: Yale University Press, 1984) for a helpful summary of the ancient debate; for the original sources collected, see Molly

Whittaker, ed., *Jews and Christians: Graeco-Roman Views*, Cambridge Commentaries on Writings of the Jewish and Christian World, 200 BC to AD 200 (New York: Cambridge University Press, 1984), 133–91. Also see Andrew McGowan, "Eating People: Accusations of Cannibalism Against Christians in the Second Century," *JECS* 2 (1994): 413–42. On the accusation of *superstitio*, see L. F. Janssen, "'Superstitio' and the Persecution of Christians," *VC* 33 (1979): 131–59. A particularly interesting reading of the anti-Christian rhetoric in the service of historical reconstruction may be found in Margaret Y. MacDonald, *Early Christian Women and Pagan Opinion: The Power of the Hysterical Woman* (New York: Cambridge University Press, 1996).

39. The relationship of Christians to the imperial cult is the most important of these religio-political elements. On this relationship, see Fergus Millar, "The Imperial Cult and the Persecutions," in *Le culte des souverains dans l'empire romain*, ed. Willem den Boer (Geneva: Fondation Hardt, 1973), 143–75. An intriguing reading of the relationship between Christian martyrs and the imperial cult as one where power is negotiated rather than monolithically exercised may be found in Allen Brent, "Ignatius of Antioch and the Imperial Cult," *VC* 52 (1998): 30–58. Brent argues that Ignatius of Antioch's passage to Rome for martyrdom functions as a performative counterprocession in the style of the imperial cult procession. The performative character of martyrdom will be taken up further in chapter 4.

40. Timothy D. Barnes, "Pre-Decian *Acta Martyrum*," *JTS*, n.s., 19 (1968): 509–31, assesses the historicity of the nine pre-Decian texts that "have been accepted as wholly authentic by competent scholars of the present century" (509). See also Bisbee, *Pre-Decian Acts*.

41. *Martyrium Polycarpi* (hereafter, *Mart. Pol.*; Musurillo, *Acts of the Christian Martyrs*, 2–21; Bastiaensen et al., *Atti e passioni*, 3–31). The date of Polycarp's martyrdom is the subject of some controversy. The introduction to the edition in Bastiaensen et al. points out that scholars have placed the date anywhere between 22 February 156 and 23 February 167 (see Bastiaensen et al., 4). See also Musurillo's summary of the different positions on the dating of the text, concluding that "where there are so many indefinite factors to be reckoned with, we cannot in the light of the present evidence be certain" (xiii; see also the relevant bibliography collected at lxiii n. 5). For a general review of the state of research on this text, see Boudewijn Dehandschutter, "The *Martyrium Polycarpi*: A Century of Research," *ANRW* 2.27.1 (1993): 485–522.

42. *Mart. Pol.* 3.2 (where the crowd shouts, "Away with the atheists!") and 9.2 (where the governor seeks to persuade Polycarp to recant, urging him to signal that change of heart through uttering this same sentence).

43. *Mart. Pol.* 3.1.

44. *Mart. Ptol. et Luc.*, 9–13.

45. *Mart. Ptol. et Luc.* 14: denial and avoidance as unsuited to a true Christian (ὧν οὐδὲν πρόσεστι τῷ ἀληθινῷ Χριστιανῷ).

46. *Mart. Ptol. et Luc.* 15: Λούκιός τις καὶ αὐτὸς ὢν Χριστιανὸς ὁρῶν τὴν ἀλόγως οὕτω γενομένην κρίσιν.

47. *Mart. Ptol. et Luc.* 16: ὀνόματος δὲ Χριστιανοῦ προσωνυμίαν ὁμολογοῦντα.

48. *Mart. Ptol. et Luc.* 20.

49. Worthy of note here is also the role that martyrdom plays in the conversion of others.

50. There are three recensions of this text, collected and translated in Musurillo as recensions A, B, and C (Musurillo, *Acts of the Christian Martyrs*, 42–61)—the shorter, medium, and long versions. Bastiaensen et al. include only recension A (Bastiaensen et al., *Atti e passioni*, 47–57) in their collection. See also Giuseppe Lazzati, *Gli sviluppi della letteratura sui martiri nei primi quattro secoli* (Torino: Società Editrice Internazionale, 1956), 119–27; R. Knopf, G. Krüger, and G. Ruhbach, *Ausgewählte Märtyrerakten*, 4th ed. (Tübingen: Mohr [Siebeck], 1965), 15–18, 125–29. See Barnes, "Pre-Decian *Acta Martyrum*," 515–17, for a discussion and bibliography of these different versions of the text. Recension A is generally accepted as the most reliable. On the emphasis on Christian confession in the martyr acts, see Adelbert Hamman, "La confession de la foi dans les premiers actes des martyrs," in *Epektasis: Mélanges patristiques offerts au Cardinal Jean Daniélou*, ed. Jacques Fontaine and Charles Kannengiesser (Paris: Beauchesne, 1972), 99–105.

51. Barnes, "Pre-Decian *Acta Martyrum*," 528: "In the present state of the evidence, therefore, the historian is justified in supposing that the earliest known versions of six pre-Decian *acta* [including the short recension of this text] preserve as accurate a report of what happened as may be expected from a contemporary." See also Rudolf Freudenberger, "Die *Acta Iustini* als historisches Dokument," in *Humanitas—Christianitas: Walther v. Loewenich zum 65. Geburtstag*, ed. Karlmann Beyschlag, Gottfried Maron, and Eberhard Wolfel (Witten: Luther-Verlag, 1968), 24–31.

52. *Acta Iustini* 5.1–3.

53. *Acta Iustini* 5.4.

54. *Acta Iustini* 5.6.

55. *Acta Iustini* 1: "In the time of the lawless ordinances of idolatry [Ἐν τῷ καιρῷ τῶν ἀνόμων προσταγμάτων τῆς εἰδωλολατρείας]."

56. P. Franchi de' Cavalieri, *Note agiografiche*, Studi e Testi 33 (Vatican City: Bibliotheca Apostolica Vaticana, 1920), 5–6; Freudenberger, "Die *Acta Iustini*," 24, 29; and Hilhorst, in Bastiensen et al., 391. Note also that recensions B and C amplify the characterization of the context: "In the time of the lawless defenders of idolatry, impious ordinances against the pious Christians were put up in city and countryside. This was to coerce them to pour libations to empty idols" (1.1–2, recension B); "While the wicked Antoninus wielded the sceptre of the Roman Empire, Rusticus happened to be the despicable prefect of Rome, a terrible man, a plague, and filled with all impiety" (1.1, recension C), with many references to the necessity of sacrificing to the Roman gods sprinkled throughout the text. It is clear that as versions of this text multiplied, their claims grew more amplified as well.

57. Eusebius, *Hist. Eccl.* 5.1.4–5.2.8. On this martyrology, see Marcel LeGlay, ed., *Les martyrs de Lyon (177): Lyon, 20–23 Septembre 1977*, Colloques internationaux du CNRS 575 (Paris: Éditions du CNRS, 1978); Juan de Churruca, "Confesseurs non condamnés à mort dans le procès contre les chrétiens de Lyon l'année 177," *VC* 38 (1984): 257–70; Marie-Louise Guillaumin, " 'Une jeune fille qui s'appelait Blandine': Aux origines d'une tradition hagiographique," in *Epektasis: Mélanges patristiques offerts au Cardinal Jean*

Danielou, ed. Jacques Fontaine and Charles Kannengiesser (Paris: Beauchesne, 1972), 93–98; Heinrich Kraft, "Die Lyoner Märtyrer und der Montanismus," in *Pietas: Festschrift für Bernhard Kötting*, ed. Ernst Dassmann and K. Suso Frank, JAC Ergänzungsband 8 (Munich: Aschendorff, 1980), 250–66; Annick Lalleman, "Le parfum des martyrs dans les Actes des martyrs de Lyon et le Martyre de Polycarpe," *StPatr* 16:2 (1985): 186–92. On the ongoing influence of martyrological traditions in Gaul, see Brigitte Beaujard, "Cités, évêques et martyrs en Gaule à la fin de l'époque romaine," in *Les fonctions des saintes dans le monde occidental (IIIe—XIIIe siècle): Actes du colloque organisé par l'École française de Rome avec le concours de l'Université de Rome "La Sapienza,"* Collection de l'École Française de Rome 149 (Rome: École Française de Rome/Palais Farnèse, 1991), 175–91.

58. Eusebius, *Hist. Eccl.* 5.1.9. The language used here is identical to that found in *Mart. Ptol. et Luc.* 15, where Lucius challenges the reasonableness of the judgment against Ptolemaeus. Lucius and Vettius Epagathus, the young man in this account, suffer the same fate.

59. Eusebius, *Hist. Eccl.* 5.1.14. These accusations appear elsewhere in anti-Christian polemics; see, for example, Minucius Felix, *Oct.* 9.5–7. See note 38 above (Wilken and Whittaker). On torture in Eusebius, see José Carlos Bermejo Barrera, "Les discours de la torture chez Eusèbe de Césarée," *Quaderni di Storia* 17, no. 34 (1991): 63–102.

60. Eusebius, *Hist. Eccl.* 5.1.25: "ἦγεν ἐπὶ κόλασιν ἀναγκάζων εἰπεῖν τὰ ἄθεα περὶ ἡμῶν."

61. Eusebius, *Hist. Eccl.* 5.1.33.

62. Eusebius, *Hist. Eccl.* 5.1.44. It was precisely such an inquiry that produced the famous exchange between Pliny, governor of Bithynia, and the emperor Trajan in the early second century.

63. Eusebius, *Hist. Eccl.* 5.1.50.

64. Eusebius, *Hist. Eccl.* 5.1.47.

65. Eusebius, *Hist. Eccl.* 5.1.58. The text here paraphrases Rev. 22:11. The Eusebius text has "Let the lawless one (ὁ ἄνομος) still be lawless, and let the righteous one (ὁ δίκαιος) still be righteous." Rev. 22:11 reads, "Let the unrighteous one (ὁ ἀδικῶν) still be unrighteous and the filthy (ὁ ῥυπαρὸς) still be filthy and let the righteous (ὁ δίκαιος) still do justice and the holy one (ὁ ἅγιος) still be made holy."

66. See Blandina's repeated confession recorded at *Hist. Eccl.* 5.1.19: "I am a Christian, and nothing bad occurs among us [Χριστιανή εἰμι καὶ παρ᾽ ἡμῖν οὐδὲν φαῦλον γίνεται]"; and Attalus's final Latin address to the crowd at *Hist. Eccl.* 5.1.52: "This which you are doing is cannibalism, but we neither eat human beings nor do anything else that is bad [Ἰδοῦ τοῦτό ἐστιν ἀνθρώπους ἐσθίειν, ὃ ποιεῖτε ὑμεῖς· ἡμεῖς δὲ οὔτε ἀνθρώπους ἐσθίομεν οὐθ᾽ ἕτερόν τι πονηρὸν πράσσομεν]."

67. Musurillo, *Acts of the Christian Martyrs*, 86–89; Bastiaensen et al, *Atti e passioni*, 97–105. For a more recent critical edition with introduction, translation, and commentary, see Fabio Ruggiero, *Atti dei Martiri Scilitani: Introduzione, Testo, Traduzione, Testimonianze e Commento*, Atti della Accademia Nazionale dei Lincei 388, *Memorie* ser. 9, vol. 1, no. 2 (Rome: Accademia Nazionale dei Lincei, 1991), 35–138. On the historicity of the text, see Rudolf Freudenberger, "Die *Akten der scilitanischen Märtyrer* als historisches Dokument," *Wiener Studien* 86 (1973): 196–215.

68. Musurillo, *Acts of the Christian Martyrs*, 106–31; Bastiensen et al., *Atti e passioni*, 107–47. Also see *Passion de Pérpetue et de Félicité suivi des Actes*, ed. and trans. Jacqueline Amat, SC 417 (Paris: Éditions du Cerf, 1996). This text is discussed in much greater detail in the next chapter.

69. *Pass. SS. Scil.* 14.

70. *Pass. Perp.* 6.6.

71. On martyrdom as social control, see Donald Riddle, *The Martyrs: A Study in Social Control* (Chicago: University of Chicago Press, 1931).

72. Judith Perkins has explored the elevation of suffering as a critical category of subject formation in the second century in *The Suffering Self: Pain and Narrative Representation in the Early Christian Era* (New York: Routledge, 1995).

73. Michel Foucault, *Power/Knowledge: Selected Interviews and other Writings, 1972–1977*, ed. Colin Gordon, trans. Colin Gordon et al. (New York: Pantheon, 1980); Michel Foucault, *Politics, Philosophy, Culture: Interviews and Other Writings, 1977–1984*, ed. Lawrence D. Kritzman, trans. Alan Sheridan et al. (New York: Pantheon, 1988); Michel Foucault, *Power*, vol. 3 of *Essential Works of Foucault, 1954–1984*, ed. James D. Faubion (New York: New Press, 1999). See also Michel Foucault, *Dits et écrits*, 4 vols., ed. Daniel Defert and François Ewald (Paris: Gallimard, 1994), esp. vol. 4 (covering the years 1980–1988).

74. James C. Scott, *Domination and the Arts of Resistance: Hidden Transcripts* (New Haven, Conn.: Yale University Press, 1990).

75. For specific details concerning the edicts of Decian (in 249) and Diocletian (in 303 and 304), see Rives, "The Decree of Decius," and Ste. Croix, "Aspects of the 'Great' Persecution."

76. *Passio Iuli Veterani* (Musurillo, *Acts of the Christian Martyrs*, 260–65) is considered by scholars to be genuine (see Musurillo, xxxix, for discussion).

77. *Passio Iuli Veterani* 1.2.

78. *Passio Iuli Veterani* 3.1.

79. *Passio Iuli Veterani* 3.3.

80. *Passio Iuli Veterani* 4.5.

81. *Passio Sancti Felicis Episcopi* (Musurillo, *Acts of the Christian Martyrs*, 266–71); conflict over the books is at 2–5, 12–15, 24, 27; conflict over primacy of imperial or divine law is at 16–17; Felix's closing prayer in which he figures himself as a willing sacrifice is at 30.

82. *Passio Sanctae Crispinae* (Musurillo, *Acts of the Christian Martyrs*, 302–09); the charge is made at 1.1; Crispina's religious commitment is called *superstitio* at 1.4, 1.6, 4.1; Crispina and Anullinus debate over *praecepta* at 1.6.

83. See, for example, the *Martyrdom of Saintly Dasius* (Musurillo, *Acts of the Christian Martyrs*, 272–79), although this text, preserved solely in an eleventh-century manuscript, is judged by Musurillo (xl–xli) and others as a late source; also, *Martyrdoms of Agapê, Irenê, Chionê at Saloniki* (Musurillo, *Acts of the Christian Martyrs*, 280–93), which emphasizes the demonic source of persecution and the repeated accusation against the Christian women of madness. See also Eusebius, *Mart. Pal.*

84. The accusation of madness against opponents is not limited to Christian characterizations of their Roman persecutors. Subsequently, the accusation of "madness"

emerges in Christian polemics against heretics. For a substantive treatment of this rhetoric as it emerged in late ancient legal discourses, see Ferdinando Zuccotti, *"Furor Haereticorum": Studi sul trattamento giuridico della follia e sulla persecuzione della eterodossia religiosa nella legislazione del tardo impero romano*, Università degli studi di Milano, Facoltà di giurisprudenza, Pubblicazioni dell'istituto di diritto romano 26 (Milan: Giuffrè, 1992). Also see Laura Nasrallah, *An Ecstasy of Folly: Prophecy and Authority in Early Christianity* (Cambridge, Mass.: Harvard University Press, 2003).

85. Rives, "The Decree of Decius"; Richard Gordon, "The Veil of Power: Emperors, Sacrificers, and Benefactors," in *Pagan Priests: Religion and Power in the Ancient World*, ed. Mary Beard and John North (Ithaca, N.Y.: Cornell University Press, 1990), 201–34, esp. 207–8.

86. Stanley K. Stowers, "Greeks Who Sacrifice and Those Who Do Not: Toward an Anthropology of Greek Religion," in *The Social World of the First Christians: Essays in Honor of Wayne A. Meeks*, ed. L. Michael White and O. Larry Yarbrough (Minneapolis: Fortress Press, 1995), 293–333, explores the "seemingly persistent fundamental aspects of sacrifice concerning procreation, gender, descent, and place that make sacrifice a powerful means of organizing all kinds of social relations" (294).

87. Williams, *Jesus' Death as Saving Event*; Seeley, *The Noble Death*.

88. See Pliny, *Ep.* 10.97, where the emperor Trajan suggests that sacrifice can function as the authenticating sign of recantation.

89. Origen, *Exhort. Mart.* 30. English translation in Origen, *An Exhortation to Martyrdom; On Prayer; First Principles: Book IV; Prologue to the Commentary on the Song of Songs; Homily XXVII on Numbers*, trans. and intro. Rowan A. Greer (New York: Paulist Press, 1979), 41–79; quotation at 62. Greek original, *Eis martyrion protreptikos*, in Origen, *Werke*, 12 vols., GCS 2:3–47.

90. "οὕτως αἱ "ψυχαὶ τῶν πεπελεκισμένων" ἕνεκεν τῆς μαρτυρίας Ἰησοῦ" (Origen, GCS 2.27.3–4), a partial quotation of Rev. 20:4: "τὰς ψυχὰς τῶν πεπελεκισμένων διὰ τὴν μαρτυρίαν Ἰησοῦ καὶ διὰ τὸν λόγον τοῦ θεοῦ. . . .'"

91. Ignatius, *Rom.* 2.2; 4.2. Ignatius of Antioch, in J. B Lightfoot, *The Apostolic Fathers*, part 2, *S. Ignatius, S. Polycarp*, 129–201.

92. Ignatius, *Eph.* 21.1; *Smyrn.* 10.2; *Pol.* 2.3; 6.1. The Greek word Ignatius uses here (ἀντίψυχον) is extremely rare: see BAGD, 76; BDAG, 91. As commentators have long noted, the term appears twice in an important Jewish martyrological text, 4 Maccabees (at 6:29 and 17:21). On the relationship between 4 Maccabees and Ignatius and other Christian martyrological texts, see Otto Perler, "Das vierte Makkabäerbuch, Ignatius von Antiochien und die ältesten Märtyrerberichte," *RivAC* 25 (1949): 47–72.

93. *Mart. Pol.* 14.1–3 (Lightfoot translation):

ὁ δὲ ὀπίσω τὰς χεῖρας ποιήσας καὶ προσδεθείς, ὥσπερ κριὸς ἐπίσημος ἐκ μεγάλου ποιμνίου εἰς προσφοράν, ὁλοκαύτωμα δεκτὸν τῷ θεῷ ἡτοιμασμένον, ἀναβλέψας εἰς τὸν οὐρανὸν εἶπεν· Κύριε ὁ θεὸς ὁ παντοκράτωρ, ὁ τοῦ ἀγαπητοῦ καὶ εὐλογητοῦ παιδός σου Ἰησοῦ Χριστοῦ πατήρ . . . σὲ αἰνῶ, εὐλογῶ σε ὅτι κατηξίωσάς με τῆς ἡμέρας καὶ ὥρας ταύτης, τοῦ λαβεῖν μέρος ἐν ἀριθμῷ τῶν μαρτύρων ἐν τῷ ποτηρίῳ τοῦ Χριστοῦ [σου], εἰς ἀνάστασιν ζωῆς αἰωνίου ψυχῆς τε καὶ σώματος ἐν ἀφθαρσίᾳ πνεύματος ἁγίου· ἐν οἷς προσδεχθείην ἐνώπιόν σου σήμερον ἐν θυσίᾳ πίονι καὶ προσδεκτῇ, καθὼς προητοίμασας καὶ προεφανέρωσας καὶ ἐπλήρωσας, ὁ ἀψευδὴς καὶ ἀληθινὸς θεός . . . σὲ εὐλογῶ, σὲ δοξάζω, διὰ τοῦ αἰωνίου καὶ ἐπουρανίου ἀρχιερέως Ἰησοῦ Χριστοῦ.

94. Eusebius, *Hist. Eccl.* 5.1.51–52.

95. Eusebius, *Hist. Eccl.* 5.1.56.

96. Frances M. Young, *The Use of Sacrificial Ideas in Greek Christian Writers from the New Testament to John Chrysostom*, Patristic Monograph Series 5 (Philadelphia: Philadelphia Patristic Foundation, 1979), 223–38; Theo Hermans, *Origène: Théologie sacrificielle du sacerdoce des chrétiens*, ThH 102 (Paris: Beauchesne, 1996), 195–205; Robert J. Daly, *Christian Sacrifice: The Judaeo-Christian Background Before Origen*, The Catholic University of America Studies in Christian Antiquity 18 (Washington, D.C.: Catholic University of America, 1978), 124–27, 149–50, 302–3, 320–21, 378–88, 493–94, and elsewhere.

97. The persistent contrast that some Christian theologians draw between Judaism (figured as the literal, carnal, material, as rote) and Christianity (figured as the spiritual, as meaningful) turns up in some of these discussions. Even when some forms of Judaism are allowed to cross over into the realm of the spiritual, the interpretive framework remains intact. See, for example, Daly, *Christian Sacrifice*, 4–5: "We are using the word ["spiritualization"] in the much broader sense which includes all those movements and tendencies within Judaism and Christianity which attempted *to emphasize the true meaning of sacrifice, i.e. the inner, spiritual, or ethical significance of the cult over against the merely material or merely external understanding of it*" (emphasis mine).

98. Joan Wallach Scott, "Gender: A Useful Category for Historical Analysis," in *Gender and the Politics of History*, by Joan Wallach Scott (New York: Columbia University Press, 1988), 42, argues for the centrality of "gender" as a signifier for power.

99. The literature here is quite extensive. See Stuart G. Hall, "Women Among the Early Martyrs," in *Martyrs and Martyrologies: Papers Read at the 1992 Summer Meeting and the 1993 Winter Meeting of the Ecclesiastical History Society*, ed. Diane Wood (Oxford: Blackwell, 1993), 1–22; Chris Jones, "Woman, Death, and the Law During the Christian Persecution," in *Martyrs and Martyrologies: Papers Read at the 1992 Summer Meeting and the 1993 Winter Meeting of the Ecclesiastical History Society*, ed. Diane Wood (Oxford: Blackwell, 1993), 23–34; Rachel Moriarty, " 'Playing the Man': The Courage of Christian Martyrs, Translated and Transposed," in *Gender and Christian Religion*, ed. R. N. Swanson (Suffolk: Boydell Press, 1998), 1–12; Elizabeth A. Castelli, " 'I Will Make Mary Male': Pieties of the Body and Gender Transformation of Early Christian Women in Late Antiquity," in *Bodyguards: The Cultural Contexts of Gender Ambiguity*, ed. Julia Epstein and Kristina Straub (New York: Routledge, 1991), 29–49; Elizabeth A. Castelli, "Visions and Voyeurism: Holy Women and the Politics of Sight in Early Christianity," in *Protocol of the Colloquy of the Center for Hermeneutical Studies, 6 December 1992*, n.s., 2, ed. Christopher Ocker (Berkeley: Center for Hermeneuti-

cal Studies, 1994), 1–20; Margaret R. Miles, *Carnal Knowing: Female Nakedness and Religious Meaning in the Christian West* (Boston: Beacon Press, 1989); among others. Related to these, see also Stephen D. Moore and Janice Capel Anderson, "Taking It Like a Man: Masculinity in 4 Maccabees," *JBL* 117 (1998): 249–73.

100. A notable exception is Joyce Salisbury, *Perpetua's Passion: The Death and Memory of a Young Roman Woman* (New York: Routledge, 1997), though the argument that the executions of the Carthaginian Christians documented in the *Pass. Perp.* constituted a conscious act of human sacrifice may exceed the limits of the evidence.

101. Mary Beard, John North, and Simon Price, *Religions of Rome*, vol. 1, *A History* (New York: Cambridge University Press, 1998), 214–15.

102. The discussion of Greek sacrifice and its social effects is apropos here; see Stowers, "Greeks Who Sacrifice."

103. The issue of spectacle emerges again in this study in chapter 4, where I focus on the question of Christian appropriation of the spectacular in generating and sustaining the collective memory of martyrdom.

104. Paul Plass, *The Game of Death in Ancient Rome: Arena Sport and Political Suicide* (Madison: University of Wisconsin Press, 1995). See René Girard, *Violence and the Sacred*, trans. Patrick Gregory (Baltimore: Johns Hopkins University Press, 1977). It should be noted that Girard's theory of sacrifice has been critiqued from various quarters, primarily for its lack of empirical and historical grounding and for its tendency to enshrine a peculiarly Christian theological perspective. See Burton Mack, "Introduction: Religion and Ritual," in *Violent Origins: Walter Burkert, René Girard, and Jonathan Z. Smith on Ritual Killing and Cultural Formation*, ed. Robert G. Hamerton-Kelly (Stanford, Calif.: Stanford University Press, 1987), 6–22; also see Stowers, "Greeks Who Sacrifice," 296–97.

105. Plass, *Game of Death*, 60.

106. Ibid., 3.

107. Ibid., 9: "As a result [of the fact that societies have to learn to cope with disorder], violence or, more generally, disorder falls under an axiom of anomaly, that is, an abnormal or disruptive factor formally institutionalized in one way or another to be internalized, *in a process characteristic of any immune system*" (italics mine); ibid., 10: "Each in its own way [arena violence and political suicide] thus *administered a dose of cultured (in the medical-biological sense) violence, working like an immune system to bring the body politic back into balance*" (italics mine).

108. Alison Futrell, *Blood in the Arena: The Spectacle of Roman Power* (Austin: University of Texas Press, 1997).

109. Ibid., 4–7. On the games as a technology for establishing and maintaining Roman hegemony, see also Monique Clavel-Lévêque, *L'empire en jeux: Espace symbolique et pratique sociale dans le monde romain* (Paris: Éditions du CNRS, 1984); Monique Clavel-Lévêque, "L'espace des jeux dans le monde romain: Hégémonie, symbolique et pratique sociale," *ANRW* 2.16.3 (1986): 2406–563.

110. Futrell, *Blood in the Arena*, 2.

111. On "ethnographic analogy" as a method, see ibid., 169–70; for comparative examples of human sacrifice, see ibid., 170–84; for critiques of the secularization

hypothesis, see ibid., 169–70, 206–7; for the functionalist definition of religion, see ibid., 77–78 and 255n1.

112. Ibid., 170: "I propose that the amphitheater was a politicized temple that housed the mythic reenactment of the cult of Roman statehood. The struggle of the gladiator embodied an idealized and distilled version of the military ethic of *Romanitas*. His death served as a foundation sacrifice that answered the crisis of empire, validating the Roman struggle for power and offering a model for understanding the basis of Roman power."

113. Festus, 318 M: "*At homo sacer is est, quem populus iudicavit ob maleficium*," in Sextus Pompeius Festus, *De verborum significatu quae supersunt cum Pauli epitome*, ed. Wallace M. Lindsay, Bibliotheca Scriptorum Graecorum et Romanorum Teubneriana (Lipsius: Teubner, 1913; reprint, Hildesheim/New York: Georg Olms, 1978), 424; Futrell, *Blood in the Arena*, 189–90.

114. Futrell, *Blood in the Arena*, 189–90.

115. James B. Rives, "Human Sacrifice Among Pagans and Christians," *JRS* 85 (1995): 65–85.

116. Beard, North, Price, *Religions of Rome*, 1:233–34.

117. Pliny, *Nat.* 30.3.13: "It is beyond calculation how great is the debt owed to the Romans, who swept away the monstrous rites, in which to kill a man was the highest religious duty and for him to be eaten a passport to health. [*Nec satis aestimari potest quantum Romanis debeatur, qui sustulere monstra, in quibus hominem occidere religiosissimum erat, mandi vero etiam saluberrimum.*]" Translation from Pliny, *Natural History with an English Translation in Ten Volumes*, trans. H. S. Jones, LCL (Cambridge: Harvard University Press, 1975), 8:286–87.

118. Livy, 22.57.1–6. In the year 216 BCE, Rome was suffering from "great disasters" and "a number of prodigies," including the conviction of two vestal virgins, Opimia and Floronia, of unchastity. One of these was buried alive near the Colline Gate; the other committed suicide. "Since in the midst of so many misfortunes this pollution was, as happens at such times, converted into a portent, the decemvirs were commanded to consult the Books, and Quintus Fabius Pictor was dispatched to Delphi, to enquire of the oracle with what prayers and supplications they might propitiate the gods, and what would be the end of all their calamities. In the meantime, by the direction of the Books of Fate, some unusual sacrifices [*sacrifica aliquot extraordinaria*] were offered; amongst others a Gaulish man and woman and a Greek man and woman were buried alive in the Cattle market, in a place walled in by stone, which even before this time had been defiled with human victims, a sacrifice wholly alien to the Roman spirit [*minime Romano sacro*]"; translation from Livy, *Livy in Fourteen Volumes*, trans. B. O. Foster, LCL (Cambridge, Mass.: Harvard University Press, 1982), 5:384–87.

119. Plutarch, *Quaest. Rom.* 83 (*Mor.* 283F–284C). In Plutarch, *Plutarch's Moralia in Sixteen Volumes*, trans. Frank Cole Babbitt, LCL (Cambridge, Mass.: Harvard University Press, 1972), 4:124–28.

120. Beard, North, Price, *Religions of Rome*, 1:81. Futrell believes that Livy and others (including modern scholars) protest too much with their insistence that the burial alive of the vestal virgin, in one case, or of two Greeks and two Gauls, in another, were

not sacrificial. Such a claim leaves the ritual character of the executions unexplored and the political and ideological work that ritual killing does—whatever the context or semantic field—uninterrogated. See Futrell, *Blood in the Arena*, 205.

121. It is worth noting that in both accounts, with significant differences in detail, the demand for the ritual killing of human victims is called for because of (reports or accusations of) violations of women's sexual virtue. (See Futrell's discussion at 197–203.) Livy mentions only the accusations of unchastity against the vestal virgins. Plutarch describes "a certain maiden, Helvia ['Ελβίαν τινὰ παρθένον]," struck by lightning while riding on horseback, her body left naked ("for her tunic had been pulled far up as if purposely"), her clothing and jewelry strewn about, and her mouth left open so that her tongue stuck out. This event is interpreted as a sign that the vestal virgins and even the equestrian ranks have been disgraced and corrupted. Here, three vestals—Aemilia, Licinia, and Marcia—are accused, convicted, and punished. But the Sibylline books require further restorative ritual activity: the sacrifice of "certain strange and alien spirits two Greeks and two Gauls, buried alive on the spot."

122. In a related vein but from a historically distant vantage point, some scholars have argued that capital punishment in the United States functions as a form of sacrifice. See, most recently, Brian K. Smith, "Capital Punishment and Human Sacrifice," *JAAR* 68 (2000): 3–25. James McBride has made the even more provocative argument that capital punishment qua sacrifice is ultimately unconstitutional in the U.S. context because it amounts to the establishment of religion by the state. See James McBride, "Capital Punishment as the Unconstitutional Establishment of Religion: A Girardian Reading of the Death Penalty," *Journal of Church and State* 37 (1995): 263–87.

123. For a broader retheorization of sacrifice in light of this insight, see Nancy Jay, *Throughout Your Generations Forever: Sacrifice, Religion, and Paternity* (Chicago: University of Chicago Press, 1992).

124. Beard, North, Price, *Religions of Rome*, 1:297. They cite Olivier de Cazanove, "*Exesto*: L'incapacité sacrificielle des femmes à Rome," *Phoenix* 41 (1987): 159–73; and John Scheid, "The Religious Roles of Roman Women," in *A History of Women from Ancient Goddesses to Christian Saints*, ed. Pauline Schmitt Pantel (Cambridge, Mass.: Harvard University Press), 379–80. Scheid raises the exception of the sacrifices offered by Roman matrons to Fortuna Muliebris at the archaic boundary of Rome on July 6, a practice preserved only in an etiological myth (388–90). His conclusion, however, is that "the extraordinary nature of this cult therefore does not contradict the general rule stated above [that women were excluded from Roman sacrificial practice]" (390).

125. Staples, *From Good Goddess to Vestal Virgins*, 154.

126. Staples, *From Good Goddess to Vestal Virgins*, 186–87n94. The passage in question is Festus 82 M (Festus, *De verborum significatu*, 72): "*Exesto, extra esto. Sic enim lictor in quibusdam sacris clamitabat: hostis, vinctus, mulier, virgo exesto.*" Staples insists that "Festus is explicit on the point that the formula was not a general one. . . . If women were excluded from *certain sacrifices* the implication must surely be that there were others in which women could participate." Staples goes on to argue that vestal virgins, whose status was anomalous with respect both to gender and to citizenship, were especially well positioned as ritual agents to act for the collective. Their role in

preparing the *mola salsa*, the salted meal that was sprinkled on sacrificial victims, placed them (in Staples's argument) in the midst of Roman sacrificial practice (154).

127. See Mathew Kuefler, *The Manly Eunuch: Masculinity, Gender Ambiguity, and Christian Ideology in Late Antiquity* (Chicago: University of Chicago Press, 2001).

128. *Mart. Pol.* 9.1. For a discussion of the problems of culture-bound translation of this sentence, see Moriarty, " 'Playing the Man' ". Although I find myself in considerable sympathy with Moriarty's caution against reading our own historical period's gender awareness back into ancient texts, it seems to me that the ancient sources betray considerable gender awareness all their own—and the arena was most certainly a site for the production and maintenance of idealized masculinity. It does not seem to me to be so great a stretch to imagine that the use of "ἀνδρίζου" here means to work with the notion that courage and endurance are masculine values.

129. See Josh. 1:6, 7, 9; Deut. 31:6, 7, 23; Pss. 26:14; 30:25; Dan. 10:19.

130. This is not true only for Christian sources. See, for example, Minoo Moallem's work on Islamic martyrdom and its masculine coding: "Transnationalism, Feminism, and Fundamentalism," in *Women, Gender, Religion: A Reader*, ed. Elizabeth A. Castelli with Rosamond C. Rodman (New York: Palgrave, 2001), 126–34; and Moallem, *Between Warrior Brother and Veiled Sister: Islamic Fundamentalism and the Cultural Politics of Patriarchy* (Berkeley and Los Angeles: University of California Press, 2004, forthcoming).

131. *Pass. Perp.* 10. See also Tertullian, *Mart.* 4, with its catalog of brave women choosing death rather than dishonor (Lucretia, the wife of Hasdrubal, Cleopatra, the Athenian courtesan who bit off her tongue and spat it into the face of the tyrant so that she would not be tempted to betray her friends).

132. Clement's treatment of martyrdom is explored briefly in Annewies van den Hoek, "Clement of Alexandria on Martyrdom," in *StPatr* 26 (1993): 324–41. She emphasizes the direct relationship between martyrdom and gnosis in Clement's thought; see 327.

133. *Gos. Thom.* 114. See *The Gospel of Thomas: The Hidden Sayings of Jesus*, ed. and trans. Marvin Meyer (San Francisco: HarperSan Francisco, 1992).

134. Castelli, " 'I Will Make Mary Male.' "

135. Clement of Alexandria, *Strom.* 4.8.58.2–4. Greek text: Clément d'Alexandrie, *Les Stromates: Stromate IV*, ed. Annewies van den Hoek, trans. Claude Mondésert, SC 463 (Paris: Cerf, 2001). English translation here and elsewhere adapted from *ANF* 2:409–41, quotation at 421.

136. Clement of Alexandria, *Strom.* 4.8.67.4–68.2.

137. Clement of Alexandria, *Strom.* 4.8.59.

138. Clement of Alexandria, *Strom.* 4.8.60.1.

139. Clement of Alexandria, *Strom.* 4.8.62.4.: "ἐκτὸς εἰ μὴ καταμαλακισθεῖεν."

140. Clement of Alexandria, *Strom.* 4.8.61.2. ὑπομονή is a virtue generally associated with martyrdom from 4 Maccabees on. See Brent D. Shaw, "Body/Power/Identity: Passions of the Martyrs." *JECS* 4 (1996): 269–312.

141. Shaw, "Body/Power/Identity," 279.

142. Clement of Alexandria, *Strom.* 4.8.61.2.

143. Clement of Alexandria, *Strom.* 4.8.61.3.

144. I use the term "ethnographic" here to suggest a pattern of observing "others" based on a comparative method that is present in the discourse of Clement and other early Christian writers. Of course, this practice bears only partial resemblance to Enlightenment and post-Enlightenment forms of ethnography, but using the same language to describe Clement's practice is intended to tune the ear to the implied claims about authority and subjectivity embedded in his discourse of the other.

145. Clement of Alexandria, *Strom.* 4.8.62.2.

146. Clement of Alexandria, *Strom.* 4.8.62.3.

147. Annewies van den Hoek points out the precursor texts to Clement's citation of the Amazons, the Sarmatian women, and the dogs: Plato, *Leg.* 7.804d–806c and *Rep.* 5.451d. See her "Clement of Alexandria on Martyrdom," 336–37. Clement goes on in this text to assert women's equal claim on moral perfection (through modesty and the control of desire), mobilizing a range of biblical, mythological, and historical examples drawing upon many different classical and Christian sources. See *Strom.* 4.19.118.1–123.1.

148. See note 99, above.

149. Origen, *Exhort. Mart.* 14 (GCS 2.14.22–32; *An Exhortation to Martyrdom*, trans. Greer, 51–52): "τούτου δὲ ἕνεκεν εἰ μαρτυρῶ, ἐβουλόμην καὶ τέκνα καταλιπεῖν μετὰ ἀγρῶν καὶ οἰκιῶν, ἵνα καὶ παρὰ τῷ θεῷ καὶ πατρὶ τοῦ κυρίου ἡμῶν Ἰησοῦ Χριστοῦ, ἐξ οὗ πᾶσα πατριὰ ἐν οὐρανοῖς καὶ ἐπὶ γῆς ὀνομάζεται," πολλαπλασιόνων καὶ ἁγιωτέρων τέκνων χρηματίσω πατὴρ ἤ, ἵν' ὡρισμένως εἴπω, ἑκατονταπλασιόνων. εἴπερ δέ εἰσι πατέρες, περὶ ὧν εἴρηται τῷ Ἀβραάμ· "σὺ δὲ ἀπελεύσῃ πρὸς τοὺς πατέρας σου μετ' εἰρήνης τραφεὶς ἐν γήρᾳ καλῷ," εἴποι ἄν τις (οὐκ οἶδα εἰ ἀληθεύων)· τάχα ἐκεῖνοι πατέρες εἰσὶ μαρτυρήσαντές ποτε καὶ ἀφέντες τέκνα, ἀνθ' ὧν πατέρες γεγόνασι πατέρων τοῦ πατριάρχου Ἀβραὰμ καὶ ἄλλων τοιούτων πατριαρχῶν· εἰκὸς γὰρ τοὺς ἀφέντας τέκνα καὶ μαρτυρήσαντας οὐ νηπίων ἀλλὰ πατερῶν γίνεσθαι πατέρας.

150. Elizabeth A. Clark, "Sex, Shame, and Rhetoric: En-Gendering Early Christian Ethics," *JAAR* 59 (1991): 221–45, traces the history of this rhetorical move—using Christian women's virtue to shame Christian men—in a range of early Christian texts.

151. See Elizabeth A. Castelli, "Gender, Theory, and the Rise of Christianity: A Response to Rodney Stark," *JECS* 6 (1998): 227–57, for a summary of this debate and a survey of the evidence and scholarship.

3. THE MARTYR'S MEMORY: AUTOBIOGRAPHY AND SELF-WRITING IN IGNATIUS, PERPETUA, AND PIONIUS

1. Throughout this chapter, I use the concept of "askesis" to talk about self-formation in the martyrological tradition. I am influenced by Richard Valantasis's broad definition of "asceticism" as "performances within a dominant social environment intended to inaugurate a new subjectivity, different social relations, and an alternative symbolic universe." See Richard Valantasis, "Constructions of Power in Asceticism," *JAAR* 63 (1995): 797.

2. Georg Misch, *A History of Autobiography in Antiquity*, trans. E. W. Dickes and

Georg Misch, 2 vols. (London: Routledge and Kegan Paul, 1950). On the eighteenth-century, probably German, origin of the term "autobiography," see Misch, *A History of Autobiography*, 5, and the accompanying note. Misch's history begins with ancient Near Eastern and Egyptian inscriptions and official records, works through classical Greek sources, and devotes significant attention to Hellenistic, Roman, and late antique sources in which the figure of the interiorized individual is increasingly prominent. See also Arnaldo Momigliano, *The Development of Greek Biography* (Cambridge, Mass.: Harvard University Press, 1993); and Patricia Cox Miller, *Biography in Late Antiquity: A Quest for the Holy Man*, Transformation of the Classical Heritage 5 (Berkeley: University of California Press, 1983).

3. Thomas J. Heffernan, "Philology and Authorship in the *Passio Sanctarum Perpetuae et Felicitatis*," *Traditio* 50 (1995): 320.

4. See, for example, Misch, esp. vol. 2, part 2, chapter 3, "The Development of Autobiography in the Philosophic and Religious Movement," 2:355–537.

5. In two of the three texts, the question of authorship is not straightforward. For the purposes of my argument, whether the actual authors and the potentially fictive self-narrators are one and the same is of less consequence since the argument about the "I" who speaks here is an argument about a literary figure.

6. The promised fourth volume of Foucault's *History of Sexuality* concerned early Christianity, but its publication was foreclosed by Foucault's untimely death in 1984. Some fragments of the promised volume appear in Jeremy R. Carrette, ed., *Religion and Culture: Michel Foucault* (New York: Routledge, 1999), 153–97; and in Michel Foucault, *Dits et écrits 1954–1988*, ed. Daniel Defert and François Ewald with Jacques Lagrange (Paris: Gallimard, 1994), vol. 4 (1980–1988), hereafter abbreviated as *Dits et écrits*.

7. Michel Foucault, "L'écriture de soi," *Corps écrit* no. 5, "L'autoportrait" (Febraury 1983): 3–23; reprinted in *Dits et écrits* 4:415–30. Translated as "Self Writing" by Paul Rabinow in Foucault, *Ethics: Subjectivity and Truth*, vol. 1 of *Essential Works of Foucault, 1954–1984* (New York: The New Press, 1994), 207–22.

8. Foucault, "Self Writing": *Ethics*, 209–10; *Dits et écrits* 4:418.

9. LSJ, 1889. According to Lampe, ὑπόμνημα is "1) memorial, reminder; of the sign of the cross at baptism; 2) record; minutes of a trial (Eus. *P.e.* 4.2; Pall. *V. Chrys.* 1); of a synod, ib. 14; of Christ's trial, A. *Pil.* A proem; ref. Last Judgment Chrys. *Hom. 56.4 in Mt.* (7.572A); account, of an apocryphal gospel, Or. *Cels.* 2.13; of Acts of Pilate, Eus. *HE* 1.9.3; copy; petition; 3) commentary; 4) division, section. ὑπομνηματικός serving as a commentary, exegetical; ὑπόμνησις = remembering, recollection; commemoration (liturg., of the eucharist); reminding, reminder, of icons; testimony" (Lampe, 1451–52).

10. Heffernan, "Philology and Authorship," 321: "The *hypomnema* is a vehicle that could combine some of the formal characteristics of autobiography and the jottings of diary. It was believed in antiquity to be the appropriate form for a style of writing that was unliterary. . . . *Hypomnemata* belonged to no genre, and therefore were not under an obligation to obey any prescriptive rhetorical canons. . . . What needs to be underscored, however, is that *hypomnema* is the term classical authors used to describe their autobiographical works."

11. Foucault, "Self Writing": *Ethics*, 216; *Dits et écrits* 4:425.

12. Foucault, "Self Writing": *Ethics*, 217; *Dits et écrits* 4:426.

13. Foucault, "Self Writing": *Ethics*, 207–8; *Dits et écrits* 4:416.

14. Note that Misch's thesis is quite similar. In his formulation of the general movement from more public forms of self-writing to increasingly interiorized forms of private writing, the late-ancient Christian autobiography par excellence, Augustine's *Confessions*, is not a radical departure or innovation toward interiority but rather the pinnacle and culmination of a long, complex cultural development that had long been aimed toward this end.

15. Foucault, "Self Writing": *Ethics*, 221; *Dits et écrits* 4:430.

16. Michel Foucault, "Technologies of the Self," in *Technologies of the Self: A Seminar with Michel Foucault*, ed. Luther H. Martin, Huck Gutman, and Patrick H. Hutton (Amherst: University of Massachusetts Press, 1988), 16–49. The essay appears as "Les techniques de soi," trans. Fabienne Durand-Bogaert, in *Dits et écrits: 1954–1988*, ed. Daniel Defert and François Eward, with Jacques Lagrange (Paris: Gallimard, 1994), 4:783–813, and in an amended English version in Foucault, *Ethics: Subjectivity and Truth*, ed. Paul Rabinow, vol. 1 of *Essential Works of Foucault, 1954–1984* (New York: The New Press, 1994), 223–51. Citations in this chapter, unless otherwise noted, will be from this latter English edition.

17. Foucault, "Technologies of the Self": *Ethics*, 224; *Dits et écrits* 4:784.

18. Foucault, "Technologies of the Self": *Ethics*, 225; *Dits et écrits* 4:785. Although this is a shift in Foucault's focus, the change may not be an absolute one. See the discussion in Daniel Boyarin and Elizabeth A. Castelli, "Foucault's *The History of Sexuality*: The Fourth Volume, or, A Field Left Fallow for Others to Till," *JHS* 10 (2001): 357–74.

19. For example, see Foucault, "On the Genealogy of Ethics: An Overview of Work in Progress," *Ethics: Subjectivity and Truth*, ed. Paul Rabinow, vol. 1 of *Essential Works of Foucault, 1954–1984* (New York: The New Press, 1994), 270–71: "What interests me about the classical concept of the care of the self is that we see here the birth and development of a certain number of ascetic themes ordinarily attributed to Christianity. Christianity is usually given credit for replacing the generally tolerant Greco-Roman lifestyle with an austere lifestyle marked by a series of renunciations, interdictions, or prohibitions. Now, we can see that in this activity of the self on itself, the ancients developed a whole series of austerity practices that the Christians later directly borrowed from them. So we see that this activity became linked to a certain sexual austerity that was subsumed directly into the Christian ethic. We are not talking about a moral rupture between tolerant antiquity and austere Christianity." (The French version is "À propos de la généalogie de l'éthique: Un aperçu du travail en cours," *Dits et écrits*, 4:383–411, quotation at 401–2.)

20. Foucault developed his understanding of Christian confession in a course of study, *Du gouvernement des vivants*, in 1979–1980 at the Collège de France. The course précis appears in *Dits et écrits* 4:125–29; translated as "On the Government of the Living," *Ethics*, 81–85, and in *Religion and Culture: Michel Foucault*, ed. Jeremy R. Carrette (New York: Routledge, 1999), 154–57. He also lectured on the topic of Christian notions of confession in 1980 at Dartmouth and Berkeley. A transcription of this lecture, "Christianity and Confession," may be found as part of "About the Beginning of the Hermeneutics of the Self," in Carrette, ed., *Religion and Culture*, 169–81.

21. The influence of Pierre Hadot, the holder of the chair in the History of Hel-

lenistic and Roman Thought at the Collège de France, on Foucault's work on ancient ascetics and ethics is worthy of note. See Arnold I. Davidson, "Introductory Remarks to Pierre Hadot," in *Foucault and His Interlocutors*, ed. Arnold I. Davidson (Chicago: University of Chicago Press, 1997), 195–202; and Pierre Hadot, "Forms of Life and Forms of Discourse in Ancient Philosophy," trans. Arnold I. Davidson and Paula Wissing, in *Foucault and his Interlocutors*, ed. Arnold I. Davidson (Chicago: University of Chicago Press, 1997), 203–24. See also Arnold I. Davidson, "Ethics as Ascetics: Foucault, the History of Ethics, and Ancient Thought," in *Foucault and the Writing of History*, ed. Jan Goldstein (Oxford: Blackwell, 1994), 63–80, and Pierre Hadot, *Philosophy as a Way of Life: Spiritual Exercises from Socrates to Foucault*, trans. Michael Chase, ed. Arnold I. Davidson (Oxford: Blackwell, 1995).

22. Foucault, "Technologies of the Self": *Ethics*, 245; *Dits et écrits* 4:807–8.

23. See, for example, Marcel Viller, "Le martyre et l'ascèse," *Revue d'ascétique et de mystique* 6 (1925): 105–42; Edward Malone, *The Monk and the Martyr: The Monk as the Successor to the Martyr*, Studies in Christian Antiquity 12 (Washington, D.C.: Catholic University Press, 1950); Sebastian P. Brock, "Early Syrian Asceticism," *Numen* 20 (1973): 2; David Knowles, *Christian Monasticism* (New York: McGraw Hill, 1969), 12.

24. For a succinct discussion of this historiographical problem, see Elizabeth A. Clark, *Reading Renunciation: Asceticism and Scripture in Early Christianity* (Princeton, N.J.: Princeton University Press, 1999), 18–27.

25. See, for example, Leif E. Vaage and Vincent L. Wimbush, eds., *Asceticism and the New Testament* (New York: Routledge, 1999).

26. Foucault, "Friendship as a Way of Life," in *Ethics: Subjectivity and Truth*, ed. Paul Rabinow, vol. 1 of *Essential Works of Foucault, 1954–1984* (New York: The New Press, 1994), 137, published originally in French as "De l'amitié comme mode de vie," *Gai Pied*, no. 25 (April 1981): 38–39, reprint, *Dits et écrits: 1954–1988*, 4 vols., ed. Daniel Defert and François Eward, with Jacques Lagrange (Paris: Gallimard, 1994), 4:165.

27. I am using "askesis" here in its broad Foucaultian sense of "transformative work on the self" and in line with Valantasis's definition (cited above, note 1), not in its more narrow historical sense as a religious practice within early Christianity.

28. See, for example, David Seeley, *The Noble Death: Graeco-Roman Martyrology and Paul's Concept of Salvation*, JSNTSup 28 (Sheffield: JSOT Press, 1990), 83–141. More generally, see also Michel Spanneut, *Le Stoïcisme des pères de l'église de Clément de Rome à Clément d'Alexandrie*, Patristica Sorbonensia 1 (Paris: Seuil, 1957).

29. The authenticity of this text has been widely assumed by most modern scholars, though it is by no means universally recognized as having been composed by the hand of Perpetua. See Heffernan, "Philology and Authorship," and Ross S. Kraemer and Shira L. Lander, "Perpetua and Felicitas," in *The Early Christian World*, ed. Philip F. Esler (New York: Routledge, 2000), 2:1048–68, esp. 1051–58. I refer in this discussion to the first-person speaker of this text as Perpetua, whether or not the historical authenticity of her "I" can be established with certainty.

30. Ignatius's letters can be found in a collection of early Christian writings entitled *The Apostolic Fathers*. Two bilingual (Greek-English) editions are most readily accessible: *The Apostolic Fathers: Greek Texts and English Translations of Their Writings*, trans. J. B. Lightfoot and J. R. Harmer, 2nd ed., ed. and rev. Michael W. Holmes (Grand

Rapids, Mich.: Baker Book House, 1992), 129–201; and *Apostolic Fathers*, 2 vols., trans. Kirsopp Lake, LCL (Cambridge, Mass.: Harvard University Press, 1927), 1:165–277. Extensive English commentary on the letters may be found in William R. Schoedel, *Ignatius of Antioch*, Hermeneia Commentary (Philadelphia: Fortress Press, 1985). For a review of scholarship on Ignatius, see Charles Munier, "Où en est la question d'Ignace d'Antioche? Bilan d'un siècle de recherches, 1870–1988," *ANRW* 2.27.1 (1993): 359–484, and William R. Schoedel, "Polycarp of Smyrna and Ignatius of Antioch," *ANRW* 2.27.1 (1993): 272–358. On the theology of martyrdom in Ignatius's letters, see Karin Bommes, *Weizen Gottes: Untersuchungen zur Theologie des Martyriums bei Ignatius von Antiochien* (Cologne/Bonn: Peter Hanstein, 1976). See also Judith Perkins, *The Suffering Self: Pain and Narrative Representation in the Early Christian Era* (New York: Routledge, 1995), 189–92; and S. Zanartu, "Les concepts de vie et de mort chez Ignace d'Antioche," *VC* 33 (1979): 324–41.

31. The question of the dating of the letters is summarized in J. B. Lightfoot, *Apostolic Fathers*, part 2, *S. Ignatius, S. Polycarp*, 3 vols. (London: Macmillan, 1885; 2nd ed., 1889; reprint, Grand Rapids, Mich.: Baker, 1981), 2:2:435–72. Eusebius of Caesarea set the date around 107 to 108 (in his *Chronicon*; for his narrative account, see his *Hist. Eccl.* 3.36). Helmut Koester, *Introduction to the New Testament*, vol. 2, *History and Literature of Early Christianity* (Philadelphia: Fortress Press, 1984), 281, places the death in the second decade of the second century. Lightfoot straddles the two positions, arguing that the martyrdom took place "within a few years of A.D. 110, before or after" (2:1:30).

32. Ignatius, *Rom.* 4.1–2 (Lake's LCL translation; used, but adapted, throughout).

33. G. E. M. de Ste. Croix, "Why Were the Early Christians Persecuted?" *Past and Present* 26 (1963): 24.

34. James Moffatt, "Ignatius of Antioch: A Study in Personal Religion," *JR* 10 (1930): 170.

35. L. W. Barnard, "The Background of St. Ignatius of Antioch," *VC* 17 (1963): 193.

36. W. H. C. Frend, *Martyrdom and Persecution in the Early Church: A Study of a Conflict from the Maccabees to Donatus* (Oxford: Basil Blackwell, 1965), 197.

37. Schoedel, *Ignatius*, 173, in his commentary on *Rom.* 3.1 argues that the verb "ἐντέλλομαι" "does not imply formal authority." Whether formal authority is implied or not by Ignatius's use of the verb, it seems uncontroversial to suggest that some power to command is implied by the rhetoric of the statement itself.

38. E.g., Thomas F. Heffernan, *Sacred Biography: Saints and their Biographers in the Middle Ages* (New York: Oxford University Press, 1988), 58.

39. Schoedel, *Ignatius*, 175–76.

40. Ignatius, *Rom.* 2.1.

41. Ignatius, *Rom.* 1.2, "For I am afraid of your love [φοβοῦμαι γὰρ τὴν ὑμῶν ἀγάπην] lest it do me wrong."

42. Ignatius, *Rom.* 3.2–3; my emphasis.

43. Ignatius, *Rom.* 6.2.

44. Ignatius, *Rom.* 7.2.

45. Richard A. Bower, "The Meaning of ΕΠΙΤΥΧΑΝΩ in the Epistles of St. Ignatius of Antioch," *VC* 28 (1974): 1–14.

46. Ignatius, *Rom.* 5.3.

47. Ignatius, *Rom.* 5.1.

48. LSJ, s.v. "ἐθέλω," 479; BAGD, s.v. "θέλω," 354–55; Lampe, s.v. "θέλω," 623. See also the constellation of words in Lampe beginning with "ἐθελο–," 406–7, for the double-edged character of "ἐθέλω/θέλω" (both willing and willful).

49. Ignatius, *Rom.* 4.3.

50. Ignatius, *Rom.* 3.2. Schoedel, *Ignatius*, 173, suggests that here "willing" is tantamount to "acting," building upon the prior contrast between word and deed.

51. Ignatius, *Rom.* 6.1.

52. Ignatius, *Rom.* 6.2.

53. Ignatius, *Rom.* 7.2.

54. Ignatius, *Rom.* 4.3.

55. Ignatius, *Rom.* 5.1.

56. Schoedel, *Ignatius*, 180.

57. Ignatius, *Rom.* 5.3.

58. Ignatius, *Rom.* 9.2. The LCL translation offers the euphemism for "ἔκτρωμα," "born out of time." See *TDNT*, s.v. "ἔκτρωμα," 2:465–67.

59. Schoedel, *Ignatius*, 13–14.

60. Ignatius, *Rom.* 2.2.

61. BAGD, s.v. "σπένδω," 761; BDAG, 937. Phil. 2:17: "Even as I am to be poured as a libation upon the sacrificial offering of your faith, I am glad and rejoice with you all"; 2 Tim. 4:6: "For I am already on the point of being sacrificed; the time of my departure has come." (Of course, this last text is only fictively in the voice of Paul.)

62. Schoedel consistently argues against overemphasizing the sacrificial—especially the expiatory—dimensions of Ignatius's language, both here and in his other letters. See, for example, his discussion at Schoedel, *Ignatius*, 63–64, of Ignatius, *Eph.* 8.1.

63. Ignatius, *Rom.* 4.2; note that some manuscripts have "a sacrifice to God" rather than simply "a sacrifice."

64. BAGD, s.v. "περίψημα," 653; BDAG, 808.

65. Perler, "Das vierte Makkabäerbuch, Ignatius von Antiochien und die ältesten Märtyrerberichte," *RivAC* 25 (1949): 47–72. BAGD, s.v. "ἀντίψυχον," 76; BDAG, 91. The two relevant passages in 4 Maccabees are 6:29 and 17:21. The term appears in Ignatius at *Eph.* 21.1 ("I am your ransom and that of those whom you sent in honor of God to Smyrna"); *Smyrn.* 10.2 ("My spirit is your ransom, and my bonds too, which you neither despised nor were ashamed by"); *Pol.* 2.3 ("With respect to everything I am your ransom, I and my bonds which you loved"); *Pol.* 6.1 ("I am ransom for those who submit to the bishops, presbyters, and deacons").

66. Ignatius is not the first to express such sentiments. The New Testament's Apocalypse accounts for the current sufferings of the righteous by pointing to their future vindication, where the blood of the martyred saints under the altar in heaven graphically marks the triumphant promise of a new Jerusalem.

67. *Passio sanctarum Perpetuae et Felicitatis*, ed. and critical text by C. J. M. J. van Beek (Nijmegen: Dekker & Van De Vegt, 1936); Herbert Musurillo, ed. and trans., *The Martyrdom of Perpetua and Felicitas*, in *The Acts of the Christian Martyrs* (Oxford: Clarendon Press, 1972), 106–31; *Passio Perpetuae et Felicitatis*, critical text by A. A. R. Bastiaensen, trans. Gioachino Chiarini, in *Atti e passioni dei martiri*, ed. A. A. R. Bas-

tiaensen, et al. (Milan: Mondadori, 1987. 4th ed., 1998), 107–47 (text and translation); 412–52 (extensive commentary). See also *Passio SS. Perpetuae et Felicitatis latine et graece*, critical text by P. Franchi de' Cavalieri, *Scritti agiografici* 1 (1893–1900; published in 1962 [Studi e testi 221]): 41–155; *Passion de Perpétue et de Félicité suivi des Actes*, intro., ed., trans., annot., and index. Jacqueline Amat, SC 417 (Paris: Éditions du Cerf, 1996); *The Martyrdom of Perpetua*, trans. Rosemary Rader, in *A Lost Tradition: Women Writers of the Early Church*, comp. and trans. Patricia Wilson-Kastner, G. Ronald Kastner, Ann Millin, Rosemary Rader, and Jeremiah Reedy (Washington, D.C.: University Press of America, 1981), 19–32.

The scholarly literature on Perpetua is extensive. Overviews include: Henri Leclercq, "Perpétue et Félicité," *DACL* 14, no. 1 (1939): 393–444; Åke Fridh, *Le problème de la Passion des saintes Perpétue et Félicité*, Studia Graeca et Latina Gothoburgensia 26 (Stockholm: Almqvist & Wiksell, 1968); Eugenio Corsini, "Proposte per una lettura della *Passio Perpetuae*," in *Forma futuri: Studi in onore del Cardinale Michele Pellegrino* (Torino: Bottega d'Erasmo, 1975), 481–541; W. H. C. Frend, "Blandina and Perpetua: Two Early Christian Heroines," in *Les martyrs de Lyon (177): Lyon, 20–23 septembre 1977*, ed. Marcel LeGlay, Colloques internationales de CNRS 575 (Paris: Editions du CNRS, 1978), 167–77; Maurice Testard, "La Passion des saintes Perpétue et Félicité: Témoignages sur le monde antique et le christianisme," *Bulletin de l'Association Guillaume Budé* (1991): 56–75; Brent D. Shaw, "The Passion of Perpetua," *Past and Present* 139 (1993): 3–45; Joyce Salisbury, *Perpetua's Passion: The Death and Memory of a Young Roman Woman* (New York: Routledge, 1997).

68. M. Poirier, "Note sur la *Passio sanctarum Perpetuae et Felicitatis*: Félicité, était-elle vraiment l'esclave de Perpétue?" *StPatr* 10, no. 1 (1970): 306–9; Rudolf Freudenberger, "Probleme römischer Religionspolitik in Nordafrika nach der *Passio SS. Perpetuae et Felicitatis*," *Helikon* 13–14 (1973–74): 174–83; L. F. Pizzolato, "Note alla *Passio Perpetuae et Felicitatis*," *VC* 34 (1980): 105–19; Rosa Mentxaka, "La persécution du christianisme à l'époque de Septime Sévère: Considérations juridiques sur la *Passion de Perpétue et Félicité*," in *Églises et pouvoir politique: Actes des journées internationales d'histoire du droit d'Angers, 30 mai–1er juin 1985* (Angers: Presse de l'Université, 1987), 63–82; Alvyn Pettersen, "Perpetua: Prisoner of Conscience," *VC* 41 (1987): 139–53; Teresa Sardella, "Strutture temporali e modelli di cultura rapporti tra antitradizionalismo storico e modello martiriale nella *Passio Perpetuae et Felicitatis*," *Augustinianum* 30 (1990): 259–78; James B. Rives, "The Piety of a Persecutor," *JECS* 4 (1996): 1–25.

69. Valeria Lomanto, "Rapporti fra la *Passio Perpetuae* e *Passiones* africane," in *Forma futuri: Studi in onore del Cardinale Michele Pellegrino* (Torino: Bottega d'Erasmo, 1975), 566–86; James W. Halporn, "Literary History and Generic Expectations in the *Passio* and the *Acta Perpetuae*," *VC* 45 (1991): 223–41; Heffernan, "Philology and Authorship"; Kraemer and Lander, "Perpetua and Felicitas," 1051–58.

70. Franz Joseph Dölger, "Antike Parallelen zum leidenden Dinocrates in der *Passio Perpetuae*," *Antike und Christentum* 2 (1930): 1–40; Franz Joseph Dölger, "Gladiatorenblut und Martyrerblut, Eine Szene der *Passio Perpetuae* in kultur- und religionsgeschichtlicher Bedeutung," *Bibliothek Warburg, Vorträge* 1923–24 (1926): 196–214; Franz Joseph Dölger, "Der Kampf mit dem Aegypter in der Perpetua Vision: Das Martyrium als Kampf mit dem Teufel," *Antike und Christentum* 3 (1932): 177–88;

Jaakko Aronen, "Pythia Carthaginensis o immagini cristiane nella visione di Perpetua?" in *L'Africa romana VI: Atti del VI convegno di studio, Sassari 16–18 dicembre 1988*, 2 vols., ed. Attilio Mastino (Sassari: Dip. di Storia dell'Università degli studi di Sassari, 1989), 2:643–48.

71. Renzo Petraglio, "Des influences de l'Apocalypse dans la 'Passio Perpetuae' 11–13," in *L'apocalypse de Jean: Traditions exégetiques et iconographies, IIIe–XIIIe siècles*, ed. Renzo Petraglio (Geneva: Droz, 1979), 15–29; Renzo Petraglio, *Lingua latina e mentalità biblica nella Passio sanctae Perpetuae: Analisi di caro, carnalis, e corpus* (Brescia: Morcelliana, 1976).

72. Michel Meslin, "Vases sacrés et boissons d'éternité dans les visions des martyrs africains," in *Epektasis: Mélanges patristiques offerts au Cardinal Jean Daniélou*, ed. Jacques Fontaine and Charles Kannengiesser (Paris: Beauchesne, 1972), 139–53; Clementina Mazzucco, "Il significato cristiano della 'libertas' proclamata dai martiri della Passio Perpetuae," in *Forma futuri: Studi in onore del Cardinale Michele Pellegrino* (Torino: Bottega d'Erasmo, 1975), 542–65; M. P. Ciccarese, "Le più antiche rappresentazioni del purgatorio dalla Passio Perpetuae alla fine del IX secolo," *Romanobarbarico: Contributi allo studio dei rapporti culturali tra mondo latino e mondo barbarico* 7 (1982–1983): 33–76; A. Ferrarini, "Visioni, sangue e battesimo: La Passio Perpetuae," in *Atti della Settimana Sangue e antropologia nella letteratura cristiana (Roma, 29 novembre–4 dicembre 1982)* (Rome: Ed. Pia Unione del Preziosissimo Sangue, 1983), 1055–81; A. P. Orbán, "The Afterlife in the Visions of the Passio SS Perpetuae et Felicitatis," in *Fructus centesimus: Mélanges offerts à Gerard J. M. Bartelink à l'occasion de son soixante-cinquième anniversaire*, ed. A. A. R. Bastiaensen, A. Hilhorst, and C. H. Kneepkens, Instrumenta Patristica 19 (Steenbrugis: Abbatia S. Petri, 1989), 269–77; Peter Habermehl, *Perpetua und der Ägypter oder Bilder des Bösen in frühen afrikanischen Christentum: Ein Versuch zur Passio sanctarum Perpetuae et Felicitatis*, TUGAL 140 (Berlin: Akademie Verlag, 1992).

73. Louis Robert, "Une vision de Perpétue Martyre à Carthage en 203," *CRAI* (1982): 227–76; Cées Mertens, "Les premiers martyrs et leur rêves: Cohésion de l'histoire et des rêves dans quelques 'Passiones' de l'Afrique du Nord," *RHE* 81 (1986): 5–46; Jacqueline Amat, "L'authenticité de songes des la Passion de Perpétue et de Félicité," *Augustinianum* 29 (1989): 177–91; Franca Ela Consolino, "Sogni e visioni nell'agiografia tardoantica: Modelli e variazioni sul tema," *Augustinianum* 29 (1989): 237–56; R. Perraymond, "Alcune visioni nell'arte cristiana antica: Abramo, Giacobbe, Ezechiele, pastor d'Erma, Felicita e Perpetua," *Augustinianum* 29 (1989): 549–63; Patricia Cox Miller, "Perpetua and Her Diary of Dreams," in *Dreams in Late Antiquity* (Princeton, N.J.: Princeton University Press, 1994), 148–83; Christine Trevett, *Montanism: Gender, Authority, and the New Prophecy* (New York: Cambridge University Press, 1996), 176–83.

74. Mary R. Lefkowitz, "Motivations for St. Perpetua's Martyrdom," *JAAR* 44 (1976): 417–21; Marie-Louise von Franz, *Passio Perpetuae: Das Schicksal einer Frau zwischen zwei Gottesbilden* (Zurich: Daimon, 1982); Mary Ann Rossi, "The Passion of Perpetua, Everywoman of Late Antiquity," in *Pagan and Christian Anxiety: A Response to E. R. Dodds*, ed. Robert C. Smith and John Lounibos (Lanham, Md.: University Press of America, 1984), 53–86; Rebecca Lyman, "Perpetua: A Christian Quest for Self," *Journal of Women and Religion* 8 (1989): 26–33; Margaret Miles, " 'Becoming Male':

Women Martyrs and Ascetics," in *Carnal Knowing: Female Nakedness and Religious Meaning in the Christian West* (Boston: Beacon Press, 1989), 53–77; Mieke Bal, "Perpetual Contest," in *On Storytelling*, ed. David Jobling (Sonoma, Calif.: Polebridge Press, 1991), 227–41; Elizabeth A. Castelli, " 'I Will Make Mary Male': Pieties of the Body and Gender Transformation of Early Christian Women in Late Antiquity," in *Bodyguards: The Cultural Contexts of Gender Ambiguity*, ed. Julia Epstein and Kristina Straub (New York: Routledge, 1991), 29–49; Elizabeth A. Castelli, "Visions and Voyeurism: Holy Women and the Politics of Sight in Early Christianity," in *Protocol of the Colloquy of the Center for Hermeneutical Studies, 6 December 1992*, n.s., 2, ed. Christopher Ocker (Berkeley: Center for Hermeneutical Studies, 1994), 1–20; Edward Peter Nolan, "Vibia Perpetua Martyr and a Feminine Style of Revelation," in *Cry Out and Write: A Feminine Poetics of Revelation* (New York: Continuum, 1994), 32–45; Maureen A. Tilley, "The Passion of Perpetua and Felicity," in *Searching the Scriptures*, vol. 2, *A Feminist Commentary*, ed. Elisabeth Schüssler Fiorenza (New York: Crossroad, 1994), 829–58; Gillian Clark, "Bodies and Blood: Late Antique Debate on Martyrdom, Virginity, and Resurrection," in *Changing Bodies, Changing Meanings: Studies on the Human Body in Antiquity*, ed. Dominic Montserrat (London/New York: Routledge, 1997), 99–115; M. Eleanor Irwin, "Gender, Status, and Identity in a North African Martyrdom," in *Gli imperatori Severi: Storia, archeologia, religione*, ed. Enrico Dal Covolo and Giancarlo Rinaldi (Rome: LAS, 1999), 251–60. See Kraemer and Lander (cited in note 29) on the contested authenticity of the authorship of the text.

75. R. Braun, "Nouvelle observations linguistiques sur le rédacteur de la *Passio Perpetuae*," *VC* 33 (1979): 105–17. The traditional attribution of this frame narrative to the North African presbyter Tertullian does not represent the scholarly consensus.

76. The redactor/narrator describes Perpetua with a good deal of detail and attention dedicated to her social standing: *Pass. Perp.* 2.1–2: "*Apprehensi sunt adolescentes catechumeni: Revocatus et Felicitas, conserva eius, Saturninus et Secundulus; inter hos et Vibia Perpetua, honeste nata, liberaliter instituta, matronaliter nupta, habens patrem et matrem et fratres duos, alterum aeque catechumenum, et filium infantem ad ubera.* [Some young catechumens were arrested: Revocatus and Felicitas, his fellow-slave, Saturninus and Secundulus. And with them Vibia Perpetua, of high rank, liberally educated, a respectable married woman, having a father and mother and two brothers, one of them likewise a catechumen, and an infant son at the breast.]"

77. Salisbury, *Perpetua's Passion*, 5–57, gives a good overview of what Perpetua's material, cultural, legal, and religious circumstances would have been, both the constraints that confined her and the opportunities her class status would have afforded her.

78. *Pass. Perp.* 3.2 (translation adapted from Musurillo, *The Acts of the Christian Martyrs*, 106–31).

79. See *Pass. Perp.* 2.1–2, 3.5.

80. *Pass. Perp.* 3.5.

81. *Pass. Perp.* 3.6.

82. *Pass. Perp.* 3.9.

83. Note that in the next chapter Perpetua's father addresses her "no longer as a daughter [*filia*] but as a *domina*" (5.5).

84. *Pass. Perp.* 4.2.

85. Miller, *Dreams in Late Antiquity*, 151, understands this verb to emphasize not only "that dreaming is a linguistic event, a kind of discourse" but also "that the dream is a *particular* kind of discourse, one associated with imaginative story-telling, with a 'fabled' or poeticized perspective."

86. *Oxford Latin Dictionary*, s.v. "*postulo*," 1415: "1 To ask for (generally as something to which one is entitled), demand . . . 4 To look for as due, expect . . . 5 (of inanim[ate] or abst[ract] things) To demand, require."

87. "*Et postulaui, et ostensum est mihi hoc* [And I asked, and this is what was revealed to me]" (4.2). On the use of "*ostensio*" and related terms to indicate "a figurative revelation that explains divine secrets," see Miller, *Dreams in Late Antiquity*, 151; Jacqueline Amat, *Songes et visions: L'au delà dans la littérature latine tardive* (Paris: Études Augustiniennes, 1985), 68.

88. Miles, *Carnal Knowing*, 60; Tilley, "The Passion of Perpetua and Felicity," 839.

89. *Pass. Perp.* 5.10.

90. *Pass. Perp.* 5.6.

91. *Pass. Perp.* 6.2. The Latin text contains a suitable double entendre: "the others, when questioned, confessed," the text says (*interrogati ceteri confessi sunt*). They simultaneously confess their guilt before the state and their faith before God.

92. Dölger, "Antike Parallelen zum leidenden Dinocrates."

93. Ciccarese, "Le più antiche rappresentazioni del purgatorio."

94. *Pass. Perp.* 7.2–3. Compare the introduction to the first vision, "*ostensum est mihi hoc*," at 4.2.

95. *Pass. Perp.* 8.1.

96. *Pass. Perp.* 8.4.

97. *Pass. Perp.* 9.2.

98. *Pass. Perp.* 9.3.

99. *Pass. Perp.* 10.7. This transformation is probably the most extensively glossed detail in the text. See Castelli, " 'I Will Make Mary Male' " and "Visions and Voyeurism" for detailed analysis and bibliography.

100. The entire vision is found at *Pass. Perp.* 10.1–13; the interpretation at 10.14: "*et intellexi me non ad bestias, sed contra diabolum esse pugnaturam; sed sciebam mihi esse uictoriam.*"

101. *Pass. Perp.* 10.15.

102. Heffernan, "Philology and Authorship," 320: "Autobiography and diary were considered by the ancient rhetoricians to be outside genre, and thus outside rhetoric."

103. Heffernan, "Philology and Authorship," 325, makes the distinction between the "publicly interpreted world of autobiography" and "the private world of diary," which he codes as masculine and feminine, political and domestic, teleological and immediate, concerned with rational thought and intimate dreams.

104. Heffernan, "Philology and Authorship," 325.

105. *Martyrium Pionii*, ed. A. Hilhorst, trans. Silvia Ronchey, in *Atti e passioni dei Martiri*, ed. A. A. R. Bastiaensen et al., 149–91 (text and translation), 453–77 (notes and commentary); Louis Robert, ed. and trans., *Le martyre de Pionios, Prêtre de Smyrne*, ordered and completed by G. W. Bowersock and C. P. Jones (Washington,

D.C.: Dumbarton Oaks Research Library and Collection, 1994); *The Martyrdom of Pionius the Presbyter and his Companions*, in Musurillo, *The Acts of the Christian Martyrs*, xxviii–xxx (introduction), 136–67 (text and translation). Musurillo's English translation is flawed at points; see corrections by Hilhorst in Bastiaensen et al.; Robert, *Le martyre de Pionios*; and Jan den Boeft and Jan Bremmer, "*Notiunculae Martyrologicae* III: Some Observations on the *Martyria* of Polycarp and Pionius," *VC* 39 (1985): 110–30. The English translation here is my own. On Pionius as rhetor, see Laurent Pernot, "Saint Pionios, martyr et orateur," in *Du héros païen au saint chrétien: Actes du colloque organisé par le Centre d'analyse des rhétoriques religieuses de l'Antiquité (C.A.R.R.A.), Strasbourg, 1er–2 décembre 1995*, ed. Gérard Freyburger and Laurent Pernot (Paris: Institut d'Études Augustiniennes, 1997), 111–23.

106. Note that although most manuscripts have ταῖς χηρείαις, a few have ταῖς μνείαις (D* F G t vg^mss; Ambst); see Nestle-Aland, *Novum Testamentum Graecae*, 27th ed., on Rom 12:13. This same substitution appears in the preface to the longer recension of Eusebius, *Mart. Pal.*; see Praef. 2: "So for our part, we who need the help of their prayers and are commanded also in the book of the Apostles *to communicate in the commemoration of the saints*."

107. Note that "σύγγραμμα" is distinguished by at least one writer from "ὑπόμνημα": LSJ, s.v. "ὑπόμνημα," 2.5.c, 1889: "Galen distinguishes ὑπομνήματα [clinical *notes*] from συγγράμματα of Hippocrates, 16.532, 543; and the συγγράμματα of Hp. From his own *commentaries* (ὑπομνήματα) on them, ib. 811." *Syngrammata*, then, are more substantive and complete texts.

108. C. J. Cadoux, *Ancient Smyrna* (Oxford: Oxford University Press, 1938), 389n1: "There is nothing whatever impossible about the writing having been done in gaol . . . , or about its consisting of Pionios' own notes of his experiences, conversations and speeches (in short the substance of *Mart. Pion.* ii–xviii)." Hippolyte Delehaye, *Les passions des martyrs et les genres littéraires*, Subsidia Hagiographica 13b (Brussels: Société des Bollandistes, 1966), 26–33, esp. 30–32, where Delehaye argues, "Il ne suffira pas de dire que la forme même de la narration exclut l'hypothèse d'un mémoire écrit par Pionius; que celui-ci aurait parlé à la première personne, alors qu'il est toujours question de lui à la troisième. Cette difficulté n'est pas fort grave. Le rédacteur a transposé son document, sans se rendre compte de ce qu'il lui faisait perdre en interèt et en importance" (31). More recently, see Hilhorst, in Bastiaensen et al., *Atti e passioni*, 150: "Il testo di questo *Martirio* fu redatto a Smirne (ma l'autore è ignoto) poco tempo dopo gli avvenimenti descritti, e comunque nella seconda metà del terzo secolo. Esso sarebbe fondato su un documento autobiografico redatto da Pionio stesso, e complessivamente è di grande valore, nonostante alcuni rimaneggiamenti e amplificazioni" (150). The most recent commentary on Pionius also asserts the authenticity of an autobiographical text underlying the text as we currently have it: Robert, *Le Martyre de Pionios*, 49–50: "Ce document de Pionios doit être le texte fondamental du récit du *martyrium* jusqu'au moment de la mort du saint. . . . On suppose que Pionios écrivit son récit quand il était dans la prison en attendant la mort" (49). See also Robin Lane Fox, *Pagans and Christians* (New York: Alfred K. Knopf, 1987), 460–92, who calls Pionius's text his "diary" (473, 475) and who argues that "the bulk of it was so exact because Pionius had written it himself in prison" (472) and, later, "from Homer to the Dead Sea,

Susannah to the witch of Endor, Pionius's speeches have taken us on a tour of the culture of a mid-third-century Christian. They are not the invention of a later editor: they survived in his own prison diary, sermons, not visionary dreams" (483).

Standing outside this scholarly consensus is Musurillo, the editor and translator of the primary English translation of the martyr acts who dates the text later than other commentators ("shortly before or after 300") and reads it as a historically muddled creation dependent upon fashionable (but historically unreliable) rhetorical and literary models. He makes no mention of the potential autobiographical content of the text. See Musurillo, *Acts of the Christian Martyrs*, xxviii–xxix: "The document seems reminiscent of the baroque rhetoric of the late Cynic diatribe. . . . A certain atmosphere of the Hellenistic novel pervades the piece . . . and this, together with its obvious literary merits, helped to preserve it" (xxix).

109. For a comprehensive survey of the historical evidence concerning the decree of Decius, see James B. Rives, "The Decree of Decius and the Religion of Empire," *JRS* 89 (1999): 135–54.

110. *Mart. Pion.* 4.2.

111. *Mart. Pion.* 12.2.

112. *Mart. Pion.* 12.1.

113. This title, usually translated "temple warden," refers generally to an official in a temple or, alternately, to a city to indicate the presence of an important religious cult there. In the context of the imperial cult in Asia Minor in this period, the title indicates both an important civic office for the person who holds the title and also the presence of a temple devoted to the imperial cult. Hence, Polemon's title indicates both his own civic and religious importance and the importance of the temple in Smyrna. See Simon R. F. Price, *Rituals and Power: The Roman Imperial Cult in Asia Minor* (Cambridge: Cambridge University Press, 1984), 64–5.

114. *Mart. Pion.* 4.1.

115. *Mart. Pion.* 4.2.

116. Christian writers before Pionius also use this metaphor of desertion to describe Christians turning away from the church. See *1 Clement* 21.4, 28.2; Ignatius, *Pol.* 6.2; *Mart. Pauli* 4. See also the commentary of Robert, ed. and trans., *Le Martyre de Pionios*, 57; Hilhorst, in Bastiaensen et al., 456. On "ἀστόχημα" as "missing the mark" in both literal and figurative senses, see LSJ and Lampe, s.v. "ἀστόχημα."

117. Homer, *Od.* 22.412.

118. Deut. 22.4; Prov. 24.17.

119. Also see 4.8, where Pionius says, "For even if we are their enemies, *as they say*, but [we are also] human beings, moreover, wronged ones." E. Leigh Gibson, "Jewish Antagonism or Christian Polemic: The Case of the *Martyrdom of Pionius*," *JECS* 9 (2001): 339–58, situates the text in the historical situation in Smyrna.

120. *Mart. Pion.* 4.7.

121. When found in early Christian literature more broadly, it is often used in the context of persecution (describing roles on both sides of the conflict, both persecuted and persecutor) as well as in the more metaphorical context of spiritual contest and struggle. See Lampe, s.v. "ἀγών."

122. "They say that we have time for bold speech [παρρησίας]. Yes, but did we

injure [ἠδικήσαμεν] anyone? Did we kill anyone? Did we persecute anyone? Did we coerce anyone to perform service to idols? . . . Who coerced the Jews to be consecrated to Beelphegor? [Josh. 22:17; Ps. 106:28] Or to eat from the sacrifice for the dead? Or to perform sexual immorality with the daughters of foreigners? [Num. 25:1–2] Or to burn their sons and daughters for idols? Or to murmur against God; or to slander Moses? [Exod. 16:2–3] Or to be ungrateful to benefactors? Or to turn back in their hearts to Egypt? Or, when Moses went up to receive the law, to say to Aaron, 'Make for us gods, and make a calf,' [Exod. 32:1–4] and everything else they did? For they are able to deceive. Then let them read to you the book of Judges, of Kings, Exodus, and everything in which they are shamed/refuted/proven wrong [ἐλέγχονται]" (*Mart. Pion.* 4.9–12).

123. At 4.18–23. The punishments include the barrenness of Palestine and the Dead Sea and even the fact that bodies will float in the Dead Sea: "For it doesn't want to receive a human being lest because of a human being it be censured again" (4.20). Pionius also identifies volcanic eruptions and the story of the flood, a story shared by both biblical tradition and Graeco-Roman mythology, as signs of God's wrath.

124. *Mart. Pion.* 4.17: "Κρίσις γὰρ τῷ κόσμῳ ἐπίκειται, περὶ ἧς πεπληροφορήμεθα διὰ πολλῶν."

125. This text may be the earliest testimony to Christian pilgrimage. For later sources on the authority that comes from seeing the holy places with one's own eyes, see E. D. Hunt, *Holy Land Pilgrimage in the Later Roman Empire (A.D. 312–460)* (Oxford: Clarendon Press, 1982), 99–100. On the authority of pilgrims' eyewitnessing more generally, see Georgia Frank, *The Memory of the Eyes: Pilgrims to Living Saints in Christian Late Antiquity* (Berkeley: University of California Press, 2000).

126. *Mart. Pion.* 4.18.

127. At *Mart. Pion.* 13.2.

128. See 3 Macc. 2:5; Jude 7; 2 Peter 2:6.

129. *Mart. Pion.* 4.24.

130. This alignment between the two opponents of the Christians appears later in Pionius's second speech, where he makes a brief reference to "Susanna ambushed by the lawless elders" at 12.5. Early Christian interpretation of the story of Susanna and the elders often read it allegorically so that Susanna equals "the church" while the elders equal "the pagans and the Jews." See, for example, Hippolytus [Hippolyte], *Comm. in Dan.* 1.14.5–6: "Susanna prefigures [προετυποῦτο] the Church. . . . The two elders represent as types [εἰς τύπον] the two peoples who scheme against the church: one the people of the circumcision and the other the people of the nations."

131. *Mart. Pion.* 5.1.

132. *Mart. Pion.* 5.3.

133. Musurillo, *Acts of the Christian Martyrs,* xxix.

134. Ronald F. Hock and Edward N. O'Neil, *The Chreia in Ancient Rhetoric,* Texts and Translations 27, Graeco-Roman Religion Series 9 (Atlanta: Scholars Press, 1986).

135. *Mart. Pion.* 7.3–4. The syntax of these sentences is punning: Polemon says, "Be persuaded by us," or "Obey us [πείσθητι ἡμῖν]"; Pionius responds, "If only I were able to persuade you [ὑμᾶς πεῖσαι]." The interchange between Pionius and the laughing

men is also put carefully—the men say, "You do not have such power to cause us who are living to burn [Οὐδὲν ἔχεις τοιοῦτο ποιῆσαι ἵνα ζῶντες καῶμεν]," and Pionius responds, "It is much worse to be burned being dead [Χεῖρόν ἐστι πολὺ ἀποθανόντας καυθῆναι]."

136. *Mart. Pion.* 7.6: "Σὺ μὲν ὅ οὐθέλεις μέλλεις πάσχειν· αἱ γὰρ μὴ ἐπιθύουσαι εἰς πορνεῖον ἵστανται." The condemnation of Christian women to brothels is discussed in Friedrich Augar, *Die Frau im römischen Christenprocess: Ein Beitrag zur Verfolgungsgeschichte der christlichen Kirche im römischen Staat*, TUGAL 28.4c = n.F. 13.4c (Leipzig: J. C. Hinrichs, 1905), cited also by Hilhorst, in Bastiaensen, et al., 461–62, and Robert, *Le Martyre de Pionios*, 68–69. The fact that the threat of sexual violence is a narrative figure most often in stories about Christian women (often virgins) should not blind us to the fact that sexual violence, forced prostitution, or the threat of one or the other operated as a technology of coercion and/or humiliation in (especially young) men's experiences as well. See David Tombs, "Crucifixion, State Terror, and Sexual Abuse," *USQR* 53, nos. 1–2 (1999): 89–109.

137. See especially Fox's reconstruction and Robert's commentary in *Le martyre de Pionios*. Also see Gibson, "Jewish Antagonism or Christian Polemic."

138. *Mart. Pion.* 12.5 (Susanna); 12.6 (Esther); 13.2 (Sodom and Gomorrah). See note 130, above, for more on the Susanna material in the broader context of early Christian exegesis.

139. *Mart. Pion.* 13.2.

140. Isaiah 1:15: "αἱ γὰρ χεῖρες ὑμῶν αἵματος πλήρεις." Note that Pionius's warning that Christians not become ἄρχοντες Σοδόμων or λαὸς Γομόρρας cites Isaiah's epithets in 1:10.

141. *Mart. Pion.* 13.8. On this curious passage, see Stephen Gero, "Jewish Polemic in the *Martyrium Pionii* and a 'Jesus' Passage from the Talmud," *JJS* 29 (1978): 164–68.

142. *Mart. Pion.* 14.1–14. The "witch" is more literally a female oracle or "ventriloquist" (ἐγγαστρίμυθος).

143. *Mart. Pion.* 14.15: "Ὅπως ἄν ᾖ, ἡμεῖς ὑμῶν τῶν χωρὶς ἀνάγκης ἐκπορνευσάντων καὶ εἰδωλολατρησάντων κρείττονές ἐσμεν."

144. *Mart. Pion.* 2.1–3. On the assumption that Pionius has seen the inevitability of their arrest in a dream, commentators focus on the repetition of "εἶδεν" in 2.2 and 2.3 and the parallel experience in the *Mart. Pol.* to which the martyrdom of Pionius and the others is explicitly linked in 2.1.

145. *Mart. Pion.* 2.4. Musurillo seems to have misunderstood this passage; see his note at 137n1.

146. *Mart. Pion.* 6.3. At 6.1, Alexander is described as "τις ἀγοραῖος πονηρὸς ἀνὴρ"; Musurillo, 145, as incorrectly translates "ἀγοραῖος" as "a lawyer."

147. *Mart. Pion.* 6.4: "καὶ οὕτως ὁ Ἀλεξάνδρος ἐφιμώθη."

148. *Mart. Pion.* 8.1: "Κεκέλευσαι ἢ πείθειν ἢ κολάζειν· οὐ παίθεις, κόλαζε."

149. *Mart. Pion.* 8.2–3.

150. *Mart. Pion.* 8.4. Strikingly, this is one of the few places in any of the ancient literature documenting the conflict between Christians and Roman authorities where a Christian is commanded to sacrifice *to* the emperor. Even more remarkably, the com-

mand is offered here, not as a provocation, but as a plausible and less egregious alternative to offering sacrifice to the Roman gods. The other three examples of Christians commanded to sacrifice to the emperor all derive from Eusebius, two from the Syriac *Mart. Pal.* (1.1; 1.54) and one from *Hist. Eccl.* (7.15). See Price, *Rituals and Power*, 207–33, esp. 216–22, where the meanings of such sacrifices are set in religious and political context.

Elsewhere in this *Martyrdom*, one encounters the strategy of the state authority seeking to make this problem of Christian resistance to go away with a command to render an innocuous sacrifice. In the court transcription of Pionius's trial before the proconsul Quintilian, the official tries to make common cause with Pionius, saying, " 'We worship (σέβομεν) all the gods and heaven and the gods who are in heaven. Do you devote yourself to the air? Sacrifice to it' " (*Mart. Pion.* 19.10). What is clear is that the conflict here lies between two competing theories of sacrifice and religious piety, with the antisacrificial commitment of Christians illegible to their opponents.

151. *Mart. Pion.* 15.3.

152. For the legal context here, see Peter Garnsey, "The Criminal Jurisdiction of Governors," *JRS* 58 (1968): 51–59.

153. *Mart. Pion.* 15.4–6.

154. *Mart. Pion.* 16.6: "Ὁ δὲ Πιόνιος ἐβόα· Θεοσέβειαν αἰδέσθητε, δικαιοσύνην τιμήσατε, τὸ ὁμοιοπαθὲς ἐπίγνωτε, τοῖς νόμοις ὑμῶν κατακολουθήσατε· ἡμᾶς κολάζετε ὡς μὴ πειθομένους, καὶ ὑμεῖς ἀπειθεῖτε· κολάζειν ἐκελεύσθητε, οὐ βιάζεσθαι." A similar appeal to the common condition of human beings made by one persecuted to his persecutors may be found in 4 Macc 12.13 ("οὐκ ἠδέσθης ἄνθρωπος ὢν, θηριωδέστατε, τοὺς ὁμοιοπαθεῖς καὶ ἐκ τῶν αὐτῶν γεγονότας στοιχείων γλωττοτομῆσαι").

155. *Mart. Pion.* 17.2–3. The text records three names—Socrates, Aristides, and Anaxarchos—as the relevant examples. The examples of Socrates and Aristides are self-evident; the figure of Anaxarchos, whose story is preserved in Diogenes Laertius, *Lives of Eminent Philosophers*, 2 vols., trans. R. D. Hicks, LCL (Cambridge, Mass.: Harvard University Press, 1980), 9.58–60, is less transparent. A companion of Alexander the Great, he offended a tyrant at whose order he was executed; he is mentioned by Celsus as an example of a heroic death and aligned with Socrates by Origen (Origen, *Cels.* 7.53, 56). Robert, *Le Martyre de Pionios*, 98–99, argues that Pionius may have meant Anaxagoras, a friend of Pericles who was accused of atheism and exiled: "Dans le *Martyre*, cela [Anaxagoras] va bien avec Socrate et Aristide le Juste, tous les trois personnifications de la vertu injustement persécutée par les Athéniens, eux-mêmes citoyens de la ville de la culture grecque par excellence."

156. *Mart. Pion.* 17.3: "ἐκενοδόξουν καθ' ὑμᾶς ὅτι καὶ φιλοσοφίαν καὶ δικαιοσύνην καὶ καρτερίαν ἤσκησαν."

157. *Mart. Pion.* 18.1–2.

158. *Mart. Pion.* 18.13–14.

159. As some of the students with whom I have read these texts over the past several years have done, especially with Ignatius and Perpetua.

160. Augustine, *Serm.* 280.1; *Serm.* 282.2; Elizabeth Alvilda Petroff, ed., *Medieval Women's Visionary Literature* (New York: Oxford University Press, 1986), 70–76;

Judith A. Scheffler, ed., *Wall Tappings: An International Anthology of Women's Prison Writings, 200 to the Present*, 2nd ed. (New York: Feminist Press, 2002).

4. MARTYRDOM AND THE SPECTACLE OF SUFFERING

1. Eusebius quotes Romans 12:13 ("communicate in the commemoration of the saints") here, reading μνείαις for χρείαις, as does *Mart. Pion.* 1.1.

2. Eusebius, *Mart. Pal.*, longer recension (Syriac), preface, 2. The English translation appears in Eusebius, *The Ecclesiastical History and The Martyrs of Palestine*, trans. Hugh Jackson Lawlor and John Ernest Leonard Oulton (London: Society for Promoting Christian Knowledge, 1927), 1:329. Lawlor and Oulton use the Syriac text in Eusebius, *History of the Martyrs in Palestine*, ed. and trans. William Cureton (London/Edinburgh: Williams and Norgate; Paris: C. Borrani, 1861).

3. Augustine, *Serm.* 51.2. Augustine calls up a similar contrast in other sermons as well: *Serm.* 280.2 (On the birthday of the martyrs Perpetua and Felicity); *Serm.* 301A.7 (On the solemnity of the holy Maccabees: preached in Bulla Regia).

4. These writers' arguments will be explored in a subsequent section. For scholarly treatments of their critiques, see Jean-Baptiste Eriau, *Pourquoi les pères de l'église ont condamné le théâtre de leur temps* (Paris: Honoré Champion, 1914); J. H. Waszink, "Pompa Diaboli," *VC* 1 (1947): 13–41; B. H. Vandernberghe, "Saint Jean Chrysostome et les spectacles," *ZRGG* 7 (1955): 34–46; Heiko Jürgens, *Pompa Diaboli: Die lateinischen Kirchenväter und das antike Theater*, Tübinger Beiträge zur Altertumswissenschaft 46 (Stuttgart: Kohlhammer, 1972); Werner Weismann, *Kirche und Schauspiele: Die Schauspiele im Urteil der lateinischen Kirchenväter unter besonderer Berücksichtigung von Augustin*, Cassiciacum 27 (Würzberg: Augustinus-Verlag, 1972); Renato Nitti, "L'homo ludens nella paideia classica e cristiana: La funzione etico-pedagogica del divertimento nella patristica dei primi secoli," *Nicolaus: Rivista di teologia ecumenico-patristica* 8 (1980): 439–51; Christine Catharina Schnusenberg, *The Relationship Between the Church and the Theatre* (Lanham, Md.: University Press of America, 1988); Paul-Albert Février, "Les chrétiens dans l'arène," in *Spectacula I: Gladiateurs et amphithéatres: Actes du colloque tenu à Toulouse et à Lattes les 26, 27, 28 et 29 mai 1987*, ed. Claude Domerge, Christian Landes, and Jean-Marie Pailler (Lattes: Editions Imago, 1990), 265–73; Michel Matter, "Jeux d'amphithéâtre et réactions chrétiennes de Tertullien à la fin du Ve siècle," in *Spectacula I: Gladiateurs et amphithéatres: Actes du colloque tenu à Toulouse et à Lattes les 26, 27, 28 et 29 mai 1987*, ed. Claude Domerge, Christian Landes, and Jean-Marie Pailler (Lattes: Editions Imago, 1990), 259–64; Robert A. Markus, "Die *spectacula* als religiöses Konfliktfeld städtischen Lebens in der Spätantike," *FZPhTh* 38 (1991): 253–71; Martino Menghi, "Tertulliano e il De spectaculis," *Lexis* 9–10 (1992): 189–209; T. D. Barnes, "Christians and the Theater," in *Roman Theater and Society*, ed. William J. Slater (Ann Arbor: University of Michigan Press, 1996), 161–80; Costas Panayotakis, "Baptism and Crucifixion on the Mimic Stage," *Mnemosyne*, ser. 4, 50 (1997): 302–19. See, most recently, Blake Leyerle, *Theatrical Shows and Ascetic Lives: John Chrysostom's Attack on Spiritual Marriage* (Berkeley: University of California Press, 2001), esp. 42–74; Mathew Kuefler, *The Manly Eunuch: Masculinity, Gender Ambiguity, and Christian Ideology in Late Antiquity* (Chicago: University of Chicago Press, 2001), 210–14.

5. The arena stood out for special critique not only for Christian authors but also for the rabbis. See, for example, t. 'Avod. Zar. 2:5–7; y. 'Avod. Zar. 1:7 (40a); b. 'Avod. Zar. 18b. See Martin Jacobs, "Theatres and Performances as Reflected in the Talmud Yerushalmi," in The Talmud Yerushalmi and Graeco-Roman Culture, ed. Peter Schäfer, TSAJ 71 (Tübingen: Mohr [Siebeck], 1998), 1:327–47. I am grateful to Beth Berkowitz for bringing the rabbinic texts and this essay to my attention.

6. G. Lafaye, "Gladiator," in Dictionnaire des antiquités grecques et romaines d'après les textes et les monuments, ed. C. Daremberg, E. Saglio, and M. Pottier (Paris: Hachette, 1896), 2.2:1563–99; G. Lafaye, "Venatio," in Dictionnaire des antiquités grecques et romaines d'après les textes et les monuments, ed. C. Daremberg, E. Saglio, and M. Pottier (Paris: Hachette, 1914), 5:680–709; H. J. Leon, "Morituri te salutamus," TAPA 70 (1939): 46–50; Louis Robert, Les gladiateurs dans l'Orient grec, Bibliothèque de l'École des hautes études 289 (Paris: Librairie ancienne Honoré Campion, 1940); Jacques Aymard, Essai sur les chasses romaines des origines à la fin du siècle des Antonins (Cynegetica), Bibliothèque des Écoles françaises d'Athènes et de Rome 171 (Paris: Boccard, 1951); Roland Auguet, Cruelty and Civilization: The Roman Games (London: George Allen and Unwin, 1972); Paul Veyne, Le pain et le cirque: Sociologie historique d'un pluralisme politique (Paris: Seuil, 1976); Georges Ville, La gladiature en Occident des origines à la morte de Domitien, Bibliothèque des Écoles françaises d'Athènes et de Rome 245 (Rome: École Française de Rome, 1981); Keith Hopkins, "Murderous Games," in Death and Renewal: Sociological Studies in Roman History (Cambridge: Cambridge University Press, 1983), 2:1–30; M. Adele Cavallaro, Spese e spettacoli: Aspetti economici-strutturali degli spettacoli nella Roma giulio-claudia, Antiquitas 34 (Bonn: Habelt, 1984); Monique Clavel-Lévêque, L'empire en jeux: Espace symbolique et pratique sociale dans le monde romain (Paris: Éditions du CNRS, 1984); Monique Clavel-Lévêque, "Rituels de mort et consommation de gladiateurs: Images de domination et pratiques imperialistes de reproduction," in Hommages à Lucien Lerat, ed. Hélène Walter (Paris: Société d'Éditions "Les Belles Lettres," 1984), 189–208; Florence Dupont, L'acteur-roi ou le théâtre dans la Rome antique (Paris: Société d'Éditions "Les Belles Lettres," 1985); S. P. Oakley, "Single Combat in the Roman Republic," CQ 35 (1985): 392–410; Monique Clavel-Lévêque, "L'espace des jeux dans le monde romain: Hégémonie, symbolique et pratique sociale," ANRW, 2.16.3 (1986): 2406–563; F. Hinard, "Spectacle des exécutions et espace urbain," in L'urbs: Espace urbain et histoire, Ier s. av. J.C.–IIIe s. ap. J.C. Atti del colloquio internazionale CNRS, EFR, Rome 9–12 maggio 1985, Collection de l'École Française de Rome 98 (Rome: École Française de Rome, 1987), 111–25; Ernst Baltrusch, "Die Verstaatlichung der Gladiatorenspiele," Hermes 116 (1988): 324–37; Jean-Claude Golvin, L'amphithéâtre romain: Essai sur la théorisation de sa forme et de ses fonctions, 2 vols., Publications du Centre Pierre Paris 18 (Paris: Boccard, 1988); A. M. Reggiani, ed., Anfiteatro Flavio: Immagine, testimonianze, spettacoli (Rome: Edizione Quasar, 1988); Alexander Scobie, "Spectator Security and Comfort at Gladiatorial Games," Nikephoros 1 (1988): 191–243; Carlin A. Barton, "The Scandal of the Arena," Representations 27 (1989): 1–36; K. M. Coleman, "Fatal Charades: Roman Executions Staged as Mythological Enactments," JRS 80 (1990): 44–73; Pierre Flobert, "Quelques survivances de la gladiature," Voces 1 (1990): 71–76; Jean-Claude Golvin and Christian Landes, Amphithéâtres et gladiateurs (Paris: Éditions

du CNRS, 1990); Marcel LeGlay, "Les amphithéâtres: *Loci religiosi*?" in *Spectacula I: Gladiateurs et amphithéâtres: Actes du colloque tenu à Toulouse et à Lattes les 26, 27, 28 et 29 mai 1987*, ed. Claude Domergue, Christian Landes, and Jean-Marie Pailler (Lattes: Editions Imago, 1990), 217–29; Cinzia Vismara, *Il supplizio come spettacolo*, Vita e costumi dei Romani antichi 11 (Rome: Museo della civiltà romana/Quasar, 1990); Claude Domergue, Christian Landes, and Jean-Marie Pailler, eds., *Spectacula I: Gladiateurs et amphithéâtres: Actes du colloque tenu à Toulouse et à Lattes les 26, 27, 28 et 29 mai 1987* (Lattes: Editions Imago, 1990); Katherine Welch, "Roman Amphitheatres Revived," *JRA* 4 (1991): 272–81; Christian Landes and Véronique Kramérovskis, eds., *Spectacula II: Le théâtre antique et ses spectacles: Actes du colloque tenu au Musée Archéologique Henri Prades de Lattes les 27, 28, 29, et 30 avril 1989* (Latte: Musée archéologique Henri Prades, 1992); Thomas E. J. Wiedemann, *Emperors and Gladiators* (London: Routledge, 1992); Magnus Wistrand, *Entertainment and Violence in Ancient Rome: The Attitudes of Roman Writers of the First Century A.D.* (Göteburg: Acta Universitatis Gothoburgensis, 1992); Carlin A. Barton, *The Sorrows of the Ancient Romans: The Gladiator and the Monster* (Princeton, N.J.: Princeton University Press, 1993); Florence Dupont, "Ludions, Lydioi: Les danseurs de la pompa circensis: Exégèse et discours sur l'origine des jeux à Rome," in *Spectacles sportifs et scéniques dans le monde étrusco-italique: Actes de la table ronde organisée par l'equipe de recherches étrusco-italiques de l'UMR 126 (CNRS, Paris) et l'École Française de Rome, Rome 3–4 mai 1991* (Rome: École Française de Rome, 1993), 189–210; Michael B. Hornum, *Nemesis, the Roman State, and the Games* (Leiden: Brill, 1993); Katherine Welch, "The Roman Arena in Late-Republican Italy: A New Interpretation," *JRA* 7 (1994): 59–80; Shelby Brown, "Explaining the Arena: Did the Romans 'Need' Gladiators?" *JRA* 8 (1995): 376–84; Paul Plass, *The Game of Death in Ancient Rome: Arena Sport and Political Suicide* (Madison: University of Wisconsin Press, 1995); John C. Edmondson, "Dynamic Arenas: Gladiatorial Presentations in the City of Rome and the Construction of Roman Society During the Early Empire," in *Roman Theatre and Society*, ed. William J. Slater (Ann Arbor: University of Michigan Press, 1996), 69–112; Erik Gunderson, "The Ideology of the Arena," *ClAnt* 15 (1996): 113–51; Alison Futrell, *Blood in the Arena: The Spectacle of Roman Power* (Austin: University of Texas Press, 1997); Donald G. Kyle, *Spectacles of Death in Ancient Rome* (New York: Routledge, 1998); Richard C. Beacham, *Spectacle Entertainments of Early Imperial Rome* (New Haven, Conn.: Yale University Press, 1999); Paul Veyne, "Païens et chrétiens devant la gladiature," *MEFRA* 111 (1999): 883–917.

7. Especially relevant here are Futrell, *Blood in the Arena*; Plass, *The Game of Death in Ancient Rome*; Gunderson, "The Ideology of the Arena"; Clavel-Lévêque, *L'empire en jeux*; and Shelby Brown, "Death as Decoration: Scenes from the Arena on Roman Domestic Mosaics," in *Pornography and Representation in Greece and Rome*, ed. Amy Richlin (New York: Oxford University Press, 1992), 180–211.

8. It seems to be a virtual requirement in the literature on the arena to dwell upon the portraits of violence there and then to pass a reassuring, distancing judgment upon it in which "we" are not implicated in "their" violence. It is difficult to avoid observing in the secondary literature on martyrs and gladiators the contradictory rhetoric of lurid description followed immediately by moral distancing culminating in a plea to understand the Romans "in their own terms." So, Auguet, *Cruelty and Civilization*,

13–15: "In one sense, these pictures, a little morbid and shocking, teach us a lesson: that the life of a man has not always had the value that our own morality strives to give it. In the past it could be a mere episode, and death the instrument of a collective pleasure. . . . These scenes impress themselves on us because they are monstrous and inexplicable. Their apparent pointlessness incites us little by little to attribute the violence they reveal to some cruelty in the Roman nature, a prejudice which even closer contact with the ancient world may only correct with difficulty. . . . Later on, we shall try to find an explanation for this paradox in a civilization which, granting nothing to pleasure or to fantasy, ended by organizing the most unseemly and maddest extravagances." Similar discussions appear in Hopkins, "Murderous Games," 5 ("The welter of blood in gladiatorial and wild-beast shows, the squeals of the victims and of slaughtered animals are completely alien to us and almost unimaginable.") and Barton, *Sorrows of the Ancient Romans*, 11 ("The Roman fascination with the gladiator confounds us: we see him as a twisted 'athlete' in a twisted 'sport,' the embodiment of Roman sadism, brutality, and callousness. We can hear only his scream; we cannot hear the song within the sorrow."). See also Brown, "Explaining the Arena" and "Death as Decoration"; Coleman, "Fatal Charades"; Ville, *La Gladiature*, 227; and elsewhere.

In the summer of 1996, while working on portions of this project, I was part of an NEH seminar on "the art of ancient spectacle" at the American Academy in Rome. In the seminar itself, there was both great interest in the question of what actually happened in Roman arenas *and* great reticence to import modern language like "cruelty" and "brutality" to describe what went on there—paralleling the responses of many other scholars to this difficult material. But what was also striking was the fact that I was taking part in this seminar in the late twentieth century in Italy, caught up in present-day politics as much as in ancient Roman imperial sources. Indeed, on the very day when our seminar discussed "cruelty" and "brutality" in the Roman arena, an Italian court ruled against the extradition of an Italian citizen to the United States to stand trial for a murder of which he was accused in Florida. The rationale for this decision lay in the fact that the Italian court would not place an Italian citizen in a judicial situation in which he or she could be sentenced to death, a punishment that Italy and every other developed country in the world has decreed to be inhumane. As one thinks about the politics and ethics of persecution, martyrdom, and state-sponsored executions, it seemed important to notice the ironies embedded in the juxtaposition of these two events on a single Roman summer day.

9. Kyle, *Spectacles of Death*.

10. On the infamy of the people in the arena, see Ville, *La Gladiature*, 339–43; also see Futrell, *Blood in the Arena*, 47. On the condemned becoming "slaves to the penalty," see David Potter, "Martyrdom as Spectacle," in *Theater and Society in the Classical World*, ed. Ruth Scodel (Ann Arbor: University of Michigan Press, 1993), 65 (with ancient sources).

11. Clavel-Lévêque, "L'espace des jeux dans le monde romain," 2406. (Her argument in this essay follows closely the volume published two years earlier, *L'empire en jeux*.)

12. Clavel-Lévêque, "L'espace des jeux dans le monde romain," 2410–11.

13. This view has been expressed by many interpreters of the games: see Auguet, *Cruelty and Civilization*, 23; Veyne, *Le pain et le cirque*, 390–94.

14. Clavel-Lévêque, "L'espace des jeux dans le monde romain," 2472.

15. Clavel-Lévêque, "L'espace des jeux dans le monde romain," 2473.

16. Plass, *The Game of Death in Ancient Rome*.

17. René Girard, *Violence and the Sacred*, trans. Patrick Gregory (Baltimore: Johns Hopkins University Press, 1977), originally published as *La violence et le sacré* (Paris: Grasset, 1972). See also Robert G. Hamerton-Kelly, ed., *Violent Origins: Walter Burkert, René Girard, and Jonathan Z. Smith on Ritual Killing and Cultural Formation* (Stanford, Calif.: Stanford University Press, 1987).

18. Plass, *The Game of Death*, 10: "Each in its own way [arena violence and political suicide] thus administered a dose of cultured (in the medical-biological sense) violence, working like an immune system to bring the body politic back into balance." Later, at 59, "A principle of homeopathy is operative in concentrated doses of violence for responding to crises of all kinds, with concentration taking extensive or intensive, quantitative or qualitative, forms." At 60: "Crucifixion was another tool for managing violence through homeopathic counterterror."

19. Plass, *The Game of Death*, 3.

20. Plass, *The Game of Death*, 19, 21.

21. Gunderson, "The Ideology of the Arena," 115.

22. Michel Foucault, *Surveiller et punir* (Paris: Gallimard, 1975), 228–64; English translation: *Discipline and Punish: The Birth of the Prison*, trans. Alan Sheridan (New York: Vintage, 1979), 195–228. Foucault's discussion of premodern and modern forms of penalty and punishment also influences the reading of the arena in Potter, "Martyrdom as Spectacle," 53–88, and Futrell, *Blood in the Arena*, 47.

23. Gunderson, "The Ideology of the Arena," 115–16.

24. Louis Althusser, "Ideology and the Ideological State Apparatus (Notes Toward an Investigation)," in *Lenin and Philosophy and Other Essays*, trans. Ben Brewster (New York: Monthly Review Press, 1971), 127–86. Gunderson's discussion of Althusser, including a critique of aspects of his theory, appears in Gunderson, "The Ideology of the Arena," 116–18.

25. Gunderson, "The Ideology of the Arena," 117.

26. Dupont, *L'acteur-roi*, discussed in Gunderson, "The Ideology of the Arena," 118–19.

27. Gunderson, "The Ideology of the Arena," 149.

28. Futrell, *Blood in the Arena*, 47, 169–210. She is not the first or only scholar to argue for the sacrificial dimensions of Roman capital punishment; see also Theodor Mommsen, *Römischen Strafrecht*, 4 vols., Systematisches Handbuch der deutschen Rechtswissenschaft, 1 Abt. (Leipzig: Duncker & Humblot, 1899), 900–904.

29. Futrell, *Blood in the Arena*, 170.

30. But see sources collected in Wistrand, *Entertainment and Violence*, for evidence of such critique.

31. See Jennifer Glancy, *Slavery in Early Christianity* (New York: Oxford University Press, 2002).

32. Athenagoras, *Leg.* 35.1.

33. Theophilus, *Autol.* 3.15.

34. Theophilus, *Autol.* 3.15.

35. Tatian, *Or. Graec.* 22.2–3. The latter part of the passage reads, "ἕνα κατήγορον <ὄντα> πάντων τῶν θεῶν, δεισιδαιμονίας ἐπιτομήν, διάβολον ἡρωϊκῶν πράξεων, φόνων ὑποκριτήν, μοιχείας ὑπομνηματιστήν, θησαυρὸν μανίας, κιναίδων παιδευτήν, καταδικαζομένων ἀφορμήν, καί<τοι> τὸν τοιοῦτον ὑπὸ πάντων ἐπαινούμενον."

36. Tatian, *Or. Graec.* 22–24. The rhetorical importance of sexual accusations for early Christian writers has been discussed in detail by Jennifer Wright Knust, "Abandoned to Lust: The Politics of Sexual Slander in Early Christian Discourse," Ph.D. diss., Columbia University, 2000.

37. A similar critique of the spectacles as scenes of madness, debauchery, fakery, and changeability may be found in Minucius Felix, *Oct.* 37.11–12.

38. See Bernadette J. Brooten, *Love Between Women: Early Christian Reponses to Female Homoeroticism* (Chicago: University of Chicago Press, 1996), on connection between 1 Cor. 11:2–16 and Rom. 1:18–32, 252, 265; on Tertullian's discussion of these passages in *Cor.*, 315–16.

39. Tertullian, *Cor.* 6.

40. Latin text in Quinti Septimi Florentis Tertulliani, *Opera*, CCSL (Turnholt: Brepols, 1972), 1:225–53. See also Tertullian, *Apology and De Spectaculis* and Minucius Felix, *Octavius*, trans. T. R. Glover and G. H. Rendall, LCL (Cambridge, Mass.: Harvard University Press, 1984), 229–301; Tertullien, *Les Spectacles*, ed. and trans. Marie Turcan, SC 332 (Paris: Editions du Cerf, 1986). Many authors have noted the highly polemical character of Tertullian's rhetoric in this treatise. Jean-Claude Fredouille, who retraces Tertullian's own attendance at the spectacles in earlier life, argues that the treatise can be read as "an intellectual and moral expiation of his past turpitudes" (see Fredouille, *Tertullien et la conversion de la culture antique* [Paris: Études Augustiniennes, 1972], 148). In addition to the commentary in Turcan, see also Robert D. Sider, "Tertullian, On the Shows: An Analysis," *JTS*, n.s., 29 (1978): 339–65.

41. Tertullian, *Spect.* 1.

42. Tertullian, *Spect.* 5–13. See also Tertullian, *Apol.* 15.4–6 and *Idol.* 12 on the religious dimensions of the spectacles. This point is made by numerous other Christian critics as well. See, for example, Irenaeus, *Adv. haer.* 1.1.12; Novatian, *Spect.* 2.1.

43. Tertullian, *Spect.* 20–23.

44. Tertullian, *Spect.* 14–20. See also Tertullian, *Apol.* 38.4: "Your public games, too, we renounce, as heartily as we do their origins; we know these origins lie in superstition; we leave on one side the matters with which they are concerned. We have nothing to do, in speech, sight, or hearing, with the madness of the circus, the shamelessness of the theater, the savagery of the arena, the vanity of the gymnasium" (LCL trans.).

45. Tertullian, *Spect.* 24–28.

46. Tertullian, *Spect.* 29–30.

47. Simon Goldhill, "The Erotic Eye: Visual Stimulation and Cultural Conflict," in *Being Greek Under Rome: Cultural Identity, the Second Sophistic, and the Development of Empire*, ed. Simon Goldhill (New York: Cambridge University Press, 2001), 154–94,

explores the politics of the gaze in the late second century and situates Christian writers (Tertullian and Clement) within a broader cultural frame. On Tertullian, see 181–84. Thanks to Jennifer Glancy for bringing this essay to my attention.

48. Tertullian, *Spect.* 21 (LCL trans.).

49. Lactantius, *Inst.* 6.20.10: "For, although a man be condemned deservedly, whoever reckons it a pleasure for him to be strangled in his sight defiles his own conscience, just as surely as if he were a spectator and participant of a murder which is performed secretly [*nam qui hominem quamuis ob merita damnatum in conspectu suo iugulari prop uoluptate computat, conscientam suam polluit, tam scilicet quam si homicidii quo fit occulte spectator et particeps fiat*]."

50. Augustine, *Conf.* 6.7–8.

51. Clement of Alexandria, *Paed.* 3.11 (76.3–77.1), trans. *ANF* 2:289.

52. John Chrysostom, *Stat.*, *Hom.* 3.11. For a more general discussion of John Chrysostom on the gaze, see Blake Leyerle, "John Chrysostom on the Gaze," *JECS* 1 (1993): 159–74.

53. Tertullian, *Spect.* 20.

54. Cyprian, *Don.* 1 (PL 4:196–97): "*Contemptis voluptariae visionis illecebris, in me oculus tuus fixus est.*"

55. Cyprian, *Don.* 6 (PL 4:204–5).

56. Cyprian, *Don.* 6 (PL 4:205A).

57. Cyprian, *Don.* 7 (PL 4.206A).

58. Cyprian, *Don.* 7 (PL 4:207A): "*et in tam impiis spectaculis tamque diris et funestis esse se non putant oculis parricidas.*"

59. Cyprian, *Don.* 8 (PL 4:211A).

60. I am grateful to Michael Swartz for raising the interesting question, in a response to a conference paper I delivered on this topic, of the degree to which different communities in late antiquity were in competition to provide entertainment to potential adherents. Thinking about the liturgy of memory as a form of somber entertainment has been fruitful.

61. Clement of Alexandria, *Strom.* 4.3.

62. See, for example, Clement of Alexandria, *Strom.* 4.7.51; Eusebius, *Praep. Evang.* 12.10.6; Origen, *Exhort. Mart.* 18; among others.

63. Augustine, *City of God*, 14.9.

64. This text by Tertullian is one of his latest, written after his break with the Catholic church and during his Montanist period. Claude Rambaux, *Tertullien face aux morales des trois premiers siècles* (Paris: Société d'Édition "Les Belles Lettres," 1979), 367–406, discusses this text in some detail in relation to its purported "heterodox" elements. See also the discussion of this text in Christine Trevett, *Montanism: Gender, Authority, and the New Prophecy* (New York: Cambridge University Press, 1996), 126–28.

65. Tertullian, *Fug.* 9.4: " '*Publicaris*' inquit, '*bonum tibi est; qui enim non publicatur in hominibus, publicatur in Domino. Ne confundaris; iustitia te producit in medium. Quid confunderis laudem ferens? Potestas fit, cum conspiceris ab hominibus.*' Sic et alibi: '*Nolite in lectulis nec in aborsibus et febribus mollibus optare exire, sed in martyriis, uti glorificetur qui est passus pro uobis.*' " A similar argument also appears in Tertullian's

treatise on the soul: "Observe, then, the difference between a heathen and a Christian in their death: if you have to lay down your life for God, as the Paraclete counsels, it is not in gentle fevers and on soft beds, but in the sharp pains of martyrdom: you must take up the cross and bear it after your Master, as he himself instructed you. The sole key to unlock Paradise is your own life's blood" (*An.* 55.4).

66. Tertullian, *Spect.* 29.5.

67. Tertullian, *Spect.* 30.3–5, 7.

68. Rambaux, *Tertullien*, 183, observes that this passage and some others like it demonstrate how difficult it was "even for a man like Tertullian, to liberate himself from the sadism that taunted the spectators in the amphitheater."

69. The discussion by Gunderson outlined above, invoking Foucault's *Discipline and Punish*, is apropos here.

70. For the educative aspect of arena contests, see for example, Cicero, *Tusc.* 22.17.41: "A gladiatorial show is apt to seem cruel and brutal to some eyes, and I incline to think that it is so, as now conducted. But in the days when it was criminals who crossed swords in the death struggle, *there could be no better schooling against pain and death at any rate for the eye*" (my emphasis).

71. Potter, "Martyrdom as Spectacle," 53. See also Leonard L. Thompson, "The Martyrdom of Polycarp: Death in the Roman Games," *JR* 82 (2002): 27–52, for a similar argument about the spectacle of martyrdom.

72. *Mart. Pol.* 12.3; Eusebius, *Hist. Eccl.* 5.1.3–5.2.8.

73. *Pass. Perp.* 20.2: "*horruit populus alteram respiciens puellam delicatam, alteram a partu recentem stillantibus mammis.*"

74. Minucius Felix, *Oct.* 37.1.

75. Minucius Felix, *Oct.* 37.3, 6. Minucius argues that reason and God bolster the martyr's willing suffering, and both make the suffering legible not as misery but as triumph over death.

76. Origen, *Exhort. Mart.* 18. See also Cyprian, *Ep.* 10.2.3, where Cyprian describes the torture and suffering of some Christians as the *spectaculum domini*. In *The Letters of St. Cyprian of Carthage*, 1:232n15, Clarke observes, "Cyprian is so insistent throughout this epistle on the theme of *Christus in martyre* that we are perhaps to translate this phrase quite literally. The *spectaculum was* the Lord's (not 'for the Lord')."

77. One could pursue this theme throughout the homiletic and panegyric traditions. See Hippolyte Delehaye, *Les passions des martyrs et les genres littéraires*, Subsidia Hagiographica 13b (Brussels: Société des Bollandistes, 1966), 133–70. Some examples: John Chrysostom's panegyrics on the saints (PG 50); Gregory Nazianzus, *Oratio* 15, *In Machabaeorum laudem* (PG 35); Augustine's many sermons on the saints: *Serm.* 273–305A, 306–340A. François Heim, "Les panégyriques des martyrs ou l'impossible conversion d'un genre littéraire," *RevScRel* 61 (1987): 105–28, points out that the appearance of martyr panegyrics coincides with the disappearance of panegyrics devoted to emperors, appropriating and transforming a longstanding and recognizable genre.

78. See, for example, Coleman, "Fatal Charades."

79. Auguet, *Cruelty and Civilization*, 104.

80. On this point, see Alexander E. Hooke, "Spectacles of Morality, Spectacles of Truth," *ISPh* 30, no. 2 (1998): 19–35.

81. Allen Brent, "Ignatius of Antioch and the Imperial Cult," *VC* 52 (1998): 30–58. Brent supports his thesis with several different arguments and bodies of evidence: Ignatius's use of the language and ideology of sacrifice, the echoes of language from the imperial mysteries, Ignatius's title, "Theophorus [God-bearer]," and the use throughout his letters of titles drawn from imperial diplomacy and ambassadorial ranks. See Brent, 32, for a summary of the argument.

82. I do not use the term "parodic" here to suggest that there is anything particularly comedic in Ignatius's performance. But to the degree that it involves a measure of mimicry (imitation, but with a difference), Ignatius's performance undermines the dominant meanings that accrue to public processions by resembling them and yet not completely assimilating to them. The power of mimicry and parody to undermine authority and apparently fixed power dynamics has been widely theorized by both psychoanalytic and postcolonial theorists. See Homi Bhabha, *The Location of Culture* (New York: Routledge, 1994), 85–92 ("Of Mimicry and Man: The Ambivalence of Colonial Discourse"); Luce Irigaray, *Speculum de l'autre femme* (Paris: Minuit, 1974); and, on Irigaray's strategic use of mimicry and mimesis, Elizabeth Weed, "The Question of Style," in *Engaging with Irigaray: Feminist Philosophy and Modern European Thought*, ed. Carolyn Burke, Naomi Schor, and Margaret Whitford (New York: Columbia University Press, 1994), 79–109, esp. 80–86.

83. This discussion builds on Elizabeth A. Castelli, "Visions and Voyeurism: Holy Women and the Politics of Sight in Early Christianity," in *Protocol of the Colloquy of the Center for Hermeneutical Studies, 6 December 1992*, n.s., 2, ed. Christopher Ocker (Berkeley: Center for Hermeneutical Studies, 1994), 1–20.

84. *Pass. Perp.* 18.2.

85. *Pass. Perp.* 18.4.

86. *Pass. Perp.* 20.2.

87. *Pass. Perp.* 20.7; 20.9.

88. The martyr as rhetor is a Christian topos with a wide reach. See, for example, the portraits of the martyrs Lawrence and Romanus in Prudentius's *Peristephanon* 2 and 10. For analysis of the Romanus portrait, see Robert Levine, "Prudentius' Romanus: The Rhetorician as Hero, Martyr, Satirist, and Saint," *Rhetorica* 9 (1991): 5–38.

89. Augustine, *Serm.* 280.1.

90. Augustine, *Serm.* 280.2.

91. Augustine, *Serm.* 280.2.

92. Historian T. D. Barnes characterizes the antitheatrical rhetoric this way: "from the Severan age onward, Christian preachers and Christian writers regularly condemned the theater, theatrical performances, and those who attended them. But such condemnations are entirely predictable and therefore uninteresting—except as evidence that Christians habitually indulged in the behavior condemned" (Barnes, "Christians and the Theater," 163–64). For a more generous and subtle assessment of the importance of the rhetorical aspects of these condemnations, see Blake Leyerle,

"John Chrysostom's View of the Theater," in *Theatrical Shows and Ascetic Lives*, 42–74, especially the discussion of theatrical gender-bending as anarchic at 43–44 and 72–73.

93. *Pass. Perp.* 10.7. The complexities of ethnicity and gender that are condensed into this one scene have invited considerable commentary by scholars. See chapter 3, note 74 for the feminist literature on this passage. On the figure of the Egyptian as a marker for the devil, see Peter Habermehl, *Perpetua und der Ägypter oder Bilder des Bösen in frühen afrikanischen Christentum: Ein Versuch zur Passio sanctarum Perpetuae et Felicitatis*, TUGAL 140 (Berlin: Akademie Verlag, 1992); David Brakke, "Ethiopian Demons: Male Sexuality, the Black-Skinned Other, and the Monastic Self," *JHS* 10 (2001): 501–35; Gay Byron, *Symbolic Blackness and Ethnic Difference in Early Christian Literature* (London: Routledge, 2002).

94. Eusebius, *Hist. Eccl.* 5.1.41.

95. See Elizabeth A. Castelli, "'I Will Make Mary Male': Pieties of the Body and Gender Transformation of Early Christian Women in Late Antiquity," in *Bodyguards: The Cultural Contexts of Gender Ambiguity*, ed. Julia Epstein and Kristina Straub (New York: Routledge, 1991), 29–49.

96. In addition to other examples already mentioned, see Augustine, *Serm.* 313A.3 ("The Effects of the vice of curiosity, the lust of the eyes").

97. *Acta Sanctorum*, "September," 5:252–86. Situating Euphemia's cult within the broader framework of the cult of the martyrs, see Hippolyte Delehaye, *Les origines du culte des martyrs*, 2nd ed., Subsidia Hagiographica 20 (Brussels: Société des Bollandistes, 1933), 93, 152, 206, 220, 237, 299, 325–27, 330, 332, 338, 356, 389, 401.

98. The discussion here is adapted from my introduction to a translation of Asterius of Amasea's homily on the martyrdom of Euphemia. See Asterius of Amasea, *Ekphrasis on the Holy Martyr Euphemia*, trans. Elizabeth A. Castelli, in *Religions of Late Antiquity in Practice*, ed. Richard Valantasis (Princeton, N.J.: Princeton University Press, 2000), 463–68. The date of her death is also recorded in the *Martyrologium Hieronymianum*. See *Martyrologium Hieronymianum ad fidem codicum adiectis prolegomenis*, ed. Giovanni Battista de Rossi and Louis Duchesne (Brussels: Typis Polleunis et Ceuterick, 1894), 121.

99. *Itinerarium Aetheriae* 23.7. See Egeria [Éthérie], *Journal de Voyage*, text est., intro., and trans. Hélène Pétré, SC 21 (Paris: Éditions du Cerf, 1971), 186.

100. Gerontius, *Vitae Melaniae Iunioris* 53. See *Vie de Sainte Mélanie*, ed., intro., and trans. Denys Gorce, SC 90 (Paris: Éditions du Cerf, 1962), 228.

101. Jacobus de Voragine, *The Golden Legend: Readings on the Saints*, trans. William Granger Ryan, 2 vols. (Princeton, N.J.: Princeton University Press, 1993), 2:181–83.

102. For more information on the figure of Euphemia as a patron of orthodox theology, see Giovanni Lucchesi, "Eufemia di Calcedonia," *Bibliotheca Sanctorum* 5 (1964): 154–60; and Alfons M. Schneider, "Sankt Euphemia und das Konzil von Chalkedon," in *Das Konzil von Chalkedon: Geschichte und Gegenwart*, ed. Aloys Grillmeier and Heinrich Bacht (Würzburg: Echter-Verlag), 1:291–302.

103. François Halkin, *Euphémie de Chalcédoine: Légendes byzantines*, Subsidia Hagiographia 41 (Brussels: Société des Bollandistes, 1965).

104. It should be noted, however, that the story returns to make unglossed and uninterrogated appearances in scholarly circles from time to time. For example, in the

authoritative *Sources Chrétiennes* bilingual edition of Egeria's pilgrimage diary, in the footnote to the reference to Euphemia's martyrium (see above, note 99), the translator states without hesitation that Euphemia died in the arena (see 186n1). The note cites, without further comment, two articles from the authoritative multivolume encyclopedia of Christian history from the early twentieth century, the *Dictionnaire d'archéologie chrétienne et de liturgie*—Henri Leclercq, "Euphémie (Sainte)," in *DACL* 5 (1922): 745–46, and Leclercq's description of the basilica of Saint Euphemia at *DACL* 3 (1914): 91–95, a section of his full article, "Chalcedoine," *DACL* 3 (1914): 90–130.

105. O. J. Schrier, "À propos d'une donnée négligée sur la mort de Ste. Euphémie," *AnBoll* 102 (1984): 329–53.

106. Victor of Rouen, *De laude sanctorum* 6:36–37: "*hic Eufemiam, quae quondam masculato animo sub percussore uirgo non palluit*" (CCSL ed. 64:78).

107. Paulinus of Nola, *Carm.* 27, vv. 430–31: "*Et quae Chalcidicis Euphemia martyr in oris, / Signat virgineo sacratum sanguine littus.*" See also Schrier, 337, 342.

108. Preface to the Milanese rite for St. Euphemia, in Angelo Paredi, *I prefazi ambrosiani: Contributo alla storia della liturgia latina* (Milan: Società editrice "Vita e pensiero," 1937), 191. The relevant passage concerning Euphemia's death is "*Novissime gladii mucrone confossa, carnea relinquens claustra, caelesti choro iungitur laeta.*" Discussed by Schrier, "Une donnée négligée," 336–37.

109. Schrier, "Une donnée négligée," 345.

110. Asterius of Amasea, *Hom.* 11: *Ekphrasis on the Martyrdom of Saint Euphemia*, in *Asterius of Amasea, Homilies I-XIV: Text, Introduction and Notes,* ed. C. Datema (Leiden: Brill, 1970), 149–55. See also the Latin translation of the sermon in *Acta Sanctorum,* "September," 5: 283–84. In addition to my English translation, cited at note 98, see Cyril Mango, *The Art of the Byzantine Empire, 312–1453: Sources and Documents* (Englewood Cliffs, N.J.: Prentice-Hall, 1972), 37–39. The intended audience of the homily is the subject of some scholarly debate; see Wolfgang Speyer, "Die Euphemia-Rede des Asterios von Amaseia: Eine Missionschrift für gebildete Heiden," *JAC* 14 (1971): 39–47.

111. On the rhetorical form *ekphrasis,* see Glanville Downey, "Ekphrasis," *RAC* 4 (1959): 922–43.

112. Liz James and Ruth Webb, " 'To Understand Ultimate Things and Enter Secret Places': Ekphrasis and Art in Byzantium," *Art History* 14 (1991): 1–17. Thanks to Henry Maguire for recommending this article to me.

113. James and Webb, 4; from Aphthonius, *Progymnasmata.* All of the ancient rhetorical handbooks have recently appeared in English translation: George A. Kennedy, ed. and trans., *Progymnasmata: Greek Textbooks of Prose Composition and Rhetoric,* Writings from the Greco-Roman World 10 (Atlanta: SBL, 2003).

114. James and Webb, 4–5; see also 8.

115. James and Webb, 7–11.

116. The encounter with a painting as the inspiration for a story is itself a literary device familiar from the Greek romance tradition. See, for example, the proem from *Daphnis and Chloe* or the beginning of Achilles Tatius, *The Adventures of Leucippe and Clitophon.*

117. The figure of Medea was often invoked as an exemplary embodiment of mixed

and competing emotions. See Henry Maguire, "Truth and Convention in Byzantine Descriptions of Works of Art," *DOP* 28 (1974): 132. Moreover, the figure of Medea had a rich interpretive and reception history in antiquity in both Greek and Roman cultures. For a discussion of some of the ancient discussion, see James J. Clauss and Sarah Iles Johnston, eds., *Medea* (Princeton, N.J.: Princeton University Press, 1997).

118. Asterius, *Hom.* 11.3.3.

119. Representations of martyrs' suffering in both art and rhetoric drew upon available visual and verbal vocabularies, especially those concerning war and torture. See Henry Maguire, *Art and Eloquence in Byzantium* (Princeton, N.J.: Princeton University Press, 1981), 24–42.

120. Asterius, *Hom.* 11.4.2.

121. Asterius, *Hom.* 11.4.4.

122. Asterius, *Hom.* 11.3.2: "ἐρυθριῶσα τὰς ὄψεις τῶν ἀρρένων."

123. Asterius, *Hom.* 11.3.3: "ἔστ᾽ ἂν ἐθεασάμην τῆς γυναικὸς ἐκείνης τῆς Κολχίδος τὸ δρᾶμα."

124. 308A–309B. See Charles Joseph Hefele, *Histoire des conciles d'après les documents originaux,* trans. Henri Leclercq (Paris: Letouzey et Ané, 1910), vol. 3, part 2, book 18, chapter 2, 741–98, esp. 765–68. For English translation, see Daniel J. Sahas, *Icon and Logos: Sources in Eighth-Century Iconoclasm. An Annotated Translation of the Sixth Session of the Seventh Ecumenical Council (Nicea, 787), containing the Definition of the Council of Constantinople (754) and its refutation, and the Definition of the Seventh Ecumenical Council* (Toronto: University of Toronto Press, 1986), 129–31.

125. Marcus Aurelius, *Med.* 11.3. The clause that appears in square brackets in the quotation has been considered by many commentators to be an interpolation. Even if it is a scribal addition, however, it is quite likely that Marcus had Christians in mind even if he did not name them explicitly. For a broader assessment of Marcus's attitudes toward Christians, see P. A. Brunt, "Marcus Aurelius and the Christians," in *Studies in Latin Literature and Roman History,* Collection Latomus 164.1, ed. C. Deroux (Brussels: Latomus, 1979), 483–520.

126. The Christian privileging of spectacles of martyrological violence is not limited, of course, to late antiquity but carries on into the Middle Ages and the Renaissance with even greater graphic force. See, for example, Jody Enders, *The Medieval Theater of Cruelty: Rhetoric, Memory, Violence* (Ithaca, N.Y.: Cornell University Press, 1999), and Mitchell B. Merback, *The Thief, the Cross, and the Wheel: Pain and the Spectacle of Punishment in Medieval and Renaissance Europe* (Chicago: University of Chicago Press, 1998).

127. Goldhill, "The Erotic Eye," 180.

5. LAYERS OF VERBAL AND VISUAL MEMORY: COMMEMORATING THECLA THE PROTOMARTYR

The epigraph to this chapter is drawn from *Thaumata tēs hagias kai [prōto]martyros Theklas* 44, 8–11, in Gilbert Dagron, *Vie et miracles de Sainte Thècle: Texte grec, traduction et commentaire,* Subsidia Hagiographica 62 (Bruxelles: Société des Bollandistes,

1978), 404–5, my translation. The last clause is: "ὥσπερ ἔκ τινος βυθοῦ τοῦ μακροῦ χρόνου καὶ τῆς λήθης ἀναλεγόμενος τὰ θαύματα."

1. See the title of this anonymous author's two-volume work: *Praxeis tēs hagias apostolou kai martyros tou Christou Theklas, kai thaumata* (Acts of Saint Thecla, apostle and martyr of Christ, and miracles), in Dagron, *Vie et Miracles*, 167. The text repeats the epithets ἀπόστολος and [πρωτο]μάρτυς throughout. (N.B.: Although *Praxeis* is more literally translated as "acts" rather than as "life," in future citations here, I will refer to volume 1 of this work as the *Life*, following Dagron's translation, in order to distinguish more easily between the second- or third-century Apocryphal Acts and the fifth-century text discussed here.)

2. Dagron, 19: "Les évêques passent, l'hagiographie de Thècle demeure: mais, isolé, suspens, s'identifiant à une entreprise qui occupe trente ou quarante ans de sa vie, où ne se distinguent plus littéraire, piété et autobiographie, et qui va nous parvenir sans son nom."

3. *Life*, prologue 36–40 (Dagron, 170–71): "Οὐχ ὡς ἂν μὴ ἐξίτηλα, μηδὲ ἄδηλα τῷ μακρῷ χρόνῳ γένηται—βέβαια γὰρ ἀεὶ καὶ πάγια καὶ ἀθάνατα μένει τὰ τῶν ἁγίων ἔργα παρὰ Θεοῦ φυλαττόμενα, εἴς τε οἰκεῖον ἀεὶ κλέος, καὶ ἀνθρώπων τῶν ἐν γῇ ἔτι στρεφομένων ὠφέλειαν."

4. Herodotus, *Hist.* 1.1. See the earlier discussion of Herodotus in chapter 1 of this volume.

5. *Life*, prologue 29–36 (Dagron, 170–71).

6. Stephen J. Davis, *The Cult of St. Thecla: A Tradition of Women's Piety in Late Antiquity* (New York: Oxford University Press, 2001), provides an excellent account of the textual and material evidence for the Thecla cult in Egypt and Asia Minor and also puts forward a persuasive historical reconstruction of the cult as an example of women's religion in the period.

7. (*Praxeis Paulou kai Theklēs*), in *Acta Apostolorum Apocrypha*, ed. Ricardus Adelbertus Lipsius and Maximilianus Bonnet, part 1: *Acta Petri, Acta Pauli, Acta Petri et Pauli, Acta Pauli et Theclae, Acta Thaddaei*, ed. Ricardus Adelbertus Lipsius (Hildesheim: Georg Olms, 1959), 235–72. English translation in *New Testament Apocrypha*, rev. ed., ed. Wilhelm Schneemelcher; trans. R. McL. Wilson (Louisville, Ky.: Westminster/John Knox Press, 1992), 2:213–70. Hereafter, the text will be cited as *ATh*.

8. See bibliography collected in Jan Bremmer, ed., *The Apocryphal Acts of Paul and Thecla*, Studies of the Acts of the Apostles 2 (Kampen: Kok Pharos, 1996).

9. For a summary of the debate, see Shelly Matthews, "Thinking of Thecla: Issues in Feminist Historiography," *JFSR* 17, no. 2 (Fall 2001): 39–55.

10. Stevan L. Davies, *The Revolt of the Widows: The Social World of the Apocryphal Acts* (Carbondale: Southern Illinois University Press, 1980); Ross S. Kraemer, "The Conversion of Women to Ascetic Forms of Christianity," *Signs* 6 (1980): 298–307; Dennis Ronald MacDonald, *The Legend and the Apostle: The Battle for Paul in Story and Canon* (Philadelphia: Westminster Press, 1983); Ruth Albrecht, *Das Leben der heiligen Makrina auf dem Hintergrund der Thekla-Traditionen: Studien zu dem Ursprungen des weiblichen Mönchtums in 4. Jahrhundert in Kleinasien* (Göttingen: Vandenhoeck & Ruprecht, 1986); Virginia Burrus, *Chastity as Autonomy: Women in the Stories of the*

Apocryphal Acts (Lewiston, N.Y.: Edwin Mellen Press, 1987). Some scholars have rejected this historical reconstruction as feminist special pleading. See, for example, Lynne C. Boughton, "From Pious Legend to Feminist Fantasy: Distinguishing Hagiographical License from Apostolic Practice in the *Acts of Paul/Acts of Thecla*," *JR* 71 (1991): 362–83, and Peter W. Dunn, "Women's Liberation, the *Acts of Paul*, and Other Apocryphal Acts of the Apostles," *Apocrypha* 4 (1993): 245–61. See Matthews, "Thinking of Thecla," for a discussion of this literature. And also see Steve Nolan, "Narrative as a Strategic Resource for Resistance: Reading the *Acts of Thecla* for Its Political Purposes," in *Narrativity in Biblical and Related Texts/La narrativité dans la Bible et les textes apparentés*, ed. G. J. Brooke and J.-D. Kaestli, Bibliotheca Ephemeridum Theologicarum Lovaniensium 149 (Leuven: Leuven University Press/Peeters, 2000), 225–42.

11. Kate Cooper, *The Virgin and the Bride: Idealized Womanhood in Late Antiquity* (Cambridge, Mass.: Harvard University Press, 1996).

12. Cooper, *The Virgin and the Bride*, 19: "If we assume for the sake of argument that wherever a woman is mentioned a man's character is being judged—and along with it what he stands for—we can begin to see the rhetorical possibilities afforded by a female point of identification in a literature aimed at defending, or undermining, such sanctified Greco-Roman institutions as marriage, the family, and even the city itself."

13. Cooper, *The Virgin and the Bride*, 45–67 (a chapter concerning the Apocryphal Acts as a whole with numerous examples drawn from the *ATh*).

14. Matthews, "Thinking of Thecla," 50.

15. Claude Lévi-Strauss, *Structural Anthropology* (New York: Basic Books, 1963), 61; quoted in Matthews, "Thinking of Thecla," 51.

16. Matthews, "Thinking of Thecla," 51.

17. Davis, *The Cult of St. Thecla*, 18–19.

18. Davis, *The Cult of St. Thecla*, 19.

19. See the discussion below of hagiographic and ethical literature. See also Dagron, *Vie et Miracles*. On the artistic evidence, see Claudia Nauerth and Rüdiger Warns, *Thekla: Ihre Bilder in der frühchristlichen Kunst* (Wiesbaden: Otto Harrassowitz, 1981). Some examples of this evidence are discussed below.

20. In putting the matter this way, I want simultaneously to notice a distinction between Christian and Greek and Roman (e.g., "pagan") romance literature without inscribing that difference in absolute terms. I agree here with Kate Cooper's argument that the traditional distinction drawn between Jewish and Christian romances, on the one hand (as "religious" literature), and Greek and Roman romances, on the other (as "secular" literature), serves modern scholars' presuppositions about the relative status of Jewish/Christian and classical literature rather than drawing a distinction that signifies appropriately for antiquity. See her discussion in *The Virgin and the Bride*, 22. See also Melissa Aubin, "Reversing Romance? The *Acts of Thecla* and the Ancient Novel," in *Ancient Fiction and Early Christian Narrative*, ed. Ronald F. Hock, J. Bradley Chance, and Judith Perkins, SBL Symposium Series 6 (Atlanta: Scholars Press, 1998), 257–72, which focuses on the ironic uses to which Christian writers put the ancient romance form in the service of troubling the categories that romance sought to reinscribe.

21. Cooper, *The Virgin and the Bride*, 21, with a quotation summarizing the genre

from B. P. Reardon, ed., *Collected Ancient Greek Novels* (Berkeley: University of California Press, 1989), 2.

22. Cooper, *The Virgin and the Bride*, 44: "Desire remains, but its object is now a reunion with the divine and a return to the heavenly country, the homeland of the saints. The romance of late antiquity takes the form of a saint's life, in which the chaste desire of the legitimately married hero and heroine has metamorphosed into the otherworldly passion by which a Christian saint embraces a childless death." On "Death as a Happy Ending," see Judith Perkins, *The Suffering Self: Pain and Narrative Representation in the Early Christian Era* (New York: Routledge, 1995), 15–40.

23. The repetitions and doubling in the structure of the narrative has suggested to some interpreters the folkloric character of the *Acts*. See, for example, Dagron, *Vie et Miracles*, 36. More generally, on the folkloric character of the Apocryphal Acts, see MacDonald, *The Legend and the Apostle*, 27–33; Burrus, *Chastity as Autonomy*.

24. The ending of the *Acts* is actually more complicated than this, with some manuscripts providing an ending in which Thecla does not die but rather is absorbed into the earth. See *ATh* 44–45 (Lipsius, 270–71). See also the alternate ending in which, threatened by rape, Thecla escapes into a rock (Lipsius, 271–72).

25. The root "μάρτυς" appears in the text only once, in the last sentence: *ATh* 43 (Lipsius, 269): "καὶ διαμαρτυραμένη ἀπῆλθεν εἰς Σελεύκειαν [and after she bore witness, she went away to Seleucia]."

26. *ATh* 5–6 (Lipsius, 238–40). I have emphasized the explicitly ascetic macarisms here. Note that the following claims are also made: blessed are those who tremble at the words of God, those who have received the wisdom of Jesus Christ, those who have secured their baptism, those who understand Jesus Christ, those who through love of God have departed from the form of this world, and the merciful.

27. *ATh* 8; 13; 19.

28. *ATh* 16.

29. *ATh* 15; 20.

30. *ATh* 17.

31. *ATh* 9: "κρατεῖται ἐπιθυμίᾳ καινῇ καὶ πάθει δεινῷ . . . ἑάλωται ἡ παρθένος."

32. *ATh* 10: Thamyris speaking: "καὶ ποῖόν σε πάθος κατέχει ἔκπληκτον"; Theokleia speaking: "Τέκνον, τί τοιαύτη κάτω βλέπουσα κάθησαι, καὶ μηδὲν ἀποκρινομένη ἀλλὰ παραπλήξ."

33. *ATh* 10.

34. *ATh* 20.

35. *ATh* 21.

36. *ATh* 22.

37. *ATh* 19.

38. The Greek term here is "στοργή," which LSJ suggests is used most frequently of the affection experienced by parents and children and only rarely sexual love. Patristic literature uses the term to refer to familial love, love between God and human beings, and love for one's bishop; see Lampe, s.v. "στοργή."

39. *ATh* 26 (Lipsius, 254).

40. See also Davis, *The Cult of St. Thecla*, 23–26, on "ξένος," its secondary meaning as "wanderer" or "refugee," and its potential affiliation with the early Christian social practice of itinerancy.

41. *ATh* 44–45 (Lipsius, 270–71); see also the twelfth-century manuscript edited by Grabius with a longer ending (Lipsius, 271–72; the manuscript tradition is discussed at xciv–cvi).

42. Tertullian, *Bapt.* 17 (CSEL 20:215): "Petulantia autem mulieris, quae usurpauit docere, utique non etiam tinguendi ius sibi pariet, nisi si quae noua bestia euenerit similis pristinae, ut, quemadmodum illa baptismum auferebat, ita aliqua per se eum conferat. Quodsi quae Pauli perperam inscripta sunt exemplum Theclae ad licentiam mulierum docendi tinguendique defendunt, sciant in Asia presbyterum, qui eam scripturam construxit, quasi titulo Pauli de suo cumulans, conuictum atque confessum id se amore Pauli fecisse loco decessisse. Quam enim fidei proximum uideretur, ut is docendi et tinguendi daret feminae potestatem qui ne discere quidem constanter mulieri permisit? taceant, inquit, et domi maritos suos consulant." The right to teach and baptize is an episcopal right and, as Tertullian argues just before this text, "*episcopatus aemulatio schismatum mater est* [emulating the episcopal [office] is the mother of schism]." See Schneemelcher, 2:214–15, on this text and the manuscript problems involved; see also Davis, *The Cult of St. Thecla*, 7–8, 12–14.

43. See Albrecht, *Das Leben der heiligen Makrina*, for a catalog of the references to Thecla in early Christian and medieval literature. Also see Davis, *The Cult of St. Thecla*. The most important early references to Thecla in hagiographic literature are found in Gregory of Nyssa, *Vita Macrinae* 2; Pseudo-Athanasius, *Vita Syncleticae* 8; *Vita Olympiadis* 1. In works of ascetic theory, Thecla is frequently cited: Methodius, *Symp.* 8, 1, 170; 8, 17, 232; 11, 282; Ambrose, *De virg.* 2, 3; Jerome, *Ep.* 22, 41. For other examples, see the introduction to Gregory of Nyssa, *Vie de Sainte Macrine*, trans. Pierre Maraval, SC 178 (Paris: Les Editions du Cerf, 1971), 146n2. In Gregory of Nazianzus, *Or.* 4.69, Thecla appears in a list of otherwise all-male apostolic martyrs (John, Peter, Paul, James, Stephen, Luke, Andrew); also noted by Davis, *The Cult of St. Thecla*, 5.

44. *ATh* 21: Thecla is in the arena and looks for Paul "as a lamb in the desert looks around for the shepherd," and sees instead "the Lord sitting as Paul," from which she takes solace. Notice here that her steady gaze results in his ascension into heaven. *ATh* 26: When Alexander approaches Thecla in Antioch, Paul denies her, saying: "I do not know the woman of whom you speak, nor is she mine." When Alexander persists, Thecla again looks around for Paul, who seems to have disappeared. She finds him several chapters later, after her torment in the arena in Antioch, when he again seems to doubt her; see *ATh* 40.

45. Robert P. Casey, "Der dem Athanasius zugeschriebene Traktat Περὶ παρθενίας," *Sitzungsberichte der Preussischen Akademie der Wissenschaften* 33 (1935): 1022–45: introduction at 1022–26; Armenian text at 1026–34; German translation at 1035–45. For the passage in question, see lines 191–220. A Syriac version of the text may be found at J. Lebon, "Athanasiana Syriaca I: Un Λόγος περὶ παρθενίας attribué à saint Athanase d'Alexandrie," *Museon* 40 (1927): 209–18. David Brakke has translated the Syriac text, which he compared with Casey's Armenian text. See David Brakke, *Athanasius and the Politics of Asceticism* (Oxford: Clarendon Press, 1995), appendix C,

"On Virginity," 303–9. The Syriac version is incomplete and does not include the passage where Thecla is mentioned. For discussion, see Davis, *The Cult of St. Thecla*, 87–94.

46. Davis, *The Cult of St. Thecla*, 89 (emphasis in the text).

47. Davis, *The Cult of Saint Thecla*, 90; *ATh* 5: "Blessed are those who keep the flesh pure, they will become a temple of God"; Athanasius, *De virg.* 117–21 (Casey, 1030). Davis notes (at 90n33) that an additional parenthetical statement—"(for they have become the temple of God)"—appears in the Syriac version of this text. See Lebon, "Athanasiana Syriaca I," 215, and Brakke, *Athanasius*, 307.

48. Davis is especially interested in reconstructing the historical situation of women's piety from this text, arguing at 91–92, that "in this context, I do not think Athanasius' use of the *ATh* is simply a whim of intertextual fancy. Instead, I believe he is responding to the *actual exegetical interests of female monks living in Alexandria*" (emphasis in the text).

49. Davis, *The Cult of St. Thecla*, 93–94, citing at 94n45 Abraham Malherbe's documentation of the link between memory and mimesis; see Abraham Malherbe, "Hellenistic Moralists and the New Testament," *ANRW* 2.26.1 (1992): 282–83.

50. Athanasius, *De virg.* 200 (Casey, 1033; trans. at 1044).

51. Pseudo-Athanasius, *Vita Syncleticae* (PG 28:1487–1558); translated by Elizabeth A. Castelli as "The Life and Activity of the Holy and Blessed Teacher Syncletica," in *Ascetic Behavior in Greco-Roman Antiquity: A Sourcebook*, ed. Vincent L. Wimbush (Philadelphia: Fortress Press, 1990), 265–311.

52. Pseudo-Athanasius, *Vit. Syn.* 8 (Castelli, "Life and Activity," 269–70).

53. In addition to these examples and the ones named in note 44, above, see also Pseudo-Chrysostom, *Panegyric to Thecla* (PG 50:745–48); Michel Aubineau, "Le panégyrique de Thècle, attribué à Jean Chrysostome (*BHG* 1720): La fin retrouvée d'un texte mutilé," *AnBoll* 93 (1975): 349–62; and Dennis R. MacDonald and Andrew D. Scrimgeour, "Pseudo-Chrysostom's Panegyric to Thecla: The Heroine of the *Acts of Paul* in Homily and Art," *Semeia* 38 (1986): 151–59.

54. MacDonald and Scrimgeour mistakenly, in my view, reductively characterize this narrative as a simple paraphrase of the *ATh*. See their "Pseudo-Chrysostom's Panegyric," 152.

55. *Life*, prologue 1–3 (Dagron, 168–69).

56. *Life*, prologue 33–34; 41 (Dagron, 170–71).

57. *Life*, prologue 25–28 (Dagron, 170–71).

58. *Life*, prologue 19–23 (Dagron, 168–89).

59. *Life*, 3.50 (Dagron, 182–83), where the three categories are linked. At *Life* 5.22–24 (Dagron, 186–87), Paul's traitorous companions, Demas and Hermogenes, assure Thamyris that Paul is a cheat and a wanderer (ἀπατεὼν καὶ πλάνος ἐστί) whose project is the disruption of social customs and social order. Thamyris pleads with Thecla to stop listening to "this stranger and wanderer" at 4.19 (Dagron, 184–85). Subsequently, Thamyris brings Paul before the proconsul and accuses him of numerous crimes, calling him a wanderer and a guilty one who invents "laws that are new and foreign to nature": "ὁ ἀπατεὼν οὗτος καὶ ἀλιτήριος, καὶ τῶν καινῶν καὶ ἀλλοτρίων τῆς φύσεως νόμων εὑρετής." See *Life* 6.14–15 (Dagron, 190–91). Later still, the proconsul

chides Thecla for listening to "that old stranger" (παρὰ τοῦ ξένου τούτου καὶ γέροντος ἀκήκοας). See *Life* 11.48–49 (Dagron, 214–15).

60. *Life* 3.56–57 (Dagron, 182–83); 11.3 (Dagron, 212–13). See also Theokleia's speech at 12.15–24 (Dagron, 216–17) where she accuses Thecla of taking up the shameful life of a prostitute and a servant, inflicting shame on her country, her family, and the city.

61. *Life* 4.10–15 (Dagron, 182–85).

62. *Life* 15.38–40 (Dagron, 230–31).

63. *Life* 15.46–47 (Dagron, 230–31).

64. *Life* 15.49–55 (Dagron, 230–31).

65. *Life* 6.37–38 (Dagron, 190–91): "ξένος γὰρ καὶ πᾶσιν ἡμῖν ἄγνοστὸς ἐστιν ὁ ἄνθρωπος".

66. *Life* 6.38–51 (Dagron, 190–93).

67. *Life* 6.61–62 (Dagron, 192–93).

68. *Life* 7.14–15 (Dagron, 194–95).

69. *Life* 7.28–29 (Dagron, 194–97).

70. *Life* 7.65–67 (Dagron, 198–99).

71. Rom. 1:18–32; 1 Cor. 7; Lev. 18.

72. Jennifer Wright Knust, "Abandoned to Lust: The Politics of Sexual Slander in Early Christian Discourse," Ph.D. diss., Columbia University, 2000.

73. *Life* 21.40–44 (Dagron, 254–55).

74. *Life* 21.45–50 (Dagron, 254–55).

75. *Life* 7.55–77 (Dagron, 196–99).

76. *Life* 1.1–5 (Dagron, 170–71).

77. *Life* 1.9–18 (Dagron, 172–73).

78. *Life* 9.17–18 (Dagron, 202–3): "ἤδη δὲ καὶ τὸν σταυρὸν ἀραμένην πρὸς τὸν εὐαγγελικὸν παρεσκευάσθαι δρόμον."

79. *Life* 9.26 (Dagron, 204–5): "Μηδὲν ἔτι θῆλυ φρονήσῃς καὶ ἄναδρον."

80. *Life* 9.49 (Dagron, 206–7).

81. *Life* 9.50 (Dagron, 206–7).

82. *Life* 9.53–59 (Dagron, 206–7).

83. *Life* 9.60–65 (Dagron, 206–7).

84. *Life* 9.65–69 (Dagron, 206–7).

85. *Life* 9.69–70 (Dagron, 206–7): "καὶ γὰρ καὶ ζήσας καὶ τελειωθεὶς μάρτυς οὐδὲν ἧττον ἐκείνῳ φοβερός."

86. *Life* 9.72–80 (Dagron, 206–7).

87. *Life* 12.20–22 (Dagron, 216–17).

88. *Life* 12.30–32 (Dagron 218–19).

89. *Life* 12.51–59 (Dagron, 218–21).

90. *Life* 12.62–65 (Dagron, 220–21).

91. *Life* 12.71–75 (Dagron, 220–21).

92. Françoise Meltzer, *For Fear of the Fire: Joan of Arc and the Limits of Subjectivity* (Chicago: University of Chicago Press, 2001), has suggested that it is precisely this dimension of the martyr's story that renders it the object of a postmodern "nostalgia for certainty." As she puts it, "I have found that in 'secular' contemporary texts there is a fascination with figures for whom the gift of the body through death is the logical

consequence of conviction—the early Christian martyrs, for example. Contemporary theoretical writings seem to yearn for, even as they are bewildered by, an imagined past when the body and mind were presumed to be unsyncopated—when the body, in other words, whether reviled or seen as a companion, bore upon itself the beliefs of the mind and indeed served as something like a vessel specific to these beliefs" (7).

93. *Life* 12.50–51; 57–58 (Dagron 218–21).

94. *Life* 15.61–68 (Dagron, 232–33).

95. *Life* 15.12 (Dagron, 228–29).

96. *Life* 16.2–3 (Dagron, 232–33).

97. *Life* 16.27–32 (Dagron, 234–37). See also Ambrose, *Virg.* 2.3.20, where Thecla's virginity is so powerful that it inspired an exchange of natures between the beasts and the human spectators: "Oblivious of its own nature, it [the beast] had put on ours, which men had abandoned. You could see, by a certain exchange of natures, men goading a beast who were clothed in animal savagery, and the beast, eagerly kissing the virgin's feet, teaching men how they should behave. . . . their nature did not possess them, although they were savage. In adoring a martyr they taught what it meant to be religious." Translation from Boniface Ramsey, *Ambrose, "On Virgins"* (New York: Routledge, 1997), 96.

98. It is perhaps worth noting that Thecla's status as "martyr" is not always completely legible to the audience. See, for example, *Life* 16.34–40 (Dagron, 236–37), where the women protest her torture but see her "not as a *martyr* but as a *woman* suffering pitiably and having exacted from her irrational justice for the sake of chastity, solemnity, and not sending her body to prostitution and licentiousness" (my emphasis).

99. *Life* 19.34–38 (Dagron, 246–47).

100. *Life* 19.40–41 (Dagron, 246–47).

101. *Life* 19.47–51 (Dagron, 246–47).

102. *Life* 22 (Dagron, 254–61).

103. *Life* 26.2–7 (Dagron, 270–71).

104. Dagron, 271n1: "Cette longue profession de foi de Thècle, ponctuée de formules identiques, a entraîné d'assez nombreuses perturbations dans la tradition manuscrite, et il n'est pas toujours facile de distinguer ce qui est omission et ce qui est adjonction."

105. *Life* 26.60–62 (Dagron, 274–75).

106. *Life* 26.62–66 (Dagron, 274–75).

107. *Life* 28.1–3 (Dagron, 278–81): "Εὐαγγελισαμένη δὲ τὸν σωτήριον λόγον, καὶ πολλοὺς μὲν κατηχήσασα καὶ σφραγισαμένη καὶ στρατολογήσασα τῷ Χριστῷ, πολλῷ δ᾽ αὖ πλείω θαυματουργήσασα." *Life* 28.36 (Dagron, 280–81): "ὦ παρθένε καὶ μάρτυς καὶ ἀπόστολε."

108. *Life* 28.5–15 (Dagron, 280–81).

109. Robin Margaret Jensen, *Understanding Early Christian Art* (New York: Routledge, 2000).

110. Mary Charles Murray, "Art and the Early Church," *JTS*, n.s., 28 (1977): 303–45. Murray outlines her project in this way: "It is universally held to be a fact that the early Church was hostile to art. . . . However, it is the purpose of this paper to investigate whether this accepted fact has any foundation in reality, or whether it is simply an

example of the phenomenon by which repeated assertion raises to the level of established truth what was initially a matter of scholarly opinion.

"The reason why a matter of conjecture should appear to be a matter of fact is not hard to find: repetition has not only standardized the content of the theory, but the form in which it receives presentation has by now become classical" (303).

111. Jensen, *Understanding*, 13–15, 27–31.

112. Jensen, *Understanding*, 30.

113. Many of these images are catalogued in Henri Leclercq, "Thècle," *DACL* 15 (1953): 2225–36, at section 6 ("Monuments divers"), 2234–36. For a critical analysis of a wide-ranging collection of early Christian examples, see Nauerth and Warns, *Thekla*. See also Claudia Nauerth, "Nachlese von Thekla-Darstellungen," in *Studien zur spätantiken und frühchristlichen Kunst und Kultur des Orients*, Göttinger Orientforschungen, II. Reihe: Studien zur spätantiken und frühchristlichen Kunst 6, ed. Guntram Koch (Wiesbaden: Harrassowitz, 1982), 14–18, and Rüdiger Warns, "Weitere Darstellungen der heiligen Thekla," in *Studien zur frühchristlichen Kunst II*, Göttinger Orientforschungen, II. Reihe: Studien zur spätantiken und frühchristlichen Kunst 8, ed. Guntram Koch (Wiesbaden: Harrassowitz, 1986), 75–137. For later examples, see Louis Réau, "Thècle d'Iconium ou de Tarragone," in *Iconographie de l'art chrétien*, vol. 3, *Iconographie des saints* (Paris: Presses Universitaires de France, 1959), 1250–52. See also a stone/limestone relief tentatively identified as Thecla from the collection at the Brooklyn Museum (40.299; *ICA* System Number 0089142), published in *Pagan and Christian Egypt: Egyptian Art from the First to the Tenth Century A.D.: Exhibited at the Brooklyn Museum by the Department of Ancient Art, January 23–March 9, 1941* (Brooklyn: Brooklyn Museum/Brooklyn Institute of Arts and Sciences, 1941), 27, pl. 49; and in *Late Egyptian and Coptic Art: An Introduction to the Collections in the Brooklyn Museum* (Brooklyn: Brooklyn Museum/Brooklyn Institute of Arts and Sciences, 1943), 18, pl. 20.

114. The exploration of early Christian art in general needs to be undertaken within an interpretive framework that acknowledges its broader artistic, cultural, and historical contexts. See André Grabar, *Christian Iconography: A Study of Its Origins*, The A. W. Mellon Lectures in the Fine Arts, 1961; Bollingen Series 35.10 (Princeton, N.J.: Princeton University Press, 1968), xliii–xliv: "It goes without saying that at the beginning of the Christian experiment in iconography, the inspiration could have come only from the art of other religions or from profane art. . . . From its beginnings Christian imagery found expression entirely, almost uniquely, in the general language of the visual arts and with the techniques of imagery commonly practiced within the Roman Empire from the second to the fourth century. . . . We become aware how essential the contribution of the Greco-Latin iconographic language has been to Christian imagery at all periods, even down to our own." An important recent study of the intersections of Roman imperial society, culture, and art with Christian ideas and modes of representation is Jaś Elsner, *Imperial Rome and Christian Triumph: The Art of the Roman Empire, AD 100–450* (New York: Oxford University Press, 1998).

115. The first publication of this vault tomb appears in Théocharis Pazaras, "Δύο παλαιοχριστιανικοὶ τάφοι ἀπὸ τὸ δυτικὸ νεκροταφεῖο τῆς Θεσσαλονίκης," Μακεδονικὰ 21 (1981): 379–87, and figures 1–9. It is also discussed in Nikolaos G. Laskaris, *Monuments funéraires paléochrétiens (et byzantins) de Grèce* (Athens: Les Édi-

tions Historiques Stéfanos D. Basilopoulos, 2000), 517–24, and figures D, 14–16. For dating, see Laskaris, 523–24. See also *Index of Christian Art* (http://ica.princeton.edu), system number 0042836.

116. The identification of the Daniel scene is much more certain: although the face of the human figure is disfigured, the name "ΔΑΝΙΗΛ" appears above the head, and two lions frame the figure (with the word "ΛΕΩΝ" identifying them). The panel bearing the Noah portrait is badly damaged, with the portrait of a bird in the upper left corner identified with the inscription "ΠΕΡΙΣΤΕΡΑ" ("dove") underneath it. Interpreters have argued that the damaged panel most likely represents Noah, both because of the frequent pairing of Daniel with Noah in Jewish iconography and because the most likely icnonographic alternative (Jesus' baptism) would have shown the dove over Jesus' head, not flying off to his side. See Laskaris, *Monuments funéraires*, 520.

117. Laskaris, *Monuments funéraires*, 520–21.

118. Laskaris, *Monuments funéraires*, 518.

119. Laskaris, *Monuments funéraires*, 521.

120. The fact that Thecla is the sole nonbiblical character here interestingly parallels her status in Athanasius, *De virg.*, discussed above.

121. Laskaris, *Monuments funéraires*, 519. See the discussion of the pairing of Thecla and Daniel, below, for more examples from other genres of ancient Christian art.

122. The most famous sarcophagus portrait of Daniel is likely that found on the sarcophagus of Junius Bassus. See below.

123. Alison Moore Smith, "The Iconography of the Sacrifice of Isaac in Early Christian Art," *AJA*, 2d ser., 26 (1922): 159–73; Isabel Speyart van Woerden, "The Iconography of the Sacrifice of Abraham," *VC* 15 (1961): 214–55; Ernst Dassmann, *Sündenvergebung durch Taufe, Buße und Martyrerfürbitte in den Zeugnissen frühchristlicher Frömmigkeit und Kunst*, Münsterische Beiträge zur Theologie 36 (Münster: Aschendorff, 1973), 184–95.

124. On representations of Noah in early Christian art, see Henri Leclercq, "Arche," *DACL* 1 (1907): 2709–32; J. Fink, *Noe der Gerechte in der frühchristlichen Kunst* (Münster-Cologne: Böhlau, 1955); R. P. J. Hooyman, "Die Noe-Darstellung in der frühchristlichen Kunst," *VC* 12 (1958): 113–35; Peter Franke, "Bemerkungen zur frühchristlichen Noe-ikonographie," *RivAC* 49 (1973): 171–82; Dassmann, *Sündenvergebung durch Taufe*, 208–221. On representations of Adam and Eve in Early Christian art, see A. Breymann, *Adam und Eva in der Kunst des christlichen Alterthums* (Wolfenbüttel: J. Zwissler, 1893); Henri Leclercq, "Adam et Ève," *DACL* 1 (1907): 509–19; and Dieter Korol, "Zum Bild der Vertreibung Adams und Evas in der neuen Katakombe an der Via Latina und zur anthropomorphen Darstellung Gottvaters." *JAC* 22 (1979): 175–90. On the Good Shepherd image in funereal art, see Henri Leclercq, "Pasteur (Bon)," *DACL* 13 (1937–38): 2272–390; and Johannes Quasten, "Der Gut Hirte in frühchristlicher Totenliturgie und Grabeskunst," in *Miscellanea Giovanni Mercati*, Studi et testi 121 (Vatican City: Biblioteca Apostolica Vaticana, 1946), 1:373–406.

125. Jensen, *Understanding*, 68, 195n4, for concurring and dissenting views on the status and interpretive range of grave and catacomb paintings in general.

126. Jensen, *Understanding*, 6.

127. Jensen, *Understanding*, 6–7.

128. See the numeric tally in Graydon Snyder, *Ante Pacem: Archaeological Evidence of Church Life Before Constantine* (Macon, Ga.: Mercer University Press, 1985), 43.

129. The Saint Just de Valcabrère sarcophagus fragments were excavated in 1988; see the archeological report: Christine Dieulafait, *Rapport de fouilles de sauvetage effectuées à Saint-Just-de-Valcabrère en 1988* (n.p.: Service régional de l'archéologie de Midi-Pyrénées, 1988). See also Jean-Luc Schenck, "Saint-Just de Valcabrère," in *Pulchra Imago: Fragments d'archéologie chrétienne. Catalogue d'exposition, Saint-Bertrand-de-Comminges, 30 mars–11 nov. 1991* (Toulouse: Musée archéologique départemental de Saint-Bertrand-de-Comminges, 1991), 43–47; Christine Dieulafait and Jean Guyon, "Sous le signe des dieux dans la mouvance chrétienne? Heroïsation mythologique ou scènes originales d'un décor chrétien sur la face principale d'une cuve," in *Pulchra Imago: Fragments d'archéologie chrétienne. Catalogue d'exposition, Saint-Bertrand-de-Comminges, 30 mars–11 nov. 1991* (Toulouse: Musée archéologique départemental de Saint-Bertrand-de-Comminges, 1991), 61–65, full photograph on 60, detail on 65; Jean-Luc Schenck, "Valcabrère: Église Saint-Just," in *Les premiers monuments chrétiens de la France*, vol. 2, *Sud-Ouest et Centre* (Paris: Picard, 1996), 200–206, photograph of the fragment on 201. The fragment also appears in the *Index of Christian Art* (system number 0061809). The scene in question is listed in the *ICA* as "unidentified," but offers the possibility that the fragment includes a representation of Thecla (as nude orant) and Paul (holding an open scroll) with a lion between them, facing the female figure. In general, the scholarly literature that discusses this fragment identifies the figure as an unnamed nude female orant, not as Thecla, though one ingenious interpreter provocatively suggests that the nude female figure is actually Daniel, carved in error by the artist who made the mistake either because his original intention was to carve a figure of Eve or because he became confused after seeing portraits of the youthful Daniel with long hair: see Dolores del Amo Guinovart, "Frontal de Sarcófago de Valcabrère con la Adoración de Los Magos," *Antiquité Tardive* 7 (1999): 369.

130. *ATh* 21 (Lipsius, 250).

131. Boston Museum of Fine Arts, *Romans and Barbarians* (Boston: Museum of Fine Arts, 1976), 202, fig. 236; Kurt Weitzmann, ed., *Age of Spirituality: Late Antique and Early Christian Art, Third to Seventh Century. Catalogue of the Exhibition at the Metropolitan Museum of Art, November 19, 1977, through February 12, 1978* (New York: Metropolitan Museum of Art in association with Princeton University Press, 1979), 574–75, fig. 513. The provenance of this object has not been identified with precision, though the Kurt Weitzmann catalogue notes a resemblance between its style and that of some sculptures from Oxyrhynchus and Ahnas (575); Davis, *The Cult of St. Thecla*, 172, describes it as "probably from Oxyrhynchus." This relief, along with a series of other artistic artifacts and text fragments, is situated by Davis within his history of pilgrimage and devotion to Thecla in Egypt; see *The Cult of St. Thecla*, 172–73n73, 235, fig. 29. See also the description and discussion in Nauerth and Warns, *Thekla*, 31–34, fig. 14.

132. Kurt Weitzmann, *Age of Spirituality*, 574: "ropes lead to a lion and lioness posed heraldically beside her." Nauerth and Warns, *Thekla*, 31–32: "Thekla scheint wie auf einem Wappen hoheitsvoll zu schweben und der zeitlichen wie räumlichen Sphäre entrückt zu sein."

133. The catalogue entry for this object notes that the iconography here is relatively

rare, and that the figures of the angels are not found on other objects commemorating Thecla. See Kurt Weitzmann, *Age of Spirituality*, 574.

134. Kurt Weitzmann, *Age of Spirituality*, 575, notes: "this relief must undoubtedly have been placed in an architectural setting."

135. *ATh* 28; 33.

136. The representation of a figure flanked by two lions is standard iconography for Daniel. Several examples appear in Kurt Weitzmann, *Age of Spirituality*, e.g., 413, fig. 371 (where he appears as a classical nude at the top of a long rectangular plaque including several different biblical scenes); 420–21, fig. 377 (a fourth-century gold glass bowl bearing five scenes from the Hebrew Bible, including Daniel); 427–29, fig. 386 (the fourth-century sarcophagus of Junius Bassus, lower register, fourth niche from the left), on which see Elizabeth Struthers Malbon, *The Iconography of the Sarcophagus of Junius Bassus* (Princeton, N.J.: Princeton University Press, 1990); 429–30, fig. 387 (fourth-century casket from Pannonia, panels repeating the image of Daniel flanked by lions in between palm trees); 469–70, fig. 421 (a late fifth- or sixth-century ivory pyxis, perhaps from Syria-Palestine, portraying Daniel flanked by lions but with a winged and protecting angel [see Dan. 6:22] to one side); 485, fig. 436 (fifth-century ivory pyxis with the familiar figure of Daniel in the orant position, flanked by two lions). This same iconography of the figure of Daniel in the lions' den also appeared in Christian catacombs, notably the Priscilla and Callisto catacombs in Rome. On representations of Daniel in the catacombs, see J. Stevenson, *The Catacombs: Rediscovered Monuments of Early Christianity* (London: Thames and Hudson, 1978), 80. For a recent summary of the archaeology, history, and scholarship on these catacombs, see Philippe Pergola, *Le catacombe romane: Storia e topografia* (Rome: Carocci, 1998), 130–37 (Priscilla), 196–203 (Callisto). Also see A. Nestori, *Repertorio topografico delle pitture delle catacombe romane*, 2nd rev. and aug. ed., Roma sotterranea cristiana 5 (Vatican City: PIAC, 1993), 22–31, on the paintings in the catacomb of Priscilla. See also the Brescia Lipsanotheca, where the figure of Daniel flanked by the lions completes a complex typological exegesis in which Daniel prefigures Christ. See C. J. Watson, "The Program of the Brescia Casket," *Gesta* 20 (1981): 283–981; and Jaś Elsner, *Art and the Roman Viewer: The Transformation of Art from the Pagan World to Christianity* (New York: Cambridge University Press, 1995), 280–84.

137. Berlin, Frühchristlich-byzantinische Sammlung, no. 3263; Robert Forrer, *Die frühchristlichen Alterthümer aus dem Gräberfelde von Achmim-Panopolis* (Strasburg: F. Lohbauer, 1893), 15–16, plate 12; Nauerth and Warns, *Thekla*, 51–53 (with further bibliography) and fig. 19; mentioned as evidence for the Thecla cult in Egypt by Davis, *The Cult of Thecla*, 172. This object has been missing since World War II.

138. Forrer, *Die frühchristlichen Alterthümer*, 16.

139. Nauerth and Warns, *Thekla*, 51–53; Davis, *The Cult of Saint Thecla*, 172; 234, fig. 28.

140. On the connection between the three youths in the furnace and early Christian martyrdom, see: Reinhard Seeliger, "*Palai martyres*: Die Drei Junglinge im Feuerofen als Typos in der spätantiken Kunst, Liturgie und patristischen Literatur: Mit einigen Hinweisen zur Hermeneutik der christlichen Archeologie," in *Liturgie und Dichtung: Ein interdisziplinäres Kompendium*, ed. Hansjakob Becker and Reiner

Kaczynski (Sankt Ottilien: EOS Verlag, 1983), 257–334; Jensen, *Understanding*, 79–84, who cites a range of early Christian sources: *1 Clem.* 45.7; Tertullian, *Idol.* 15; *Scorp.* 8; *Adv. Marc.* 4.41; Origen, *Exhort. Mart.* 33; Cyprian, *Laps.* 19; *Unit. eccl.* 12; *Ep.* 6.3; 58.5; 57.8; 61.2. (Apart from the Roman context of 1 Clement, the other writers are all north Africans.)

141. For a discussion of the representation of Daniel in ancient north African art, see J. W. Salomonson, *Voluptatem Spectandi non perdat sed mutat: Observations sur l'iconographie du martyre en Afrique Romaine* (Amsterdam: North-Holland Publishing Company, 1979), esp. 55–90.

142. This oscillation and mirror-imaging of Thecla and Daniel is materially suggested by the uncertain identification of a fifth- or sixth-century sculpture mold from Daphne (near Antioch), now at the Princeton Art Museum (5464 s303). See Richard Stillwell, ed., *Antioch-on-the-Orontes*, vol 2, *The Excavations of 1933–1936*, Publications of the Committee for the Excavation of Antioch and Its Vicinity (Princeton, N.J.: Published for the Committee by the Department of Art and Archaeology of Princeton University, 1938), 178; 225 plate 21. The image on the obverse of this object is described by the *Index of Christian Art* as being *either* Daniel in the lions' den *or* Thecla with wild beasts. See *ICA* System Number 0099431.

143. See Davis, *Cult of Saint Thecla*, appendix A, 195–200, and, for illustrations, 215–20, figs. 7–12.

144. Josef Wilpert, "Menasfläschen mit der Darstellung der hl. Thekla zwischen den wilden Tieren," *RQ* 20 (1906): 86–92; C. M. Kaufmann, *Zur Ikonographie der Menasampullen* (Cairo: F. Diemer, Finck and Baylaender, 1910).

145. Originally published in O. M. Dalton, *Catalogue of Early Christian Antiquities and Objects from the Christian East in the Department of British and Mediaeval Antiquities and Ethnography of the British Museum* (London: British Museum, 1901), no. 882, pl. 32. The object is also discussed in Nauerth and Warns, *Thekla*, 35–42. See also Davis, *Cult of Saint Thecla*, appendix A, no. 12. The date of this object is uncertain according to Dalton; the *ICA* assigns it to the period of the fifth through seventh centuries (*ICA* system number 0090106).

146. *ATh* 32–35 (Lipsius, 258–62).

147. Nauerth and Warns, *Thekla*, 40, argue that on all the ampullae there is an object in the shape of an "o" which they interpret as a small fire or flame. They acknowledge that the image on this particular object is especially subtle. They connect this image with *ATh* 35, where fire is brought to prod the bulls on in their murderous task, fire that in turn burns the ropes that bind Thecla's feet and frees her. If Nauerth and Warns are correct in their analysis of this image, then there is a small but significant visual reminder that Thecla's story is not only about constraint and suffering but also about miraculous rescue.

148. *ATh* 34 (Lipsius, 260): "Τότε εἰσβάλλουσιν πολλὰ θηρία, ἑστώσης αὐτῆς καὶ ἐκτετακυίας τὰς χεῖρας καὶ προσευχομένης."

149. *ATh* 35 (Lipsius, 262).

150. See Jan Willem Salomonson, *Spätrömische Rote Tonware mit Reliefverzierung aus Nordafrikanischen Werkstätten* (Rome: Nederlands Historisch Instituut te Rom,

1969), 46, fig. 55; 47, fig. 56; 48, fig. 57. See also Salomonon, *Voluptatem,* 48–49, pl. 39, 40, 41; Nauerth and Warns, *Thekla,* 38.

151. See Nauerth and Warns, *Thekla,* 25–30; Kurt Weitzmann, *Age of Spirituality,* 576–78, no. 516; Davis, *Cult of Saint Thecla,* 119–20; 219, fig. 11; 220, fig. 12.

152. Nauerth and Warns, *Thekla,* 25.

153. Nauerth and Warns, *Thekla,* 30. This interpretation goes back to Kurt Weitzmann and is not currently considered authoritative.

154. Nauerth and Warns, *Thekla,* 27 (my translation).

155. For example, Kaufmann, *Zur Ikonographie der Menasampullen.* See also Davis, *The Cult of Saint Thecla,* 120–36.

156. Davis, *The Cult of Saint Thecla,* 114–20 (on the pilgrimage ampullae); also see appendix A, "A Catalogue of Published Ampullae with Saint Thecla," 195–200. On the artistic evidence more generally as evidence for the spread and extent of the Thecla cult, see 112–94.

157. Davis, *The Cult of Saint Thecla,* 133–36.

158. Elsner, *Art and the Roman Viewer,* 251.

159. Averil Cameron, *Christianity and the Rhetoric of Empire,* Sather Classical Lectures 55 (Berkeley: University of California Press, 1991), 150–51, quotation at 151.

6. RELIGION AS A CHAIN OF MEMORY: CASSIE BERNALL
OF COLUMBINE HIGH AND THE AMERICAN LEGACY
OF EARLY CHRISTIAN MARTYRDOM

1. *Time,* "The Monsters Next Door: A Special Report on the Colorado School Massacre," 3 May 1999.

2. On guns and gun control: Handgun Control, Inc./Center to Prevent Handgun Violence, *Progress Report* (Fall 1999), included articles such as "The Nation After Littleton" and "Enough Is Enough" (an opinion piece by HCI/CPHV cofounder Sarah Brady). Meanwhile, the National Rifle Association's Independence Institute published, online, *Special Report on the Columbine Murders,* comprising a wide array of articles and Internet resources offering "The Truth About Guns," the observation that "Gun Control Won't Stop the Madness," Oliver North's MSNBC commentary, "Don't Blame the NRA for Littleton." See http://www.i2i.org/SuptDocs/Crime/Columbine. htm. Gun culture, popular culture, adolescent cruelty, and alienation turned up regularly in the press coverage of the events. See *Time,* 3 May 1999, "The Monsters Next Door," whose cover featured black-and-white photographs of the dead and color photographs of the two killers. Featured articles included "The Danger of Cliques," "Life Imitates the Movies," and "Round Up the Usual Suspects [on gun culture]." See also *US News & World Report,* "The Lessons of Littleton," 3 May 1999, 16–26; and Mark Jacobson, Michael Wolff, and Nancy Jo Sales, "Kid Culture in the Age of Columbine," *New York,* 17 May 1999, 24–34. On media complicity, see Thomas de Zengotita, "The Gunfire Dialogues," *Harper's,* July 1999, 55–58. The music of Marilyn Manson was at times blamed for the Littleton shootings. The musician published a spirited defense: "Columbine: Whose Fault is It?" *Rolling Stone,* 24 June 1999, 23–24, 77. On the culture

wars, religion in schools, etc., see Fred Barnes, "God, Gary, and the GOP," *The Weekly Standard*, 24 May 1999, 13: "Harris and Klebold gave the Hitler salute and produced violent videos, but were never reprimanded. But had a teacher 'hung the Ten Commandments in her room, she would have been in the principal's office that day.'" At Rachel Scott's funeral, the pastor Bruce Porter preached, "I want to say to you here today that prayer was established again in our public schools last Tuesday"; see Andrew Walsh, "Preaching the Word in Littleton," *Religion in the News* 2, no. 2 (Summer 1999): 6. See also Don Feder, "National Day of Prayer Survives Amid Attack on Religion by Courts," *Insight on the News*, 29 May 2000, 46, which poses the sarcastic question: "Since she admitted to a belief in God on public property, did Cassie violate the Constitution?" For another perspective on the implications of Columbine for the culture wars, see George Plasketes, "Things to Do in Littleton When You're Dead: A Post-Columbine Collage," *Popular Music and Society* 23, no. 3 (Fall 1999): 9–24.

3. I am not alone in exploring the links between ancient Mediterranean martyrdom and the contemporary scene. See also E. Leigh Gibson, "The Making of Modern Martyrs: The Martyrs of Columbine," in *The Bible in the Twenty-First Century: Actors and Scenes of Violence*, ed. Athalya Brenner (New York: Continuum, 2004), forthcoming; Jan Willem van Henten, "Internet Martyrs and Violence Vicitms and/or Perpetrators," in *Vocabularies of Violence*, ed. Jonneke Bekkenkamp and Yvonne Sherwood (New York: Continuum, 2004), forthcoming. I am grateful to these two scholars for sharing their works-in-progress with me.

4. Another student killed at Columbine, Rachel Scott, has also emerged as a martyr figure. I focus on the example of Cassie Bernall because she was the first to garner public attention and the figure whose story stirred the most serious controversy. For a complete analysis of both Cassie's and Rachel's stories, see Justin Watson, *The Martyrs of Columbine: Faith, Tragedy, and Politics* (New York: Palgrave, 2002).

5. On the death of Cassie Bernall at Columbine High, see J. Bottum, "A Martyr Is Born," *The Weekly Standard, Special Report: Littleton*, 10 May 1999, 12–14. Bottum goes on to cite Christian scholars who have mentioned various early Christian women saints—Eulalia, Catherine of Alexandria, Crispina, and Rhipsime—in relation to Cassie. See also Kenneth L. Woodward with Sherry Keene-Osborn and Claire Kirk, "The Making of a Martyr," *Newsweek*, 14 June 1999, 64, which also makes parallels between Columbine and early Christian martyrdom.

6. J. Bottum, "Awakening at Littleton," *First Things* 95 (August/September 1999): 28–32; online version available at http://www.firstthings.com/ftissues/ft9908/articles/bottum.html. Author's emphasis.

7. By Cassie Bernall's funeral on April 26, six days after the shootings, she was already being declared a martyr. See Janet Bingham, "Cassie Bernall Died for Faith," *Denver Post*, 27 April 1999; Amy Goldstein, "In Colorado, Questions About Accomplices, 'Martyrs'; Deaths Seen in Christian Context," *Washington Post*, 27 April 1999. An early martyrological account may be found in Matt Labash, "'Do You Believe in God?' 'Yes.': On the Life and Death of Cassie Bernall," *The Weekly Standard*, 10 May 1999, 20–25.

8. Bottum, "A Martyr Is Born."

9. Quoted in Goldstein, "In Colorado, Questions About Accomplices, 'Martyrs' ";
Bingham, "Cassie Bernall Died for Faith." See also Bottum, "A Martyr is Born."

10. David Van Biema, "A Surge of Teen Spirit," *Time Magazine,* 31 May 1999, 58–59.

11. Bottum, "Awakening at Littleton," 31.

12. Bottum, "Awakening at Littleton," 28. See also Dave Cullen, "The Rumor That
Won't Go Away: Jocks Say Littleton Killers Were Gay, but Friends Deny It," *Salon,* 24
April 1999, available at http://www.salon.com/news/feature/1999/04/24/rumors; and
Dave Cullen, "Gay Leaders Fear Littleton Backlash," *Salon,* 27 April 1999, available at
http://www.salon.com/news/feature/1999/04/27/gay. See also Anthony Chase, "Violent Reaction: What Do Teen Killers Have in Common?" *In These Times,* 9 July 2001:
"Interviews with Columbine students indicate that the possible homosexuality of Klebold and Harris is used to confirm that they were freaks or monsters—not to open the
dialogue on tolerance and diversity. The implication is that the abuse the pair suffered
in life is justified by the deed they finally committed."

13. William Kristol, "Good and Evil in Littleton," *The Weekly Standard,* 10 May
1999, 7. Al Gore, the vice president at the time, argued that the killers "simply made a
choice in favor of evil over good. We have a mandate to choose good over evil. They
did not." See Fred Barnes, "Born-Again Gore," *The Weekly Standard,* 10 May 1999, 14.
At the end of Barnes's article, he writes: "On Littleton, he's on the side of good, Christianity, and morality." See also *National Review,* " 'A Wave of Evil,' " *National Review,*
11 October 1999. On "madness" as the root of the problem, see Bottum, "Awakening at
Littleton," 30, who called Harris and Klebold "insane criminals" and distinguished
them from the image of Cassie the martyr by saying, "Harris and Klebold form an
image to engender insanity." Meanwhile, Labash called them "a couple of crazed Goth
geeks," in his " 'Do You Believe in God?' " 22.

14. Sharon Begley, "Why the Young Kill," *Newsweek,* 3 May 1999, 32–35.

15. Including, I should note, students of mine at Barnard and Columbia. See the
glib and sarcastic dismissal of such feelings in *The Weekly Standard,* "Americans
United for Blame Shifting," *The Weekly Standard,* 7 June 1999, 3. By contrast, see
Chase, "Violent Reaction," 16, which begins: "I recall the feelings of hatred and fantasies of revenge I harbored as a teen-ager in the rural Hudson River Valley, where certain classmates tormented me because they thought I was gay. . . . Those memories
return to me each time I hear that yet another teen-age boy has taken a gun into a high
school and opened fire, leaving his community terrorized and bewildered. I do not feel
bewildered. The memory of my own revenge fantasies, Bosch-like in their terror,
return to me vividly, even now, 30 years after my days at Van Wyck Junior High
School."

16. Jean Bethke Elshtain, "Heartland of Darkness," *The New Republic,* 17 January
2000, 36, 38.

17. One of the cocreators of this television series is an alumnus of Columbine High
School and is interviewed in Michael Moore's documentary "Bowling for Columbine."

18. Gary Burns, "Marilyn Manson and the Apt Pupils of Littleton," *Popular Music
and Society* 23, no. 3 (Fall 1999): 3–8.

19. Bottum, "Awakening at Littleton." Elsewhere, Bottum makes a similarly struc-

tured argument indicting the Columbine killers as examples of the perilous slackening of high culture and its reduction and domestication: "They are like suburban high-school Raskolnikovs or imitation Underground Men—characters wrenched from a Dostoyevsky novel and dulled down into something unspeakably murderous, vulgar, and boring" (J. Bottum, "Columbine, Again," *The Weekly Standard*, 27 December 1999, 7).

20. Kristol, "Good and Evil in Littleton," 7. Kristol concludes his editorial with the observation: "Modernity began with Machiavelli. The great interpreter of Machiavelli, the late Leo Strauss, concluded his book on that unbelievably brilliant and subtle 'teacher of evil' with the suggestion that we could only ascend from the dead-end of Machiavellian modernity by returning to an earlier notion of 'the primacy of the good.'"

21. Elshtain, "The Heartland of Darkness," 33–38.

22. Quoted in Bottum, "Awakening at Littleton," 30; Misty Bernall, *She Said Yes: The Unlikely Martyrdom of Cassie Bernall* (Farmington, Penn.: Plough Publishing Company, 1999), 63, 73.

23. Bernall, *She Said Yes*. Subsequent editions of the book have appeared from Word Publishers and, more recently, Pocket Books. It is also available as an audiobook and a video.

24. See also Labash, "'Do You Believe in God?'" 22: "In fact, this faith, Cassie's faith, rejects randomness entirely. It affirms instead that seemingly arbitrary events are orchestrated, for reasons that may remain unknown."

25. Licia Fiol-Matta, *A Queer Mother for the Nation: The State and Gabriela Mistral* (Minneapolis: University of Minnesota Press, 2001), 112.

26. Elena Giannarelli, "Il παιδαριογέρων nella biografia cristiana," *Prometheus* 14 (1988): 279–84; Elena Giannarelli, "Sogni e visioni dell'infanzia nelle biografie dei santi: Fra tradizione classica e innovazione cristiana," *Augustinianum* 29 (1989): 213–35; Anna Benvenuti Papi and Elena Giannarelli, *Bambini santi: Rappresentazioni dell'infanzia e modelli agiografici* (Torino: Rosenberg & Sellier, 1991).

27. The second pattern is more frequently associated with female saints whose fallenness is frequently figured in sexual terms. For some primary sources, see Sister Benedicta Ward, *The Harlots of the Desert: A Study of Repentance in Early Monastic Sources* (Kalamazoo, Mich.: Cistercian Publications, 1987).

28. Bernall, *She Said Yes*, 95.

29. Bernall, *She Said Yes*, 55.

30. The church identifies itself as an evangelical Presbyterian church. See its Web site at http://www.westbowleschurch.com.

31. Bernall, *She Said Yes*, 63–64.

32. Bernall, *She Said Yes*, 100.

33. Bernall, *She Said Yes*, 30.

34. Bernall, *She Said Yes*, 31.

35. Bernall, *She Said Yes*, 107.

36. Bernall, *She Said Yes*, 124.

37. See also Labash, "'Do You Believe in God?'" 24, on a paragraph Cassie had

underlined in a book for Bible study, which Labash quotes and then glosses: "What some call eerie prescience, others label divine appointment."

38. Bernall, *She Said Yes*, 115.

39. Bernall, *She Said Yes*, 31.

40. Ibid., 111. This story was first reported by Matt Labash in *The Weekly Standard* (" 'Do You Believe in God?' " 23): " 'She wanted to cut off her hair and give it to this place that makes hair for kids who go through chemo,' says Sara Romes, a 15-year-old member of Cassie's youth group. 'She wanted to cut it off pretty short, so that there would be enough to supply three or four kids.' "

41. "Cassie may be a martyr to others, but to me, she'll always be my little girl." Misty Bernall, quoted in http://www.cassiebernall.org/questions.htm; accessed 24 October 1999, now expired.

42. Just months before the shootings at Columbine, Dr. King was honored at Westminster Abbey by the installation of a towering statue commemorating his martyrdom, alongside nine other twentieth-century Christian martyrs (including, for example, Archbishop Oscar Romero of El Salvador). See Jenny E. Heller, "Westminster Abbey Elevates 10 Foreigners," *New York Times*, 22 September 1998.

43. Bernall, *She Said Yes*, 139–40.

44. Bottum, "A Martyr Is Born." See also Labash, " 'Do You Believe in God?' " 22, which calls up several early Christian examples—"Stephen stoned outside the city gates while praying for his executioners, Peter crucified upside down, John the Baptist handed his head"—observing that "some skeptics" might challenge the analogy between Cassie's death and "the dramatic demises of our first-century martyrs."

45. Elshtain, "Heartland of Darkness," 34.

46. John Foxe, *The New Foxe's Book of Martyrs*, ed. Harold J. Chadwick (Bridge-Logos Publishers, 2001): "newly expanded to include martyrs through 1996," according to the advertisement in the Christian Book Distributors online catalogue (Christianbook.com). Thanks to Simon Steiner for bringing this book to my attention.

47. John Wagner, ed., *The Big Book of Martyrs* (New York: Paradox Press, 1997). Thanks to Elizabeth Branon for bringing this book to my attention.

48. DC Talk and The Voice of the Martyrs, *Jesus Freaks: Stories of Those Who Stood for Jesus: The Ultimate Jesus Freaks* (Tulsa, Okla.: Albury Publishing, 1999). Thanks to Rosamond Rodman for bringing this book to my attention.

49. Bernall, *She Said Yes*, 134.

50. Quoted in Dave Cullen, " 'I Smell the Presence of Satan,' " *Salon*, 15 May 1999, available at http://salon.com/news/feature/1999/05/15/evangelicals/print.html.

51. Bernall, *She Said Yes*, 101.

52. Bernall, *She Said Yes*, 108.

53. Bernall, *She Said Yes*, 72.

54. Bernall, *She Said Yes*, 93; my emphasis.

55. Dave Cullen, "Who Said 'Yes'?" *Salon*, 30 September 1999, available at http://www.salon.com/news/feature/1999/09/30/bernall/print.html.

56. Reported in various media outlets: Dave Cullen, "Inside the Columbine High Investigation: Everything You Know About the Littleton Killings Is Wrong," *Salon*,

23 September 1999, available at http://www.salon.com/news/feature/1999/09/23/ columbine, was the first to report the controversy. Soon afterwards, the *Denver Post* began covering the controversy: Susan Besze Wallace, "Faith in Cassie's Last Words Wavers," *Denver Post*, 25 September 1999; and Susan Besze Wallace, "Schnurr's Memory Corroborated by Other Witnesses," *Denver Post*, 28 September 1999. For a strongly worded denunciation of the perpetuation of the martyrdom story, see Jon Carroll, "She Didn't Say Anything," *San Francisco Chronicle*, 4 October 1999.

57. For a complete assessment of the available testimony and evidence, see Justin Watson, "Defenders and Debunkers: 'What Really Happened?' " in his *The Martyrs of Columbine*, 115–45.

58. Hanna Rosin, "Columbine Miracle: A Matter of Belief; The Last Words of Littleton Victim Cassie Bernall Test a Survivor's Faith—and Charity," *The Washington Post*, 14 October 1999; Dave Shiflett, "It Ain't Gospel," *Salon*, 17 February 2000, available at http://www.salon.com/news/feature/2000/02/17/ramsey.

59. Chris Zimmerman, quoted at http://www.cassiebernall.org/questions.htm (accessed 24 October 1999, now expired) and in Art Toalston, "Cassie Bernall's Parents Recount Efforts to Achieve Accuracy in Book," *Southern Baptist Website*, 29 September 1999, http://www.sbc.net/articles/1999/09/29/bpa1.asp; accessed 24 October 1999, now expired. See now *BP news*, 29 September 1999, http://www.bpnews.net/bpnews. asp?id=333.

60. "From the Publisher," page facing "Table of Contents," *She Said Yes*, x.

61. Sean Kelly, "Bernalls Defend Book's Accuracy," *Denver Post*, 26 September 1999; also quoted in Toalston, "Cassie Bernall's Parents." See also Dan Luzadder and Katie Kerwin McCrimmon, "Accounts Differ on Question to Bernall," *Denver Rocky Mountain News*, 24 September 1999.

62. Quoted in Michael Janofsky, "Far Beyond Columbine, Rancor and Tension: Shootings' Legacy is Passionate Discord," *New York Times*, 4 October 1999.

63. Cullen, "Inside the Columbine High Investigation."

64. Dave Cullen, *Cloud Over Columbine: How the Press Got It Wrong and the Police Let It Happen* (New York: Random House, 2002).

65. Matthew Heimer, "Adding Up the Facts," *Brill's Content* 2, no. 6 (July/August 1999): 92–93.

66. Wendy Murray Zoba, *Day of Reckoning: Columbine and the Search for America's Soul* (Grand Rapids, Mich.: Brazos Press, 2000).

67. Elshtain, "Heartland of Darkness," 35.

68. "Is Cassie Bernall a Martyr? An Orthodox Christian Answer," www. orthodox.net/articles/is-cassie-bernall-a-martyr.html (accessed 10/24/99) argued that "Belief in God is not a sole criterion for salvation, but belonging to the body of Christ, that is the [orthodox] church is. Cassie's firm belief, which we absolutely admire, in her religion was most likely based on the bible only, however, the bible does not save. It only points to Christ, and his church, which DOES save. . . . Cassie is a HERO, and I rejoice because of her confession. . . . I cannot pray to her as a martyr, and I cannot deny that she is a martyr, and is blessed. I simply (as an Orthodox Christian, obedient to the church), cannot answer the question, and am content with this. God knows."

69. Robert E. Reccord, quoted in Toalston, "Cassie Bernall's Parents." A similar

argument was made, using St. Thérèse of Lisieux as an analogy by Eileen McNamara, "No Doubting One Girl's Faith," *Boston Globe*, 10 October 1999.

70. Vincent Crapanzano, *Serving the Word: Literalism in America from the Pulpit to the Bench* (New York: New Press, 2000).

71. Http://www.revdwpoc.org/cassiepledge.html; accessed 9 December 1999, now expired. It is worth noting that the Cassie Pledge has subsequently disappeared from the Internet, raising questions about both its ephemeral status and the character of this form of memory work.

72. Nebraska Fellowship of Christian Athletes, "Seeing Christ at Columbine: In Memory of Cassie Bernall," http://www.fca.ilsweb.com/CassieBernall.htm (accessed 7/30/99). Other memorial Web sites included one in which a small picture of Cassie morphs digitally into an image of a bloodied and crucified Christ (http://www.slip.net?~holtonj/ [accessed 7/30/99]) and another entitled, "In Memory of Cassie Rene Bernall," with an image of Cassie's smiling face at the top of a cloud-encircled staircase, the face of a bearded man (presumably Jesus) above her head (http://www.cwdzyns.com/Cassie%20Bernall%20Memorial/cassie_bernall.htm [accessed 7/30/99]). This site, like so many others devoted to Cassie's memory, has since disappeared.

73. Also announced in the "Spotlight" feature of *Billboard* magazine, 18 December 1999. Thanks to Simon Steiner for bringing this music to my attention and keeping me informed about Christian popular culture more generally. See also *Whatever It Takes: The 'She Said Yes' Project*, a multi-artist CD released in 2000 (Deborah Evans Price, "Higher Ground," *Billboard*, 30 December 2000).

74. Jim Yardley, "Church's Haunted House Draws Fire," *New York Times*, 29 October 1999. Also see *Hell House: A Documentary Film*, dir. George Ratliff, prod. Zachary Mortenson, New York, Mixed Greens films, 2001.; www.hellhousemovie.com.

75. Susan Besze Wallace, "Columbine Crosses Return for Play," *Denver Post*, 19 November 1999.

76. Bruce Nolan, "Columbine Cast as Morality Play: Slick Church Production Held Over for Months," *New Orleans Times-Picayune*, 20 February 2000.

77. Sandy Shore, "A Girl's Faith Leaves Enduring Legacy: Columbine Victim Seen as Martyr," *New Orleans Times-Picayune*, Orleans edition, 15 May 1999: "In Catonsville, Md., Kristen Eppard, 15, was so moved by Bernall's story that she plans to take Cassie's name when she is confirmed Sunday at the Church of the Good Shepherd."

78. http://www.yesibelieve.com/yes_promo.html; accessed 9 December 1999. Note that the "Yes I Believe" site is currently a site for "Spiritual Wear," which sells Christian apparel.

79. http://www.yesibelieve.com/yes_newsletter.html.

80. http://www.yesibelieve.com/yes_retail.html.

81. http://www.yesibelieve.com/yes_bernall_foundation.html.

82. Cindy Brovsky, "Forever Changed: Columbine Is Not Alone in Its Grief, as People from Afar Have Reached out with Heartfelt Messages," *Denver Post*, 25 April 1999; Gustav Niebuhr and Jodi Wilgoren, "From the Shock of Violent Deaths, New and More Public Rites of Mourning," *New York Times*, 28 April 1999; Nancy Gibbs, "Special Report: The Littleton Massacre," *Time*, 3 May 1999, 36.

83. Lorraine Adams, "Columbine Crosses Can't Bear Weight of Discord: Memorials Embrace Gunmen, Divide Mourners," *Washington Post*, 3 May 1999, Final Edition.

84. Jim Kirksey, "Original Crosses for Victims to Go on Tour," *Denver Post*, 3 June 1999, Rockies Edition. Gayle White, "Evangelism Effort Prelude to Baptists' Meeting," *Atlanta Journal-Constitution*, 13 June 1999 (reporting the presence of the crosses at the annual convention of the Southern Baptist Convention in Atlanta). Matt Labash, "Among the Crusaders: The Saga of a Columbine Father, an Illinois Carpenter, and Their Evangelical Roadshow," *The Weekly Standard*, 24 April 2000; see also Wallace, "Columbine Crosses Return for Play."

85. Percy Ednalino, "Crosses May Return to Hill Site," *Denver Post*, 15 April 2001, Rockies Edition; Percy Ednalino, "Columbine Crosses Spark Dispute," *Denver Post*, 18 April 2001, Final Edition.

86. Dan Haley, "Protesters Fell Church's Trees: Pair Linked to Columbine High Killers Chopped Down," *Denver Post*, 27 September 1999; Janofsky, "Far Beyond Columbine."

87. *New York Times*, "Columbine Lawsuit Filed," *New York Times*, 5 October 1999.

88. See, for example, Labash, "Among the Crusaders."

89. Elshtain, "Heartland of Darkness," 36, 38.

90. Elshtain, "Heartland of Darkness," 36.

91. Donna Schaper, "Sacred Spaces," *Cross Currents* 50 (2000): 221–25.

92. Crapanzano, *Serving the Word*, 2–3, offers a ten-point summary of the elements of "literalism" in both religious and legal contexts.

93. Jeffrey Goldberg, "Washington Discovers Christian Persecution," *New York Times Magazine*, 21 December 1997, 46–52, 60, 64–65.

94. Peter Steinfels, "Evangelicals Lobby for Oppressed Christians," *New York Times*, 15 September 1996; Peter Steinfels, "The State Department's Decision to Establish a Panel on Religious Persecution Around the World Immediately Raises Questions of Sincerity," *New York Times*, 16 November 1996.

95. Steven Erlanger, "U.S. Assails China Over Suppression of Religious Life," *New York Times*, 22 July 1997; Steven Lee Myers, "Elsewhere in the World, the Right to Worship Freely Hasn't a Prayer," *New York Times*, 27 July 1997.

96. *Freedom from Religious Persecution Act of 1998*, 105th Cong., 2nd sess., H.R. 2431 (known as the Wolf-Specter Bill); Rev. Jay Lintner, "The Right's Holy War," *The Nation*, 20 July 1998, 6–7.

97. *International Religious Freedom Act*, 105th Cong., 2nd sess., S.B. 1868 (known as the Nickles-Lieberman Bill); Eric Schmitt, "Bill to Punish Nations Limiting Religious Beliefs Passes Senate," *New York Times*, 10 October 1998.

98. Laurie Goodstein, "Christians Gain Support in Fight on Persecution," *New York Times*, 9 November 1998. See also Katha Pollitt, "Religious Right, Religious Rights," *The Nation*, 13 October 1997, 10.

99. Francis X. Clines, "A Religious Tilt Toward the Left," *New York Times*, 16 September 1996.

100. Eyal A. Naveh, *Crown of Thorns: Political Martyrdom in America from Abraham Lincoln to Martin Luther King, Jr.* (New York: New York University Press, 1990);

Richard Slotkin, *Regeneration Through Violence: The Mythology of the American Frontier, 1600–1860* (Middletown, Conn.: Wesleyan University Press, 1973).

101. Harriet Martineau, "The Martyr Age in the United States," *London and Westminster Review* 32 (December 1838–April 1839): 1–59. Reprinted in Harriet Martineau, *Writings on Slavery and the American Civil War*, ed. Deborah Anna Logan (DeKalb: Northern Illinois University Press, 2002), 44–80.

102. A cursory search of a periodicals database for the terms "Matthew Shepard" and "martyr" produces hundreds of citations from newspapers and magazines across the country and, indeed, the globe. See Guy Trebay, "Beyond the Fence: Conjuring the Lives of Martyr Matthew Shepard," *Village Voice*, 3 November 1998. Conservative gay columnist Andrew Sullivan cautioned against the politics of victimization, which he saw as a necessary correlate to the claim of Matthew Shepard's martyrdom (mentioning Cassie Bernall in passing). See Andrew Sullivan, "Afterlife," *The New Republic*, 22 November 1999, 6.

103. The most substantive journalistic account of this story is John Gregory Dunne, "The Humboldt Murders," *New Yorker*, 13 January 1997, 44–62. See also David L. Kirp, "Martyrs and Movies," *American Prospect*, 20 December 1999, 52–53 (on *Boys Don't Cry*, the feature film based on the story). Also see Erin Runions, "Why Girls Cry: Gender Melancholia and Sexual Violence in Ezekiel 16 and *Boys Don't Cry*," in *How Hysterical: Identification and Resistance in the Bible and Film* (New York: Palgrave, 2003), 114–34.

104. Pam Belluck, "Hate Groups Seeking Broader Reach: Articulate and Middle Class Recruits Fit New, Moderated Image," *New York Times*, 7 July 1999.

105. Christian Berthelsen, "Hundreds Remember Slain Letter Carrier," *New York Times*, 15 August 1999.

106. Elshtain, "Heartland of Darkness," 34.

107. Elshtain, "Heartland of Darkness," Eulalia's story is first told in Prudentius, *Peristephanon* 3. On the subsequent sources for the portrait of Eulalia, see Anne-Marie Palmer, *Prudentius on the Martyrs* (Oxford: Oxford University Press, 1989), 239–41; On the literary portrait of Eulalia, see John Petruccione, "The Portrait of St. Eulalia of Mérida in Prudentius' *Peristephanon*," *AnBoll* 108 (1990): 81–104; Elizabeth A. Castelli, "Imperial Reimaginings of Christian Origins: Epic in Prudentius's Poem for the Martyr Eulalia," in *Reimagining Christian Origins*, ed. Elizabeth A. Castelli and Hal Taussig (Valley Forge, Penn.: Trinity Press International, 1996), 173–84. Agnes's story is preserved in Prudentius, *Peristephanon* 14. There are earlier testimonia concerning Agnes, including important texts by Ambrose. On the sources, see Palmer, *Prudentius on the Martyrs*, 250–55. On Prudentius and the cult of the martyrs more generally, see Michael Roberts, *Poetry and the Cult of the Martyrs: The* Liber Peristephanon *of Prudentius* (Ann Arbor: University of Michigan Press, 1993). On the theological and ideological interests of the Agnes tradition, see Virginia Burrus, "Reading Agnes: The Rhetoric of Gender in Ambrose and Prudentius," *JECS* 3 (1995): 25–46.

108. Bottum, "A Martyr Is Born."

109. Woodward, "The Making of a Martyr," 64.

110. Alessandra Stanley, "French Bishop, Disciplined Over 'Gay Pride' Issue, Still Speaks Out in Rome," *New York Times* 4 July 2000.

111. The comments were made in an interview with the Italian magazine, *30 Giorni*. They were initially reported in Rory Carroll, "Media Revel in Abuse Scandal, Says Cardinal: Man Tipped as Next Pope Says US Coverage of Paedophile Priests Resembles Persecutions Under Stalin and Hitler," *Manchester Guardian,* 10 June 2002. See also Gary Wills, "The Bishops at Bay," *New York Review of Books,* 15 August 2002, 10 (which erroneously reports the cardinal's comment as referring to the Decian persecution).

112. This insight belongs to Michal Govrin, "Theological Writing of Second-Generation Survivors," paper presented at the Genocide, Religion, and Modernity Conference at the U.S. Holocaust Museum, Washington, D.C., 11–13 May 1997. Used with permission of the author.

EPILOGUE

1. See now Margaret Cormack, ed., *Sacrificing the Self: Perspectives on Martyrdom and Religion* (New York: Oxford University Press, 2001).

2. Eyal J. Naveh, *Crown of Thorns: Political Martyrdom in America from Abraham Lincoln to Martin Luther King, Jr.* (New York: New York University Press, 1990). This connection is a long-recognized one: see Harriet Martineau, "The Martyr Age in the United States," *London and Westminster Review* 32 (December 1838–April 1839): 1–59; reprint, Harriet Martineau, *Writings on Slavery and the American Civil War,* ed. Deborah Anna Logan (DeKalb: Northern Illinois University Press, 2002), 44–80.

3. Benjamin Weiser, "Life for Terrorist in Embassy Attack," *The New York Times,* 13 June 2001. See also the follow-up story, Benjamin Weiser, "A Jury Torn and Fearful in 2001 Terrorism Trial," *The New York Times,* 5 January 2003. This latter story documents the complex role of religious conviction in the jurors' deliberations and the fact that at least two jurors consulted with their pastors during the sentencing phase of the trial. The larger question of the intersections of violence and religion in this crime and its judicial aftermath must be left to another discussion.

4. Francis X. Clines, "A Religious Tilt Toward the Left," *The New York Times,* 16 September 1996.

5. Barbara Kingsolver, *The Poisonwood Bible* (San Francisco: Harper Flamingo, 1998), 410.

6. Søren Kierkegaard, *Papers and Journals,* 352; quoted in Hent de Vries, *Religion and Violence: Philosophical Perspectives from Kant to Derrida* (Baltimore: Johns Hopkins University Press, 2002), 169.

7. Françoise Meltzer, *For Fear of the Fire: Joan of Arc and the Limits of Subjectivity* (Chicago: University of Chicago Press, 2001), 34–35.

8. Talal Asad, *Genealogies of Religion: Discipline and Reasons of Power in Christianity and Islam* (Baltimore: Johns Hopkins University Press, 1993), 12.

9. See also Michael C. Kearl and Anoel Rinaldi, "The Political Uses of the Dead as Symbols in Contemporary Civil Religions," *Social Forces* 61 (1983): 693–708.

10. For further consideration of the visibility and legibility of suffering, see Arthur Kleinman, Veena Das, and Margaret Lock, eds., *Social Suffering* (Berkeley: University of California Press, 1997); Luc Boltanski, *Distant Suffering: Morality, Media, and Politics,* trans. Graham Burchell (New York: Cambridge University Press, 1999); Stanley

Cohen, *States of Denial* (London: Polity Press, 2001); and Sven Lindqvist, *A History of Bombing*, trans. Linda Haverty Rugg (New York: New Press, 2001).

11. Hent de Vries, *Religion and Violence*, 1.

12. See now Robert Gibbs and Elliot Wolfson, eds., *Suffering Religion* (New York: Routledge, 2002).

BIBLIOGRAPHY

PRIMARY SOURCES AND REFERENCE WORKS

Achilles Tatius. *Adventures of Leucippe and Clitophon.* Trans. S. Gaselee. LCL. Cambridge: Harvard University Press, 1969.

Acta Apostolorum Apocrypha. See Lipsius.

Acta Pauli et Theclae. In Lipsius, 235–72.

Acta Sanctorum. Ed. Johannes Bolland, Godefridus Henschenius, Daniel von Papenbroeck, et al. 64 vols. Reprint ed. Brussels: Culture et civilisation, 1965–.

Acts of the Christian Martyrs. See Musurillo.

Ambrose. *De virginibus.* PL 16.187–234. Excerpted English translation by Boniface Ramsey as "On Virgins," in *Ambrose,* ed. and trans. Boniface Ramsey (New York: Routledge, 1997), 71–116.

Ante-Nicene Fathers. 10 vols. Ed. Alexander Roberts and James Donaldson. Rev. A. Cleveland Coxe. Reprint edition. Peabody, Mass.: Hendrickson, 1994.

The Apostolic Fathers. 2 vols. Trans. Kirsopp Lake. LCL. Cambridge, Mass.: Harvard University Press, 1927.

The Apostolic Fathers: Greek Texts and English Translations of Their Writings. Trans. J. B. Lightfoot and J. R. Harmer. 2nd ed., ed. and rev. Michael W. Holmes. Grand Rapids, Mich.: Baker Book House, 1992.

Asterius of Amasea. *Ekphrasis on the Holy Martyr Euphemia.* Trans. Elizabeth A. Castelli. In *Religions of Late Antiquity in Practice,* ed. Richard Valantasis, 463–68. Princeton, N.J.: Princeton University Press, 2000.

———. *Homilies I–XIV: Text, Introduction, and Notes.* Ed. C. Datema. Leiden: Brill, 1970.

Athenagoras. *Legatio pro Christianis.* Ed. Miroslav Marcovich. PTS 31. Berlin: Walter de Gruyter, 1990. English translation: *ANF* 2:129–48.

Atti e passioni dei martiri. See Bastiaensen et al.

Aubineau, Michel. "Le panégyrique de Thècle, attribué à Jean Chrysostome (*BHG* 1720): La fin retrouvée d'un texte mutilé." *AnBoll* 93 (1975): 349–62.

Aufstieg und Niedergang der römischen Welt: Geschichte und Kultur Roms im Spiegel der neueren Forschung. Ed. H. Temporini and W. Haase. Berlin: Walter de Gruyter, 1972–.

Augustine. *City of God*. Trans. Henry Bettenson. Intro. John O'Meara. New York: Penguin, 1984.

———. *Confessiones*. CCSL 27. Published in English as *Confessions*, trans. R. Pine-Coffin. London: Penguin, 1961.

———. *Sermons*. English translation: *The Works of Saint Augustine: A Translation for the Twenty-first Century*. Part 3, 11 vols. Intro. Cardinal Michele Pellegrino. Trans. Edmund Hill. Ed. John E. Rotelle. Brooklyn: New City Press, 1990–1997.

Ausgewählte Märtyrerakten. See Knopf, Krüger, and Ruhbach, eds.

Bastiaensen, A. A. R., A. Hilhorst, G. A. A. Kortekaas, A. P. Orbán, and M. M. van Assendelft, eds. *Atti e passioni dei martiri*. Milan: Mondadori, 1987. 4th ed., 1998.

Bauer, Walter, William F. Arndt, F. Wilbur Gingrich, and F. W. Danker. *Greek-English Lexicon of the New Testament and Other Early Christian Literature*. 2nd ed. Chicago: University of Chicago Press, 1979.

Cabrol, Fernand, and Henry Leclercq, eds. *Dictionnaire d'archéologie chrétienne et de liturgie*. 15 vols. Paris: Letouzet et Ané, 1907–1953.

Casey, Robert P. "Der dem Athanasius zugeschriebene Traktat Περὶ παρϑενίας." *Sitzungsberichte der Preussischen Akademie der Wissenschaften* 33 (1935): 1022–45.

Cicero. *Tusculan Disputations*. Trans. John E. King. Rev. ed. LCL. Cambridge: Harvard University Press, 1945.

Clement of Alexandria (Clément d'Alexandrie). *Le Pédagogue, Livre I*. Intro. Henri-Irénée Marrou. Trans. Marguerite Harl. SC 70. Paris: Éditions du Cerf, 1960. English translation: *ANF* 2: 209–36.

——— (Clément d'Alexandrie). *Le Pédagogue, Livre II*. Trans. Claude Mondésert. Annot. Henri-Irénée Marrou. SC 108. Paris: Éditions du Cerf, 1965. English translation: *ANF* 2: 237–70.

——— (Clément d'Alexandrie). *Le Pédagogue, Livre III*. Trans. Claude Mondésert and Chantal Matray. Annot. Henri-Irénée Marrou. SC 158. Paris: Éditions du Cerf, 1970. English translation: *ANF* 2: 271–96.

——— (Clément d'Alexandrie). *Protrepticus*. Supplements to *VC* 34. Ed. M. Marcovich. Leiden: Brill, 1995. English translation: *ANF* 2: 171–206.

——— (Clemens Alexandrinus). *Stromata. Buch I-VI*. Ed. Otto Stählin; new ed., Ludwig Früchtel; 4th ed., Ursula Treu. Berlin: Akademie-Verlag, 1985.

——— (Clément d'Alexandrie). *Les Stromates: Stromate IV*. Ed. Annewies van den Hoek. Trans. Claude Mondésert. SC 463. Paris: Éditions du Cerf, 2001.

Cyprian. *De Lapsis and De Ecclesiae Catholicae Unitate*. Ed. and trans. Maurice Bévenot, S.J. Oxford: Clarendon Press, 1971.

———. *Epistolae*. Ed. Wilhelm August Hartel. CSEL 3.2. English translation: *The Letters of St. Cyprian of Carthage*. 4 vols. Trans. and annot. G. W. Clarke. ACW 43, 44, 46, 47. New York: Newman Press, 1984–1989.

Dagron, Gilbert, ed. and trans. *Vie et miracles de Sainte Thècle: Texte grec, traduction et commentaire*. Subsidia Hagiographica 62. Bruxelles: Sociète des Bollandistes, 1978.

Danker, Frederick William, ed. *A Greek-English Lexicon of the New Testament and*

Other Early Christian Literature. 3rd ed. Chicago: University of Chicago Press, 2000.

Daphnis and Chloe; Parthenius. Trans. George Thornley; rev. and aug. J. M. Edmonds. LCL. Cambridge: Harvard University Press, 1962.

Digesta Iustiniani. Ed. Theodor Mommsen and P. Krueger. Trans. Alan Watson. Philadelphia: Univeristy of Pennsylvania Press, 1985.

Diodorus of Sicily in Twelve Volumes. Trans. C. H. Oldfather. LCL. Cambridge: Harvard University Press, 1933. Reprint, 1989.

Diogenes Laertius. *Lives of Eminent Philosophers.* 2 vols. Trans. R. D. Hicks. LCL. Cambridge: Harvard University Press, 1980.

Egeria [Éthérie]. *Journal de voyage.* Ed., intro., and trans. Hélène Pétré. SC 21. Paris: Éditions du Cerf, 1971.

Eusebius of Caesarea. *Ecclesiastical History.* 2 vols. Trans. Kirsopp Lake. LCL. Cambridge: Harvard University Press, 1975.

——. *The Ecclesiastical History and the Martyrs of Palestine.* Trans. Hugh Jackson Lawlor and John Ernest Leonard Oulton. 2 Vols. London: Society for Promoting Christian Knowledge, 1927.

—— (Eusèbe de Césarée). *Histoire Ecclésiastique, livres VIII–X et Les Martyrs en Palestine,* ed., trans., and annot. Gustave Bardy, SC 55 (Paris: Éditions du Cerf, 1958), 121–74.

——. *History of the Martyrs in Palestine.* Syriac text, ed. and trans. William Cureton. London/Edinburgh: Williams and Norgate; Paris: C. Borrani, 1861.

——. *Praeparatio Evangelica.* GCS 43: 1 (1954), GCS 43: 2 (1956).

—— (Eusèbe de Césarée). *La préparation évangélique.* 9 vols. Trans. Jean Sirinelli et al. SC 206, 215, 228, 262, 266, 292, 307, 338, 369. Paris: Editions du Cerf, 1974–.

Festus, Sextus Pompeius. *De verborum significatu quae supersunt cum Pauli epitome.* Ed. Wallace M. Lindsay. Bibliotheca Scriptorum Graecorum et Romanorum Teubneriana. Lipsius: Teubner, 1913. Reprint, Hildesheim/New York: Georg Olms, 1978.

Gerontius. *Vitae Melaniae Iunioris.* See *Vie de Sainte Mélanie.*

Glare, P. G. W., ed. *Oxford Latin Dictionary.* Oxford: Clarendon Press, 1982.

The Gospel of Thomas: The Hidden Sayings of Jesus. Ed. and trans. Marvin Meyer. San Francisco: Harper San Francisco, 1992.

Gregory of Nazianzus. *Orationes.* PG 35:395–1252; 36:11–664.

Gregory of Nyssa. *Vita Macrinae/Vie de Sainte Macrine.* Trans. Pierre Maraval. SC 178. Paris: Cerf, 1971.

Herodotus. *Histories, Books I–II.* Trans. A. D. Godley. LCL. Cambridge: Harvard University Press, 1926. Reprint, 1996.

Hippolytus (Hippolyte). *Commentaire en Daniel.* Intro. Gustave Bardy. Ed. and trans. Maurice Lefèvre. SC 14. Paris: Éditions du Cerf, 1947.

Hock, Ronald F., and Edward N. O'Neil. *The Chreia in Ancient Rhetoric.* Texts and Translations 27; Graeco-Roman Religion Series 9. Atlanta: Scholars Press, 1986.

Ignatius of Antioch. See Lightfoot, J. B., *Apostolic Fathers.*

Index of Christian Art. URL: http://ica.princeton.edu.

Irenaeus. *Adversus Haereses.* PG 7.1.

Itinerarium Aetheriae. See Egeria.

Jerome. *Epistolae/Lettres.* 8 vols. Ed. and trans. Jerome Labourt. Paris: Société d'Édition Belles Lettres, 1949–63.

John Chrysostom. *Against the Games and Theatres.* PG 56:263–70. English translation in Mayer and Allen, 118–25.

——. *Homilies on 1 Corinthians. NPNF* 12: 1–269.

——. *Homilies on 1 Thessalonians. NPNF* 13: 323–75.

——. *Homilies on the Gospel of Saint Matthew. NPNF* 10.

——. *Homilies on the Statues. NPNF* 9: 315–489.

Kennedy, George A., ed. and trans. *Progymnasmata: Greek Textbooks of Prose Composition and Rhetoric.* Writings from the Greco-Roman World 10. Atlanta: SBL, 2003.

Kittel, G., and G. Friedrich, eds. *Theological Dictionary of the New Testament.* Trans. G. W. Bromiley. 10 vols. Grand Rapids, Mich.: Eerdmans, 1964–76.

Kluser, T., et al., eds. *Reallexicon für Antike und Christentum.* Stuttgart: Hiesemann, 1959–.

Knopf, Rudolf, Gustav Krüger, and Gerhard Ruhbach, eds. *Ausgewählte Märtyrerakten.* 4th ed. Tübingen: Mohr (Siebeck), 1965.

Lactantius. *Divine Institutes.* In L. Caeli Firmiani Lactanti, *Opera Omnia.* Ed. Samuel Brandt and Georgius Laubman. CSEL. Prague: Tempsky, 1890. Published in English as *The Divine Institutes, Books I-VII,* trans. Mary Francis McDonald, The Fathers of the Church (Washington, D.C.: Catholic University of America Press, 1964).

——. *De Mortibus Persecutorum.* Ed. and trans. J. L. Creed. Oxford: Clarendon Press, 1984.

Lampe, G. W. H., ed. *A Patristic Greek Lexicon with Addenda et Corrigenda.* Oxford: Clarendon Press, 1961.

Lazzati, Giuseppe. *Gli sviluppi della letteratura sui martiri nei primi quattro secoli.* Torino: Società Editrice Internazionale, 1956.

Lebon, J. "Athanasiana Syriaca I: Un Λόγος περὶ παρθενίας attribué à saint Athanase d'Alexandrie." *Museon* 40 (1927): 205–48.

Liddell, H. G., R. Scott, and H. S. Jones. *A Greek-English Lexicon.* 9th ed. with revised supplement. Oxford: Oxford University Press, 1996.

Lightfoot, J. B. *Apostolic Fathers.* Part 2, *S. Ignatius, S. Polycarp.* 3 vols. London: Macmillan, 1885. 2nd ed., 1889. Reprint, Grand Rapids, Mich: Baker, 1981.

Lipsius, Ricardus Adelbertus, ed. *Acta Pauli et Theclae.* In *Acta Apostolorum Apocrypha. Pars Prior: Acta Petri, Acta Pauli, Acta Petri et Pauli, Acta Pauli et Theclae, Acta Thaddaei,* 235–72. Hildesheim: Georg Olms, 1959. Translated by R. McL. Wilson in *New Testament Apocrypha,* ed. Wilhelm Schneemelcher, rev. ed. (Louisville, Ky.: Westminster/John Knox Press, 1992), 2:213–70.

Livy. *Livy in Fourteen Volumes.* Trans. B. O. Foster. LCL. Cambridge: Harvard University Press, 1919. Reprint, 1976.

Mango, Cyril. *The Art of the Byzantine Empire, 312–1453: Sources and Documents.* Englewood Cliffs, N.J.: Prentice-Hall, 1972.

Marcus Aurelius. *Ad se ipsum.* Ed. J. Dalphen. Leipzig: Teubner, 1979. Translated into English by Maxwell Staniforth as *Meditations* (Harmondsworth: Penguin, 1964).

The Martyrdom of Perpetua. Trans. Rosemary Rader. In *A Lost Tradition: Women Writers of the Early Church*, comp. and trans. Patricia Wilson-Kastner, G. Ronald Kastner, Ann Millin, Rosemary Rader, and Jeremiah Reedy, 19–32. Washington, D.C.: University Press of America, 1981.

Martyrologium Hieronymianum ad fidem codicum adiectis prolegomenis. Ed. Giovanni Battista de Rossi and Louis Duchesne. Brussels: Typis Polleunis et Ceuterick, 1894.

Mayer, Wendy, and Pauline Allen. *John Chrysostom*. London: Routledge, 2000.

Methodius. *Symposium Decem Virginem/Le Banquet*. Trans. Victor-Henry Debidour. SC 95. Paris: Cerf, 1963.

Migne, J.-P., ed. *Patrologiae cursus completus [Series Graeca]*. 161 vols. Paris: Migne, 1857–66.

——. *Patrologiae cursus completus [Series Latina]*. 221 vols. Paris: Migne, 1844–64.

Minucius Felix. *Octavius*. Ed. and trans. Jean Beaujeu. 2nd rev. corr. ed. Paris: Société d'Édition "Les Belles Lettres," 1974. English translation: *ANF* 4:173–98.

Musurillo, Herbert, ed. and trans. *The Acts of the Christian Martyrs*. Oxford: Clarendon Press, 1972.

Nicene and Post-Nicene Fathers. Ed. Philip Schaff and Henry Wace. 28 vols. Reprint ed. Peabody, Mass.: Hendrickson, 1994.

Novatian. *De Spectaculis*. In *Novatiani Opera*, ed. G. F. Diercks. CCSL 4. Turnholt: Brepols, 1972. Published in English as Novatian, *The Trinity, The Spectacles, Jewish Foods, In Praise of Purity, Letters*, trans. Russell J. DeSimone, The Fathers of the Church (Washington, D.C.: Catholic University of America, 1972), 113–33.

Novum Testamentum Graece. Ed. Eberhard Nestle, Kurt Aland, and Barbara Aland. 27th ed. Stuttgart: Deautch Bibelstiftung, 1993.

Origen. *Eis martyrion protreptikos*. In *Werke*. GCS.

——. *An Exhortation to Martyrdom; On Prayer; First Principles: Book IV; Prologue to the Commentary on the Song of Songs; Homily XXVII on Numbers*. Trans. and intro. Rowan A. Greer. New York: Paulist Press, 1979.

—— (Origène). *Commentaire sur Saint Jean*. 4 vols. Ed., trans., and annot. Cécile Blanc. SC 120, 157, 222, 290. Paris: Cerf, 1969–82.

——. *Contra Celsum*. Rev. and corr. ed. Trans. and ed. by Henry Chadwick. New York: Cambridge University Press, 1986 [1953].

Paredi, Angelo. *I prefazi ambrosiani: Contributo alla storia della liturgia latina*. Milan: Società editrice "Vita e pensiero," 1937.

Passio sanctarum Perpetuae et Felicitatis. Ed. and critical text C. J. M. J. van Beek. Nijmegen: Dekker & Van De Vegt, 1936.

Passio SS. Perpetuae et Felicitatis latine et graecae. Ed. P. Franchi de' Cavalieri. *Scritti agiografici* 1 (1893–1900; published in 1962 [Studi e testi 221]): 41–155.

Passion de Pérpetue et de Félicité suivi des Actes. Intro., ed., trans., annot., and index. Jacqueline Amat. SC 417. Paris: Éditions du Cerf, 1996.

Paulinus of Nola. *Carmina*. CSEL 30. English translation: ACW 40 (1975).

Pliny. *Letters and Panegyricus in Two Volumes*. Trans. Betty Radice. LCL. Cambridge: Harvard University Press, 1969.

——. *Natural History with an English Translation in Ten Volumes.* Trans. H. S. Jones. LCL. Cambridge: Harvard University Press, 1975.

Plutarch. *Plutarch's Lives in Eleven Volumes.* Trans. Bernadette Perrin. LCL. Cambridge: Harvard University Press, 1914–1926.

——. *Plutarch's Moralia in Sixteen Volumes.* Trans. Frank Cole Babbitt. LCL. Cambridge: Harvard University Press, 1972.

Prudentius. *Peristephanon (Crowns of Martyrdom).* In *Prudentius,* trans. H. J. Thomson. 2 vols. LCL. Cambridge, Mass.: Harvard University Press, 1953.

Pseudo-Athanasius. *Vita Syncleticae.* PG 28:1487–1558. Translated by Elizabeth A. Castelli as "The Life and Activity of the Holy and Blessed Teacher Syncletica," in *Ascetic Behavior in Greco-Roman Antiquity: A Sourcebook,* ed. Vincent L. Wimbush (Philadelphia: Fortress Press, 1990), 265–311.

Pseudo-Chrysostom. *Panegyric to Thecla.* PG 50:745–48. See also Aubineau.

Reardon, B. P., ed. *Collected Ancient Greek Novels.* Berkeley: University of California Press, 1989.

Robert, Louis, ed. and trans. *Le martyre de Pionios, Prêtre de Smyrne.* Ordered and completed by G. W. Bowersock and C. P. Jones. Washington, D.C.: Dumbarton Oaks Research Library and Collection, 1994.

Ruggiero, Fabio. *Atti dei Martiri Scilitani: Introduzione, Testo, Traduzione, Testimonianze e Commento.* Atti della Accademia Nazionale dei Lincei 388. *Memorie* ser. 9, vol. 1, no. 2. Rome: Accademia Nazionale dei Lincei, 1991.

Sahas, Daniel J. *Icon and Logos: Sources in Eighth-Century Iconoclasm. An Annotated Translation of the Sixth Session of the Seventh Ecumenical Council (Nicea, 787), containing the Definition of the Council of Constantinople (754) and its refutation, and the Definition of the Seventh Ecumenical Council.* Toronto: University of Toronto Press, 1986.

Schneemelcher, Wilhelm. *New Testament Apocrypha.* Rev. ed. Vol. 2, *Writings Relating to the Apostles, Apocalypses, and Related Subjects.* Trans. R. McL. Wilson. Louisville, Ky.: Westminster/John Knox Press, 1992.

Suetonius. *Suetonius.* Trans. J. C. Rolfe. 2 vols. LCL. Cambridge, Mass.: Harvard University Press, 1951.

Tacitus. *The Histories; The Annals.* Trans. Clifford F. Moore and John Jackson. 4 vols. Cambridge, Mass.: Harvard University Press, 1925–37.

Tatian. *Oratio ad Graecos.* PTS 43. Ed. Miroslav Marcovich. Berlin: Walter de Gruyter, 1995.

Tertullian (Quinti Septimi Florentis Tertulliani). *Opera. Pars I: Opera Catholica; Adversus Marcionem.* CCSL. Turnholt: Brepols, 1954. *See individual entries below.*

——. *Ad martyras.* In CCSL, 1–8. English translation in *ANF* 3:693–96.

——. *Apologeticum.* In CCSL, 77–172.

——. *Apology; De spectaculis.* Minucius Felix. *Octavius.* Trans. T. R. Glover and G. H. Rendall. LCL. Cambridge, Mass.: Harvard University Press, 1984.

——. *De anima.* In CCSL, 781–869. English translation: *ANF* 3:181–235.

——. *De baptismo.* In CSEL 20:201–218. English translation: *ANF* 3:669–79.

——. *De corona.* In CCSL, 1037–66. English translation: *ANF* 3:93–104.

——. *De cultu feminarum.* In CCSL, 341–70. English translation: *ANF* 4:14–26.

———. *De fuga in persecutione.* In CCSL, 1133–56. English translation: *ANF* 4:116–26.

———. *De idololatria.* In CCSL, 1099–124. English translation: *ANF* 3:61–77.

———. *De spectaculis.* In CCSL, 225–54. Published in French as (Tertullien,) *Les specta-cles (De spectaculis)*, intro., ed., trans., and annot. Marie Turcan, SC 332 (Paris: Éditions du Cerf, 1986).

———. *Scorpiace.* In CCSL, 1967–98. Tertulliano. *Scorpiace.* A cura di Giovanna Azzali Bernardelli. Florence: Nardini Editore, 1990. English translation: *ANF* 3:633–48.

Thaumata tēs hagias kai [prōto]martyros Theklas. See Dagron.

Theophilus. *Ad Autolycum.* Ed. Miroslav Marcovich. PTS 44. Berlin: Walter de Gruyter, 1995.

Valantasis, Richard, ed. *Religions of Late Antiquity in Practice.* Princeton, N.J.: Princeton University Press, 2000.

Victor of Rouen (Victricii Rotomagensis). *De Laude Sanctorum.* Ed. I. Mulders and R. Demeulenaere. CCSL 64 (1985): 55–93. French translation in René Herval, *Origines chrétiennes de la IIe Lyonnaise gallo-romaine à la Normandie ducale (IVe—XIe siè-cles) avec le texte complet et la traduction intégrale du* De Laude Sanctorum *de Saint Victrice (396)*, 108–53. Paris: Picard, 1966.

Vie de Sainte Mélanie. Ed., intro., and trans. Denys Gorce. SC 90. Paris: Éditions du Cerf, 1962.

Vie et miracles de Sainte Thècle. See Dagron.

Vita Olympiadis/La vie anonyme d'Olympias. In John Chrysostom, *Epistolae ad Olympiadem/Lettres à Olympias.* 2nd aug. ed. with *Vita Olympiadis/La vie anonyme d'Olympias.* Trans. Anne-Marie Malingrey. SC 13bis. Paris: Cerf, 1968.

Voragine, Jacobus de. *The Golden Legend: Readings on the Saints.* Trans. William Granger Ryan. 2 vols. Princeton, N.J.: Princeton University Press, 1993.

Wilson-Kastner, Patricia, G. Ronald Kastner, Ann Millin, Rosemary Rader, and Jere-miah Reedy. *A Lost Tradition: Women Writers of the Early Church.* Washington, D.C.: University Press of America, 1981.

SECONDARY SOURCES

Adams, Lorraine. "Columbine Crosses Can't Bear Weight of Discord: Memorials Embrace Gunmen, Divide Mourners." *Washington Post*, 3 May 1999, Final Edition.

Aguilar, Paloma. *Collective Memory of the Spanish Civil War: The Case of the Political Amnesty in the Spanish Transition to Democracy.* Madrid: Centro de Estudios Avanzados en Ciencias Sociales, Instituto Juan March de Estudios e Investiga-ciones, 1996.

Albrecht, Ruth. *Das Leben der heiligen Makrina auf dem Hintergrund der Thekla-Tra-ditionen: Studien zu dem Ursprungen des weiblichen Monchtums in 4. Jahrhundert in Kleinasien.* Göttingen: Vandenhoeck & Ruprecht, 1986.

Allard, Paul. *Histoire des persécutions.* 1903–1908. 3rd ed., revised and augmented. Rome: "L'Erma" di Bretschneider, 1971.

Alonso, Ana Maria. "The Effects of Truth: Re-Presentations of the Past and the Imag-ining of Community." *Journal of Historical Sociology* 1 (1988): 33–57.

Althusser, Louis. "Ideology and the Ideological State Apparatus (Notes Toward an

Investigation)." In *Lenin and Philosophy and Other Essays*, 127–86. Trans. Ben Brewster. New York: Monthly Review Press, 1971.

Amat, Jacqueline. "L'authenticité des songes de la Passion de Perpétue et de Félicité." *Augustinianum* 29 (1989): 177–91.

———. *Songes et visions: L'au delà dans la littérature latine tardive.* Paris: Études Augustiniennes, 1985.

Annales: Économies Sociétés Civilisations. Special section, "Archives Orales: Une autre histoire?" *Annales: Économies Sociétés Civilisations* 35 (1980): 124–99.

Antze, Paul, and Michael Lambek, eds. *Tense Past: Cultural Essays in Trauma and Memory.* New York: Routledge, 1996.

Arias, Arturo, ed. *The Rigoberta Menchù Controversy.* Minneapolis: University of Minnesota Press, 2001.

Arieti, James A. *Discourses on the First Book of Herodotus.* London: Littlefield Adams Books, 1995.

Aronen, Jaakko. "Pythia Carthaginensis o immagini cristiane nella visione di Perpetua?" In *L'Africa romana VI: Atti del VI convegno di studio, Sassari 16–18 dicembre 1988.* 2 vols. Ed. Attilio Mastino, 2:643–48. Sassari: Dip. di Storia dell'Università degli studi di Sassari, 1989.

Asad, Talal. *Genealogies of Religion: Discipline and Reasons of Power in Christianity and Islam.* Baltimore: Johns Hopkins University Press, 1993.

Assmann, Jan. "Collective Memory and Cultural Identity." Trans. John Czaplicka. *New German Critique* 65 (Spring–Summer 1995): 125–33. Originally published as "Kollektives Gedächtnis und kulturelle Identität," in *Kultur und Gedächtnis*, ed. Jan Assmann and Tonio Hölscher (Frankfurt am Main, 1988), 9–19.

———. *Das kulturelle Gedächtnis: Schrift, Erinnerung und politische Identität in frühen Hochkulturen.* Munich: C. H. Beck, 1992.

Aubin, Melissa. "Reversing Romance? The *Acts of Thecla* and the Ancient Novel." In *Ancient Fiction and Early Christian Narrative*, ed. Ronald F. Hock, J. Bradley Chance, and Judith Perkins, 257–72. SBL Symposium Series 6. Atlanta: Scholars Press, 1998.

Augar, Friedrich Augar. *Die Frau im römischen Christenprocess: Ein Beitrag zur Vergolgungsgeschichte der christlichen Kirche im römischen Staat.* TUGAL 28.4c = n.F. 13.4c. Leipzig: J. C. Hinrichs, 1905.

Auguet, Roland. *Cruelty and Civilization: The Roman Games.* London: George Allen and Unwin, 1972.

Aymard, Jacques. *Essai sur les chasses romaines des origines à la fin du siècle des Antonins (Cynegetica).* Bibliothèque des Écoles françaises d'Athènes et de Rome 171. Paris: Boccard, 1951.

Bal, Mieke. "Perpetual Contest." In *On Storytelling*, ed. David Jobling, 227–41. Sonoma, Calif.: Polebridge Press, 1991.

Bal, Mieke, Jonathan Crewe, and Leo Spitzer, eds. *Acts of Memory: Cultural Recall in the Present.* Hanover, N.H.: Dartmouth College/University Press of New England, 1999.

Baltrusch, Ernst. "Die Verstaatlichung der Gladiatorenspiele." *Hermes* 116 (1988): 324–37.

Barnard, L. W. "The Background of St. Ignatius of Antioch." *VC* 17 (1963): 193–206.

Barnes, Fred. "Born-Again Gore." *The Weekly Standard*, 10 May 1999, 14–16.

———. "God, Gary, and the GOP." *The Weekly Standard*, 24 May 1999, 13–14.

Barnes, T. D. "Christians and the Theater." In *Roman Theatre and Society*, ed. William J. Slater, 161–80. Ann Arbor: University of Michigan Press, 1996.

———. "Legislation Against the Christians." *JRS* 58 (1968): 32–50.

———. "Pre-Decian *Acta Martyrum*." *JTS*, n.s., 19 (1968): 509–31.

Barthel, Diane L. *Historic Preservation: Collective Memory and Historical Identity*. New Brunswick, N.J.: Rutgers University Press, 1996.

Barton, Carlin A. "Savage Miracles: Redemption of Lost Honor in Roman Society and the Sacrament of the Gladiator and the Martyr." *Representations* 45 (1994): 41–71.

———. "The Scandal of the Arena." *Representations* 27 (1989): 1–36.

———. *The Sorrows of the Ancient Romans: The Gladiator and the Monster*. Princeton, N.J.: Princeton University Press, 1993.

Bastide, Roger. "Mémoire collective et sociologie du bricolage." *L'année sociologique*, 3rd ser., 21 (1970): 65–108.

Bauman, Richard A. *Crime and Punishment in Ancient Rome*. New York: Routledge, 1996.

Baumeister, Theofried. *Die Anfänge der Theologie des Martyriums*. Münster: Aschendorff, 1980.

———. *Genese und Entfaltung der altkirchlichen Theologies des Martyriums*. New York: Peter Lang, 1991.

Beacham, Richard C. *Spectacle Entertainments of Early Imperial Rome*. New Haven, Conn.: Yale University Press, 1999.

Beamish, Thomas D., Harvey Molotch, and Richard Flacks. "Who Supports the Troops? Vietnam, the Gulf War, and the Making of Collective Memory." *Social Problems* 43 (1995): 344–60.

Beard, Mary, John North, and Simon Price. *Religions of Rome*. Vol. 1: *A History*. New York: Cambridge University Press, 1998.

Beaujard, Brigitte. "Cités, évêques et martyrs en Gaule à la fin de l'époque romaine." In *Les fonctions des saintes dans le monde occidental (IIIe—XIIIe siècle): Actes du colloque organisé par l'École française de Rome avec le concours de l'Université de Rome "La Sapienza,"* 175–91. Collection de l'École Française de Rome 149. Rome: École Française de Rome/Palais Farnèse, 1991.

Begley, Sharon. "Why the Young Kill." *Newsweek*, 3 May 1999, 32–35.

Belluck, Pam. "Hate Groups Seeking Broader Reach: Articulate and Middle Class Recruits Fit New, Moderated Image." *New York Times*, 7 July 1999.

Ben-Yehuda, Nachman. *The Masada Myth: Collective Memory and Mythmaking in Israel*. Madison: University of Wisconsin Press, 1995.

Berger, Ronald J. *Constructing a Collective Memory of the Holocaust: A Life History of Two Brothers' Survival*. Boulder: University Press of Colorado, 1995.

Bergson, Henri. *Matter and Memory*. Trans. N. M. Paul and W. S. Palmer. New York: Zone Books, 1988.

Bermejo Barrera, José Carlos. "Les discours de la torture chez Eusèbe de Césarée." *Quaderni di Storia* 17, no. 34 (1991): 63–102.

Bernall, Misty. *She Said Yes: The Unlikely Martyrdom of Cassie Bernall.* Farmington, Penn.: Plough Publishing Company, 1999.

Berthelsen, Christian. "Hundreds Remember Slain Letter Carrier." *New York Times,* 15 August 1999.

Besier, Gerhard. "Bekenntis—Widerstand—Martyrium als historisch-theologische Kategorien." In *Bekenntnis, Widerstand, Martyrium,* ed. Gerhard Besier and Gerhard Ringshausen, 126–47. Göttingen: Vandenhoeck & Ruprecht, 1986.

Bhabha, Homi. *The Location of Culture.* New York: Routledge, 1994.

Bingham, Janet. "Cassie Bernall Died for Faith." *Denver Post,* 27 April 1999.

Bickermann, Elias. "La chaîne de la tradition pharisienne." *RB* 59 (1952): 44–54.

Biema, David Van. "A Surge of Teen Spirit." *Time,* 31 May 1999, 58–59.

Bisbee, Gary A. *Pre-Decian Acts of the Martyrs and Commentarii.* HDR 22. Philadelphia: Fortress Press, 1988.

Bloch, Marc. "Mémoire collective, tradition et coutume." *Revue de Synthèse Historique* 40 (1925): 73–83.

Bodnar, John. *Remaking America: Public Memory, Commemoration, and Patriotism in the Twentieth Century.* Princeton: Princeton University Press, 1992.

Boeft, Jan den, and Jan Bremmer. "*Notiunculae Martyrologicae.*" *VC* 35 (1981): 43–56.

———. "*Notiunculae Martyrologicae* II." *VC* 36 (1982): 383–402.

———. "*Notiunculae Martyrologicae* III: Some Observations on the *Martyria* of Polycarp and Pionius." *VC* 39 (1985): 110–30.

———. "*Notiunculae Martyrologicae* IV." *VC* 45 (1991): 105–22.

———. "*Notiunculae Martyrologicae* V." *VC* 36 (1992): 146–64.

Boeschoten, Riki van. *From Armatolik to People's Rule: Investigation into the Collective Memory of Rural Greece, 1750–1949.* Amsterdam: A. M. Hakkert, 1991.

Boltanski, Luc. *Distant Suffering: Morality, Media, and Politics.* Trans. Graham Burchell. New York: Cambridge University Press, 1999.

Bommes, Karin. *Weizen Gottes: Untersuchungen zur Theologie des Martyriums bei Ignatius von Antiochien.* Cologne/Bonn: Peter Hanstein, 1976.

Boston Museum of Fine Arts. *Romans and Barbarians.* Boston: Museum of Fine Arts, 1976.

Bottum, J. "A Martyr Is Born." *The Weekly Standard. Special Report: Littleton,* 10 May 1999, 12–14.

———. "Columbine, Again." *The Weekly Standard,* 27 December 1999, 7.

———. "Awakening at Littleton." *First Things* 95 (August/September 1999): 28–32.

Boughton, Lynne C. "From Pious Legend to Feminist Fantasy: Distinguishing Hagiographical License from Apostolic Practice in the *Acts of Paul/Acts of Thecla.*" *JR* 71 (1991): 362–83.

Bourguet, Marie Noëlle, Lucette Valensi, and Nathan Wachtel, eds. "Between History and Memory." Special issue of *History and Anthropology* 2, no. 2 (October 1986).

Bower, Richard A. "The Meaning of ΕΠΙΤΥΧΑΝΩ in the Epistles of St. Ignatius of Antioch." *VC* 28 (1974): 1–14.

Bowersock, G. W. *Martyrdom and Rome*. New York: Cambridge University Press, 1995.

Boyarin, Daniel. *Dying for God: Martyrdom and the Making of Christianity and Judaism*. Stanford: Stanford University Press, 1999.

Boyarin, Daniel, and Elizabeth A. Castelli. "Foucault's *The History of Sexuality*: The Fourth Volume, or, A Field Left Fallow for Others to Till." *JHS* 10 (2001): 357–74.

Boyarin, Jonathan. *Storm from Paradise: The Politics of Jewish Memory*. Minneapolis: University of Minnesota Press, 1992.

——, ed. *Remapping Memory: The Politics of TimeSpace*. Minneapolis: University of Minnesota, 1994.

Boyer, M. Christine. *The City of Collective Memory: Its Historical Imagery and Architectural Entertainments*. Cambridge: MIT Press, 1994.

Brakke, David. *Athanasius and the Politics of Asceticism*. Oxford: Clarendon Press, 1995.

——. "Ethiopian Demons: Male Sexuality, the Black-Skinned Other, and the Monastic Self." *JHS* 10 (2001): 501–35.

Braun, R. "Nouvelle observations linguistiques sur le rédacteur de la *Passio Perpetuae*." *VC* 33 (1979): 105–17.

Brekelmans, Antonius J. *Martyrerkranz: Eine symbolgeschichtliche Untersuchung im frühchristlichen Schrifttum*. Analecta Gregoriana 150. Rome: Libreria Editrice dell'Università Gregoriana, 1965.

Bremmer, Jan. "'Christianus sum': The Early Christian Martyrs and Christ." In *Eulogia: Mélanges offerts à Antoon A. R. Bastiaensen à l'occasion de son soixante-cinquième anniversaire*, ed. G. J. M. Bartelink, A. Hilhorst, and C. H. Kneepkens, 11–20. Steenbrugge: in Abbatia S. Petri; The Hague: Nijhoff, 1991.

——, ed. *The Apocryphal Acts of Paul and Thecla*. Studies of the Acts of the Apostles 2. Kampen: Kok Pharos, 1996.

Brent, Allen. "Ignatius of Antioch and the Imperial Cult." *VC* 52 (1998): 30–58.

Breymann, A. *Adam und Eva in der Kunst des christlichen Alterthums*. Wolfenbüttel: J. Zwissler, 1893.

Brock, Sebastian. "Early Christian Asceticism." *Numen* 20 (1973): 1–19.

Brooten, Bernadette J. *Love Between Women: Early Christian Responses to Female Homoeroticism*. Chicago: University of Chicago Press, 1996.

Brovsky, Cindy. "Forever Changed: Columbine Is Not Alone in Its Grief, as People from Afar Have Reached out with Heartfelt Messages." *Denver Post*, 25 April 1999.

Brown, Peter. *The Cult of the Saints: Its Rise and Function in Latin Christianity*. Chicago: University of Chicago Press, 1981.

——. *Power and Persuasion in Late Antiquity: Towards a Christian Empire*. Madison: University of Wisconsin Press, 1992.

Brown, Shelby. "Death as Decoration: Scenes from the Arena in Roman Domestic Mosaics." In *Pornography and Representation in Greece and Rome*, ed. Amy Richlin, 180–211. New York: Oxford University Press, 1992.

——. "Explaining the Arena: Did the Romans 'Need' Gladiators?" *JRA* 8 (1995): 376–84.

Brox, Norbert. *Zeuge und Märtyrer: Untersuchungen zur frühchristlichen Zeugnis-Terminologie.* SANT 5. Munich: Kösel, 1961.

Bruner, Edward M., and Phyllis Gorfain. "Dialogic Narration and the Paradoxes of Masada." In *Text, Play, and Story: The Construction and Reconstruction of the Self and Society,* ed. Stuart Plattner and Edward M. Bruner, 56–75. Washington, D.C.: American Ethnological Society, 1984.

Brunt, P. A. "Marcus Aurelius and the Christians." In *Studies in Latin Literature and Roman History,* ed. C. Deroux, 483–520. Collection Latomus 164.1. Brussels: Latomus, 1979.

Burke, Peter. "History as Social Memory." In *Memory: History, Culture and the Mind,* ed. Thomas Butler, 97–113. New York: Basil Blackwell, 1989. Reprinted in Peter Burke, *Varieties of Cultural History* (Ithaca, N.Y.: Cornell University Press), 43–59.

Burns, Gary. "Marilyn Manson and the Apt Pupils of Littleton." *Popular Music and Society* 23, no. 3 (Fall 1999): 3–8.

Burrus, Virginia. *Chastity as Autonomy: Women in the Stories of the Apocryphal Acts.* Lewiston, N.Y.: Edwin Mellen Press, 1987.

———. "Reading Agnes: The Rhetoric of Gender in Ambrose and Prudentius." *JECS* 3 (1995): 25–46.

Buruma, Ian. *The Wages of Guilt: Memories of War in Germany and Japan.* New York: Farrar, Straus, Giroux, 1994.

Butler, Thomas, ed. *Memory: History, Culture, and the Mind.* New York: Basil Blackwell, 1989.

Butterweck, Christel. *"Martyriumssucht" in der Alten Kirche? Studien zur Darstellung und Deutung frühchristlicher Martyrien.* Tübingen: Mohr (Siebeck), 1995.

Byron, Gay. *Symbolic Blackness and Ethnic Difference in Early Christian Literature.* London: Routledge, 2002.

Cadoux, C. J. *Ancient Smyrna.* Oxford: Oxford University Press, 1938.

Cameron, Averil. *Christianity and the Rhetoric of Empire: The Development of Christian Discourse.* Sather Classical Lectures 55. Berkeley: University of California Press, 1991.

———. *The Later Roman Empire.* Cambridge, Mass.: Harvard University Press, 1993.

———, ed. *History as Text: The Writing of Ancient History.* London: Duckworth, 1989.

Campenhausen, Hans von. *Die Idee des Martyriums in der alten Kirche,* 2nd ed. Göttingen: Vandenhoeck & Ruprecht, 1964.

Cantarella, Eva. *I supplizi capitali in Grecia e a Roma: Origini e funzioni delle pene di morte nell'antichità classica.* Milano: Rizzoli, 1991. Reprint, 1996.

Carrette, Jeremy R., ed. *Religion and Culture: Michel Foucault.* New York: Routledge, 1999.

Carroll, Jon. "She Didn't Say Anything." *San Francisco Chronicle,* 4 October 1999.

Carroll, Rory. "Media Revel in Abuse Scandal, Says Cardinal: Man Tipped as Next Pope Says US Coverage of Paedophile Priests Resembles Persecutions Under Stalin and Hitler." *Manchester Guardian,* 10 June 2002.

Carruthers, Mary. *The Book of Memory: A Study of Memory in Medieval Culture.* Cambridge Studies in Medieval Literature 10. New York: Cambridge University Press, 1990.

Caruth, Cathy, ed. *Trauma: Explorations in Memory*. Baltimore: Johns Hopkins University Press, 1995.

Cassidy, Richard J. *Christians and Roman Rule in the New Testament: New Perspectives*. New York: Crossroad, 2001.

———. *Paul in Chains: Roman Imprisonment and the Letters of St. Paul*. New York: Crossroad, 2001.

Castelli, Elizabeth A. "Asterius of Amasea: Ekphrasis on the Holy Martyr Euphemia." In *Religions of Late Antiquity in Practice*, ed. Richard Valantasis, 463–66. Princeton, N.J.: Princeton University Press, 2000.

———. "Gender, Theory, and *The Rise of Christianity*: A Response to Rodney Stark." *JECS* 6 (1998): 227–57.

———. " 'I Will Make Mary Male': Pieties of the Body and Gender Transformation of Early Christian Women in Late Antiquity." In *Bodyguards: The Cultural Contexts of Gender Ambiguity*, ed. Julia Epstein and Kristina Straub, 29–49. New York: Routledge, 1991.

———. "Imperial Reimaginings of Christian Origins: Epic in Prudentius's Poem for the Martyr Eulalia." In *Reimagining Christian Origins: A Colloquium Honoring Burton L. Mack*, ed. Elizabeth A. Castelli and Hal Taussig, 173–84. Valley Forge, Penn.: Trinity Press International, 1996.

———. "Visions and Voyeurism: Holy Women and the Politics of Sight in Early Christianity." In *Protocol of the Colloquy of the Center for Hermeneutical Studies, 6 December 1992*, n.s., 2. Ed. Christopher Ocker, 1–20. Berkeley: Center for Hermeneutical Studies, 1994.

Castelli, Elizabeth A., and Hal Taussig, eds. *Reimagining Christian Origins: A Colloquium Honoring Burton L. Mack*. Valley Forge, Penn.: Trinity Press International, 1996.

Cavalieri, P. Franchi de'. *Note agiografiche*. Studi e Testi 33. Vatican City: Bibliotheca Apostolica Vaticana, 1920.

Cavallaro, M. Adele. *Spese e spettacoli: Aspetti economici-strutturali degli spettacoli nella Roma giulio-claudia*. Antiquitas 34. Bonn: Habelt, 1984.

Cazanove, Olivier de. "*Exesto*: L'incapacité sacrificielle des femmes à Rome." *Phoenix* 41 (1987): 159–73.

Certeau, Michel de. *The Writing of History*. Trans. Tom Conley. New York: Columbia University Press, 1988.

Chase, Anthony. "Violent Reaction: What Do Teen Killers Have in Common?" *In These Times*, 9 July 2001.

Churruca, Juan de. "Confesseurs non condamnés à mort dans le procès contre les chrétiens de Lyon l'année 177." *VC* 38 (1984): 257–70.

Ciccarese, M. P. "Le più antiche rappresentazioni del purgatorio dalla *Passio Perpetuae* alla fine del IX secolo." *Romanobarbarico: Contributi allo studio dei rapporti culturali tra mondo latino e mondo barbarico* 7 (1982–1983): 33–76.

Clark, Elizabeth A. *Reading Renunciation: Asceticism and Scripture in Early Christianity*. Princeton, N.J.: Princeton University Press, 1999.

——. "Sex, Shame, and Rhetoric: En-Gendering Early Christian Ethics." *JAAR* 59 (1991): 221–45.

——. "Women, Gender, and the Study of Christian History." *CH* 70 (2001): 395–426.

Clark, Gillian. "Bodies and Blood: Late Antique Debate on Martyrdom, Virginity, and Resurrection." In *Changing Bodies, Changing Meanings: Studies on the Human Body in Antiquity,* ed. Dominic Montserrat, 99–115. London/New York: Routledge, 1997.

Clauss, James J., and Sarah Iles Johnston, eds. *Medea.* Princeton, N.J.: Princeton University Press, 1997.

Clavel-Lévêque, Monique. *L'empire en jeux: Espace symbolique et pratique sociale dans le monde romain.* Paris: Éditions du CNRS, 1984.

——. "L'espace des jeux dans le monde romain: Hégémonie, symbolique et pratique sociale." *ANRW* 2.16.3 (1986): 2406–563.

——. "Rituels de mort et consommation de gladiateurs: Images de domination et pratiques imperialistes de reproduction." In *Hommages à Lucien Lerat,* ed. Hélène Walter, 189–208. Paris: Société d'Éditions "Les Belles Lettres," 1984.

Clines, Francis X. "A Religious Tilt Toward the Left." *New York Times,* 16 September 1996.

Cohen, Aryeh. "Toward an Erotics of Martyrdom." *Journal of Jewish Thought and Philosophy* 7 (1998): 227–56.

Cohen, Shaye J. D. *The Beginnings of Judaism: Boundaries, Varieties, Uncertainties.* Berkeley: University of California Press, 1999.

Cohen, Stanley. *States of Denial.* London: Polity Press, 2001.

Coleman, K. M. "Fatal Attractions: Roman Executions Staged as Mythological Enactments." *JRS* 80 (1990): 44–73.

Collins, Adela Yarbro. *Crisis and Catharsis: The Power of the Apocalypse.* Philadelphia: Westminster, 1984.

Confino, Alon. "Collective Memory and Cultural History: Problems of Method." *AHR* 102 (1997): 1386–403.

Connerton, Paul. *How Societies Remember.* New York: Cambridge University Press, 1989.

Consolino, Franca Ela. "Sogni e visioni nell'agiografia tardoantica: Modelli e variazioni sul tema." *Augustinianum* 29 (1989): 237–56.

Cooke, Lynne, Bice Curiger, Greg Hilty, Lynne Richards, and Hayward Gallery. *Doubletake: Collective Memory and Current Art.* London: South Bank Centre, 1992.

Cooper, Kate. *The Virgin and the Bride: Idealized Womanhood in Late Antiquity.* Cambridge, Mass.: Harvard University Press, 1996.

Cormack, Margaret, ed. *Sacrificing the Self: Perspectives on Martyrdom and Religion.* New York: Oxford University Press, 2001.

Corsini, Eugenio. "Proposte per una lettura della *Passio Perpetuae.*" In *Forma futuri: Studi in onore del Cardinale Michele Pellegrino,* 481–541. Torino: Bottega d'Erasmo, 1975.

Craig, John E. "Maurice Halbwachs à Strasbourg." *Revue française de sociologie* 20 (1979): 273–92.

Crane, Susan A. "Writing the Individual Back into Collective Memory." *AHR* 102 (1997): 1372–85.

Crapanzano, Vincent. *Serving the Word: Literalism in America from the Pulpit to the Bench*. New York: New Press, 2000.

Crary, Jonathan. "Spectacle, Attention, Counter-Memory." *October* 50 (1989): 97–107.

Cullen, Dave. *Cloud Over Columbine: How the Press Got It Wrong and the Police Let It Happen*. New York: Random House, 2002.

———. "Gay Leaders Fear Littleton Backlash." *Salon*, 27 April 1999. Available at http://www.salon.com/news/feature/1999/04/27/gay.

———. "Inside the Columbine High Investigation: Everything You Know About the Littleton Killings Is Wrong." *Salon*, 23 September 1999. Available at http://www. salon.com/news/feature/1999/09/23/columbine.

———. " 'I Smell the Presence of Satan.' " *Salon*, 15 May 1999. Available at http://salon. com/news/feature/1999/05/15/evangelicals/print.html.

———. "The Rumor That Won't Go Away: Jocks Say Littleton Killers Were Gay, but Friends Deny It." *Salon*, 24 April 1999. Available at http://www.salon.com/news/feature/1999/04/24/rumors.

———. "Who Said 'Yes'?" *Salon Magazine*, 30 September 1999. Available at http://www. salon.com/news/feature/1999/09/30/bernall/print.html.

Cunningham, Scott. *"Through Many Tribulations": The Theology of Persecution in Luke-Acts*. JSNTSup 142. Sheffield: Sheffield Academic Press, 1997.

Dalton, O. M. *Catalogue of Early Christian Antiquities and Objects from the Christian East in the Department of British and Mediaeval Antiquities and Ethnography of the British Museum*. London: British Museum, 1901.

Daly, Robert J. *Christian Sacrifice: The Judaeo-Christian Background Before Origen*. Catholic University of America Studies in Christian Antiquity 18. Washington, D.C.: Catholic University of America, 1978.

Darwish, Mahmoud. *Memory for Forgetfulness: August, Beirut, 1982*. Trans. Ibrahim Muhawi. Berkeley: University of California Press, 1982.

Dassmann, Ernst. *Sündenvergebung durch Taufe, Buße und Martyrerfürbitte in den Zeugnissen frühchristlicher Frömmigkeit und Kunst*. Münsterische Beiträge zur Theologie 36. Münster: Aschendorff, 1973.

Davidson, Arnold I. "Ethics as Ascetics: Foucault, the History of Ethics, and Ancient Thought." In *Foucault and the Writing of History*, ed. Jan Goldstein, 63–80. Oxford: Blackwell, 1994.

———. "Introductory Remarks to Pierre Hadot." In *Foucault and His Interlocutors*, ed. Arnold I. Davidson, 195–202. Chicago: University of Chicago Press, 1997.

———, ed. *Foucault and His Interlocutors*. Chicago: University of Chicago Press, 1997.

Davies, Stevan L. *The Revolt of the Widows: The Social World of the Apocryphal Acts*. Carbondale: Southern Illinois University Press, 1980.

Davis, Natalie Zemon, and Randolph Starn, eds. "Collective Memory and Counter-memory." Special issue of *Representations* 26 (Spring 1989).

Davis, Stephen J. *The Cult of Saint Thecla: A Tradition of Women's Piety in Late Antiquity*. New York: Oxford University Press, 2001.

DC Talk and The Voice of the Martyrs. *Jesus Freaks: Stories of Those Who Stood For Jesus: The Ultimate Jesus Freaks.* Tulsa, Okla.: Albury Publishing, 1999.

Dehandschutter, Boudewijn. "The *Martyrium Polycarpi*: A Century of Research." *ANRW* 2.27.1 (1993): 485–522.

Delehaye, Hippolyte. *Les origines du culte des martyrs.* 2nd ed. Subsidia Hagiographica 20. Brussels: Société des Bollandistes, 1933.

———. *Les passions des martyrs et les genres littéraires.* Subsidia Hagiographica 13b. Brussels: Société des Bollandistes, 1966.

Dieulafait, Christine. *Rapport de fouilles de sauvetage effectuées à Saint-Just-de-Valcabrère en 1988.* N.p.: Service régional de l'archéologie de Midi-Pyrénées, 1988.

Dieulafait, Christine, and Jean Guyon. "Sous le signe des dieux dans la mouvance chrétienne? Heroïsation mythologique ou scènes originales d'un décor chrétien sur la face principale d'une cuve." In *Pulchra Imago: Fragments d'archéologie chrétienne. Catalogue d'exposition, Saint-Bertrand-de-Comminges, 30 mars–11 nov. 1991*, 61–65. Toulouse: Musée archéologique départemental de Saint-Bertrand-de-Comminges, 1991.

Digeser, Elizabeth DePalma. *The Making of a Christian Empire: Lactantius and Rome.* Ithaca, N.Y.: Cornell University Press, 2000.

Dinshaw, Carolyn. *Getting Medieval: Sexualities and Communities, Pre- and Postmodern.* Durham, N.C.: Duke University Press, 1999.

Dölger, Franz Joseph. "Antike Parallelen zum leidenden Dinocrates in der *Passio Perpetuae*." *Antike und Christentum* 2 (1930): 1–40.

———. "Gladiatorenblut und Martyrerblut, Eine Szene der *Passio Perpetuae* in kultur- und religionsgeschichtlicher Bedeutung." *Bibliothek Warburg, Vorträge* 1923–24 (1926): 196–214.

———. "Der Kampf mit dem Aegypter in der Perpetua Vision: Das Martyrium als Kampf mit dem Teufel." *Antike und Christentum* 3 (1932): 177–88.

Domergue, Claude, Christian Landes, and Jean-Marie Pailler, eds. *Spectacula I: Gladiateurs et amphithéâtres: Actes du colloque tenu à Toulouse et à Lattes les 26, 27, 28, et 29 mai 1987.* Lattes: Editions Imago, 1990.

Dunne, John Gregory. "The Humboldt Murders." *New Yorker*, 13 January 1997, 44–62.

Dower, J. W. "The Bombed: Hiroshimas and Nagasakis in Japanese Memory." *Diplomatic History* 19 (1995): 275–95.

Downey, Glanville. "Ekphrasis." *RAC* 4 (1959): 922–43.

Droge, Arthur J., and James D. Tabor. *A Noble Death: Suicide and Martyrdom Among the Christians and Jews in Antiquity.* San Francisco: HarperSan Francisco, 1992.

Dunn, Peter W. "Women's Liberation, the *Acts of Paul*, and Other Apocryphal Acts of the Apostles." *Apocrypha* 4 (1993): 245–61.

Dupont, Florence. *L'acteur-roi ou le théâtre dans la Rome antique.* Paris: Société d'Éditions "Les Belles Lettres," 1985.

———. "Ludions, Lydioi: Les danseurs de la pompa circensis: Exégèse et discours sur l'origine des jeux à Rome." In *Spectacles sportifs et scéniques dans le monde étrusco-italique: Actes de la table ronde organisée par l'equipe de recherches étrusco-italiques de l'UMR 126 (CNRS, Paris) et l'École française de Rome, Rome 3–4 mai 1991*, 189–210. Rome: École Française de Rome, 1993.

Edmondson, John C. "Dynamic Arenas: Gladiatorial Presentations in the City of Rome and the Construction of Roman Society during the Early Empire." In *Roman Theatre and Society*, ed. William J. Slater, 69–112. Ann Arbor: University of Michigan Press, 1996.

Ednalino, Percy. "Columbine Crosses Spark Dispute." *Denver Post*, 18 April 2001, Final Edition.

———. "Crosses May Return to Hill Site," *Denver Post*, 15 April 2001, Rockies Edition.

Edwards, Catharine. *Writing Rome: Textual Approaches to the City*. New York: Cambridge University Press, 1996.

Edwards, Mark J., Martin Goodman, S. R. F. Price, and Christopher Rowland, eds. *Apologetics in the Roman Empire: Pagans, Jews, and Christians*. Oxford: Clarendon Press, 1999.

Elshtain, Jean Bethke. "Heartland of Darkness." *The New Republic*, 17 January 2000, 33–38.

Elsner, Jaś. *Art and the Roman Viewer: The Transformation of Art from the Pagan World to Christianity*. New York: Cambridge University Press, 1995.

———. "Cultural Resistance and the Visual Image: The Case of Dura Europos." *CPh* 96 (2001): 269–304.

———. *Imperial Rome and Christian Triumph: The Art of the Roman Empire, AD 100–450*. New York: Oxford University Press, 1998.

Enders, Jody. *The Medieval Theater of Cruelty: Rhetoric, Memory, Violence*. Ithaca, N.Y.: Cornell University Press, 1999.

Eriau, Jean-Baptiste. *Pourquoi les pères de l'église ont condamné le théâtre de leur temps*. Paris: Honoré Champion, 1914.

Erlanger, Steven. "U.S. Assails China Over Suppression of Religious Life." *New York Times*, 22 July 1997.

Fay, Brian, Philip Pomper, and Richard T. Vann, eds. *History and Theory: Contemporary Readings*. Malden, Mass.: Blackwell, 1998.

Feder, Don. "National Day of Prayer Survives Amid Attack on Religion by Courts." *Insight on the News*, 29 May 2000, 46.

Feldman, Allen. "Strange Fruit: The South African Truth Commission and the Demonic Economics of Violence." *Social Analysis* 46, no. 3 (2002): 234–65.

Fentress, James, and Chris Wickham. *Social Memory*. Cambridge: Blackwell, 1992.

Ferguson, Everett. "Early Christian Martyrdom and Civil Disobedience." *JECS* 1 (1993): 73–83.

———, ed. *Church and State in the Early Church*. New York: Garland, 1993.

Ferrarini, A. "Visioni, sangue e battesimo: La Passio Perpetuae." In *Atti della Settimana Sangue e antropologia nella letteratura cristiana (Roma, 29 novembre–4 dicembre 1982)*, 1055–81. Rome: Ed. Pia Unione del Preziosissimo Sangue, 1983.

Février, Paul-Albert. "Les chrétiens dans l'arène." In *Spectacula I: Gladiateurs et amphithéatres: Actes du colloque tenu à Toulouse et à Lattes les 26, 27, 28, et 29 mai 1987*, ed. Claude Domerge, Christian Landes, and Jean-Marie Pailler, 265–73. Lattes: Editions Imago, 1990.

———. "Martyre et Sainteté." In *Les fonctions des saints dans le monde occidental (IIIe–XIIIe siècle): Actes du colloque organisé par l'École Française de Rome avec le concours de l'Université de Rome "La Sapienza," 27–29 octobre 1988*, 51–80. Rome: École Française de Rome, 1991.

Fink, J. *Noe der Gerechte in der frühchristlichen Kunst.* Münster-Cologne: Böhlau, 1955.

Finley, M. I. "Myth, Memory, and History." *History and Theory* 4 (1965): 281–302. Expanded reprint in *The Use and Abuse of History*, by M. I Finley, 11–33. New York: Viking Press, 1971.

Finnegan, Ruth. "Tradition, but What Tradition and for Whom?" *Oral Tradition* 6 (1991): 104–24.

Fiol-Matta, Licia. *A Queer Mother for the Nation: The State and Gabriela Mistral.* Minneapolis: University of Minnesota Press, 2001.

Fischer, Michael M. J. "Ethnicity and the Post-Modern Arts of Memory." In *Writing Culture: The Poetics and Politics of Ethnography*, ed. James Clifford and George E. Marcus, 194–233. Berkeley: University of California Press, 1986.

Flobert, Pierre. "Quelques survivances de la gladiature." *Voces* 1 (1990): 71–76.

Fornara, Charles W. *The Nature of History in Ancient Greece and Rome.* Berkeley: University of California Press, 1983.

Forrer, Robert. *Die frühchristlichen Alterthümer aus dem Gräberfelde von Achmim-Panopolis.* Strasburg: F. Lohbauer, 1893.

Forster, Kurt. "Aby Warburg's History of Art: Collective Memory and the Social Mediation of Images." *Daedalus* 105, no. 1 (Winter 1976): 169–76.

Foucault, Michel. "About the Beginning of the Hermeneutics of the Self." In *Religion and Culture: Michel Foucault*, ed. Jeremy R. Carrette, 169–81. New York: Routledge, 1999.

———. *Dits et écrits: 1954–1988.* 4 vols. Ed. Daniel Defert and François Eward, with Jacques Lagrange. Paris: Gallimard, 1994.

———. "L'écriture de soi." *Corps écrit* no. 5, "L'autoportrait" (February 1983): 3–23. Reprinted in Foucault, *Dits et écrits: 1954–1988*, 4:415–30. Translated as "Self Writing" by Paul Rabinow in Foucault, *Ethics: Subjectivity and Truth*, vol. 1 of *Essential Works of Foucault, 1954–1984*, 207–22. New York: The New Press, 1994.

———. *Ethics: Subjectivity and Truth*, ed. Paul Rabinow. Vol. 1 of *Essential Works of Foucault, 1954–1984.* New York: The New Press, 1994.

———. "Friendship as a Way of Life." In *Ethics: Subjectivity and Truth*, ed. Paul Rabinow, vol. 1 of *Essential Works of Foucault, 1954–1984*, 135–40. New York: The New Press, 1994. Published originally in French as "De l'amitié comme mode de vie," *Gai Pied*, no. 25 (April 1981): 38–39; reprint, *Dits et écrits: 1954–1988*, 4 vols., ed. Daniel Defert and François Eward, with Jacques Lagrange, 4:163–67. Paris: Gallimard, 1994.

———. *Language, Counter-Memory, Practice: Selected Essays and Interviews.* Ed. Donald F. Bouchard, trans. Donald Bouchard and Sherry Simon. Ithaca, N.Y.: Cornell University Press, 1977.

———. "On the Genealogy of Ethics: An Overview of Work in Progress." In *Ethics: Subjectivity and Truth*, ed. Paul Rabinow. Vol. 1 of *Essential Works of Foucault, 1954–1984*, 253–80. New York: The New Press, 1994. Translated from the French, "Á propos de la généalogie de l'éthique: Un aperçu du travail en cours," in *Dits et écrits: 1954–1988*, 4 vols., ed. Daniel Defert and François Eward, with Jacques

Lagrange, 4:383–411. Paris: Gallimard, 1994. Originally published in English as "On the Genealogy of Ethics: An Overview of Work in Progress," in Hubert L. Dreyfus and Paul Rabinow, *Michel Foucault: Beyond Structuralism and Hermeneutics*, 2nd ed., 229–52. Chicago: University of Chicago Press, 1983.

———. *Politics, Philosophy, Culture: Interviews and Other Writings, 1977–1984*. Ed. Lawrence D. Kritzman. Trans. Alan Sheridan et al. New York: Pantheon, 1988.

———. *Power*. Ed. James D. Faubion. Vol. 3 of *Essential Works of Foucault, 1954–1984*. New York: The New Press, 1999.

———. *Power/Knowledge: Selected Interviews and Other Writings, 1972–1977*. Ed. Colin Gordon. Trans. Colin Gordon et al. New York: Pantheon, 1980.

———. Précis for *Du gouvernement des vivants*. In Foucault, *Dits et écrits*, 4 vols. ed. Daniel Defert and François Eward, with Jacques Lagrange, 4:125–29. Paris: Gallimard, 1994. Translated as "On the Government of Living," in Foucault, *Ethics: Subjectivity and Truth*, ed. Paul Rabinow, vol. 1 of *Essential Works of Foucault, 1954–1984*, 81–85. New York: The New Press, 1994; and in *Religion and Culture: Michel Foucault*, ed. Jeremy R. Carrette, 154–57. New York: Routledge, 1999.

———. *Surveiller et punir*. Paris: Gallimard, 1975. Trans. Alan Sheridan as *Discipline and Punish: The Birth of the Prison*. New York: Vintage, 1979.

———. "Technologies of the Self." In *Technologies of the Self: A Seminar with Michel Foucault*, ed. Luther H. Martin, Huck Gutman, and Patrick H. Hutton, 16–49. Amherst: University of Massachusetts Press, 1988. Translated into French by Fabienne Durand-Bogaert as "Les techniques de soi," in *Dits et écrits: 1954–1988*, ed. Daniel Defert and François Eward, with Jacques Lagrange, 4:783–813. Paris: Gallimard, 1994. Amended English version in Foucault, *Ethics: Subjectivity and Truth*, ed. Paul Rabinow, vol. 1 of *Essential Works of Foucault, 1954–1984*, 223–51. New York: The New Press, 1994.

Fox, Robin Lane. *Pagans and Christians*. New York: Alfred K. Knopf, 1987.

Foxe, John. *The New Foxe's Book of Martyrs*. Ed. Harold J. Chadwick. Bridge-Logos Publishers, 2001.

Fraade, Steven D. *From Tradition to Commentary: Torah and Its Interpretation in the Midrash Sifre to Deuteronomy*. Albany, N.Y.: SUNY Press, 1991.

Frank, Georgia. *The Memory of the Eyes: Pilgrims to Living Saints in Christian Late Antiquity*. Berkeley: University of California Press, 2000.

Franke, Peter. "Bemerkungen zur frühchristlichen Noe-ikonographie." *RivAC* 49 (1973): 171–82.

Franz, Marie-Louise von. *Passio Perpetuae: Das Schicksal einer Frau zwischen zwei Gottesbilden*. Zurich: Daimon, 1982.

Fredouille, Jean-Claude. *Tertullien et la conversion de la culture antique*. Paris: Études Augustiniennes, 1972.

Frend, W. H. C. "Blandina and Perpetua: Two Early Christian Heroines." In *Les martyrs de Lyon (177): Lyon, 20–23 septembre 1977*, ed. Marcel LeGlay, 167–77. Colloques internationales de CNRS 575. Paris: Editions du CNRS, 1978.

———. *Martyrdom and Persecution in the Early Church: A Study of a Conflict from the Maccabees to Donatus*. Oxford: Basil Blackwell, 1965.

Freudenberger, Rudolf. "Die *Acta Iustini* als historisches Dokument." In *Humanitas—*

Christianitas: Walther v. Loewenich zum 65. Geburtstag, ed. Karlmann Beyschlag, Gottfried Maron, and Eberhard Wolfel, 24–31. Witten: Luther-Verlag, 1968.

——. "Die *Akten der scilitanischen Märtyrer* als historisches Dokument." *Wiener Studien* 86 (1973): 196–215.

——. "Probleme römischer Religionspolitik in Nordafrika nach der *Passio SS. Perpetuae et Felicitatis.*" *Helikon* 13–14 (1973–74): 174–83.

Fridh, Åke. *Le problème de la Passion des saintes Perpétue et Félicité.* Studia Graeca et Latina Gothburgensia 26. Stockholm: Almqvist & Wiksell, 1968.

Funkenstein, Amos. "Collective Memory and Historical Consciousness." *History and Memory* 1 (1989): 5–26.

Fussell, Paul. *The Great War and Modern Memory.* New York: Oxford University Press, 1975.

Futrell, Alison. *Blood in the Arena: The Spectacle of Roman Power.* Austin: University of Texas Press, 1997.

Galinsky, Karl. *Augustan Culture.* Princeton, N.J.: Princeton University Press, 1996.

Garnsey, Peter. "The Criminal Jurisdiction of Governors." *JRS* 58 (1968): 51–59.

Gedi, Noa, and Yigal Elam. "Collective Memory—What Is It?" *History and Memory* 8 (Spring/Summer 1996): 30–50.

Gero, Stephen. "Jewish Polemic in the *Martyrium Pionii* and a 'Jesus' Passage from the Talmud." *JJS* 29 (1978): 164–68.

Giannarelli, Elena. "Il παιδαριογέρων nella biografia cristiana." *Prometheus* 14 (1988): 279–84.

——. "Sogni e visioni dell'infanzia nelle biografie dei santi: Fra tradizione classica e innovazione cristiana." *Augustinianum* 29 (1989): 213–35.

Gibbs, Nancy. "Special Report: The Littleton Massacre." *Time,* 3 May 1999, 24–36.

Gibbs, Robert, and Elliot R. Wolfson, eds. *Suffering Religion.* New York: Routledge, 2002.

Gibson, E. Leigh. "Jewish Antagonism or Christian Polemic: The Case of the *Martyrdom of Pionius.*" *JECS* 9 (2001): 339–58.

——. "The Making of Modern Martyrs: The Martyrs of Columbine." In *The Bible in the Twenty-First Century: Actors and Scenes of Violence,* ed. Athalya Brenner. New York: Continuum, 2004 (forthcoming).

Gillis, John R., ed. *Commemorations: The Politics of National Identity.* Princeton, N.J.: Princeton University Press, 1994.

Girard, René. *Violence and the Sacred.* Trans. Patrick Gregory. Baltimore: Johns Hopkins University Press, 1977. Originally published as *La violence et le sacré* (Paris: Grasset, 1972).

Glancy, Jennifer. *Slavery in Early Christianity.* New York: Oxford University Press, 2002.

Goldberg, Jeffrey. "Washington Discovers Christian Persecution." *New York Times Magazine,* 21 December 1997, 46–52, 60, 64–65.

Goldhill, Simon. "The Erotic Eye: Visual Stimulation and Cultural Conflict." In *Being Greek Under Rome: Cultural Identity, the Second Sophistic, and the Development of Empire,* ed. Simon Goldhill, 154–94. New York: Cambridge University Press, 2001.

Goldstein, Amy. "In Colorado, Questions About Accomplices, 'Martyrs'; Deaths Seen in Christian Context." *Washington Post*, 27 April 1999.

Golvin, Jean-Claude. *L'amphithéâtre romain: Essai sur la théorisation de sa forme et de ses fonctions.* 2 vols. Publications du Centre Pierre Paris 18. Paris: Boccard, 1988.

Golvin, Jean-Claude, and Christian Landes. *Amphithéâtres et gladiateurs.* Paris: Éditions du CNRS, 1990.

Goodblatt, David. "Suicide in the Sanctuary: Traditions on Priestly Martyrdom." *JJS* 46 (1995): 10–29.

Goodstein, Laurie. "Christians Gain Support in Fight on Persecution." *New York Times*, 9 November 1998.

Gordon, Richard. "The Veil of Power: Emperors, Sacrificers, and Benefactors." In *Pagan Priests: Religion and Power in the Ancient World*, ed. Mary Beard and John North, 201–34. Ithaca, N.Y.: Cornell University Press, 1990.

Govrin, Michal. "Theological Writing of Second-Generation Survivors." Paper presented at the Genocide, Religion, and Modernity Conference at the U.S. Holocaust Museum, Washington, D.C., 11–13 May 1997.

Grabar, André. *Christian Iconography: A Study of Its Origins.* The A. W. Mellon Lectures in the Fine Arts, 1961. Bollingen Series 35.10. Princeton, N.J.: Princeton University Press, 1968.

Grandazzi, Alexandre. *The Foundation of Rome: Myth and History.* Trans. Jane Marie Todd. Ithaca, N.Y.: Cornell University Press, 1997.

Grégoire, Henri, with P. Orgels, J. Moreau, and A. Maricq. *Les persécutions dans l'empire romain.* 2nd ed. Academie royale de Belgique, Mémoires de la classe des lettres et des sciences morales et politiques 47.1. Brussels: Academie Royale de Belgique, 1964.

Grodzynski, Denise. "Tortures mortelles et catégories sociales: Les *Summa Supplicia* dans le droit romain aux IIIe et IVe siècles." In *Du châtiment du corps dans la cité: Supplices corporels et peine du morte dans le monde antique: Table ronde, Rome, 1982*, 361–403. Collection École Française de Rome 79. Rome: École Française de Rome, 1984.

Guillaumin, Marie-Louise. "'Une jeune fille qui s'appelait Blandine': Aux origines d'une tradition hagiographique." In *Epektasis: Mélanges patristiques offerts au Cardinal Jean Danielou*, ed. Jacques Fontaine and Charles Kannengiesser, 93–98. Paris: Beauchesne, 1972.

Guinovart, Dolores del Amo. "Frontal de Sarcófago de Valcabrère con la Adoración de Los Magos." *Antiquité Tardive* 7 (1999): 365–70.

Gunderson, Erik. "The Ideology of the Arena." *ClAnt* 15 (1996): 113–51.

Gustafson, Mark. "Condemnation to the Mines in the Later Roman Empire." *HTR* 87 (1994): 421–33.

Haaken, Janice. *Pillar of Salt: Gender, Memory, and the Perils of Looking Back.* New Brunswick, N.J.: Rutgers University Press, 1998.

Habermehl, Peter. *Perpetua und der Ägypter oder Bilder des Bösen in frühen afrikanischen Christentum: Ein Versuch zur Passio sanctarum Perpetuae et Felicitatis.* TUGAL 140. Berlin: Akademie Verlag, 1992.

Hacking, Ian. *Rewriting the Soul: Multiple Personality and the Sciences of Memory.* Princeton, N.J.: Princeton University Press, 1995.

Hadot, Pierre. "Forms of Life and Forms of Discourse in Ancient Philosophy." Trans. Arnold I. Davidson and Paula Wissing. In *Foucault and His Interlocutors*, ed. Arnold I. Davidson, 203–24. Chicago: University of Chicago Press, 1997.

——. *Philosophy as a Way of Life: Spiritual Exercises from Socrates to Foucault.* Trans. Michael Chase. Ed. Arnold I. Davidson. Oxford: Blackwell, 1995.

Halbwachs, Maurice. *Les cadres sociaux de la mémoire.* Paris: Librairie Félix Alcan, 1925. New ed., Paris: Presses Universitaires de France, 1952. Reprint: Paris: Mouton, 1975.

——. *The Collective Memory.* Trans. Francis J. Ditter and Vida Yazdi Ditter. New York: Harper & Row, 1980.

——. "Individual Consciousness and Collective Mind." *American Journal of Sociology* 44 (1939): 812–22.

——. "Individual Psychology and Collective Psychology." *American Sociological Review* 3 (1938): 615–23.

——. *La mémoire collective.* Paris: Presses Universitaires de France, 1950. 2nd rev., aug. ed., Paris: Presses Universitaires de France, 1968.

——. *On Collective Memory.* Ed. and trans. Lewis A. Coser. Chicago: University of Chicago Press, 1992.

——. *La topographie légendaire des évangiles en terre sainte: Étude de mémoire collective.* Paris: Presses Universitaires de France, 1941.

Haley, Dan. "Protesters Fell Church's Trees: Pair Linked to Columbine High Killers Chopped Down." *Denver Post*, 27 September 1999.

Halkin, François. *Euphémie de Chalcédoine: Légendes byzantines.* Subsidia Hagiographica 41. Brussels: Société des Bollandistes, 1965.

Hall, Stuart G. "Women Among the Early Martyrs." In *Martyrs and Martyrologies: Papers Read at the 1992 Summer Meeting and the 1993 Winter Meeting of the Ecclesiastical History Society*, ed. Diane Wood, 1–22. Oxford: Blackwell, 1993.

Halperin, Jean, and Georges Levitte, eds. *Mémoire et histoire: Données et debats: Actes du XXVe Colloque des intellectuels juifs de langue française.* Paris: Denoël, 1986.

Halporn, James W. "Literary History and Generic Expectations in the *Passio* and the *Acta Perpetuae.*" *VC* 45 (1991): 223–41.

Hamerton-Kelly, Robert G., ed. *Violent Origins: Walter Burkert, René Girard, and Jonathan Z. Smith on Ritual Killing and Cultural Formation.* Stanford, Calif.: Stanford University Press, 1987.

Hamman, Adelbert. "La confession de la foi dans les premiers actes des martyrs." In *Epektasis: Mélanges patristiques offerts au Cardinal Jean Daniélou*, ed. Jacques Fontaine and Charles Kannengiesser, 99–105. Paris: Beauchesne, 1972.

Handgun Control, Inc./Center to Prevent Handgun Violence. *Progress Report.* Fall 1999.

Hartmann, Geoffrey H. "Public Memory and Modern Experience." *Yale Journal of Criticism* 6 (1993): 239–47.

Hass, Kristin Ann. *Carried to the Wall: American Memory and the Vietnam Veterans Memorial.* Berkeley: University of California Press, 1998.

Haug, Frigga. *Female Sexualization: A Collective Work of Memory.* London: Verso, 1987.

Haver, William. *The Body of this Death: Historicity and Sociality in the Time of AIDS.* Stanford, Calif.: Stanford University Press, 1996.

Hefele, Charles Joseph. *Histoire des conciles d'après les documents originaux.* Trans. Henri Leclercq. Paris: Letouzey et Ané, 1910.

Heffernan, Thomas J. "Philology and Authorship in the *Passio Sanctarum Perpetuae et Felicitatis*." *Traditio* 50 (1995): 315–25.

——. *Sacred Biography: Saints and Their Biographers in the Middle Ages.* New York: Oxford University Press, 1988.

Heim, François. "Les panégyriques des martyrs ou l'impossible conversion d'un genre littéraire." *RevScRel* 61 (1987): 105–28.

Heimer, Matthew. "Adding Up the Facts." *Brill's Content* 2, no. 6 (July/August 1999): 92–93.

Hein, Laura, and Mark Selden. "Commemoration and Silence: Fifty Years of Remembering the Bomb in America and Japan." In *Living with the Bomb: American and Japanese Cultural Conflict in the Nuclear Age,* ed. Laura Hein and Mark Selden, 3–34. Armonk, N.Y.: M. E. Sharpe, 1997.

Hejl, Peter. "Wie Gesellschaften Erfahrungen machen, oder: Was Gesellschaftstheorie zum Verständnis des Gedächtnisproblems beitragen kann." In *Gedächtnis: Probleme und Perspektiven der interdisziplinären Gedächtnisforschung,* ed. Siegfried J. Schmidt, 293–336. Frankfurt: Suhrkamp, 1991.

Heller, Jenny E. "Westminster Abbey Elevates 10 Foreigners." *New York Times,* 22 September 1998.

Hell House: A Documentary Film. Dir. George Ratliff, prod. Zachary Mortenson. New York, Mixed Greens Films, 2001.

Henten, Jan Willem van. "Internet Martyrs and Violence Vicitms and/or Perpetrators." In *Vocabularies of Violence,* ed. Jonneke Bekkenkamp and Yvonne Sherwood. New York: Continuum, 2004 (forthcoming).

——. *The Maccabean Martyrs as Saviours of the Jewish People: A Study of 2 and 4 Maccabees.* Supplements to the Journal for the Study of Judaism 57. Leiden: Brill, 1997.

Henten, Jan Willem van, Boudewijn Dehandschutter, and H. J. W. van der Klaauw, eds. *Die Enstehung der jüdischen Martyrologie.* Studia Post-Biblica 38. Leiden: Brill, 1989.

Hermans, Theo. *Origène: Théologie sacrificielle du sacerdoce des chrétiens.* ThH 102. Paris: Beauchesne, 1996.

Hervieu-Léger, Danièle. *La religion pour mémoire.* Paris: Editions du Cerf, 1993. Trans. Simon Lee as *Religion as a Chain of Memory* (New Brunswick: Rutgers University Press, 2000).

Hinard, F. "Spectacle des exécutions et espace urbain." In *L'urbs: Espace urbain et histoire, Ier s. av. J.C.–IIIe s. ap. J. C. Atti del colloquio internazionale CNRS, EFR, Rome 9–12 maggio 1985,* 111–25. Collection de l'École Française de Rome 98. Rome: École Française de Rome, 1987.

Hirsch, Marianne, and Valerie Snith, eds. "Gender and Cultural Memory." Special issue of *Signs* 28, no. 1 (Autumn 2002): 1–479.

Hobsbawm, Eric, and Terence Ranger, eds. *The Invention of Tradition*. New York: Cambridge University Press, 1983.

Hoek, Annawies van den. "Clement of Alexandria on Martyrdom." *StPatr* 26 (1993): 324–41.

Hooke, Alexander E. "Spectacles of Morality, Spectacles of Truth." *ISPh* 30, no. 2 (1998): 19–35.

Hooyman, R. P. J. "Die Noe-Darstellung in der frühchristlichen Kunst." *VC* 12 (1958): 113–35.

Hopkins, Keith. "Early Christian Number and Its Implications." *JECS* 6 (1998): 185–226.

———. "Murderous Games." In his *Death and Renewal: Sociological Studies in Roman History*, 2:1–30. Cambridge: Cambridge University Press, 1983.

———. *A World Full of Gods: Pagans, Jews, and Christians in the Roman Empire*. London: Weidenfeld and Nicolson, 1999.

Horbury, William, and Brian McNeil, eds. *Suffering and Martyrdom in the New Testament: Studies Presented to G. M. Styler by the Cambridge New Testament Seminar*. Cambridge: Cambridge University Press, 1981.

Hornum, Michael B. *Nemesis, the Roman State, and the Games*. Leiden: Brill, 1993.

Hunt, E. D. *Holy Land Pilgrimage in the Later Roman Empire (A.D. 312–460)*. Oxford: Clarendon Press, 1982.

Hutton, Patrick H. "Collective Memory and Collective Mentalities: The Halbwachs-Ariès Connection." *Historical Reflections/Réflexions Historiques* 15, no. 2 (1988): 311–22.

———. *History as an Art of Memory*. Hanover, N.H.: University Press of New England, 1993.

Huyssen, Andreas. *Twilight Memories: Marking Time in a Culture of Amnesia*. New York: Routledge, 1995.

Index on Censorship. Special issue, "Memory and Forgetting." *Index on Censorship* 30:1, no. 198 (January/February 2001).

Irigaray, Luce. *Speculum de l'autre femme*. Paris: Minuit, 1974.

Irwin, M. Eleanor Irwin. "Gender, Status, and Identity in a North African Martyrdom." In *Gli imperatori Severi: Storia, archeologia, religione*, ed. Enrico Dal Covolo and Giancarlo Rinaldi, 251–60. Rome: LAS, 1999.

Irwin-Zarecka, Iwona. *Frames of Remembrance: The Dynamics of Collective Memory*. New Brunswick, N.J.: Transaction Publishers, 1994.

Jacobs, Martin. "Theatres and Performances as Reflected in the Talmud Yerushalmi." In *The Talmud Yerusalmi and Graeco-Roman Culture*, 3 vols., ed. Peter Schäfer. TSAJ 71, 1:327–47. Tübingen: Mohr (Siebeck), 1998.

Jacobson, Mark, Michael Wolff, and Nancy Jo Sales. "Kid Culture in the Age of Columbine." *New York*, 17 May 1999, 24–34.

James, Liz, and Ruth Webb. "'To Understand Ultimate Things and Enter Secret Places': Ekphrasis and Art in Byzantium." *Art History* 14 (1991): 1–17.

Janofsky, Michael. "Far Beyond Columbine, Rancor and Tension: Shootings' Legacy is Passionate Discord." *New York Times*, 4 October 1999.

Janssen, L. F. "'Superstitio' and the Persecution of Christians." *VC* 33 (1979): 131–59.

Jay, Nancy. *Throughout Your Generations Forever: Sacrifice, Religion, and Paternity.* Chicago: University of Chicago Press, 1992.

Jeffrey, Jaclyn, and Glenace Edwall, eds. *Memory and History: Essays on Recalling and Interpreting Experience.* Lanham, Md.: University Press of America, 1994.

Jensen, Robin Margaret. *Understanding Early Christian Art.* New York: Routledge, 2000.

Johnson, Thomas J. *The Rehabilitation of Richard Nixon: The Media's Effect on Collective Memory.* New York: Garland, 1995.

Jones, Chris. "Women, Death, and the Law During the Christian Persecution." In *Martyrs and Martyrologies: Papers Read at the 1992 Summer Meeting and the 1993 Winter Meeting of the Ecclesiastical History Society*, ed. Diane Wood, 23–34. Oxford: Blackwell, 1993.

Jonker, Gerdien. *The Topography of Remembrance: The Dead, Tradition, and Collective Memory in Mesopotamia.* SHR 68. Leiden: Brill, 1995.

Josipovici, Gabriel. "Rethinking Memory: Too Much/Too Little." *Judaism* 47 (1998): 232–39.

Jürgens, Heiko. *Pompa Diaboli: Die lateinischen Kirchenväter und das antike Theater.* Tübinger Beiträge zur Altertumswissenschaft 46. Stuttgart: Kohlhammer, 1972.

Kaestli, Jean-Daniel. "Mémoire et pseudépigraphie dans le christianisme de l'âge post-apostolique." *RTP* 125 (1993): 41–63.

Kammen, Michael. *Mystic Chords of Memory: The Transformation of Tradition in American Culture.* New York: Alfred A. Knopf, 1991.

Kaufmann, C. M. *Zur Ikonographie der Menasampullen.* Cairo: F. Diemer, Finck and Baylaender, 1910.

Kearl, Michael C., and Anoel Rinaldi. "The Political Uses of the Dead as Symbols in Contemporary Civil Religions." *Social Forces* 61 (1983): 693–708.

Kelley, Shawn. *Racializing Jesus: Race, Ideology, and the Formation of Modern Biblical Scholarship.* New York: Routledge, 2002.

Kelly, Sean. "Bernalls Defend Book's Accuracy." *Denver Post*, 26 September 1999.

Kingsolver, Barbara. *The Poisonwood Bible.* San Francisco: Harper Flamingo, 1998.

Kirksey, Jim. "Original Crosses for Victims to Go on Tour." *Denver Post*, 3 June 1999, Rockies Edition.

Kirp, David L. "Martyrs and Movies." *American Prospect*, 20 December 1999, 52–53.

Kleinman, Arthur, Veena Das, and Margaret Lock, eds. *Social Suffering.* Berkeley: University of California Press, 1997.

Knipfing, J. R. "The *Libelli* of the Decian Persecution." *HTR* 16 (1923): 345–90.

Knowles, David. *Christian Monasticism.* New York: McGraw Hill, 1969.

Knust, Jennifer Wright. "Abandoned to Lust: The Politics of Sexual Slander in Early Christian Discourse." Ph.D. diss., Columbia University, 2000.

Koester, Helmut. *Introduction to the New Testament.* Vol. 2, *History and Literature of Early Christianity.* Philadelphia: Fortress Press, 1984.

Korol, Dieter. "Zum Bild der Vertreibung Adams und Evas in der neuen Katakombe an der Via Latina und zur anthropomorphen Darstellung Gottvaters." *JAC* 22 (1979): 175–90.

Kraemer, Ross S. "The Conversion of Women to Ascetic Forms of Christianity." *Signs* 6 (1980): 298–307.

Kraemer, Ross S., and Shira L. Lander. "Perpetua and Felicitas." In *The Early Christian World*, ed. Philip F. Esler, 2:1048–68. New York: Routledge, 2000.

Kraft, Heinrich. "Die Lyoner Märtyrer und der Montanismus." In *Pietas: Festschrift für Bernhard Kötting*, ed. Ernst Dassmann and K. Suso Frank, 250–66. JAC Ergänzungsband 8. Munich: Aschendorff, 1980.

Krell, David Farrell. *Of Memory, Reminiscence, and Writing: On the Verge.* Bloomington: Indiana University Press, 1990.

Kristol, William. "Good and Evil in Littleton." *The Weekly Standard*, 10 May 1999, 7–8.

Kuberski, Philip. *The Persistence of Memory: Organism, Myth, Text.* Berkeley: University of California Press, 1992.

Kuchler, Susanne, and Walter Melion, eds. *Images of Memory: On Remembering and Representation.* Washington, D.C.: Smithsonian Institution Press, 1991.

Kuefler, Mathew. *The Manly Eunuch: Masculinity, Gender Ambiguity, and Christian Ideology in Late Antiquity.* Chicago: University of Chicago Press, 2001.

Kyle, Donald G. *Spectacles of Death in Ancient Rome.* New York: Routledge, 1998.

Labash, Matt. "Among the Crusaders: The Saga of a Columbine Father, an Illinois Carpenter, and Their Evangelical Roadshow." *The Weekly Standard*, 24 April 2000, 26.

——. " 'Do You Believe in God?' 'Yes.': On the Life and Death of Cassie Bernall." *The Weekly Standard*, 10 May 1999, 20–25.

Lafaye, G. "Gladiator." In *Dictionnaire des antiquités grecques et romaines d'après les textes et les monuments*, ed. C. Daremberg, E. Saglio, and M. Pottier, 2.2:1563–99. Paris: Hachette, 1896.

——. "Venatio." In *Dictionnaire des antiquités grecques et romaines d'après les textes et les monuments.* Ed. C. Daremberg, E. Saglio, and M. Pottier, 5:680–709. Paris: Hachette, 1914.

Lalleman, Annick. "Le parfum des martyrs dans les Actes des martyrs de Lyon et le Martyre de Polycarpe." *StPatr* 16:2 (1985): 186–92.

Lamberigts, M., and P. van Deun, eds. *Martyrium in Multidisciplinary Perspective: Memorial Louis Reekmans.* Leuven: Leuven University Press/Peeters, 1995.

Landes, Christian, and Véronique Kramérovskis, eds. *Spectacula II: Le théâtre antique et ses spectacles: Actes du colloque tenu au Musée Archéologique Henri Prades de Lattes les 27, 28, 29, et 30 avril 1989.* Latte: Musée archéologique Henri Prades, 1992.

Langer, Lawrence L. *Holocaust Testimonies: The Ruins of Memory.* New Haven, Conn.: Yale University Press, 1991.

Laskaris, Nikolaos G. *Monuments funéraires paléochrétiens (et byzantins) de Grèce.* Athens: Les Éditions Historiques Stéfanos D. Basilopoulos, 2000.

Late Egyptian and Coptic Art: An Introduction to the Collections in the Brooklyn Museum. Brooklyn: Brooklyn Museum/Brooklyn Institute of Arts and Sciences, 1943.

Leclercq, Henri. "Adam et Ève." *DACL* 1 (1907): 509–19.

——. "Arche." *DACL* 1 (1907): 2709–32.

——. "Chalcédoine." *DACL* 3 (1914): 90–130.

——. "Euphémie (Sainte)." *DACL* 5:1 (1922): 745–46.

——. "Martyr." *DACL* 10:2 (1932): 2359–512.

——. "Pasteur (Bon)." *DACL* 13 (1937–38): 2272–390.

——. "Perpétue et Félicité." *DACL* 14:1 (1939): 393–444.

——. "Thècle." *DACL* 15 (1953): 2225–36.

Lefkowitz, Mary R. "Motivations for St. Perpetua's Marytrdom." *JAAR* 44 (1976): 417–21.

LeGlay, Marcel. "Les amphithéâtres: *Loci religiosi?*" In *Spectacula I: Gladiateurs et amphthéatres: Actes du colloque tenu à Toulouse et à Lattes les 26, 27, 28, et 29 mai 1987*, ed. Claude Domerge, Christian Landes, and Jean-Marie Pailler, 217–29. Lattes: Editions Imago, 1990.

——, ed. *Les Martyrs de Lyon (177): Lyon, 20–23 Septembre 1977*. Colloques internationaux du CNRS 575. Paris: Éditions du CNRS, 1978.

LeGoff, Jacques. *History and Memory*. Trans. Steven Rendall and Elizabeth Claman. New York: Columbia University Press, 1992.

LeGoff, Jacques, and Pierre Nora, eds. *Constructing the Past: Essays in Historical Methodology*. New York: Cambridge University Press, 1985.

Leon, H. J. "Moritui te salutamus." *TAPA* 70 (1939): 46–50.

Levine, Robert. "Prudentius' Romanus: The Rhetorician as Hero, Martyr, Satirist, and Saint." *Rhetorica* 9 (1991): 5–38.

Lévi-Strauss, Claude. *Structural Anthropology*. New York: Basic Books, 1963.

Leyerle, Blake. "John Chrysostom on the Gaze." *JECS* 1 (1993): 159–74.

——. *Theatrical Shows and Ascetic Lives: John Chrysostom's Attack on Spiritual Marriage*. Berkeley: University of California Press, 2001.

Lincoln, Bruce. *Theorizing Myth: Narrative, Ideology, and Scholarship*. Chicago: University of Chicago Press, 1999.

Lindqvist, Sven. *A History of Bombing*. Trans. Linda Haverty Rugg. New York: New Press, 2001.

Lintner, Rev. Jay. "The Right's Holy War." *The Nation*, 20 July 1998, 6–7.

Lintott, Andrew. *Imperium Romanum: Politics and Administration*. London: Routledge, 1993.

Lipsitz, George. *Time Passages: Collective Memory and American Popular Culture*. Minneapolis: University of Minnesota Press, 1990.

Lomanto, Valeria. "Rapporti fra la *Passio Perpetuae* e *Passiones* africane." In *Forma futuri: Studi in onore del Cardinale Michele Pellegrino*, 566–86. Torino: Bottega d'Erasmo, 1975.

Long, Burke O. *Imagining the Holy Land: Maps, Models, and Fantasy Travels*. Bloomington: Indiana University Press, 2003.

Lowenthal, David. *The Past is a Foreign Country*. Cambridge: Cambridge University Press, 1985.

Lucchesi, Giovanni. "Eufemia di Calcedonia." *Bibliotheca Sanctorum* 5 (1964): 154–60.

Luzadder, Dan, and Katie Kerwin McCrimmon. "Accounts Differ on Question to Bernall." *Denver Rocky Mountain News*, 24 September 1999.

Lyman, Rebecca. "Perpetua: A Christian Quest for Self." *Journal of Women and Religion* 8 (1989): 26–33.

MacDonald, Dennis R. *The Legend and the Apostle: The Battle for Paul in Story and Canon.* Philadelphia: Westminster Press, 1983.

MacDonald, Dennis R., and Andrew D. Scrimgeour. "Pseudo-Chrysostom's Panegyric to Thecla: The Heroine of the *Acts of Paul* in Homily and Art." *Semeia* 38 (1986): 151–59.

MacDonald, Margaret Y. *Early Christian Women and Pagan Opinion: The Power of the Hysterical Woman.* New York: Cambridge University Press, 1996.

Mack, Burton. *The Christian Myth: Origins, Logic, and Legacy.* New York: Continuum, 2001.

——. "Introduction: Religion and Ritual." In *Violent Origins: Walter Burkert, René Girard, and Jonathan Z. Smith on Ritual Killing and Cultural Formation,* ed. Robert G. Hamerton-Kelly, 1–70. Stanford, Calif.: Stanford University Press, 1987.

——. *A Myth of Innocence: Mark and Christian Origins.* Philadelphia: Fortress Press, 1988.

——. *Who Wrote the New Testament? The Making of the Christian Myth.* San Francisco: Harper, 1995.

MacMullen, Ramsay. "Judicial Savagery in the Roman Empire." *Chiron* 16 (1986): 147–66.

Maguire, Henry. *Art and Eloquence in Byzantium.* Princeton, N.J.: Princeton University Press, 1981.

—— "Truth and Convention in Byzantine Descriptions of Works of Art." *DOP* 28 (1974): 111–40.

Maier, Charles S. *The Unmasterable Past: History, Holocaust, and the German National Identity.* Cambridge, Mass.: Harvard University Press, 1988.

Malbon, Elizabeth Struthers. *The Iconography of the Sarcophagus of Junius Bassus.* Princeton, N.J.: Princeton University Press, 1990.

Malherbe, Abraham. "Hellenistic Moralists and the New Testament." *ANRW* 2.26.1 (1992): 267–333.

Malone, Edward. *The Monk and the Martyr: The Monk as the Successor to the Martyr.* Studies in Christian Antiquity 12. Washington, D.C.: Catholic University Press, 1950.

Manson, Marilyn. "Columbine: Whose Fault is It?" *Rolling Stone,* 24 June 1999, 23–24, 77.

Maraval, Pierre. *Les persécutions des chrétiens durant les quatres premiers siècles.* Bibliothèque d'histoire du christianisme 30. Paris: Desclée, 1992.

Markus, Robert A. "Die *spectacula* als religiöses Konfliktfeld städtischen Lebens in der Spätantike." *FZPhTh* 38 (1991): 253–71.

Marincola, John. *Authority and Tradition in Ancient Historiography.* New York: Cambridge University Press, 1997.

Martineau, Harriet. "The Martyr Age in the United States." *London and Westminster Review* 32 (December 1838–April 1839): 1–59. Reprint, Harriet Martineau, *Writings on Slavery and the American Civil War,* ed. Deborah Anna Logan, 44–80. DeKalb: Northern Illinois University Press, 2002.

Matter, Michel. "Jeux d'amphithéâtre et réactions chrétiennes de Tertullien à la fin du

Ve siècle." In *Spectacula I: Gladiateurs et amphthéatres: Actes du colloque tenu à Toulouse et à Lattes les 26, 27, 28, et 29 mai 1987*, ed. Claude Domerge, Christian Landes, and Jean-Marie Pailler, 259–64. Lattes: Editions Imago, 1990.

Matthews, Shelly. "Thinking of Thecla: Issues in Feminist Historiography." *JFSR* 17, no. 2 (2001): 39–55.

Mazzucco, Clementina. "Il significato cristiano della 'libertas' proclamata dai martiri della *Passio Perpetuae.*" In *Forma futuri: Studi in onore del Cardinale Michele Pellegrino*, 542–65. Torino: Bottega d'Erasmo, 1975.

McBride, James. "Capital Punishment as the Unconstitutional Establishment of Religion: A Girardian Reading of the Death Penalty." *Journal of Church and State* 37 (1995): 263–87.

McGowan, Andrew. "Eating People: Accusations of Cannibalism Against Christians in the Second Century." *JECS* 2 (1994): 413–42.

McNamara, Eileen. "No Doubting One Girl's Faith." *Boston Globe*, 10 October 1999.

Meltzer, Françoise. *For Fear of the Fire: Joan of Arc and the Limits of Subjectivity.* Chicago: University of Chicago Press, 2001.

Menchù, Rigoberta. *I, Rigoberta Menchù: An Indian Woman in Guatemala.* London: Verso, 1984.

Menghi, Martino, "Tertulliano e il *De spectaculis.*" *Lexis* 9–10 (1992): 189–209.

Mentxaka, Rosa. "La persécution du christianisme à l'époque de Septime Sévère: Considérations juridiques sur la *Passion de Perpétue et Félicité.*" In *Églises et pouvoir politique: Actes des journées internationales d'histoire du droit d'Angers, 30 mai–1er juin 1985*, 63–82. Angers: Presse de l'Université, 1987.

Merback, Mitchell B. *The Thief, the Cross, and the Wheel: Pain and the Spectacle of Punishment in Medieval and Renaissance Europe.* Chicago: University of Chicago Press, 1998.

Mertens, Cées. "Les premiers martyrs et leur rêves: Cohésion de l'histoire et des rêves dans quelques 'Passiones' de l'Afrique du Nord." *RHE* 81 (1986): 5–46.

Meslin, Michel. "Vases sacrés et boissons d'éternité dans les visions des martyrs africains." In *Epektasis: Mélanges patristiques offerts au Cardinal Jean Daniélou*, ed. Jacques Fontaine and Charles Kannengiesser, 139–53. Paris: Beauchesne, 1972.

Miles, Margaret R. *Carnal Knowing: Female Nakedness and Religious Meaning in the Christian West.* Boston: Beacon Press, 1989.

Millar, Fergus. "Condemnation to Hard Labour in the Roman Empire, from the Julio-Claudians to Constantine." *Papers of the British School at Rome* 52 (1984): 127–47.

——. "The Imperial Cult and the Persecutions." In *Le culte des sourverains dans l'empire romain*, ed. Willem den Boer, 143–75. Geneva: Fondation Hardt, 1973.

Miller, Patricia Cox. *Biography in Late Antiquity: A Quest for the Holy Man.* Transformation of the Classical Heritage 5. Berkeley: University of California Press, 1983.

——. *Dreams in Late Antiquity.* Princeton, N.J.: Princeton University Press, 1994.

Misch, Georg. *A History of Autobiography in Antiquity.* Trans. E. W. Dickes and Georg Misch. 2 vols. London: Routledge and Kegan Paul, 1950.

Mizruchi, Susan L., ed. *Religion and Cultural Studies*. Princeton, N.J.: Princeton University Press, 2001.

Moallem, Minoo. *Between Warrior Brother and Veiled Sister: Islamic Fundamentalism and the Cultural Politics of Patriarchy*. Berkeley and Los Angeles: University of California Press, 2004 (forthcoming).

———. "Transnationalism, Feminism, and Fundamentalism." In *Women, Gender, Religion: A Reader*, ed. Elizabeth A. Castelli with Rosamond C. Rodman, 119–45. New York: Palgrave, 2001.

Moffatt, James. "Ignatius of Antioch: A Study in Personal Religion." *JR* 10 (1930): 169–86.

Moles, J. L. "Truth and Untruth in Herodotus and Thucydides." In *Lies and Fiction in the Ancient World*, ed. Christopher Gill and T. P. Wiseman, 88–121. Austin: University of Texas Press, 1993.

Momigliano, Arnaldo. *The Conflict Between Paganism and Christianity in the Fourth Century*. Oxford: Clarendon Press, 1963.

———. *The Development of Greek Biography*. Cambridge, Mass.: Harvard University Press, 1993.

———. "Pagan and Christian Historiography in the Fourth Century A.D." In his *Essays in Ancient and Modern Historiography*, 107–26. Oxford: Blackwell, 1977.

Mommsen, Theodor. *Römisches Strafrecht*. 4 vols. Systematisches Handbuch der deutschen Rechtswissenschaft, 1 Abt. Leipzig: Duncker & Humblot, 1899.

Moore, Stephen D., and Janice Capel Anderson. "Taking It Like a Man: Masculinity in 4 Maccabees." *JBL* 117 (1998): 249–73.

Moriarty, Rachel. " 'Playing the Man': The Courage of Christian Martyrs, Translated and Transposed." In *Gender and Christian Religion*, ed. R. N. Swanson, 1–12. Suffolk: Boydell Press, 1998.

Mortley, Raoul. "The Hellenistic Foundations of Ecclesiastical Historiography." In *Reading the Past in Late Antiquity*, ed. Graeme Clarke with Brian Croke, Raoul Mortley, and Alanna Emmett Nobbs, 225–50. Rushcutters Bay, New South Wales: Australian National University Press, 1990.

Mosse, George L. *Fallen Soldiers: Reshaping the Memory of the World Wars*. New York: Oxford University Press, 1990.

Munier, Charles. "Où en est la question d'Ignace d'Antioche? Bilan d'un siècle de recherches, 1870–1988." *ANRW* 2.27.1 (1993): 272–358.

Murray, Mary Charles. "Art and the Early Church." *JTS*, n.s., 28 (1977): 303–45.

Myers, Steven Lee. "Elsewhere in the World, the Right to Worship Freely Hasn't a Prayer." *New York Times*, 27 July 1997.

National Rifle Association/Independence Institute. *Special Report on the Columbine Murders*. Available at http://www.i2i.org/SuptDocs/Crime/Columbine.htm.

Nasrallah, Laura. *An Ecstasy of Folly: Prophecy and Authority in Early Christianity*. Cambridge, Mass.: Harvard University Press, 2003.

National Review. " 'A Wave of Evil.' " *National Review*, 11 October 1999.

Nauerth, Claudia. "Nachlese von Thekla-Darstellungen." In *Studien zur spätantiken und frühchristlichen Kunst und Kultur des Orients*, ed. Guntram Koch, 14–18. Göttinger Orientforschungen, II. Reihe: Studien zur spätantiken und frühchristlichen Kunst 6. Wiesbaden: Harrassowitz, 1982.

Nauerth, Claudia, and Rüdiger Warns. *Thekla: Ihre Bilder in der frühchristlichen Kunst.* Wiesbaden: Otto Harrassowitz, 1981.

Naveh, Eyal J. *Crown of Thorns: Political Martyrdom in America from Abraham Lincoln to Martin Luther King, Jr.* New York: New York University Press, 1990.

Neal, Arthur G. *National Trauma and Collective Memory: Major Events in the American Century.* Armonk, N.Y.: M. E. Sharpe, 1998.

Nestori, A. *Repertorio topografico delle pitture delle catacombe romane.* 2nd rev. and aug. ed. Roma sotterranea cristiana 5. Vatican City: PIAC, 1993.

New York Times. "Columbine Lawsuit Filed." *New York Times,* 5 October 1999.

Niebuhr, Gustav, and Jodi Wilgoren. "From the Shock of Violent Deaths, New and More Public Rites of Mourning." *New York Times,* 28 April 1999.

Nitti, Renato. "L'homo ludens nella paideia classica e cristiana: La funzione etico-pedagogica del divertimento nella patristica dei primi secoli." *Nicolaus: Rivista di teologia ecumenico-patristica* 8 (1980): 439–51.

Nolan, Bruce. "Columbine Cast as Morality Play: Slick Church Production Held Over for Months," *New Orleans Times-Picayune,* 20 February 2000.

Nolan, Edward Peter. "Vibia Perpetua Martyr and a Feminine Style of Revelation." In *Cry Out and Write: A Feminine Poetics of Revelation,* 32–45. New York: Continuum, 1994.

Nolan, Steve. "Narrative as a Strategic Resource for Resistance: Reading the *Acts of Thecla* for Its Political Purposes." In *Narrativity in Biblical and Related Texts/La narrativité dans la Bible et les textes apparentés,* ed. G. J. Brooke and J.-D. Kaestli, 225–42. Bibliotheca Ephemeridum Theologicarum Lovaniensium 149. Leuven: Leuven University Press/Peeters, 2000.

Nora, Pierre. "Between Memory and History: *Les lieux de mémoire.*" *Representations* 26 (1989): 7–25.

———, ed. *Les lieux de mémoire.* 3 vols. Paris: Gallimard, 1984–1992.

Oakley, S. P. "Single Combat in the Roman Republic." *CQ* 45 (1985): 392–410.

Oexle, Otto Gerhard. "Memoria als Kultur." In *Memoria als Kultur,* ed. Otto Gerhard Oexle, 9–78. Veröffentlichungen des Max-Planck-Instituts für Geschichte 121. Göttingen: Vandenhoeck & Ruprecht, 1995.

———, ed. *Memoria als Kultur.* Veröffentlichungen des Max-Planck-Instituts für Geschichte 121. Göttingen: Vandenhoeck & Ruprecht, 1995.

O'Flaherty, Wendy Doniger. *Other Peoples' Myths.* New York: Macmillan, 1988.

Olender, Maurice. *The Languages of Paradise: Race, Religion, and Philology in the Nineteenth Century.* Trans. Arthur Goldhammer. Cambridge, Mass.: Harvard University Press, 1992.

Olick, Jeffrey, and Daniel Levy. "Collective Memory and Cultural Constraint: Holocaust Myth and Rationality in German Politics." *American Sociological Review* 62 (1997): 921–36.

Olick, Jeffrey, and Joyce Robbins. "Social Memory Studies: From 'Collective Memory' to the Historical Sociology of Mnemonic Practices." *Annual Review of Sociology* 24 (1998): 105–40.

Orbán, A. P. "The Afterlife in the Visions of *Passio SS Perpetuae et Felicitatis.*" In *Fructus centesimus: Mélanges offerts à Gerard J. M. Bartelink à l'occasion de son soixante-*

cinquième anniversaire, ed. A. A. R. Bastiaensen, A. Hilhorst, and C. H. Kneep-kens, 269–77. Instrumenta Patristica 19. Steenbrugis: Abbatia S. Petri, 1989.

Osiel, Mark. *Mass Atrocity, Collective Memory, and the Law.* New Brunswick, N.J.: Transaction Publishers, 1997.

Pagan and Christian Egypt: Egyptian Art from the First to the Tenth Century A.D. Exhibited at the Brooklyn Museum by the Department of Ancient Art, January 23–March 9, 1941. Brooklyn: Brooklyn Museum/Brooklyn Institute of Arts and Sciences, 1941.

Pagels, Elaine. "Gnostic and Orthodox Views of Christ's Passion: Paradigms for the Christian's Response to Persecution?" In *Rediscovery of Gnosticism,* vol. 1, ed. Bentley Layton, 262–88. Leiden: Brill, 1980.

Palmer, Anne-Marie. *Prudentius on the Martyrs.* Oxford: Oxford University Press, 1989.

Panayotakis, Costas. "Baptism and Crucifixion on the Mimic Stage." *Mnemosyne,* ser. 4, 50 (1997): 302–19.

Papi, Anna Benvenuti, and Elena Giannarelli. *Bambini santi: Rappresentazioni dell'infanzia e modelle agiografici.* Torino: Rosenberg & Sellier, 1991.

Pazaras, Théocharis. "Δύο παλαιοχριστιανικοὶ τάφοι ἀπὸ τὸ δυτικὸ νεκροταφεῖο τῆς Θεσσαλονίκης." Μακεδονικά 21 (1981): 379–87; figs. 1–9.

Pennebaker, James W., Darío Páez, and Bernard Rimé. *Collective Memory of Political Events: Social Psychological Perspectives.* Mahwah, N.J.: Lawrence Erlbaum Associates, 1997.

Pergola, Philippe. *Le catacombe romane: Storia e topografia.* Rome: Carocci, 1998.

Perkins, Judith. *The Suffering Self: Pain and Narrative Representation in the Early Christian Era.* New York: Routledge, 1995.

Perler, Otto. "Das vierte Makkabäerbuch, Ignatius von Antiochien und die ältesten Märtyrerberichte." *RivAC* 25 (1949): 47–72.

Perlman, Michael. *Imaginal Memory and the Place of Hiroshima.* Albany, N.Y.: SUNY Press, 1988.

Pernot, Laurent. "Saint Pionios, martyr et orateur." In *Du héros païen au saint chrétien: Actes du colloque organisé par le Centre d'analyse des rhétoriques religieuses de l'Antiquité (C.A.R.R.A.), Strasbourg, 1er–2 décembre 1995,* ed. Gérard Freyburger and Laurent Pernot, 111–23. Paris: Institut d'Études Augustiniennes, 1997.

Perraymond, R. "Alcune visioni nell'arte cristiana antica: Abramo, Giacobbe, Ezechiele, pastor d'Erma, Felicita e Perpetua." *Augustinianum* 29 (1989): 549–63.

Petraglio, Renzo. "Des influences de l'Apocalypse dans la 'Passio Perpetuae' 11–13." In *L'apocalypse de Jean: Traditions exégétiques et iconographies, IIIe–XIIIe siècles,* ed. Renzo Petraglio, 15–29. Geneva: Droz, 1979.

——. *Lingua latina e mentalità biblica nella Passio sanctae Perpetuae: Analisi di caro, carnalis, e corpus.* Brescia: Morcelliana, 1976.

Petroff, Elizabeth Alvilda. *Medieval Women's Visionary Literature.* New York: Oxford University Press, 1986.

Petruccione, John. "The Portrait of St. Eulala of Mérida in Prudentius' *Peristephanon.*" *AnBoll* 108 (1990): 81–104.

Pettersen, Alvyn. "Perpetua: Prisoner of Conscience." *VC* 41 (1987): 139–53.

Pizzolato, L. F. "Note alla *Passio Perpetuae et Felicitatis.*" *VC* 34 (1980): 105–19.

Plantinga, Theodore. *How Memory Shapes Narratives: A Philosophical Essay on Redeeming the Past.* Lewiston, N.Y.: Edwin Mellen Press, 1992.

Plasketes, George. "Things to Do in Littleton When You're Dead: A Post-Columbine Collage." *Popular Music and Society* 23, no. 3 (Fall 1999): 9–24.

Plass, Paul. *The Game of Death in Ancient Rome: Arena Sport and Political Suicide.* Madison: University of Wisconsin Press, 1995.

Pobee, John S. *Persecution and Martyrdom in the Theology of Paul.* JSNTSup 6. Sheffield: JSOT Press, 1985.

Poirier, M. "Note sur la *Passio sanctarum Perpetuae et Felicitatis*: Félicité, était-elle vraiment l'esclave de Perpétue?" *StPatr* 10, no. 1 (1970): 306–9.

Pollitt, Katha. "Religious Right, Religious Rights." *The Nation,* 13 October 1997, 10.

Potter, David S. *Literary Texts and the Roman Historian.* New York: Routledge, 1999.

——. "Martyrdom as Spectacle." In *Theater and Society in the Classical World,* ed. Ruth Scodel, 53–88. Ann Arbor: University of Michigan Press, 1993.

Pouderon, Bernard, and Joseph Doré, eds. *Les apologistes chrétiens et la culture grecque.* ThH 105. Paris: Beauchesne, 1998.

Press, Gerald A. *The Development of the Idea of History in Antiquity.* McGill-Queen's Studies in the History of Ideas 2. Kingston/Montreal: McGill-Queen's University Press, 1982.

Price, Deborah Evans. "Higher Ground." *Billboard,* 30 December 2000.

Price, Simon R. F. *Rituals and Power: The Roman Imperial Cult in Asia Minor.* Cambridge: Cambridge University Press, 1984.

Quasten, Johannes. "Der Gut Hirte in frühchristlicher Totenliturgie und Grabeskunst." In *Miscellanea Giovanni Mercati,* 1:373–406. Studi et testi 121. Vatican City: Biblioteca Apostolica Vaticana, 1946.

Rajak, Tessa. "Dying for the Law: The Martyr's Portrait in Jewish-Greek Literature." In *Portraits: Biographical Representation in the Greek and Latin Literature of the Roman Empire,* ed. M. J. Edwards and Simon Swain, 39–67. Oxford: Clarendon Press, 1997.

Rambaux, Claude. *Tertullien face aux morales des trois premiers siècles.* Paris: Société d'Édition "Les Belles Lettres," 1979.

Réau, Louis. *Iconographie de l'art chrétien.* Vol. 3, *Iconographie des saints.* Paris: Presses Universitaires de France, 1959.

Reddish, Mitchell Glenn. "The Theme of Martyrdom in the Book of Revelation." Ph.D. Diss., Southern Baptist Theological Seminary, 1982.

Reggiani, A.M., ed. *Anfiteatro Flavio: Immagine, testimonianze, spettacoli.* Rome: Edizione Quasar, 1988.

Renan, Ernest. *Oeuvres complètes.* Ed. Henriette Psichari. 7th ed. 10 vols. Paris: Calmann-Levy, 1947.

——. *Vie de Jesus.* Histoire des origines du christianisme 1. Paris: M. Levy frères, 1863. 22nd ed., rev. and aug., Paris: Calmann Levy, 1893.

Riddle, Donald. *The Martyrs: A Study in Social Control.* Chicago: University of Chicago Press, 1931.

Rives, James B. "The Decree of Decius and the Religion of Empire." *JRS* 89 (1999): 135–54.

——. "Human Sacrifice Among Pagans and Christians." *JRS* 85 (1995): 65–85.

——. "The Piety of a Persecutor." *JECS* 4 (1996): 1–25.

Roach, Joseph R. *Cities of the Dead: Circum-Atlantic Performance.* New York: Columbia University Press, 1996.

Robert, Louis. *Les gladiateurs dans l'Orient grec.* Bibliothèque de l'École des hautes études 289. Paris: Librairie ancienne Honoré Campion, 1940.

——. "Une vision de Perpétue Martyre à Carthage en 203." *CRAI* (1982): 227–76.

Roberts, Michael. *Poetry and the Cult of the Martyrs: The Liber Peristephanon of Prudentius.* Ann Arbor: University of Michigan Press, 1993.

Robinson, O. F. *The Criminal Law of Ancient Rome.* Baltimore: Johns Hopkins University Press, 1995.

——. "Repressionen gegen Christen in der Zeit vor Decius—noch immer ein **Rechts**problem." *Zeitschrfit der Savigny-Stiftung für Rechtsgeschichte* 112 (1995): 352–69.

——. "The Repression of Christians in the Pre-Decian Period: A Legal Problem Still." *Irish Jurist* 25–27 (1990–92): 269–92.

Rosin, Hanna. "Columbine Miracle: A Matter of Belief; The Last Words of Littleton Victim Cassie Bernall Test a Survivor's Faith—and Charity." *The Washington Post,* 14 October 1999.

Rossi, Mary Ann. "The Passion of Perpetua, Everywoman of Late Antiquity." In *Pagan and Christian Anxiety: A Response to E. R. Dodds,* ed. Robert C. Smith and John Lounibos, 53–86. Lanham, Md.: University Press of America, 1984.

Roth, Michael S. *The Ironist's Cage: Memory, Trauma, and the Construction of History.* New York: Columbia University Press, 1995.

Rowe, William, and Vivian Shelling. *Memory and Modernity: Popular Culture in Latin America.* New York: Verso, 1991.

Runions, Erin. "Why Girls Cry: Gender Melancholia and Sexual Violence in Ezekiel 16 and *Boys Don't Cry.*" In *How Hysterical: Identification and Resistance in the Bible and Film,* 114–34. New York: Palgrave, 2003.

Sacks, Kenneth S. *Diodorus Siculus and the First Century.* Princeton, N.J.: Princeton University Press, 1990.

Saldarini, Anthony J. *Scholastic Rabbinism: A Literary Study of the Fathers According to Rabbi Nathan.* BJS 14. Chico, Calif.: Scholars Press, 1982.

Salisbury, Joyce. *Perpetua's Passion: The Death and Memory of a Young Roman Woman.* New York: Routledge, 1997.

Salomonson, Jan Willem. *Spätrömische Rote Tonware mit Reliefverzierung aus Norafrikanischen Werkstätten.* Rome: Nederlands Historisch Institut te Rom, 1969.

——. *Voluptatem Spectandi non perdat sed mutat: Observations sur l'iconographie du martyre en Afrique Romaine.* Amsterdam: North-Holland Publishing Company, 1979.

Santner, Eric L. *Stranded Objects: Mourning, Memory, and Film in Postwar Germany.* Ithaca, N.Y.: Cornell University Press, 1990.

Sardella, Teresa. "Strutture temporali e modelli di cultura rapporti tra antitradizional-ismo storico e modello martiriale nella *Passio Perpetuae et Felicitatis*." *Augustianum* 30 (1990): 259–78.

Scarry, Elaine. *The Body in Pain: The Making and Unmaking of the World*. New York: Oxford University Press, 1985.

Schaper, Donna. "Sacred Spaces." *Cross Currents* 50 (2000): 221–25.

Scheffler, Judith A., ed. *Wall Tappings: An International Anthology of Women's Prison Writings, 200 to the Present*. 2nd ed. New York: Feminist Press, 2002.

Scheid, John. "The Religious Roles of Roman Women." In *A History of Women from Ancient Goddesses to Christian Saints*, ed. Pauline Schmitt Pantel, 377–408. Cambridge, Mass.: Harvard University Press, 1992.

Schenck, Jean-Luc. "Saint-Just de Valcabrère." In *Pulchra Imago: Fragments d'archéologie chrétienne. Catalogue d'exposition, Saint-Bertrand-de-Comminges, 30 mars–11 nov. 1991*, 43–47. Toulouse: Musée archéologique départemental de Saint-Bertrand-de-Comminges, 1991.

——. "Valcabrère: Église Saint-Just." In *Les premiers monuments chrétiens de la France*. Vol. 2, *Sud-Ouest et Centre*, 200–206. Paris: Picard, 1996.

Schmitt, Eric. "Bill to Punish Nations Limiting Religious Beliefs Passes Senate." *New York Times*, 10 October 1998.

Schneider, Alfons M. "Sankt Euphemia und das Konzil von Chalkedon." In *Das Konzil von Chalkedon: Geschichte und Gegenwart*, ed. Aloys Grillmeier and Heinrich Bacht, 3 vols., 1:291–302. Würzburg: Echter-Verlag, 1951.

Schnusenberg, Christine Catharina. *The Relationship Between the Church and the Theatre*. Lanham, Md.: University Press of America, 1988.

Schoedel, William R. *Ignatius of Antioch*. Hermeneia Commentary. Philadelphia: Fortress Press, 1985.

——. "Polycarp of Smyrna and Ignatius of Antioch." *ANRW* 2.27.1 (1993): 272–358.

Schrier, O. J. "À propos d'une donnée négligée sur la mort de Ste. Euphémie." *AnBoll* 102 (1984): 329–53.

Schudson, Michael. *Watergate in American Memory: How We Remember, Forget, and Reconstruct the Past*. New York: Basic Books, 1992.

Schwartz, Barry. "The Social Context of Commemoration: A Study in Collective Memory." *Social Forces* 61 (1982): 374–402.

Schwartz, Barry, Yael Zerubavel, and Bernice M. Barnett. "The Recovery of Masada: A Study in Collective Memory." *Sociological Quarterly* 27 (1986): 147–64.

Schweitzer, Albert. *The Quest of the Historical Jesus: A Critical Study of its Progress from Reimarus to Wrede*. Trans. W. Montgomery. New York: Macmillan, 1961. Originally published in German, 1906.

Scobie, Alexander. "Spectator Security and Comfort at Gladiatorial Games." *Nikephoros* 1 (1988): 191–243.

Scott, James C. *Domination and the Arts of Resistance: Hidden Transcripts*. New Haven, Conn.: Yale University Press, 1990.

Scott, Joan W. "'Experience.'" In *Feminists Theorize the Political*. Ed. Judith Butler and Joan W. Scott, 22–40. New York: Routledge, 1992.

———. "Gender: A Useful Category for Historical Analysis." In *Gender and the Politics of History*, by Joan Wallach Scott, 28–50. New York: Columbia University Press, 1988.

———. *Gender and the Politics of History*. New York: Columbia University Press, 1988.

Seeley, David. *The Noble Death: Graeco-Roman Martyrology and Paul's Concept of Salvation*. JSNTSup 28. Sheffield: JSOT Press, 1990.

Seeliger, Reinhard. "*Palai martyres*: Die Drei Junglinge im Feuerofen als Typos in der spätantiken Kunst, Liturgie und patristischen Literatur: Mit einigen Hinweisen zur Hermeneutik der christlichen Archeologie." In *Liturgie und Dichtung: Ein interdisziplinäres Kompendium*, ed. Hansjakob Becker and Reiner Kaczynski, 257–334. Sankt Ottilien: EOS Verlag, 1983.

Shaw, Brent D. "Body/Power/Identity: Passions of the Martyrs." *JECS* 4 (1996): 269–312.

———. "The Passion of Perpetua." *Past and Present* 139 (1993): 3–45.

Sherwin-White, A. N. "The Early Persecutions and Roman Law Again." *JTS*, n.s. 3, pt. 2 (1952): 199–213. Updated version as appendix to *The Letters of Pliny*, ed. and trans. Sherwin-White, 722–87. Oxford: Oxford University Press, 1966.

———. "Why Were the Early Christians Persecuted?—An Amendment." *Past and Present* 27 (1964): 23–7.

Shiflett, Dave. "It Ain't Gospel." *Salon*, 17 February 2000. Available at http://www.salon.com/news/feature/2000/02/17/ramsey.

Shore, Sandy. "A Girl's Faith Leaves Enduring Legacy: Columbine Victim Seen as Martyr." *New Orleans Times-Picayune*, Orleans edition, 15 May 1999.

Sider, Robert D. "Tertullian, *On the Shows*: An Analysis." *JTS*, n.s., 29 (1978): 339–65.

Signer, Michael A., ed. *Memory and History in Christianity and Judaism*. Notre Dame, Ind.: University of Notre Dame Press, 2001.

Singh, Amritjit, Joseph T. Skerrett Jr., and Robert E. Hogan, eds. *Memory and Cultural Politics: New Approaches to American Ethnic Literatures*. Boston: Northeastern University Press, 1996.

Slotkin, Richard. *Regeneration Through Violence: The Mythology of the American Frontier, 1600–1860*. Middletown, Conn.: Wesleyan University Press, 1973.

Slovo, Gillian. *Red Dust*. London: Virago, 2001.

Smith, Alison Moore. "The Iconography of the Sacrifice of Isaac in Early Christian Art." *AJA*, 2d ser., 26 (1922): 159–73.

Smith, Brian K. "Capital Punishment and Human Sacrifice." *JAAR* 68 (2000): 3–25.

Smith, Lacey Baldwin. *Fools, Martyrs, Traitors: The Story of Martyrdom in the Western World*. New York: Knopf, 1997.

Snyder, Graydon. *Ante Pacem: Archaeological Evidence of Church Life Before Constantine*. Macon, Ga.: Mercer University Press, 1985.

Sordi, Marta. *The Christians and the Roman Empire*. Trans. Annabel Bedini. Norman: University of Oklahoma Press, 1986.

Spanneut, Michel. *Le Stoïcisme des pères de l'église de Clément de Rome à Clément d'Alexandrie*. Patristica Sorbonensia 1. Paris: Seuil, 1957.

Speyer, Wolfgang. "Die Euphemia-Rede des Asterios von Amaseia: Eine Missionschrift für gebildete Heiden." *JAC* 14 (1971): 39–47.

Stanley, Alessandra. "French Bishop, Disciplined Over 'Gay Pride' Issue, Still Speaks Out in Rome." *New York Times* 4 July 2000.

Staples, Ariadne. *From Good Goddess to Vestal Virgins: Sex and Category in Roman Religion*. London: Routledge, 1998.

Ste. Croix, G. E. M. de. "Aspects of the 'Great' Persecution." *HTR* 47 (1954): 75–115.

——. "Why Were the Early Christians Persecuted?" *Past and Present* 26 (1963): 6–38.

——. "Why Were the Early Christians Persecuted?—A Rejoinder." *Past and Present* 27 (1964): 28–33.

Steinfels, Peter. "Evangelicals Lobby for Oppressed Christians." *New York Times*, 15 September 1996.

——. "The State Department's Decision to Establish a Panel on Religious Persecution Around the World Immediately Raises Questions of Sincerity." *New York Times*, 16 November 1996.

Stevenson, J. *The Catacombs: Rediscovered Monuments of Early Christianity*. London: Thames and Hudson, 1978.

Stillwell, Richard, ed. *Antioch-on-the-Orontes*. Vol. 2, *The Excavations of 1933–1936*. Publications of the Committee for the Excavation of Antioch and Its Vicinity. Princeton, N.J.: Published for the Committee by the Deaprtment of Art and Archaeology of Princeton University, 1938.

Stoll, David. *Rigoberta Menchù and the Story of All Poor Guatemalans*. Boulder, Colo.: Westview Press, 1999.

Stowers, Stanley K. "Greeks Who Sacrifice and Those Who Do Not: Toward an Anthropology of Greek Religion." In *The Social World of the First Christians: Essays in Honor of Wayne A. Meeks*, ed. L. Michael White and O. Larry Yarbrough, 299–333. Minneapolis: Fortress Press, 1995.

Sturken, Marita. *Tangled Memories: The Vietnam War, the AIDS Epidemic, and the Politics of Remembering*. Berkeley: University of California Press, 1997.

——. "The Wall, the Screen, and the Image: The Vietnam Veterans Memorial." *Representations* 35 (1991): 118–42.

Sullivan, Andrew. "Afterlife." *The New Republic*, 22 November 1999, 6.

Swedenburg, Ted. *Memories of Revolt: The 1936–1939 Rebellion and the Palestinian National Past*. Minneapolis: University of Minnesota Press, 1995.

Tajra, H. W. *The Martyrdom of St. Paul: Historical and Judicial Context, Traditions, and Legends*. WUNT 2. Reihe 67. Tübingen: Mohr (Siebeck), 1994.

——. *The Trial of St. Paul: A Juridical Exegesis of the Second Half of the Acts of the Apostles*. WUNT 2. Reihe 35. Tübingen: Mohr (Siebeck), 1989.

Talbert, Charles H. "Martyrdom in Luke-Acts and the Lukan Social Ethic." In *Political Issues in Luke-Acts*, ed. Richard Cassidy and Philip J. Scharper, 99–110. Maryknoll, N.Y.: Orbis, 1983.

Terdiman, Richard. *Present Past: Modernity and the Memory Crisis*. Ithaca, N.Y.: Cornell University Press, 1993.

Teski, Marea C., and Jacob J. Climo, eds. *The Labyrinth of Memory: Ethnographic Journeys*. Westport, Conn.: Bergin & Garvey, 1995.

Testard, Maurice. "La Passion des saintes Perpétue et Félicité: témoignages sur le monde antique et le christianisme." *Bulletin de l'Association Guillaume Budé* (1991): 56–75.

Thelen, David. "Memory and American History." *Journal of American History* 75 (1989): 1117–29.

Thomas, Rosalind. *Herodotus in Context: Ethnography, Science, and the Art of Persuasion.* Cambridge: Cambridge University Press, 2000.

Thompson, Leonard L. *The Book of Revelation: Apocalypse and Empire.* New York: Oxford University Press, 1990.

———. "The Martyrdom of Polycarp: Death in the Roman Games." *JR* 82 (2002): 27–52.

Thomson, Alistair. "Unreliable Memories? The Use and Abuse of Oral History." In *Historical Controversies and Historians*, ed. William Lamont, 23–34. London: UCL Press, 1998.

Tilley, Maureen A. "The Ascetic Body and the (Un)Making of the World of the Martyr." *JAAR* 59 (1991): 467–79.

———. "The Passion of Perpetua and Felicity." In *Searching the Scriptures*, vol. 2, *A Feminist Commentary*, ed. Elisabeth Schüssler Fiorenza, 829–58. New York: Crossroad, 1994.

Time. "The Monsters Next Door: A Special Report on the Colorado School Massacre." *Time*, 3 May 1999.

Toalston, Art. "Cassie Bernall's Parents Recount Efforts to Achieve Accuracy in Book." *BPNews*, 29 September 1999. http://www.bpnews.net/bpnews.asp?id=333.

Tombs, David. "Crucifixion, State Terror, and Sexual Abuse." *USQR* 53, nos. 1–2 (1999): 89–109.

Trebay, Guy. "Beyond the Fence: Conjuring the Lives of Martyr Matthew Shepard." *Village Voice*, 3 November 1998.

Trevett, Christine. *Montanism: Gender, Authority, and the New Prophecy.* New York: Cambridge University Press, 1996.

Tutu, Archbishop Desmond. *Truth and Reconciliation Commission of South Africa Report.* Vol. 1. London: Macmillan, 1999.

US News & World Report. "The Lessons of Littleton." *US News & World Report*, 3 May 1999, 16–26.

Vaage, Leif, and Vincent L. Wimbush, eds. *Asceticism and the New Testament.* New York: Routledge, 1999.

Valantasis, Richard. "Constructions of Power in Asceticism." *JAAR* 63 (1995): 775–821.

Vandernberghe, B. H. "Saint Jean Chrysostome et les spectacles." *ZRGG* 7 (1955): 34–46.

Vergote, J. "Les principaux modes de supplice chez les anciens et dans les textes chrétiens." *Bulletin de l'Institut historique belge de Rome* 20 (1939): 141–63.

Veyne, Paul. *Did the Greeks Believe in Their Myths? An Essay on the Constitutive Imagination.* Trans. Paula Wissing. Chicago: University of Chicago Press, 1988.

———. "Païens et chrétiens devant la gladuature." *MEFRA* 111 (1999): 883–917.

———. *Le pain et le cirque: Sociologie historique d'un pluralisme politique.* Paris: Seuil, 1976.

Vidal-Naquet, Pierre. *Assassins of Memory: Essays on the Denial of the Holocaust.* Trans. Jeffrey Mehlman. New York: Columbia University Press, 1992.

Viljamaa, Toivo, Asko Timonen, and Christian Krötze, eds. *Crudelitas: The Politics of Cruelty in the Ancient and Medieval World*. Krems: Medium Aervum Quotidianum, 1992.

Ville, Georges. *La gladiature en Occident des origines à la morte de Domitien*. Bibliothèque des Écoles françaises d'Athènes et de Rome 245. Rome: École Française de Rome, 1981.

Viller, Marcel. "Le martyre et l'ascèse." *Revue d'ascétique et de mystique* 6 (1925): 105–42.

Vismara, Cinzia. *Il supplizio come spettacolo*. Vita e costumi dei Romani antichi 11. Rome: Museo della civiltà romana/Quasar, 1990.

Voisin, J.-L. "Pendus, crucifiés, *oscilla* dans la Rome païenne." *Latomus* 38 (1979): 442–50.

Vries, Hent de. *Religion and Violence: Philosophical Perspectives from Kant to Derrida*. Baltimore: Johns Hopkins University Press, 2002.

Wagner, John, ed. *The Big Book of Martyrs*. New York: Paradox Press, 1997.

Walker, J. Samuel. "History, Collective Memory, and the Decision to Use the Bomb." *Diplomatic History* 19 (1995): 319–28.

Wallace, Susan Besze. "Columbine Crosses Return for Play." *Denver Post*, 19 November 1999.

———. "Faith in Cassie's Last Words Wavers." *Denver Post*, 25 September 1999.

———. "Schnurr's Memory Corroborated by Other Witnesses." *Denver Post*, 28 September 1999.

Walsh, Andrew. "Preaching the Word in Littleton." *Religion in the News* 2, no. 2 (Summer 1999): 4–6.

Ward, Sister Benedicta. *Harlots of the Desert: A Study of Repentance in Early Monastic Sources*. Kalamazoo, Mich.: Cistercian Publications, 1987.

Warns, Rüdiger. "Weitere Darstellungen der heiligen Thekla." In *Studien zur frühchristlichen Kunst II*, Göttinger Orientforschungen, II. Reihe: Studien zur spätantiken und frühchristlichen Kunst 8, ed. Guntram Koch, 75–137. Wiesbaden: Harrassowitz, 1986.

Waszink, J. H. "Pompa Diaboli." *VC* 1 (1947): 13–41.

Watson, C. J. "The Program of the Brescia Casket." *Gesta* 20 (1981): 283–98.

Watson, Justin. *The Martyrs of Columbine: Faith, Tragedy, and Politics*. New York: Palgrave, 2002.

Weed, Elizabeth. "The Question of Style." In *Engaging with Irigaray: Feminist Philosophy and Modern European Thought*, ed. Carolyn Burke, Naomi Schor, and Margaret Whitford, 79–109. New York: Columbia University Press, 1994.

The Weekly Standard. "Americans United for Blame Shifting." *The Weekly Standard*, 7 June 1999, 3.

Weiser, Benjamin. "A Jury Torn and Fearful in 2001 Terrorism Trial." *New York Times*, 5 January 2003.

———. "Life for Terrorist in Embassy Attack." *New York Times*, 13 June 2001.

Weismann, Werner. *Kirche und Schauspiele: Die Schauspiele im Urteil der lateinischen Kirchenväter unter besonderer Berücksichtigung von Augustin*. Cassiciacum 27. Würzberg: Augustinus-Verlag, 1972.

Weitzmann, Kurt, ed. *Age of Spirituality: Late Antique and Early Christian Art, Third to*

Seventh Century. Catalogue of the Exhibition at the Metropolitan Museum of Art, November 19, 1977, through February 12, 1978. New York: Metropolitan Museum of Art in association with Princeton University Press, 1979.

Welch, Katherine. "Roman Amphitheatres Revived." *JRA* 4 (1991): 272–81.

———. "The Roman Arena in Late-Republican Italy: A New Interpretation." *JRA* 7 (1994): 59–80.

White, Gayle. "Evangelism Effort Prelude to Baptists' Meeting." *Atlanta Journal-Constitution,* 13 June 1999.

Whitehead, Colson. *John Henry Days.* New York: Doubleday, 2001.

Whittaker, Molly, ed. *Jews and Christians: Graeco-Roman Views.* Cambridge Commentaries on Writings of the Jewish and Christian World, 200 BC to AD 200. New York: Cambridge University Press, 1984.

Wiedemann, Thomas E. J. *Emperors and Gladiators.* London: Routledge, 1992.

Wilken, Robert. *The Christians as the Romans Saw Them.* New Haven, Conn.: Yale University Press, 1984.

Williams, Sam K. *Jesus' Death as Saving Event: The Origin of a Concept.* HDR 2. Missoula, Mont.: Scholars Press, 1975.

Williams, Stephen. *Diocletian and the Roman Recovery.* New York: Routledge, 1985.

Wills, Gary. "The Bishops at Bay." *New York Review of Books,* 15 August 2002, 8–11.

Wilpert, Josef. "Menasfläschen mit der Darstellung der hl. Thekla zwischen den wilden Tieren." *RQ* 20 (1906): 86–92.

Winter, Jay. *Sites of Memory, Sites of Mourning: The Great War in European Cultural History.* New York: Cambridge University Press, 1995.

Wiseman, T. P. "Lying Historians: Seven Types of Mendacity." In *Lies and Fiction in the Ancient World,* ed. Christopher Gill and T. P. Wiseman, 122–46. Austin: University of Texas Press, 1993.

Wistrand, Magnus. *Entertainment and Violence in Ancient Rome: The Attitudes of Roman Writers of the First Century A.D.* Göteburg: Acta Universitatis Gothoburgensis, 1992.

Woerden, Isabel Speyart van. "The Iconography of the Sacrifice of Abraham." *VC* 15 (1961): 214–55.

Woodman, A. J. *Rhetoric in Classical Historiography: Four Studies.* London: Croom Helm, 1988.

Woodward, Kenneth L., with Sherry Keene-Osborn and Claire Kirk. "The Making of a Martyr." *Newsweek,* 14 June 1999, 64.

Workman, Herbert B. *Persecution in the Early Church.* New York: Oxford University Press, 1980.

Xeres, Saviero. "La 'bella morte' del cristiano: La metafora agonistica in Paolo e nei primi atti dei martiri." In *Dulce et decorum est pro patria mori: La morte in combattimento nell'antichità,* ed. Marta Sordi, 281–93. Milan: Vita e Pensiero, 1990.

Yardley, Jim. "Church's Haunted House Draws Fire." *New York Times,* 29 October 1999.

Yerushalmi, Yosef Hayim. *Zakhor: Jewish History and Jewish Memory.* Seattle: University of Washington Press, 1982.

Yoneyama, Lisa. *Hiroshima Traces: Time, Space, and the Dialectics of Memory.* Berkeley: University of California Press, 1999.

Young, Francis M. *The Use of Sacrificial Ideas in Greek Christian Writers from the New Testament to John Chrysostom.* Patristic Monograph Series 5. Philadelphia: Philadelphia Patristic Foundation, 1979.

Young, James E. *The Art of Memory: Holocaust Memorials in History.* New York: Prestel, 1994.

——. *At Memory's Edge: After-Images of the Holocaust in Contemporary Art and Architecture.* New Haven, Conn.: Yale University Press, 2000.

——. *The Texture of Memory: Holocaust Memorials and Meaning.* New Haven, Conn.: Yale University Press, 1993.

——. *Writing and Rewriting the Holocaust: Narrative and the Consequences of Interpretation.* Bloomington: University of Indiana Press, 1988.

Young, Robin Darling. *In Procession Before the World: Martyrdom as Public Liturgy in Early Christianity.* The Père Marquette Lecture in Theology, 2001. Milwaukee, Wis.: Marquette University Press, 2001.

Zanartu, S. "Les concepts de vie et de mort chez Ignace d'Antioche." *VC* 33 (1979): 324–41.

Zanker, Paul. *The Power of Images in the Age of Augustus.* Trans. Alan Shapiro. Ann Arbor: University of Michigan Press, 1990.

Zelizer, Barbie. *Covering the Body: The Kennedy Assassination, the Media, and the Shaping of Collective Memory.* Chicago: University of Chicago Press, 1992.

——. "Reading the Past Against the Grain: The Shape of Memory Studies." *Studies in Mass Communication* 12 (1995): 214–39.

Zengotita, Thomas de. "The Gunfire Dialogues." *Harper's,* July 1999, 55–58.

Zerubavel, Yael. "The 'Death of Memory' and the Memory of Death: Masada and the Holocaust as Historical Metaphors." *Representations* 45 (1994): 72–100.

——. *Recovered Roots: Collective Memory and the Making of Israeli National Tradition.* Chicago: University of Chicago Press, 1995.

Zoba, Wendy Murray. *Day of Reckoning: Columbine and the Search for America's Soul.* Grand Rapids, Mich.: Brazos Press, 2000.

Zuccotti, Ferdinando. *"Furor Haereticorum": Studi sul trattamento giuridico della follia e sulla persecuzione della eterodossia religiosa nella legislazione del tardo impero romano.* Università degli studi di Milano, Facoltà di giurisprudenza, Pubblicazioni dell'istituto di diritto romano 26. Milan: Giuffrè, 1992.

INDEX

Rohrbough, Brian, 188

Roman empire, 5; citizenship, 37–38, 45–46; as diabolical, 36, 45, 49; martyrdom as contest with, 39–49; religious observance, 34, 37–38, 50. *See also* judicial apparatus; sacrifice, Roman

Roman imperial period, narrative literature, 138

Rufinus, 101

Rusticus, 44, 223n.56

sacrifice, 34; arena and, 55, 111; competition over notions of, 50–67; gender of, 59–61; Jewish, 55, 60; as literal, 51, 53, 55; as metaphor, 52–55; spectacle and, 53–54. *See also* martyrdom; sacrifice, Christian; sacrifice, Roman

sacrifice, Christian: biblical tradition of, 50–52, 60; as disordering influence on Rome, 51–55; *imitatio Christi*, 51–54; martyrdom and, 84–85; as spiritual, 54, 227n.97; theory of, 55–57

sacrifice, Roman: agency *vs.* victimhood, 51–52; Christian critique of, 67–68; Christian resistance to, 55–57; to emperor, 100, 102, 245–46n.150; exclusion of women from, 59–61, 230n.124; human sacrifice, 58–59, 229nn.117, 118, 230n.121; role of violence, 57–59; social order and, 50–51, 56–57

Ste. Croix, G. E. M. de, 38

Saint-Just de Valcabrère fragment, 161, 268n.129

saints, immunity to being forgotten, 134–35, 147

Schnurr, Valeen, 184–85

Schoedel, William R., 84

Schrier, O. J., 128

Scott, Joan, 4

Scott, Rachel, 189, 272n.4

self, 69; care of, 75, 234n.19; destruction of physical body, 80–82; disciplining of, 74–75; Stoic *vs.* Christian techniques of,

75, 77; technologies of, 6, 70–71, 74–77; transformation of, 80, 82, 85–92

self-effacement, 83–84

self-examination, 74–75

self-writing, 6; apologia, 94, 99; audience for, 102–3; Bible as source for, 72, 98–99; as discipline, 72, 73; performance and, 99–100; personal correspondence of philosophers, 72–74; reading notebooks, 71–74, 98, 233n.10; redactors, 92–93, 103, 240n.76; as response to state authority, 100–101, 246n.150; rhetorical realm, 93, 96, 98, 101, 244n.123; turn toward interiority, 70–71, 73–74, 91–92

September 11, 2001, terrorist attacks, 198, 200–203

sexual deviance, 7, 142, 150

Shaw, Brent, 64

Shepard, Matthew, 192, 279n.102

Sherman, Brad, 193

She Said Yes: The Unlikely Martyrdom of Cassie Bernall (Bernall), 177–85, 193

Shoah, 191

slave, metaphor of, 142, 148–49

Smith, Michael W., 187

Smith, Nathaniel, 193

social formation, evolutionary view of, 18, 209n.35

Social Frameworks of Memory, The (Halbwachs), 11–19, 14

social order, 5, 108–10, 141–42; Roman sacrifice and, 50–51, 56–57

Southern Baptist Convention, 191

spectacle, 6–7; Christian counterscripts, 105–6, 117–25, 132–33, 225nn.81, 82; Christian polemics against, 106, 112–17, 255n.92; costuming, 119, 123; as educational, 119, 254n.70; gaze as problematic, 114–15, 120–21; gender ambiguities, 121–22, 125–26; God's gaze and, 120, 254n.76; as idolatry, 113–14, 150–51; martyrdom as, 119–26; mental picture as, 105–6; sacrifice and, 53–54; scholarship, 107–11; as scripted ritual, 119–20; second